What Role for Government?

What Role for Government?

Lessons from Policy Research

Edited by

Richard J. Zeckhauser

and Derek Leebaert

Duke Press Policy Studies

Durham, N.C.   1983

Library of Congress Cataloging in Publication Data
Main entry under title:
What role for government?
  (Duke Press policy studies)
  Bibliography: p.
  Includes index.
    1. United States—Economic policy—1971−1981—Address-
es, essays, lectures. 2. United States—Social policy—
Addresses, essays, lectures. 3. Trade regulation—
United States—Addresses, essays, lectures. 4. Policy
sciences—Addresses, essays, lectures. I. Zeckhauser,
Richard J.   II. Leebaert, Derek.   III. Title.
IV. Series.
HC106.7.W48   1983   361.6′1′0973   82−21074
ISBN 0−8223−0496−1

Contents

Tables

Figures

What Role for Government?

Introduction: What Role for Government?

Richard J. Zeckhauser and Derek Leebaert

No constitutional convention, no legislative proclamation, no document identifies the appropriate role for government in American society. In the words of the Constitution, the purposes of government are to "establish Justice, insure domestic Tranquillity, provide for the common defence, promote the general Welfare, and secure the Blessings of Liberty to ourselves and our Posterity. . . ." There is no indication that government is to play a part in transforming or enforcing values or uplifting the citizenry. Nor is government assigned any special role in assuring the stability, productivity, and prosperity of the economy. Finally, no mission of income redistribution is identified.

The vital debates on government today, by contrast, are specifically concerned with its social roles, its participation in the economy, and its redistributive function. We have little but the evolution of society and values and the powerful but somewhat jerky hand of the political process to guide us. But surely the analytic approach to policy issues that has grown up over the past two decades has something to say on the issue of government's role.

That mode of thought, which informs most of what follows in this volume, embraces the fundamental concepts of welfare economics and relies overwhelmingly on the microeconomic approach to policy issues, its stepdaughter. Welfare economics provides a clear and precise set of principles for government action in a variety of arenas. In brief, the government is to establish the rules of the game, for example, by making voluntary contracts enforceable. And it has the further role to step in when markets fail. Such situations include the handling of externalities, such as pollution, and the provision of public goods—national defense being the quintessential example. Government may also play a role when the operation of markets is impeded (e.g., by a restricted information flow, the rationale for grading and standards programs) or in a case of market concentration, which might be addressed through antitrust policy or price regulation.

As a guide to government action, the microeconomic model falls short in at least three ways. First, in practice at least, it tells little about the extent of market failures. Although an estimated loss to society may be advanced to give political impetus to a program, the measure is rarely precise. Second, economics provides no mechanism for determining the costs or effectiveness of governmental remedies. Performance can only be estimated in retrospect: How much did the Clean Air Act do to cleanse the air? How successful has the Occupational Safety and Health Administration been in reducing occupational injuries? The costs of such programs, however, usually include a large indirect component diffused throughout the economy. Estimates of social benefits and costs usually rest on a scaffolding of weak assumptions and speculative data.

Difficulties in determining the likely accomplishments and costs of alternative government remedies would be less troubling if those who benefited from a government program were those who bore the cost. Then, at least over time, the class of affected parties would act to move government policies toward appropriate forms and appropriate levels of vigor. But when public programs help some people and through their costs hurt others, a political struggle is inevitable. Then neither the appropriate form nor the right degree of government intervention can be expected. Outcomes are likely to be particularly out of line when the contending parties have unequal access to the political process, whether because of differences in resources or in the way those resources are deployed. If interests on one side are concentrated and on the other diffuse, the former will be advantaged. Hence, the rise of the special-interest state. Finally, the political process, by picking a single winner, introduces a random component. Despite the claims of virtually every newly elected official to represent all of the people, election by a slim majority invariably gives excess weight (i.e., more than is efficient) to the interests of those who supported the winner.

Even when economics provides measures of gains and losses, and points the way to effective policy, a third difficulty limits its contribution. The norms of economics are almost as widely rejected outside the profession as they are accepted within. An appeal to principles of equity, together with some political muscle, can often win support for even a clear misallocation of resources. Reforms are commonly attacked on the grounds that some impoverished individuals will suffer—it is rarely thought necessary to show that those hurt by a policy change are poorer on average than those who gain—or even that some individuals will be worse off than they are under the status quo. (The latter argument infers a property right in the existing set of government policies.)

The potential losers include both an existing program's nominal beneficiaries, say the tenants within public or rent-subsidized housing, and the industry that provides its goods and services, in this case the construction and financial services industries. The expedient of buying off affected parties through lump sum payments, or their equivalent, has rarely been tried, in part because the recipients recognize that once an in-kind or regulatory or price control program has been converted to cash subsidy basis, it loses its legitimacy and moreover becomes subject to annual budget review. Only a budget-breaking once-and-for-all payment could be secure. In many cases too, the professional and bureaucratic cadre that administers a program may have a strong self-interest in its continuation; if a city hospital may be closed, its staff is likely to be no less vocal than the surrounding community.

The economic approach is perhaps most useful in indicating the appropriate form of government intervention, assuming that there will be intervention. Classic recommendations include: (1) When coping with externalities, use the price system rather than command and control mechanisms (e.g., price controls rather than environmental standards). (2) To enhance efficiency in service delivery, promote competition among alternative providers (e.g., provide vouchers for primary and secondary education, not just public schooling, or for portable rent subsidies in lieu of public housing). (3) In pursuit of income redistribution, (a) use cash rather than in-kind transfers (e.g., use welfare reform to cash out the benefit of subsidized medical care for the poor) and (b) employ the tax system in preference to price controls (e.g., eschew minimum wages or price controls on natural gas and favor a negative income tax for the bottom of the scale and fewer tax preference items for the top).

Some of these choices would be too extreme for even many mainline economists, but most would subscribe to the general directions for reform they illustrate. And yet only minimal progress has been made in carrying out what might be called economic approaches to policy goals. (Energy price deregulation is perhaps the area of greatest advance.) Quite simply, the losers from proposed reforms have been able to mount emotional or political arguments, or claims for justice sufficient to overcome the somewhat elusive and insufficiently understood argument of economic efficiency. Once again, the efficiency argument is unpersuasive because we lack mechanisms to compensate the losers. Even when the loss in resources may be substantial, the advantage tips to the status quo.

These persistent departures from the norms of efficiency suggest to some that government functions should be overhauled. Policy analysts usually take a more modest view: If the values or beliefs of society are clarified, they can be pursued in a more effective fashion. More analytic approaches to policy will yield better outcomes, and ultimately a superior society.

This Volume

The primary goal of this volume is to enhance discussion of public policies, and by example to demonstrate that systematic and scholarly analyses have a role to play in the national debate. The contributors have been ambitious. Although an important function of analysis is to resolve such narrow issues as where to locate a hospital, or what standard should be set for some pollutant, none of the chapters in this volume is limited to such technical exercises. The chapters derive from research presented at the 1980-81 conference of the Association for Public Policy and Management. They were selected from more than 100 papers, and were then refereed, revised, and updated.

How can we ensure that government itself plays an appropriate role, and does so effectively? Again and again the authors independently encounter common constraints on government performance—the short-run instincts of the institution, the conflicting conclusions possible from analyses using the same data, the tension between effective government action and individual freedom, and the perennial oversupply of position papers when analytical studies should guide the action.

The book is divided into five sections defined in terms of broad policy concerns: Democracy and Elections, Economic Well-Being, Health, Regulation, and Management. Some of the questions that the chapters confront are time-less: how to define the common good, what should or can be compelled, who should pay, when to compensate, and so forth. Defining what is equitable and fair is a pervasive problem, whether the task is apportioning broadcasting time among political candidates or deciding where to cut back in public programs. Other questions are more focused, although no less important, such as how to maintain the virtues of a competitive system while meeting a range of public needs. Or how to respond to constituencies that express inconsistent principles, such as the auto industry and its workers, who want less regulation of their product, but also demand import controls.

Democracy and Elections

The cornerstone of American government is the electoral process. Most citizens still adhere to the simple belief that democracy means that citizens vote for their candidates, and majority rule prevails. But is the electoral process truly democratic when television packages our candidates and their campaigns? When the presidential nominating system leads to the selection of candidates who are superb campaigners, almost apart from their skills as policy makers and managers? When a vocal interest group can seek to legislate morality for the nation by influencing electoral outcomes?

Three chapters in this volume address the question: How can we better assure that electoral processes promote democracy? Wertheimer and Huwa (abstracts of this and other chapters are provided at the beginning of each chapter) discuss the influence of television on the political process. This rela-tively new medium of communication offers voters unprecedented access to relevant information, yet selectivity in news coverage introduces some distortion in the information flow. In particular, the way primary campaigns have been reported may have an undue influence on outcomes. Paid political advertising is an effective means for providing information to voters, but its high costs unfortunately increase the dependence of candidates on donors. Proposals to reduce the distortion of politics by television are presented.

Nelson's chapter on the presidential nominating system also examines the unintended effects of the process on electoral outcomes. The historical forces that have shaped the nominating process, he shows, have not promoted the simplicity and clarity most conducive to truly democratic outcomes. Various possible reforms are discussed.

This section concludes with Fleishman's reaffirmation of the values of our democratic society in light of two quite disparate threats: (1) the growing force of those who wish to legislate personal morality, thereby threatening personal freedoms, and (2) the attempts by skeptics and radicals who recognize imper-fections in American institutions to undermine the citizenry's faith in those institutions.

Economic Well-being

Today, government is held responsible for promoting the economic well-being of the nation. How and where that responsibility should be carried out has become a primary subject for debate. We start with the poor. Have we provided them with an adequate standard of living? How can we do so, without drawing them into dependency?

Kasten and Todd show that the past decade's near-doubling of federal social welfare spending had not significantly reduced the number of people below the official poverty threshold. In particular, they show that AFDC benefits declined substantially in real terms during the 1970s. Though benefit levels are set by the states, the federal government has policy options for influencing state decisions. The authors discuss various possible strategies. Whatever the outcome of the debate on the new federalism, the issues addressed here must be considered in any attempt to reform our welfare system.

Robins, West, and Steiger provide a means to evaluate the negative income tax. Analysts ranging across the political spectrum have proposed the negative income tax as the preferred major reform of our current welfare system. In the past decade, a handful of experimental programs have tried to implement the concept on a limited scale. The authors examine the experience of these programs, and develop a general statistical procedure for assessing the impact of the negative income tax on labor supply.

The latest round of federal tax cuts has provoked frequent charges (and denials) of giveaways to the affluent. Unfortunately, statistics are rarely considered in the debate, in part because our methodologies for measuring progressivity are weak. Berliant and Strauss attack this problem, providing a novel method for measuring the progressivity of taxes across income groups and the equity of taxes within them. They test their method with data from 1973, 1975, and 1978.

In the distributional debate, unions have traditionally played the role of the worker's principal protector. But unions have rapidly been losing their members, and their status. Not surprisingly, unions have attempted to work through the government to stem these flows. Two chapters in this volume focus on labor relations and government. Bennett and Johnson argue that, because of changes in the labor force, unions will not be able to stem their membership declines by appealing directly to workers, and will adopt new techniques that rely on influencing management and government. Raphaelson examines the controversy surrounding a particular piece of labor legislation, the Davis-Bacon Act, which requires that wages paid on federally financed construction projects meet local norms. The Act is frequently cited for promoting inflation and defeating efficiency and many have urged its repeal. Reviewing the evidence and arguments, the author concludes that the decision whether to repeal the Act will depend not on its consequences for efficiency, but rather on who benefits from the Act, and who would benefit from its repeal.

Substantial inflation was the major new issue to appear on the nation's economic policy agenda in the last half dozen years. What was the source of that inflation? How effective were the Carter administration's efforts to deal with it? Cecchetti, McClain, McKee, and Saks use econometric modeling to test the impact of oil price shocks on the underlying rate of inflation and to assess the effectiveness of the Carter administration's incomes policies. Their findings suggest that the appropriate aggregate demand policy response to an external supply shock is to try to maintain the expected gap between actual and potential gross national product, rather than to adopt sharply restrictive policies. Viscusi examines the Carter program of price and pay standards more closely, concluding that it had little impact on prices and that the observed slowing of wage increases may have been due to the energy price shock rather than the Carter policy. He attributes these poor results to a lack of enforcement tools, as well as the administration's failure to integrate the program into a broader anti-inflation effort.

Health

A central debate in policy circles is the extent of the government's responsibility. What arguments are there for the provision of in-kind services as opposed to merely cash? Apart from instances of market failure, when is government intervention justified? Outside the economic arena, health is the area where the government role is most substantial, most widely accepted, and growing most rapidly. Four studies suggest ways to rationalize health care expenditures.

Graham and Vaupel start by looking at the emotionally charged question of how to value the lives saved through a given program or policy. They show that alternative methodologies often produce markedly different estimates, but that these differences generally have little significance for policy choice. Their findings also indicate that the cost of a life (or life-year) saved differs widely across programs and agencies.

One of the most effective ways to improve the nation's health, it is widely alleged, is to change the life styles of individuals. Anderson, Boardman, and Inman examine a large sample of white male twins to identify the factors associated with the adoption of health-promoting habits. Beyond socioeconomic variables, certain events, such as a heart attack, seem to have an influence on habit formation, suggesting some scope for policies related to health education and preventive medical care.

Cook pursues the discussion of life styles and examines a particular measure, taxes on liquor. He demonstrates statistically that a decline in the real price of liquor (induced historically by a failure to increase taxes with inflation) has led to more deaths due to cirrhosis and automobile accidents. By reducing consumption, Cook concludes, an increase in liquor taxes could have significant public health benefits, as well as reduce government-financed medical costs of drinkers.

How long people stay in hospitals is a major determinant of health care costs. What length of stay is appropriate for a particular type of individual with a particular health problem? Stoto develops a methodology for estimating distributions of length of stay for different populations, which should prove useful in formulating and evaluating hospital policies. More generally, his procedures can be applied to any policy, such as welfare or unemployment, where duration of stay or condition is important.

Regulation

The analysis of regulation has blossomed along with its subject. Here the key issues are not purely economic, political, or legal. What should be the balance between the carrot and the stick? On what basis should we choose between administrative command-and-control and incentive-based approaches? And a fundamental challenge to the whole policy analytic approach has even reached the level of Supreme Court debate: Should costs and benefits guide regulatory interventions?

Broder and Morall examine one of the most sensitive arenas, the regulation of carcinogens. The Occupational Safety and Health Administration and the Environmental Protection Agency have pursued different policy approaches to the problem, with EPA markedly more receptive to the use of cost-benefit analysis. The authors find that many of OSHA's regulations have been more cost-effective than might have been expected, given the agency's aversion to economic considerations. However, for both OSHA and EPA, the cost of a life saved through carcinogen regulation exceeds the estimated willingness-to-pay of direct beneficiaries.

O'Hare and Mundel focus on programs that transfer resources to lower levels of government to reward good behavior—a timely concern in this age of renewed debate on federalism. Such programs in effect regulate behavior. The authors take efficiency, maximum output per dollar spent, as their major concern, yet argue that such transfer programs should be retroactive. Otherwise, decisions are likely to be deferred until it is clear whether the higher level of government will authorize a program that would reward the contemplated action (e.g., the construction of a toxic waste facility). A program not enacted this session in not necessarily killed conclusively; thus the delay can be a long one.

The analysis identifies a previously unrecognized link among programs: Making a current program retroactive will change expectations about the retroactivity of future programs and can thus encourage "premature" good behavior in other areas. More generally, the authors show that the way a program changes our conception of government function may be as important as its specific impacts.

DeMuth probes the idea of regulation itself in a framework that melds legal and economic approaches. He reviews the major alternative conceptions of regulation that have been advanced in the recent literature, and then offers his own definition: Regulation is the prescription by government of the terms of private transactions. DeMuth points out that this definition "defines the limit of regulation's ability either to redistribute income or to improve the efficiency of markets."

Management

The great advances in policy analysis of the past twenty years have revealed the importance of new areas of research. Even if we know what policy is preferred, little may be accomplished if it is not effectively implemented and capably managed. Scholars as well as practitioners in the public policy field have recently been devoting much more attention to issues of implementation and management. Hargrove examines the various factors that affect implementation (organizational incentives, politics and bureaucracy), and tries to develop a general theory of implementation that will be useful in assessing the likely effectiveness of proposed policies.

Government policies often cannot attain their objectives without incidentally harming certain individuals. Cordes, Goldfarb, and Barth examine the rationales for compensating such individuals, and consider the practical forms such compensation might take.

In an era of government retrenchment, public managers will increasingly have to grapple with the problems of cutting back. Behn offers timely, practical suggestions for maintaining the efficiency and effectiveness of an organization while reducing its size.

Postscript

The volume concludes with Fleishman's assessment of the origins of the fledgling science of policy analysis, and its development over the past dozen years. The justification for this new discipline rests on one central tenet: Whatever roles government may assume, they will be better performed if they are better understood. Granting this, Fleishman's article sounds an optimistic note for future contributions from a profession charged to understand the way government does and can work, the profession of policy analysis and management.

The Role of Analysis

Our governmental structure requires only that beliefs and values be expressed through the electoral process, whether those beliefs are well- or ill-informed, whether those values are self-serving or public-spirited. In practice, our nation has taken minimal steps—most significantly through the support of public education—to encourage a more informed outcome of the political process. Still, the United States has soundly rejected the notion of placing educational requirements on franchise, and has refused to deviate from our representative system of government to achieve more seemingly rational political outcomes.

By contrast, it seems to be generally accepted that the policy choices made by government—particularly those of the executive branch—should be based on sound thinking and—where it will make a difference—supported by rational analysis. It is not obvious from whence this norm derives. Surely it is not the Constitution. Had our founding fathers foreseen the nature of our modern government, so intricately entwined with so many aspects of its citizens' lives, perhaps they would have laid down rules of procedure for government decision. They left no such instructions, however. (Their instructions on other matters suggest that they put more faith in systems of checks and balances that could harness men's greed to public purposes than they did in careful calculation by well-informed, dispassionate leaders and electorate.)

In reality, analysis plays far less of a role in shaping government than citizens expect and believe, and less still than policy makers allege. This divergence between imagined and real roles for analysis is able to persist because our ability to trace from policy to outcome is still so limited. Controlled experiments, the most reliable source of evidence, often pose equity problems, and are too costly to mount in most important cases. Statistical analyses that merely look at the world as it evolves are handicapped by a lack of natural variation: One cannot compare the outcomes under alternative federal policies, since only one is in effect. Further confounding the process of inference, when we look across individuals or states, are the many uncontrolled variables, usually unfortunately arranged in dependent patterns. In some instances, it is not even possible to identify whether a change in policy variable would help or hurt on a specified government objective. Would more sophisticated missiles for the U.S. reduce or increase the likelihood of our own nuclear destruction? Will additional regulations affecting hospital behavior raise or lower costs? Will a loosening of our monetary policy diminish or increase long-run rates of inflation?

It is very difficult to disprove policy analyses. Thus, when formulating policy and the instruments to manage it, our government frequently finds it politically helpful to invoke the form of analysis—"I have before me a study that shows. . ." —while at the same time discarding the spirit of analysis, dispassionate objectivity. But it need not always be this way.

Throughout this nation's history we find important scholarly studies of public policy. Alexander Hamilton's influential *Report on the Subject of Manufactures*, identifying the government's responsibilities to promote the private sector, provides an example. Whether judged in terms of insight or impact, it compares favorably with similarly oriented current assessments of policies to encourage industrial growth. But policy analysis as a major industry is predominantly a post-World War II development.

First came national security. As the strategic realities of the post-war era unfolded, a generation of thinkers, disproportionately associated with the Rand Corporation, developed insightful though simple theories of appropriate military posture and balance. As a complement to this movement, and in no small part to bring the unruly military services under civilian control, the systems analysis approach was increasingly applied to military weapons and manpower, and within the Defense Department itself. For the first time in government, microeconomic principles were applied on a wide-spread basis to areas outside traditional economic realms such as regulation, antitrust, or agriculture.

Vietnam set back the credibility of systems analysis, particularly in relation to military issues, in part because analytic techniques were misused or applied to improperly formulated problems. Many analysts who worked within the defense establishment were discredited. Those who ventured outside typically refused to work on defense matters. The nation's understanding of military issues may well have suffered appreciably from the antagonism felt by most emerging young thinkers and analysts toward the assessment of these problems. The absence of defense policy analysis in this volume reflects the paucity of nongovernment work in this field, particularly within the public policy schools at major universities. It is a serious omission, which the editors regret.

Defense issues, and their relation to more general problems of foreign policy and international relations, are crucial public concerns. Their importance starts with the need to provide security for the nation without excessively draining resources. Careful analytic work could be of great value in examining such issues as the prospects for the NATO alliance; the relative roles of conventional and nuclear capabilities in deterring or stimulating conflicts; mechanisms to reduce levels of nuclear and conventional weapons; East-West economic relations and their effects on the military balance; and the international weapons market and its relation to third-world economic development.

Defense issues also interact with domestic policy concerns: manpower problems raise controversies over conscription, women's rights, and racial balance; weapons procurement spotlights the imperfectly understood relationship between the development of military and civilian technologies. And the foreign policy issue of nuclear weapons control seems likely to have major domestic political consequences in the 1980s.

Already established in the defense area, the systematic approach to policy issues was waiting in the wings when, in the early 1960s, the nation started to grapple with issues of domestic policy. With heady optimism, the government launched a crusade to conquer the ills of poverty, inadequate education, etc. Through evaluation and systematic review, we would learn the most efficacious means to accomplish these goals. Matters did not work out that way. All too often, policy analysis became the bearer of bad news about the Great Society efforts of the 1960s and the protective regulation revolution of the 1970s: "All manpower training programs fall far short of their announced objectives; most are worthless." "OSHA has not noticeably reduced the accident rate in the workplace." "Some air pollution regulations are not only excessively costly, but counterproductive." "Busing may promote, not reduce, racial antagonisms."

There were exceptions, but policy analysis spoke mostly for lowered expectations. Not surprisingly, there have been attempts to shoot the messenger. Many an environmental activist or advocate for the poor regards systems analysis or cost-benefit analysis as the enemy. In policy circles, the feeling is widespread that analysis is inherently a conservative tool. This is not to suggest that many conservatives would embrace policy analysis. If policy analysis has pushed for lessened government intervention, that is only fortuitous. The basis for the discipline, they would probably argue, is invalid. Government should not be assigned the task of maximizing some net size of pie, according to some technical rules, as policy analysis prescribes. Rather, government actions should be a product of creative tension and struggle; they should reflect the moral, cultural, and political forces that impinge upon them.

It would be premature to conclude that policy analysis on the whole argues for lessened government intervention. So far, our opportunity to view policy analysis in action has been limited to an era in which government budgets and responsibilities were expanding in response to powerful political tides. Matters may turn in this era of retrenchment. Already we find analyses whose message is that present efforts to slash social programs are ill advised even if our only goal is to cut resource expenditures. An excessive reduction in food stamps, or maternal health care, or compensatory education programs may lead to substantially increased future expenditures on health care, prisons, or unemployment compensation. If such relationships are to be demonstrated, analysis will be required.

From time to time the political climate may favor the economic approach implicit in the analytic approach to policy. But that is more likely to be a reflection of the increased power of those who would gain from the change, rather than from an enhanced recognition of the virtues of efficiency. In the conservative clime of the moment, for example, energy price deregulation is bolstered and in-kind transfer programs are trimmed. Supporters of such measures will surely cloak themselves in the mantle of the pursuit of efficiency. But for many of them, the efficiency norm will be less compelling when providing special encouragements, such as depreciation rates in excess of true value, to business investment. Indeed for the most part, we would argue, those who are in control of some aspect of the political process will be the ones who least wish to invoke the yardstick of efficiency. For example, in the early 1970s, when protective regulation was in its heyday, cost-benefit and other such economic accoutrements were the bane of the proponents of stricter regulation. As became evident with the landmark disputes over benzene and cotton dust, industry wished to apply the balancing scales of economic cost against the values of health loss.

Now with fortunes turned, what will happen if for some new piece of environmental legislation there is the opportunity to reduce costs to business but only at greater cost to the environment? Now, we might expect, those who previously proposed the introduction of economic assessment methods would reverse their stand. Indeed, in the environmental area we may well have come full circle from the 1950s, when environmentalists first proposed the application of cost-benefit methods as a means to counter public works projects that created undercounted long-term costs to the environment.

A more sophisticated view of policy analysis is not that it serves particular sets of values, but rather that it operates as a disciplining tool for government. Its function may resemble that of certified accounting in for-profit institutions. Analysis frequently points out the excesses that those in power, with political force behind them, are tempted to undertake.

From these considerations emerges a maxim: The careful counting and weighing of all of the consequences of a policy will be in the interest of the political "outs." Policy analysis tempers the "ins' " ability to exploit their superior political position and their control of information flow. If this disciplining hypothesis proves correct, policy analysis may systematically switch sides in this era of retrenchment and become a voice for maintaining worthwhile government programs.

Government as Resource Shifter

A major challenge for government in the coming decade will be to define its function in the wrestling ring where the battles are for economic resources. What with tax advantages, antitrust decisions, tariffs, the imposition of regulations favoring one party or another, the government can no longer pretend to be playing the role of impartial referee. But should it seek to reclaim at least some portion of its impartial stance? If not, which contenders should it help? Is there any guarantee or even suggestion that our political system provides help in the right corner?

Analytic approaches to these issues suggest that concentrated interests are more likely to gain through the political process at the expense of diffuse interests. Established interest groups carry more weight than those that have the potential to be established. If so, we must expect to find governments, particularly the federal government, on the side of our large industries, many of which are losing competitive positions in world markets. This tendency will be reinforced by the appeals for preventing losses from the status quo.

The government's major role as resource shifter has more or less come upon it unsought. It is the product of thousands of small decisions, each responding to some cry of need, some demonstration of political strength, some call for equity. In not a few arenas, the government was unwittingly drawn into its predominant role. The innocuous role of guarantor is often the entree. Guaranteed mortgage programs have, through defaults, made the government the premiere landlord in many cities. Through its guarantees of deposits, government threatens to become a leading banker. Through the Pension Benefit Guarantee Corporation, and attempts to assure adequate funding of private plans, it may soon find itself a major participant in collective bargaining agreements.

In its resource-shifting role, the government may provide some direct financial support. But camouflaged assistance—loan guarantees, tariffs, restrictive agreements on imports, special dispensation on pension funding—though less efficient, usually proves more popular. Off-budget expenditures are less exposed to public scrutiny and less vulnerable to the budget-cutter's knife.

In the early 1980s we find that the government has eased into a major role as resource shifter, but without any well-established rationale, without a convincing demonstration that efforts are pushing in the appropriate direction, and with considerable suspicion that many government programs of this type are working at cross purposes.

There is widespread agreement that something should be done. There the agreement stops. Under the reindustrialization banner, we hear cries for more vigorous policies to support our major declining industries such as autos or steel. Others, arguing that established interest groups already have too much influence on the political allocation of resources, suggest that countervailing strategies must be taken. They could be of two types: First, we could compensate these interests through mechanisms such as retraining programs or relocation assistance, and thereby diminish the urgency of their claims for protection. Second, emerging industries themselves could be supported with new instruments, such as greater subsidies to research and development or government programs that guarantee them favorable access to capital.

A third group would argue that both of these approaches are misguided. Providing more instruments for government action, encouraging new supplicants for government largesse, even with a beneficial shift in power relationships, will simply lead to a further decline in market discipline. If our steel producers and genetic engineering firms are locked in battle for government or government-directed dollars, there may be no one to speak for the stormwindow firm or the pizza parlor. In its optimistic moments, this third group would argue that the government could be eased out of its inappropriate role as a shifter of resources.

In the past two decades we have learned how government can better perform many roles. Yet there seems to be a widespread perception that government functions less well than it did twenty years ago, and that its legitimacy has been diminished. Why has government lost ground despite our growing knowledge? The increasing scope and complexity of its business provides a partial explanation. More important, we would argue, the government has evolved, often without conscious attention, into a major array of activities that lie beyond its traditional mandate. With few exceptions, the public consensus required to establish new mandates has not been developed.

Whether the matter under consideration is auto emissions or auto imports, the health of individuals or the health of the economy, the central policy question for the 1980s is likely to be: What role for government?

Part I. Democracy and Elections

1. The Role of Television in American Politics

Fred Wertheimer and Randy Huwa

Abstract

In the last 30 years, television has become the primary source of news for most Americans and a dominant force in politics as well. This study attempts to assess the impact of television on the political process. The analysis is based on the premise that (a) television can be a very positive force in politics and (b) the tendencies of television to distort politics can be overcome. The study examines the role of television in three different political contexts: Presidential nominations—TV coverage of primaries tends to exaggerate the importance of early primaries and gives undue attention to winners. Correcting this distortion requires more balanced media coverage and modifications of the nominating process itself. Political programming—news, the first facet of TV political programming, tends to focus on the events of a campaign rather than on the substance: the issues and candidates' personalities. The networks can take and have taken steps to devote more attention to issue coverage. Further, public affairs broadcasting, the second major facet, provides valuable information to voters but is somewhat restricted by communications regulations. Possible remedies include repeal of the "equal time" rule and the institution of a system of free "voters time" for candidates. Paid political advertising—TV spots, though much maligned, provide candidates with an unprecedented forum for the presentation of information to voters. The increasing costs of the medium, however, threaten to reduce access and increase candidate dependence on political action committee (PAC) contributions. This study explores the modification of the existing "lowest unit rate" rule to reduce the costs of TV advertising.

> If a tree falls in the forest, and the media aren't there to cover it, has the tree really fallen?
>
> —cartoon from *Saturday Review*

The last three decades have seen a phenomenal, society-altering explosion of television. In 1950 fewer than 10 percent of American households had TV sets. Today television has an almost total market penetration—98 percent of all U.S. households have one or more TV sets, with an average of 1.67 sets per household.

The TV set is an active participant in most American homes. On the average, an American TV set is in use seven hours per day. The average American spends nearly three hours a day watching television, and on a typical evening, nearly half the population will be watching. A February 1980 poll conducted by the Roper Organization found that 91 percent of the respondents had watched some television in the previous 24 hours. For special events, as many as 75 to 80 million people may be watching the same telecast simultaneously (Graber, 1980).

In one generation, television has become the primary source of entertainment for the average American and the primary source of news as well. According to the Roper poll, television has been the chief news source for most Americans in every year since 1959. On a daily basis, the evening news programs on the three networks reached an average audience of 56 million individuals, up to 5 million in the last year alone. And polls since 1961 consistently have shown that television is the news medium that most people feel is most believable.

Not surprisingly, the use of television by politicians closely parallels the explosive development of the TV industry. In the 1980 presidential campaign, for example, television consumed more than half of the total campaign budgets of Jimmy Carter and Ronald Reagan (Bonafede, 1981). Television appears to have become the single most important strategic resource for virtually all U.S. Senate races, major statewide candidacies, and many congressional campaigns (White, 1978). TV time and production costs, which have skyrocketed in the past decade, can consume one-third to one-half of campaign expenditures in elections at all levels of government (Graber, 1980).

The importance of television in politics has reached the point at which Theodore H. White can say, "Television is the political process—it's the playing field of politics. Today the action is in the studios, not in the back rooms" (Bonafede, 1980b). In significant ways, the media provide candidates with direct access to voters and have replaced the parties as the conveyors of political information (Swerdlow, 1981). Veteran Republican campaign manager John Sears has called the news media—the press, radio, and television—the "bosses of our political system." And Phillips (1975:v) has bemoaned the emergence of a "mediacracy."

Curiously, television became a dominant force in American politics during the past three decades with relatively little public attention. We watched the daily network and local TV news programs, we saw the paid political commercials, we listened to the TV debates when they occurred. But we did so almost unconscious as a society of the profound impact that television was having on the political process, on our ability to govern and be governed.

The challenge for the American political system in the 1980s is to come to grips with television. Too often, politicians yearn for the "good old days" when political news came from the party block captain—not from Walter Cronkite— and when the candidate selection process was not open to television's probing eye. Yet there is no room for nostalgia. The TV genie is out of the bottle. Television is here—and here to stay—as an incredibly powerful communications medium. And new technological advances—increased deployment of cable systems, satellite networks, and the like—promise to perpetuate the influence of television.

This study attempts to assess the impact of television on the political process. The analysis is based on two premises. *First, television can be a very positive force in the political process.* Television has the capacity for instantly communicating more political information and discussion of issues to more people than anyone would have thought possible three decades ago. Robert MacNeil (1980:37) of public broadcasting has written, "Indisputably television has brought the electorate into more intimate contact with politicians than had ever been thought possible. Most Americans alive when he was president never actually saw Abraham Lincoln. Now millions can see and hear Jimmy Carter every day, as close as if they were sitting beside him in a cabinet meeting." As President Kennedy observed, television allows citizens to examine their public officials and candidates "close up and close to the bone, for the first time since the Greek city-states" (Senate Commerce Committee, 1971:27).

Second, the negative effects that television has had on the political process can be tempered. The peculiarities of television lead, without design or intent, to a distorted coverage of politics. Television, for example, has a unique capacity to intensify. Like the magnifying glass that a child uses to focus the sun on a blade of grass until it begins to burn up, television can bring white heat—irresistible heat—to the subject of its attention. The familiarity that television brings—the ability to view politics "up close and personal"—may breed its own form of skepticism, increasing voter indifference and contempt. As a medium that is watched rather than studied, television has a preference for the colorful and scenic setting, even though "talking heads" are a much more important part of politics. Television is also normally forced to compress politics into very small morsels. The result of these time pressures is the TV version of the short story; 60- or 90-second segments become the standard lengths for "in-depth" discussions of issues, candidates, and campaigns.

TV Looks at Politics: The Presidential Primaries

In the last 12 years, the process by which the major political parties select their presidential standardbearers has been greatly altered by the proliferation of state primary elections. In 1968 there were 16; in 1980 a presidential contender was faced with 36. An outgrowth of the Progressive era and an important vehicle for direct citizen involvement in party politics, the presidential primary also could have been invented by a director of TV spectaculars—cheering crowds, stump speeches, motorcades, and, most important, election-night coverage. In fact, the mass media may have contributed to the growth in the number of primaries; Swerdlow (1981:91) has called presidential primaries "the handmaidens of television." First, the boosterism these races bring—every state would like a visit from John Chancellor or the staff of "Today"—has encouraged the proliferation of primaries. Second, as Rubin has suggested, the media have portrayed primaries "as *the* democratic way to make nomination choices" (Patterson, 1980a:4).

In a system with this many races, it could be argued, a single primary is just one indicator of a candidate's popularity—a return from one of many units. Furthermore, a presidential primary lacks the finality of a general election—both winners and losers survive, and, because of proportional representation, most candidates are likely to pick up convention delegates.

But while the "winner-take-all" primary has been barred from presidential campaigns, the media in general and the networks in particular have developed a very close facsimile. Thomas E. Patterson's study (1980a:44) of the 1976 presidential primaries found that "no matter how close the balloting, the state's leading vote getter was awarded the headlines and most of the coverage. To finish second, even a close second, was to receive little attention from the press." Coverage of nominating primaries should resemble a series of snapshots of a continuing process; too often, primaries are presented as a series of playoff games—with one candidate the winner, the rest sent to the showers.

Patterson's study of the 1976 primaries demonstrates the media's winner-take-all coverage. In the New Hampshire primary, Jimmy Carter received 28 percent of the vote, trailed by Representative Morris Udall (D-AZ) with 23 percent and a host of others. Yet television (and newspapers) gave the victorious Carter four times the coverage they gave to each of his major rivals. The New Hampshire example was part of a general pattern. In the typical week following a primary election, 60 percent of the news coverage went to the candidate who finished first. The second-place finisher—no matter how narrow the margin of "victory"—garnered 20 percent, with 15 percent to the third-place candidate and 5 percent for number four (Patterson, 1980a).

If the media like to identify the winners of presidential primaries, then there is no winner like the first—the winner in New Hampshire. A study of three months of TV coverage of the 1976 campaign (Patterson, 1980a) found that over half of the network evening news stories discussed the New Hampshire primary. ABC political correspondent Hal Bruno complained, "We had to cover New Hampshire, but I wanted to scream that it wasn't important, that it was only a small, first step. Yet it never came through" (Bonafede, 1980a:1132). According to Michael Robinson (1978:42), "The key to winning the nomination is merely to be *declared* the winner by the networks in the New Hampshire primary."

The results of this type of coverage are obvious. Winners of early primaries quickly become front-runners with subsequent increases in media attention; losers, despite substantial promises of support in later primaries, are quickly relegated to the category of also-rans and have difficulty raising money and attracting volunteers. The principle of "one person, one vote" notwithstanding, the participants in Iowa's caucuses or New Hampshire's primary have a much greater say in the election of the major party presidential nominees than do the voters of, for instance, California or New Jersey.

To correct this imbalance, the networks should take steps to improve their coverage of presidential primaries. Television must resist the temptation to label every primary the make-it-or-break-it election, for instance, and must focus attention on delegate counts as well as primary returns.

But more importantly, the presidential nominating system itself is in need of a major overhaul. ABC's Hal Bruno concedes, "There is no question the media have an impact on the system. But the system is at fault; the media are as much a victim as anyone else. We are carried along, week after week; it's like riding a tidal wave . . . the system is an abomination; it is too long and too costly and the early primaries have an impact far out of proportion to reality" (Bonafede, 1980a:1133). By changing these procedures, the political system could do much to dilute the unintended but distorting effect that TV coverage has on the presidential nominating process. Three current proposals for modifying the primary system are to institute a national primary, a system of regional primaries, or a series of fixed dates for primaries within a certain time frame.

A National Primary

A Gallup poll taken in 1980 showed that 66 percent of the public favored a national primary, allowing voters to choose nominees by direct popular vote on a single date. While a national primary would end the undue influence of early primary states and would be the ultimate simplification of the process, it would eliminate the testing that a series of primaries provides. One of the advantages of the current crazy-quilt system is that it allows a fresh face to be tested and emerge from the pack over the course of a campaign. Competition is not limited to incumbents, well-known personalities, and candidates of the monied interests. A national primary might make it impossible for an able but relatively unknown candidate to win a nomination. In addition, a national primary would further undermine the role of political parties and their national conventions in the nominating process.

Regionial Primaries

A less drastic remedy for modifying the process is a proposal for regional primaries. Proponents of regional primaries—where all state primaries in a given region or time zone would be held on the same day—argue that they would facilitate the efficient use of media and candidate travel and would help focus attention on regional issues. Critics argue that a system of regional primaries would require significant changes in existing state primary dates and would pose the difficult problem of deciding the order of the regional primaries. This critical decision might well skew the discussion of issues or the choice of candidates, depending on which region would vote first. The discussion of energy issues, for example, might be quite different depending on whether the candidates began in the Northeast or the Southwest.

Limited Primary Dates

The most promising of the proposals designed to improve the nominating process would restrict the delegate selection process to a three-month period and limit state primaries to four or five specific dates within that period. By clustering state primaries on a few specific dates, this proposal would diminish the importance of the early individual state contests and minimize the ability of the press to call winners and losers. With a number of primaries representing various regions on the same day, credible candidates would be less likely to fall victim to early knockouts. If, for example, caucuses and primaries were held on March 25 in such states as Florida, Illinois, Iowa, New Hampshire, New York, and Washington, the mixed results would probably produce several winners. The media's ability to establish momentum and deliver death blows would be lessened.

In addition, this target date proposal, unlike the national or regional primary proposals, would provide flexibility to states in selecting primary dates. This plan could be adopted by federal legislation but might gain more widespread acceptance if proposed as amendments to Democratic and Republican party rules. Patterson has also suggested that a series of staggered dates—separated by three to four weeks—would give time for candidate travel and also "would provide the press with more space in which to report the candidates' views, since each Tuesday would not bring contests that the press felt compelled to forecast, report, and analyze." This would give voters a better opportunity to consider their election choices, for in 1976, as Patterson noted, and in 1980, "Each week was so filled with news of the latest and upcoming races that voters thought and talked about almost nothing but the candidates' success in the primaries" (Patterson, 1980a:178).

The Message of the Medium: TV Presentation of Campaigns

If television is the major source of news for most Americans, if—as Roper (1979:7–8) indicates—television is the news source through which most people become "best acquainted" with candidates for U.S. House and Senate seats and statewide offices, what kind of job is the medium doing? How well does television convey to voters information about the candidates and the issues of a campaign? To answer these questions, two facets of television must be examined. First, what picture of an election emerges from regularly scheduled TV news programs? And second, how well can voters learn about candidates and issues through special public affairs programming—candidate debates, interviews, and the like?

The News

An examination of the content of TV news coverage of political campaigns reveals that television tends to provide voters with more information on the process than the substance of campaigns. Because television deals with short story segments, because television is primarily a visual medium, because the network news is a nightly undertaking, TV news focuses on events—the results of the presidential primaries, the opinion polls, the motorcades and airport stops, on the eye-catching movement—rather than on the substance—the issues of an election, the personalities of the candidates. TV coverage emphasizes the horse-race nature of campaigns—who's ahead, by how much, and in what track conditions. Patterson's study of the 1976 presidential campaign found that the press "concentrated on the strategic game played by the candidates in their pursuit of the presidency, thereby deemphasizing questions of national policy and leadership." Patterson discovered that more than half of the election coverage dealt with the competition between the candidates—"winning and losing, strategy and organization, appearances and tactics." Only 30 percent of the coverage was devoted to a discussion of campaign issues and candidates' policy positions. While Patterson found that election coverage by all media concentrates on the strategic game rather than the issues, he also determined that "the tendencies are more pronounced on television than in the newspapers" (Patterson, 1980b:2–3).

Representatives of all players in the news drama—the candidates, their campaign aides, and the correspondents themselves—bemoan the media's fascination with the horse race. NBC's Irving R. Levine has said, "News isn't something that's reported day after day. So if Kennedy or Anderson has said it five or six times a day in stump speeches, you can't keep reporting the economic positions. . . . So you report the heckler, the change of position, the reaction to possibly some charge that has been leveled." Dan Cordtz, an ABC News correspondent, complains about the "same old here-they-come, there-they-go kind of coverage. You see the plane landing at the airport, you see the motorcade into town, and, 'oh yeah, folks, he said this.' Then a 10-second standup at the airport where the correspondent handicaps the candidate's chances" (Groff et al., 1980:73, 103–104). The *Washington Post*'s Robert Kaiser (1980: A1, A3) has divided the 1980 network election coverage into three categories—the charge-countercharge, the day-in-the-life-of-the-candidate-on-the-road story, and the handicapper's report—and has identified one common characteristic: "none of them conveys much information to voters that is likely to help a serious but undecided voter to make up his or her mind about how to vote."

One of the survivors of the press roller-coaster ride in the 1980 campaign, George Bush, has stated:

I was accused of not speaking on the issues, and the reason was that I was not perceptive enough to fail to answer all those questions about "how well are you going to do next Tuesday?" I was speaking on the issues for a year and a half in every forum, every Q and A, and every speech, and all the reporters were interested in was "When do you have to beat Reagan by?" Then they level the charge against me that I didn't talk about any issues even though it was their questions I was responding to. I learned later not to respond to those questions, and then the coverage became somewhat more substantive. It was my fault as well as theirs. Their interest was in what horse race was on next week. (*Washington Journalism Review*, 1980:28)

The steps needed to make the evening news more attentive to the issues of the campaign—and perhaps less descriptive of the horse race of the campaign itself—are not actions that can or should be mandated by Congress or the Federal Communications Commission (FCC). These are changes that appropriately can be made, and have been made, by the networks themselves. Before the 1980 campaign began, for example, ABC reporter Dan Cordtz prepared a memorandum that called for more in-depth reporting of candidates' stands on the issue. "Nobody talks about the issues," Cordtz wrote. "Why don't we compel the candidates to talk about the issues? And if they don't why don't we talk about the issues?" In partial response to Cordtz' suggestions, ABC did a series of four nightly stories outlining the candidates' stands (Groff et al., 1980:8-9).

This example is not unique. Despite preliminary suggestions that the 1980 campaign would resemble the 1976 campaign in its fixation on motion,[1] all three networks seem to have done a better job of covering the issues in 1980. All three networks devoted more attention to in-depth interviews and analyses of important campaign issues. Robinson and Sheehan (1980:16) report, "Our own predictions, as well as those of most of the critics, about noncoverage of issues, were wide of the mark. . . . The networks—all of them—did get around to talking seriously about issues as the campaigns moved closer to election day. Coverage of the early campaign, which had been a desert in terms of issues, had been transformed, if not into a bountiful garden, at least into something capable of sustaining voters hungry for news about the issues."

These efforts are hampered, of course, by the tight time constraints of a network news broadcast. No less an authority than Walter Cronkite has stated, "It has become impossible to cover the news with the half-hour show. We have a responsibility that we simply cannot discharge" (Halberstam 1981:7). One possible partial solution is expansion of the evening network news from 30 minutes to one hour. In the last 15 years, most local news shows have expanded from 15 minutes to one hour—up to two hours in many areas. This expanded format provides more opportunities for in-depth discussion of the issues, longer interviews with candidates, and reports on campaign issues by correspondents with expertise in such fields as economics, foreign affairs, and the like. A similar expansion is needed at the national level. ABC's "Nightline," which provides a 30-minute look at two or three stories, and the CBS "Sunday Morning" program illustrate the type of coverage that an expanded news program might provide.[2]

Public Affairs Broadcasting

While news broadcasts have the potential for providing voters with basic information on a daily and regular basis, special public affairs broadcasting—debates, individual interviews, and other "free time" opportunities—are generally a much richer source of information about candidates and issues. Following the September 1980 square-off between presidential contenders John Anderson and Reagan for example, Henry Brandon (1980:A15) described the true value of debates when he observed:

> In an age when candidates are being merchandised, manipulated, processed, orchestrated, motivated, cosmeticized by the image-makers, when the campaign ballet is choreographed to the music played by the opinion pollsters, when more and more reliance is placed on bought television time to show the candidates in carefully staged poses speaking to pre-rehearsed men-in-the-street and when the press is kept at arm's length to shield candidates from the hazards of off-the-cuff comments, television debates are still one of the few opportunities left to enable the general public to get a better feel for the personality, the human and political instincts and emotional stability of the candidates.

And debates draw audiences; 120 million people—89 percent of them registered voters—saw at least part of the first debate between Jimmy Carter and Gerald Ford in 1976, and an equal number saw the 1980 confrontation between Carter and Reagan.

Despite the popularity of debates—and aside from the reluctance of some office-seekers to participate—the federal communications statutes themselves are often cited as a prime obstacle to these clashes between the candidates and other forms of potentially valuable public service political broadcasting. The "equal time" rule of the Communications Act of 1934 (47 U.S.C. 315[a]) states: "If any licensee shall permit any person who is a legally qualified candidate for any public office to use a broadcasting station, he shall afford equal opportunities to all other such candidates for that office in the use of such broadcasting station." As the FCC has interpreted the section, TV stations are forbidden to sponsor candidate debates or forums unless all candidates participate (or waive their right to participate). Any qualified candidate who has been excluded from a public service program may legitimately lay claim to an equal amount of time with a comparable audience. Broadcasters argue that this requirement, designed to protect all office-seekers—particularly independent and minor party candidates—in fact serves as a disincentive to public service broadcasting. Rather than involving all candidates, the licensee simply decides to do limited or no political public service broadcasting.

Two exemptions—one for a specific campaign, one of general application—modify the equal opportunities standard. In 1960, by act of Congress, that year's presidential campaign was exempted from Section 315, allowing John F. Kennedy and Richard Nixon to debate without guaranteeing access for the other sixteen contenders. For the 1960 election, the three TV networks provided over 39 hours of free political broadcast time to presidential nominees. In 1964 and 1968, in contrast, when the equal opportunities provision was in full force— and when the candidates themselves refused to debate—the networks provided only 4.5 and 3 hours, respectively (Senate Commerce Committee, 1971).

A second general exemption is contained within the statute itself. Excluded from the equal opportunities standard are bona fide newscasts, news interviews, documentaries (if candidate appearances are incidental), and on-the-spot coverage of bona fide news events. Thus in both 1976 and 1980 the debates among the presidential candidates were hosted by the League of Women Voters and were televised in their entirety by the networks as news events.

To improve public service broadcasting generally—and thereby to make more information about candidates available to voters—the TV networks have repeatedly advocated the repeal of Section 315 (or at least an exemption for candidates for federal office). In February 1980, representatives of all three networks appeared before a House subcommittee and expressed their support for a repeal of the equal opportunities clause. NBC's Bill Monroe, for instance, stated, "It's our basic belief, of course, that outright elimination of Section 315 would be the best way to assure the American public of the kind of free, open coverage of the political process contemplated by the First Amendment" (House Commerce Committee, 1980:49). Ironically, the repeal of Section 315 was also supported by a spokesperson for the Libertarian party, who argued, "Without question this provision of the law has acted to reduce political debate in general, and specifically to inhibit access to the media by the Libertarian Party" (House Commerce Committee, 1980:78).

Despite network support for repeal of Section 315, the proposal has languished in Congress for over two decades. This is not due simply to congressional lethargy; many supporters of Section 315(a) argue that it protects the interest of minority party and underdog candidates. A spokesperson for the Media Access Project, for instance, testified that repeal of the equal opportunities clause would "authorize broadcasters to increase their domination of the minds of the listening and viewing public by discriminating among political opponents and advancing the candidacies of anyone the broadcasters choose" (House Commerce Committee, 1980:91). In arguing against repeal of Section 315, the FCC's Broadcast Bureau stated that removal of the equal opportunities clause would not necessarily stimulate coverage of political events, would greatly increase the number of complaints under the fairness doctrine, and would "once again raise the specter of broadcast favoritism" (General Accounting Office 1979:152). Congressional incumbents are also reluctant to repeal Section 315; poor coverage of their challengers only enhances the name-recognition advantage enjoyed by present office-holders.

Another proposal designed to increase candidate access to television would require TV licensees to supply a certain amount of free time to qualifying candidates. Under this proposal, all TV stations would be required to give "voters' time" (perhaps between five and eight half-hour segments) to major party presidential candidates, with shorter allotments of time for others. Similar broadcast time would also be provided to candidates for U.S. Senate and House seats. Voters' time would be exempt from Section 315; however, the equal opportunities standard (and exemptions) would apply to all other aspects of broadcast coverage of campaigns.

The voters'-time proposal would greatly increase the quantity of public service campaign broadcasting, would provide additional opportunities for debates and forums, and would give candidates relatively uninhibited access to the public airwaves. A number of difficult questions must be tackled, however, if this free-time proposal is to work. First, an equitable and fair method of apportioning time among major, minor, and new party candidates must be established. Voters' time is not designed to preserve the status quo, but providing equal broadcast opportunities to all candidates would only perpetuate the Section 315(a) morass. Second, some method of allocating responsibility for voters' time in the case of congressional candidates would have to be developed for media markets with large populations. New York City stations, for example, are the primary source of television in at least 40 congressional districts, with similar concentrations in Chicago (25) and Los Angeles (28). Third, the issue of the costs of "free" time must be addressed squarely. Production costs for public service broadcasting are in themselves significant—one hour of studio time with two or three cameras might cost $3,000. The far more costly component is the revenue lost to the station because of the cancellation of revenue-producing commercials (White, 1978:72–73). The costs of substantial amounts of voters' time would be considerable and would have to be absorbed by the licensees, passed on to commercial advertisers (through higher rates), or fully or partially offset by federal subsidies. Fourth, public affairs broadcasting of all types—and voters-time segments in particular—would have to be aired during prime time or some other high-audience time. Too often, public affairs political broadcasting is relegated to the wasteland of Sunday morning television or must compete with two National Football League contests. While presidential debates attract enough interest in their own right to draw an audience, other races are not as appealing.

Despite these difficulties, Congress and the TV industry must take steps to encourage public affairs broadcasting. Debates and in-depth interviews offer enormous potential as a means of providing citizens with a close and meaningful look at candidates. As the FCC (1980:2–3, 10) has noted, "In short, the presentation of political broadcasting, while only one of the many elements of service to the public . . . is an important facet, deserving the licensee's closest attention, because of the contribution broadcasting can thus make to an informed electorate —in turn as vital to the proper functioning of our Republic."

Paid Political Advertising: Direct Access and the PACs

A decade ago Dean Burch, then chairman of the FCC, testified, "Any effort to reform the law with regard to political broadcasting should have two major objectives. First, the legislation should promote the widest and most penetrating dissemination possible of views and issues in an election. Second, the reform should minimize the cost of campaigning for office, while at the same time preserving the traditional concept of fairness which has been the long-standing premise of political broadcast law" (Senate Commerce Committee, 1971:185). If these two goals are to be realized—and if the potential of television as a conduit of the candidate's own ideas is to be realized—then the political system must once again come to terms with the political spot commercial.

While the political spot has become a fixture of American politics, it has been much criticized and derided. TV spots, it is argued, tend to be superficial, misleading, carefully packaged, and not very informative (House Commerce Committee, 1971). Reviewing political TV spots, one campaign advisor has observed, is like "spending an afternoon in the snakehouse of the zoo or riding through a sewer in a glass-bottomed boat" (Thayer, 1973:251). Curtis B. Gans (1979:40–42), director of the Committee for the Study of the American Electorate, has called for a flat ban on TV spots, arguing, " [I]f there is one legislative remedy that might reduce the growing and pervasive American distrust with politics and the increasing desertion of Americans from the polling booth, it is this—abolish the paid political television commercial."

Despite these criticisms, the spot commercial does serve a vital function: it enables a candidate to communicate his or her message directly to the voters, unencumbered by any intervening mechanism or personality. Reagan media advisor Peter Dailey, for instance, has explained: "In our case, media advertising is critically important. It's the only time we can present the governor on our terms—that is, in a straightforward, unfiltered way. He may be on a network evening news program for 10 to 20 seconds, but what is shown is the result of somebody else's judgment and usually centers on some aberration in the campaigns" (Bonafede, 1980c: 1702). TV spots have effectively become the soapboxes of the 1980s; only through TV ads can candidates be assured that their messages will be delivered to their constituents at a time and in a manner that the candidate controls.

TV spots have a demonstrated record of effectiveness in reaching voters. A study of the use of TV spot advertising in a Michigan congressional race in 1974 (Atkins & Heald, 1976:228) found that a TV media campaign can "(1) increase the electorate's level of knowledge about the candidate and his featured issue positions, (2) elevate emphasized issues and attributes higher on the voters' agenda of decisional criteria, (3) stimulate the electorate's interest in the campaign, (4) produce more positive affect toward the candidate as a person, and

(5) intensify polarization of evaluations of the candidate." In the 1976 presidential campaign, Patterson (1980a:177) found that "candidate-controlled communication"—the debates, convention speeches, and TV advertisements—"gave voters the clearest idea of their choices."

Candidates are critically aware of the power of the paid TV advertising, and more and more campaigns are now investing in TV spots (Gans, 1979). Unfortunately, TV time is becoming more and more expensive. In 1974, for example, a 30-second evening prime time spot on a Portland, Oregon, TV station cost $55; the same time today costs $3,000. The cost of a similar ad has jumped from $509 to $3,000 in San Diego and from $1,100 to $3,000 in Baltimore (*Washington Post*, 1980). In the last two years, the cost of five minutes of TV time in rural Wisconsin has escalated from $250 to $950; Washington political consultant Joseph Rothstein estimates that spot advertising costs generally have increased 40 percent in the last year (Leff, 1980).

A sharp increase in the amount spent on campaigns—particularly at the congressional level—closely parallels the increase in the use of television by candidates and its costs. Most observers believe that the huge increase in campaign costs is directly related to the increasing use and expense of television (Alexander, 1976; Gans, 1979; and Reeves, 1980).

The increase in the price of attaining political office is not merely a subject for academic concern but has serious, potentially debilitating consequences for the health of the political system. As Gans (1979:40) has observed, escalating campaign costs—fueled by higher media expenditures—threaten to make elective office a "realistic ambition only for the very rich or for those who are willing to enter office beholden to interests and individuals who have the wherewithal" to finance a competitive campaign.

In their quest for office, congressional candidates are becoming increasingly dependent on one type of contributor with considerable wherewithal—corporate, trade association, and union political action committees (PACs). Since 1974, the number of PACs has increased from 608 to nearly 2,400. The amount of money PACs contribute to congressional campaigns has risen concomitantly —$12.5 million in 1974, $35 million in 1978, $60 million in 1980. These PAC contributions are generally gifts with a legislative purpose, made by interest groups which have legislative goals and which conduct organized Washington lobbying programs. The access these contributions bring, the "strings" tied to these PAC dollars, represent a real threat to our representative form of government (Common Cause, 1979; and Wertheimer, 1980).

By reducing the costs of TV advertising we can reduce the ever-growing congressional addiction to PAC financial support. Congress must, once again, take action to reduce the costs of TV campaigning.

In 1972, as part of an effort to keep campaign costs in check and to prevent advertising price-gouging by TV stations, Congress amended the Communications Act to require special rates for political advertising (47 U.S.C. 315[b]). During the 45 days before a primary election and in the 60 days preceding a general election, candidates are entitled to "the lowest unit charge of the station for the same class and amount of time for the same period." If, for example, a TV station regularly sells 30-second prime-time spots for $1,000 but provides a special package rate of $750 for purchases of ten or more commercials, a candidate in the period immediately before an election may be charged no more than $750, even if he or she only purchases one spot. During the remainder of the calendar year, political spots may be purchased at the rates "made for comparable use of such station by other users thereof" (FCC, 1980).

It is time for Congress to reexamine the lowest unit-rate rule in the light of increasing TV advertising costs and the increasing PAC presence in campaigns. In particular, Congress should consider amending the lowest unit-charge provision to provide TV advertising to political candidates at some fixed percentage —50 percent, for example—of the lowest unit charge. With a minimum of government interference in broadcasting and through a system that treats all office-seekers equally, Congress could reduce the cost of the one medium that provides the most direct communication between candidate and constituent.

In considering modifications to the existing lowest unit-charge standard, Congress must come to grips with the following issues:

Reimbursement for lost advertising revenues. In 1972 Congress took no steps to allow stations to recoup any advertising revenues lost through the imposition of the lowest unit-charge rule. Any resulting loss, it was felt, was part of the station's public service responsibility. This move probably reduced the availability of TV spots for political candidates. An analysis of the 1972 amendments prepared for Harvard (White, 1978:218) concluded that, "As the profitability of political broadcasting declined, somewhat less time was made available by broadcasters for political use."

As Congress considers modifications to the lowest unit-charge standard, it must determine whether a reduction in political advertising rates will result in the imposition of counter-productive quotas by broadcasters. To ward off this possibility, the Institute of Politics' Campaign Study Group at Harvard (1978) has recommended allowing licensees and the networks to deduct from gross income the difference between the actual rate charges for political spots and the average commercial rate for comparable spots. An alternative funding source could be the federal campaign finance account funded by the income tax check-off.

Limitations on reduced rates. Regardless of whether federal reimbursement funding is involved, Congress may wish to consider imposing some limitations on reduced advertising rates. The public good is not necessarily served if one or more candidates saturate a district or state with a media blitz. Congress may wish to set a threshold standard providing candidates with adequate media opportunities at the new reduced lowest rate, with additional buys beyond this minimum to be charged at the lowest existing unit rate.

Coverage of reduced lowest unit rate. The existing lowest unit-charge pro-vision applies to any qualified candidate—whether the office sought is the presidency of the nation or of the school board. As a first step, Congress might want to restrict the applicability of any new reduction in the lowest unit-rate rule to candidates for federal office, particularly if federal reimbursement is involved. Other candidates, of course, would continue to enjoy the benefit of the existing lowest unit charge.

Political parties. The lowest unit-rate rule—and any modifications of it—should be expanded to apply to *bona fide* political parties as well as candidates. Political parties should be encouraged to make public statements about issues and ideas and concepts of governing; the lowest rate would facilitate this type of activity. The lowest-rate provision, however, should *not* be made available to other nonparty groups or so-called independent expenditure efforts.

In sum, TV commercials represent an important conduit by which candidates can get their messages through to the voters unimpeded by any intervening mechanism or filter. Unfortunately, the increasing costs of the medium are responsible for steep hikes in the costs of campaigns, which in turn are strength-ening the importance of the well-heeled special interest PACs. To change the system, Congress should consider new legislation to enable candidates to purchase TV time at reduced rates. Such a provision would facilitate access for all candidates while requiring candidates to demonstrate their seriousness by paying for their time. As a marketplace solution, it would not necessitate the complex regulatory scheme that some access proposals would require. Also, by limiting the reduced-cost program to federal candidates and political parties, the proposal would put them at an advantage over the so-called independent expenditure committees and negative advertising campaigns that are being used with increasing frequency.

Conclusion

In 1971 Senator Edward Kennedy (D-MA) warned that television, "like the colossus of the ancient world . . . stands astride our political system, demanding tribute from every candidate for major public office, incumbent or challenger. Its appetite is insatiable, and its impact is unique" (Senate Commerce Commit-tee, 1971:193). Ten years later, this threatening imagery remains valid. Even though we are now in the third decade of the TV era, the political system has yet to come to grips with television. TV coverage of the presidential primaries warps the process, by its very nature giving inflated attention to early primaries and providing too little insight into campaign issues and too much information on the horse race aspects of a campaign. Public affairs broadcasting—candidate debates and in-depth interviews—can be very informative for voters, but this type of TV programming is hamstrung by regulations and high costs. While television can provide candidates with unprecedented access to voters, the ever-escalating price of TV time increases the financial pressure on office-seekers.

Yet the enormous potential of television grasped by President Kennedy—the opportunity it provides voters to learn about candidates and issues—remains as well. Through a modification of the presidential primary process, the distorting powers of television can be tempered. Through expanded and upgraded news programming and increased public affairs broadcasting, television can provide voters with substantial information about important election issues. If the costs of TV advertising are reduced, more candidates will be able to use modern technology to deliver their own messages effectively and less expensively. Coming to grips in the 1980s with the serious problems that television is causing in American politics will in turn allow us to realize the vast potential it has for benefiting us all.

2. The Presidential Nominating System: Problem and Prescriptions

Michael Nelson

Abstract

The present system of nominating presidential candidates has been shaped by intraparty conflicts over the course of the past 180 years. In this gradual evolution, little conscious effort has been made to promote simplicity and clarity, two prime values of democratic theory and sound public policy as they pertain to elections. As a result, the distinguishing qualification of the people who are elected president is a talent for getting elected president. In recent years, a variety of changes to promote simplicity and clarity in the nominating system have been proposed. Some are excessively nostalgic for days forever gone; others are halfway measures that, in seeking to promote several sets of values, would achieve none. One set of proposals—for a national primary, accompanied by televised debates and perhaps a modified voting system—seems more appropriate. But prospects for passage into law of any of these proposals probably rest on a new wave of intraparty conflicts.

A favorite indoor sport of presidential scholars is drawing up lists of qualities that the American political system demands of its candidates for chief executive. "Honesty and integrity head the list," writes Thomas Cronin in *The State of the Presidency* (1980:30), a recent and representative effort. "Intelligence, a capacity to clarify, communicate, and mobilize, as well as flexibility, compassion, and open-mindedness are also leading characteristics sought in presidential candidates." So is "moderation" on the issues.

It is hard to quarrel with Cronin's list, but it also is hard to use it as a basis for predicting which of the dozen or more candidates running for president in a given election year—honest, intelligent, compassionate Americans to the last— eventually will be chosen. For that we need to look elsewhere, not just to the players in the presidential election game, but to the rules by which they must play. As anyone who followed the election of 1980 can testify, those rules are complicated. They are so complicated, in fact, and the strategic considerations involved in manipulating them so varied, that nowadays it may be fair to say that *the distinguishing qualification of the people who are elected president is a talent for getting elected president.* This is especially true at the nomination stage, which is the concern of this essay.

Part of this talent involves skill in influencing media perceptions of how well the candidate is doing (Arterton, 1978; Matthews, 1978). With delegate selection scattered across space (50 states, several territories) and time (January through June), there is no real scoreboard in the ongoing contest, apart from the media's message as to who is up and who is down. If a candidate can get the national political press to declare him the winner even when he loses, as Representative John Anderson did after finishing second in the March 4, 1980, Massachusetts and Vermont Republican primaries, he is well on his way.[1] Conversely, it was clear that George Bush's candidacy was doomed when, on the eve of the March 11 Florida Republican primary, he threw up his hands and told reporters he did no know what a "respectable showing" would be. "I guess it is so that you people in the press say, 'he did well.'" The idea apparently is to do better than the press expects. But lowering press expectations without also reducing supporters' morale, and thus their financial contributions and personal efforts, is no mean feat.

At some point, of course, the number of delegates a candidate actually has won becomes more important than how well he seems to be doing. So the would-be nominee must know—or have staff people who know—such strategic minutiae as these:

Winning early is everything . . . On June 3, 1980, the last day of primary voting, Democrats in eight states chose 696 delegates—more than 20 percent of all delegates selected—to their party's national convention. Senator Edward Kennedy won five of these primaries, including those in California and New Jersey; President Jimmy Carter won three. Kennedy earned the votes of 46 percent of the 5.8 million electors who cast ballots that day; Carter 42 percent. These decisions were almost meaningless, however, because by most accounts the Democratic nomination was won in January and February when Carter triumphed in the Iowa caucus and the New Hampshire primary and seemed to win the Maine caucus. These three states are hardly typical of the Democratic voter population: none has a measurable black population; none has a city larger than 200,000; all voted Republican in the 1972, 1976, and 1980 elections. Yet those early Carter victories made Kennedy look like a loser, placing him on the defensive and increasing his problems in raising the resources needed to continue an effective campaign.

. . . but not the only thing . . . In 1979 George Bush spent 329 days campaigning on the road, many of them in Iowa. Shortly before the Iowa caucus, his aides began worrying about what might happen there. On January 21 their worst fears were confirmed: Bush won. This meant he would have to keep on winning; close seconds would not do. As it happened, Reagan won by better than two to one in New Hampshire, ruining Bush's chances for the nomination but sparing him the psychological strain of another Orwellian week

of "Winning is Losing." For the remaining contenders, however, there were further subtleties to be grasped.

. . . even assuming you can tell who won. On February 10 Carter earned a slim plurality in the Maine municipal Democratic party caucuses, which was taken to be a great strategic triumph. Headlines ran along the lines of: "Carter is Victor in Sen. Kennedy's Backyard." In truth, however, no convention delegates from Maine actually were chosen until the statewide party convention in mid-May, and when they were, Kennedy tied Carter, 11 to 11. Why did this real event generate no headlines and the pseudo-event of February 10 so many? Because of its timing. According to *CQ Weekly Report*, "as the lone event in the Democratic nominating process between the January 21 Iowa caucus and the February 26 New Hampshire primary, the Maine [municipal] caucus drew the attention to the candidates of the media."

Presidents get the vigorish. Primaries that involve an incumbent president are inevitably referendums on his performance. But as former Senator Eugene McCarthy (1980) points out, the Democratic party's "rules change for 1980 gives a special advantage to the incumbent." A state's delegates now are divided among only those candidates who win at least 15 percent of the primary or caucus vote. So in New Hampshire, where the opposition vote was 53 percent (38 percent for Kennedy, 10 percent for Governor Jerry Brown, and another scattered 5 percent), the president nonetheless was awarded a majority of the delegates. In Maryland, Carter's 47 percent of the popular vote won him 54 percent of the delegates; in Nebraska, 47 percent of the vote reaped 14 of 24 delegates, or 58 percent. New Hampshire, especially, was a vital victory for Carter, and the rules-induced distortion made it appear all the more so.

You can't play the game unless you know where the playing field is, unless you know who the players are. By the end of the 1980 nominating season, 36 states and territories had held primaries. Some were limited to each party's registered voters, others were open to everyone. Some chose delegates, some did not. Some chose delegates, but separately from the presidential preference vote. Some required that a candidate petition to get on the ballot, some that he petition to get off the ballot, meaning that voters did not know whose names they would encounter. Some had primaries and caucuses, still others had just caucuses. Of the caucus-only states, some chose their national convention delegates at the congressional district level, some at the state level.[2]

The Presidential Nominating System, 1800–1968

It was not always so complicated.[3] In the early years of the Republic, winning a party's nomination for president was simply a matter of persuading its members in Congress to give it to you. The congressional caucus system sprang from the same source as subsequent methods of presidential nomination: intraparty politics.

That struggles over presidential selection systems should work themselves out in this arena is not surprising; fights about rules and procedures almost always are fights about policy as well. E. E. Schattschneider, in his brilliant book *The Semi-Sovereign People* (1966:2, 3, 4, 16), described the "contagiousness of conflict" in ways that are useful in understanding the history of American presidential politics: "The number of people involved in any conflict determines what happens; every change in the number of participants, every increase or reduction in the number of participants, affects the results. . . . [Thus] the most important strategy of politics is concerned with the scope of conflict. . . . It is the *loser* who calls in outside help."

Thus, the congressional caucus was developed in 1800 when Alexander Hamilton came to the conclusion that the incumbent Federalist president, John Adams, probably could not win reelection. At that time, members of the Electoral College still voted for two men for president, with the runner-up awarded the vice-presidency. Hamilton's hope was that if Federalist electors united behind Charles Cotesworth Pinckney, a popular South Carolinian, as well as Adams, Pinckney might draw enough additional votes to squeak through as vice-president, if not president. To get the word out about Pinckney to Federalists around the country, he persuaded party members in Congress to "caucus" and recommend both Adams and Pinckney. "To support *Adams* and *Pinckney* equally is the only thing that can possibly save us from the fangs of *Jefferson*," he wrote in a letter to Theodore Sedgwick, the Federalist Speaker of the House.

The Jeffersonian Republicans of the day initially ridiculed the Federalist innovation but soon adopted it and put it to even better use themselves. Among those they chose by caucus were Thomas Jefferson, James Madison, and James Monroe, an honor roll that has persuaded at least one political scientist, Michael Robinson, to prescribe a modern-day return to "King Caucus." Robinson (1975:19887) argues that presidential nominees selected by political "peers" would tend to be "more competent intellectually and more mature emotionally" than those produced by the present system.

The caucus system had its flaws, however, as can be seen in the nation's experience with William Crawford, the last of the caucus nominees. Crawford, a Georgia planter with presidential ambitions, was secretary of the Treasury in the Monroe administration. Realizing early on, however, that his chances for advancing to the White House lay on Capitol Hill, Crawford curried favor there and turned his back on Monroe. Once, after the president expressed reservations about some of his official appointments, Crawford called him a "damned infernal old scoundrel" and broke off communication. Crawford also plotted against Secretary of State John Quincy Adams, leaking charges that Adams had appeared barefoot in church and forged changes in the original copy of the Constitution, which was in his department's custody. Crawford's scheming won him his party's nomination in 1824, but little else: 150 of the 215 Republican congressmen boycotted the nominating caucus, and Crawford ran a distant third in the election (fourth in the popular vote). Voters clearly had had their fill of King Caucus and the petty intragovernmental bickering it seemed to encourage.

After a brief period of confusion following the demise of the caucus (Andrew Jackson, for example, received his first two nominations for president from the Tennessee legislature, and was elected in 1828), the national nominating convention came into being. Searching for a way to unite geographically diffuse anti-Jackson sentiment behind a single candidate in the 1832 election, the nascent National Republican or Whig party decided to take a page from the book of the small Anti-Masonic party, which had held a national delegate convention in 1830. The practice already was widespread at the state level. The Whig convention met at Baltimore in December 1831 and nominated Henry Clay. Democrats, at the behest of President Jackson, followed suit six months later, partly because Jackson was anxious to create a forum in which he could dump Vice-President John C. Calhoun from the ticket in favor of Martin Van Buren. (Calhoun was popular in Congress and in several state legislatures.)

Primaries did not develop until early in the 20th century, when the reformers of the Progressive movement, who tended to think of party pros as "bosses" rather than "leaders," prevailed on some states to allow voters a direct voice in the process. Again, intraparty politics was a motivating force. The first state presidential primary to choose convention delegates, for example, was created in Wisconsin in 1905 to help resolve a split among the state's Republicans that had caused both the progressive supporters of Senator Robert LaFollette and his "regular" Republican foes to send their own delegations to the Republican national convention and even nominate their own slates of candidates for state office. From the standpoint of the pros, primaries were a nuisance, but a small one. In 1912, for example, Theodore Roosevelt won 10 of 12 primaries, but the Republican convention nominated William Howard Taft anyway. Democrats chose Adlai Stevenson as their nominee in 1952, even though Senator Estes Kefauver had won 12 of the 13 primaries he entered. By 1960, magnanimous Democratic pros conceded a use for primaries, as a testing ground for candidates, much as the New Haven theater audience is a dry run for Broadway-bound shows. The pros liked John Kennedy in 1960, but it took the West Virginia primary to convince them that a Catholic could be elected. Still, however, the final decision rested with them and not the primaries. As late as 1968, party pros still were able to nominate a candidate like Hubert Humphrey, who had not won a single primary.

The Presidential Nominating System, 1969 to the Present

It is Chicago, 1968. Enter American youth, protesting. It is Vietnam-time. Blood and tear gas foul the streets. . . . But in the committee rooms, the insurgents win their cause. Shamed, confused in the din of the floor, the regular delegates accept a Minority Report on Rules that they do not understand. It demands that all Democratic voters get "full, meaningful and timely opportunity to participate in the selection of delegates" to the next convention and sets up a commission to rewrite party rules. (White, 1980:71)

Theodore White's breathless prose may not fit all occasions, but most students of presidential politics would agree that it is appropriate here. The commission White refers to, headed by South Dakota Senator George McGovern and Representative Donald Fraser of Minnesota, met in 1969 in a postelection atmosphere of confusion and some desperation. Clearly, it seemed, something had gone wrong with a party system that offered a nation consumed by dissatisfaction with the Vietnam war a choice between Hubert Humphrey and Richard Nixon. Clearly, too, the solution seemed to lie in somehow "opening up" the parties, making them more "responsive" to voters at the "grass roots" so that they never could get that far out of touch again. But how?

The McGovern-Fraser Commission labored mightily, but aside from stipulating that party leaders no longer could automatically send themselves and their supporters to the national convention, it came up with no unequivocal answer to that question. Instead, it gave the state parties a choice: Either they could select their delegates in primaries, or they could select them in "open caucuses," meetings in which any and all self-professed Democrats could participate equally. The commission apparently hoped that the states would select the latter course, but, says Austin Ranney, a commission member, "we got a rude shock" (1974a:73).

Seven additional states instantly opted for a primary, raising the number of Democratic primary states to 22 in 1972. Rather than "radically revise their accustomed ways of conducting caucuses and conventions for other party matters," these state parties decided that "it would be better to split off the process for selecting national convention delegates and let it be conducted by a state-administered primary" (Ranney 1974a:73-74). Of the state parties that went the less certain, open-caucus route, some soon regretted their decision. In 1972 supporters of McGovern's candidacy for president organized thoroughly, packed the state caucuses, and took them over from the surprised party regulars; even conservative Virginia found itself represented at the national convention by a pro-McGovern delegation. (He got 30 percent of the vote there in November.) "The rules were very complicated. McGovern understood them. The other candidates didn't," says Ranney.[4]

To avoid a second round of ideological takeovers, several more caucus states switched to primaries after the 1972 election, raising the total to 30 in 1976. Then another party rules commission, this one chaired by Barbara Mikulski, mandated that starting in 1976 a state's convention delegates must be allocated according to the principle of proportional representation, in "fair reflection" of each candidate's support there. In 1976 it was Jimmy Carter who figured out the new angle. Carter knew that if he entered all the primaries he would win at least some delegates even when he finished second or third in the popular vote.

By 1980, another five state parties had converted to primaries, bringing the total to 35.

Although the Democrats have taken the lead in all this, the Republicans have followed suit quite closely. Their "DO" commission (Committee on Delegates and Organization), also appointed in 1969, ushered in similar, if less explicit rules with regard to open caucuses and such. And Republican primaries also have increased, from 16 in 1968 to 34 in 1980.

Each individual component of the present nominating system has its defenders. For example, Richard Scammon, director of the Elections Research Center, likes primaries because, he says, "the great leavening in American politics is that—and this makes us unique among the democracies of the world—our people have something to say *en masse* about who the nominees are going to be."[5] Political scientist Larry Sabato (1980) defends caucuses on grounds that "the voters who participate in the caucuses [are] treated to a political education that the simple act of voting cannot begin to match." Some even make a case for the emphasis on the early, small-state contests. "They make the system flexible," argues Milton Cummings, "so that a relatively unknown 'outsider' candidate can start small, win a few caucuses or primaries, and get national recognition."[6]

Criticisms of the Present System

However admired its parts, the nominating process as a whole has few defenders—"It's like a pizza with everything on it," in political analyst James Schuengel's apt simile. Almost everyone—journalists and their critics alike—deplores the responsibility that the hybrid nature of the system places on the media to interpret who is winning and who is not, and even to decide which candidacies should be taken seriously. Additionally, few think it proper that voters in the late-primary states have their choice circumscribed by the decisions of voters in the early-primary states. New Hampshire Republicans could choose among six serious candidates in the 1980 primary; fourteen weeks later, their copartisans in California effectively were limited to Ronald Reagan, the only contender who had not withdrawn from the race. "There's a very real sense in which this system violates the one man, one vote principle," says one scholar. "Somebody who participated in those Iowa caucuses, or voted in that New Hampshire primary, counts for 10 or 15 times as much in determining the outcome as the people who voted in California, Ohio, and New Jersey." This early-late distortion introduces an East-West bias as well: of the first 19 Democratic primaries in 1980, 16 were east of the Mississippi; of the last 16, only 7 were. Finally, there is the problem of the "faithful delegate" versus the "open convention," born of the sheer length of the process and reflected in the Rule F(3)(c) controversy at the 1980 Democratic convention. Should a delegate be free to ignore the promise he made to the citizens that elected him to vote for a particular candidate, or should he be bound to that pledge even if at the time of the convention, the political situation and perhaps the candidate's stands on the issues look very different? The nature of the process is such that it poses unhappy choices such as this.

Other criticisms of the present nominating system are directed less to the process than to its products. In what James David Barber (1980:318) calls "the great campaign stress test," the system screens for "qualities of physical endurance and superficial plausibility, but not much else." David Broder of the *Washington Post* adds that in such a protracted process, the only people willing to join the staffs of candidates are "young people who have very few other attractive alternatives." Thus, after the election, "you find in the White House, making key decisions about government, young people whose essential skills are in the tactics and logistics of a long presidential campaign." It also has been argued that the process tends to exclude the presently employed, who presumably have other things to do than campaign steadily for two years.[7] The 1976 Democratic nomination went to an unemployed ex-governor, Jimmy Carter, as did the 1980 Republican nomination, after former Governor Reagan defeated former Ambassador Bush.

The most telling criticism of the current nominating process, however, is the one we began with: It is so extraordinarily complicated that no voter reasonably could be expected to understand his place in it. "I am fully confident," says Richard Stearns, who helped engineer McGovern's 1972 nomination before becoming Kennedy's director of delegate selection in 1980, "that there aren't more than 100 people in the country who fully understand the rules." (1979).

Criteria for a Nominating System

Institutional or structural complexity in a political system certainly need not mean that it is "undemocratic," just as simplicity and clarity alone do not guarantee a democratic process. (A coin flip would be a clear and simple method of choosing officials.) The American Constitution, in fact, provided for an elaborate system of what Richard Neustadt has called "separated institutions sharing powers," in which citizens, though the well-spring of all legitimate political authority, only share in its exercise, chiefly through voting in elections. And it was characteristic of the political theories of the framers that the electoral role of the citizen in the complex political process was to be clear, if not direct, and comprehensible to him and to those who represent him. First among those principles of constitutional government that the framers subscribed to, wrote Clinton Rossiter (1968), was that "government must be plain, simple, and intelligible. The common sense of a reasonably educated man should be able to comprehend its structure and functioning." Henry Mayo notes in his *Introduction to Democratic Theory* (1960:73) that simplicity and clarity are hallmarks of all representative electoral processes:[8] "If [the] purpose of the election is to be carried out—to enable the voter to share in political power—the voter's job must not be made difficult and confusing for him. It ought, on the contrary, to be made as simple as the electoral machinery can be devised to make it."

It may be argued that the authors of the Constitution did not have candidate nominations in mind, that their notion of where citizens fit into the governing process was much more constricted. That is true, but beside the point. The framers also did not envision direct election of United States senators or universal adult suffrage. But, by allowing for amendments and for state discretion, their Constitution left open the possibility that the boundaries of popular political participation might expand. What remained constant was the principle that whatever doors of influence were opened to citizens, it should be clear to them how they could walk through.

Democratic theory, in mandating simplicity and clarity in citizen participation, treats elections as a process. But, especially to the extent that electoral rules become subjects of political controversy and government regulation, those processes also should be thought of as public policies. (Certainly they have been treated that way in the history of nominating politics.) It is useful, then, to consult the literature of policy analysis as well as that of democratic theory for guidance.

Again, one finds simplicity and clarity valued, this time as essential ingredients to sound implementation.[9] "[A]n appreciation of the length and unpredictability of necessary decision sequences in implementation should lead the designers of policy to consider more direct means for accomplishing their desired ends," wrote Jeffrey Pressman and Aaron Wildavsky (1973:143, 147). They add that "simplicity in policies is much to be desired. The fewer the steps involved in carrying out the program, the fewer the opportunities for a disaster to overtake it. The more directly the policy aims at its target, the fewer the decisions involved in its ultimate realization."

What is to be done? A Nostalgic Consensus

An institution that has attracted as much criticism as the presidential nominating system might also be expected to have generated some imaginative thinking about how to improve it, especially among the political scientists and journalists whose business it is to study the process. Instead, however, we have heard mainly assurances that clarity, simplicity, and other desired values will be restored if only we turn back the clock to the time before the 1968 reforms.

Those days were idyllic, if their modern chroniclers are to be believed; Ranney even refers to them as "the good old days." "Under the old system," as David Broder describes it, "running for president involved taking a few months off from your public office in the election year to present your credentials largely to political peers—other officeholders, party leaders, leaders of allied interest groups—and to persuade them that you were best qualified to carry the party banner." As it happens, the qualities those political peers were looking for, says political scientist Jeane Kirkpatrick, were the very qualities that made for good presidents: "the ability to deal with diverse groups, ability to work out compromises and develop consensus, and the ability to impress people who have watched a candidate over many years." And when they finally decided on someone, Ranney writes, "the delegates would follow their lead and choose him. The coalition of leaders also would see to it that the party's platform would help to unite the party and put it in the best possible position to win the election" (1978a:34).

There is nostalgia as well as history in these and similar accounts. Writing in the late 19th century, the high-water mark of party organization in this country, James Bryce reported in his classic study of *The American Commonwealth* (1959:28–29) that party pros indeed had a talent for choosing electable candidates. But he also felt compelled to explain "Why Great Men Are Not Chosen President" in terms of that very skill: "It must be remembered that the merits of a President are one thing and those of a candidate another thing. . . . It will be a misfortune to the party, as well as to the country, if the candidate elected should prove a bad President. But it is a greater misfortune to the party that it should be beaten in the impending election, for the evil of losing national patronage will have come four years sooner."

The party pros' indifference to nominating great presidents extended to an occasional inability to weed out pathological ones. Of the presidents from Taft onward that Barber analyzed in his study of *The Presidential Character* (1977), 4 of the 11 who were nominated in good old, prereform days—Woodrow Wilson, Herbert Hoover, Lyndon Johnson, and Richard Nixon—fit his category of "active-negatives," psychologically unhealthy personalities who tended to turn political crises into personal crises and thus would rigidly "persevere in a disastrous policy." Only three—Franklin Roosevelt, Harry Truman, and John Kennedy—qualified as "active-positives," that is, leaders with "personal strengths [of character] specially attuned to the presidency." In contrast, both Gerald Ford and Jimmy Carter, the first two presidents produced by the new system, score as active-positives, and Ronald Reagan as a safe if uninspiring passive-positive.[10]

Like their talent for "peer review," the party pros' ability to choose winners may have been overstated. Bryce was writing in a period of unusually close electoral competition. But in this century, 12 of the 18 presidential elections held before the McGovern-Fraser reforms were landslides in which the winner had more than twice as many electoral votes as his opponent. At least one set of party pros in each of these elections had made a poor judgment of its candidate's electability.[11]

The good old days of party politics, then, just were not that good. (A further point. Strong party organization often is prescribed as a sure antidote to "single-interest politics" and "interest-group liberalism." But as Arthur Schlesinger, Jr. [1979] points out, "lobbies were never more powerful that in those years after the Civil War when we came as near as we ever have to the beatitude of party discipline.") And good or bad, those days are gone. Commenting on recent proposals to give presidential nominations back to the party pros, Richard Scammon asks, "What party pros? I see as much of grass-roots politics in this country as anyone alive, and I can tell you, there are no party pros anymore—just ideological activists of the left and right who want to use the parties for their own purposes. If you try to turn it over to the pros, you'll guarantee that the Democrats will become the party of the ideological left and the Republicans the party of the ideological right." Advocates of counter-reformation who insist that the parties would prosper if their elected public officials—congressmen, governors, and big-city mayors—were given convention delegate status by entitlement ignore the fact that nowadays such officials rarely conduct their own campaigns through party channels.

If one accepts the argument made by Jeane Kirkpatrick, among others, that more than anything else the reforms killed the party organizations, then it seems plausible that undoing the reforms might bring them back to life. But the causes of the change run deeper, reflecting a changed society in which more prosperous, better-informed voters no longer feel a need to rely on parties either for patronage jobs or for advice on how to cast their vote, and thus are more selective in giving their loyalties. To be sure, the share of the electorate that identifies itself as either Democratic or Republican fell by 5 percentage points in the four-year period after the McGovern-Fraser and DO commissions. But it already had fallen 7 percentage points in the four previous years, the last four years of "good old days."[12] In this light, it is hard to quarrel with Barber (1980:322) when he writes that "Reformers who urge the revival of parties as abstract good things in themselves or look to the reinvigoration of the jumbo coalitions of years gone by are marching up a blind alley." He adds: "You can't recruit people to a party just because you believe we've got to have a party. Parties grow out of a purpose that draws people and politicians together."

What is to be done? Halfway Measures

If going back is not a desirable or even a feasible response to the present confusion, what would be? A variety of other proposals for change have been offered, usually by former presidential candidates.[13] Most are politically realistic in that they accept the historical trend toward the democratization of political decision-making in general and toward primaries in particular (Nelson, 1979). Most, too, are efforts to build into this trend the stated criteria for sound electoral processes that we have borrowed from democratic theory and policy analysis: they are moves toward values of clarity, simplicity, and responsiveness in the nominating system. But most proposals fall short of the goal. In their efforts to enhance yet other sets of values as well, they risk satisfying none.

The best-known regional primary bill has been introduced in recent Congresses by Senator Bob Packwood, an Oregon Republican. It proposes to divide the nation into five regions (New England, Great Lakes, Southeast, Great Plains, and West) and require any state within a region that wishes to hold a presidential primary to hold it on the same day as the other states in that region. Primaries would be permitted only on the second Tuesday of each month from March through July, one region per month. Lotteries would be held 70 days before each primary date to determine which region could vote then.

Time-zone primaries have been proposed in the Senate by former Republican presidential candidate Howard Baker. The proposal was introduced after the 1980 election. It is similar to the regional primary bill in that it would assign each state that wished to hold a primary a specified date, based on its geographical location. The major difference is that the states would be divided among time zones rather than regions.

Several advantages of the regional and time-zone primary proposals are argued. While showing a certain deference to the Constitution's federal principle, they would ease the physical and financial plight of candidates, who presently must fly all over the country to contest primaries in widely distant places. Further, both proposals would distribute randomly among the states and regions the advantages and disadvantages of being first, last, or in between on the primary calendar.

It seems likely, however, that a regional primary system would preserve some old problems and create some new ones. Too much stress still would be placed on the first primaries. To make this bias random is not to eliminate it; indeed, it would legitimate it in federal law. Further, by defining the electorate regionally, the system would encourage an emphasis in the campaign on regional issues and other sources of division. (Packwood's plan would exacerbate existing regional differences, such as those dividing the "Sunbelt" and the "Frostbelt"; Baker's might revive some, setting the coast against the inland.) As for the effort to preserve an element of federalism, it need only be said that the region, being neither state nor nation, is at best a constitutional stepchild.

Two other former candidates for the presidency, Democratic Representative Morris Udall of Arizona and Republican Representative John Ashbrook of Ohio, have proposed legislation that would borrow the first-Tuesday-only aspect of the regional primary bills while abandoning the regions. Any state that wanted to could hold its primary on the first Tuesday in March, or the first Tuesday in April, May, or June. This, too, is an effort at rationality, but it seems likely that its real effect would be that state primaries would cluster in March and June. The campaign would begin no later and end no sooner, but spring would be strangely silent.

What is to be done? Prescription

With certain refinements, a national primary would probably prove an appreciably better—that is, clearer, simpler, and more democratic—presidential nominating system.

The idea of a national primary is not new. Since 1911 and shortly after, when Representative Richard Hobson of Alabama introduced the first piece of national primary legislation and Woodrow Wilson endorsed the concept, some 125 such bills have been offered in Congress. Most have been close kin to the one introduced by Republican Senator Lowell Weicker, which would work like this:

Each major party's supporters, along with interested independents, would choose their nominee for president directly, with their votes. To get on the primary ballot, a candidate would have until June 30 of the election year to round up valid signatures equal in number to 1 percent of the turnout in the most recent presidential election (about 800,000 in 1980)—a high enough standard to screen out frivolous candidacies, but not "outsider" ones. Ballots would be cast on the first Tuesday in August. If no candidate in a party got 50 percent, there would be a runoff between the top two finishers three weeks later.[14]

By definition, a national primary would be a simpler system than the present one, or any other that has been proposed: the candidate who received a majority of votes would win. It offers the clearest connection between popular votes and outcome. But what other consequences might we reasonably expect of a national primary?

Voter participation in the nominating process would rise substantially. In part this is almost tautologically true. In 1976, for example, 28.9 million people voted in 30 state primaries, a turnout rate of 28.2 percent of the voting age population in those states. If all the other states had held primaries, and if voters in those states also had turned out at a rate of 28.2 percent, some 38.5 million people would have participated, an additional 9.6 million (Ranney 1977:20).

Actually, it seems likely that the turnout *rate* would rise in a national primary as well. Ranney has found that voters in states whose primary results are binding on delegates—where there is, in short, a direct causal relationship between votes and outcomes—turn out at a higher rate than voters in states whose primaries are advisory (Ranney 1977:27–28). In a national primary, cause and effect would be not only direct, but obvious: there would be no delegates or other intermediaries between voters and candidates. Presumably, voter turnout would rise accordingly.

In addition, a single national primary would avoid the corrosive effects of a protracted sequence of primaries. Specifically, all the candidates would be on the ballots of all the voters (no one's choice would be circumscribed by anyone else's) and no candidate would be prematurely declared the winner (no voter would feel that his vote was coming after the fact). In 1980 voter turnout rose substantially from 1976 levels in the early primaries, when the nomination contests still were up in the air (51 percent in 1980 versus 48 percent in 1976 in New Hampshire, 35 percent versus 25 percent in Vermont, 43 percent versus 33 percent in Massachusetts), but fell precipitately after that.

Participants would be more representative of ordinary party identifiers. In nomination politics, the volume of participation seems to be directly related to its representativeness. Caucus participants are substantially more affluent, educated, and ideological than their fellow partisans. Similarly, Ranney found, "each party's [state] primary voters are unrepresentative of its rank-and-file identifiers in the same ways as the caucus-convention activists but not to the same degree" (Ranney 1978a:16). The effect under the present system is that candidates for a party's nomination must make ideological or special-interest appeals that will harm them in the general election campaign. Having a larger, more representative national primary electorate would reduce this dysfunction.

Votes would count equally. The advantage, or disadvantage, of living in a particular state or voting on a particular date vanishes when everyone votes at the same time. The present violations—in spirit if not in letter—of the "one man, one vote" standard no longer would exist under a national primary.

Campaigns would change. It is too much to say, as some advocates do, that a new era of rational debate on national issues would follow adoption of a national primary. But it does seem likely that candidates would place less emphasis on local issues that are disproportionately important to crucial early states, such as gun control in New Hampshire and old-age benefits in Florida. The campaign period also presumably would become shorter. Strenuous campaigning, which now begins a year before the January Iowa caucus, might start seven months later if all voting were in August. It might begin even later: local publicity in key early states can be obtained as a reward for campaigning in the preelection year; publicity in the national media, the most valuable kind for a national primary, would not be so easy to obtain that far ahead of the election. To survive their campaigns, candidates still would need the physical endurance of athletes, but perhaps not that of marathon runners.

The strategic position of the incumbent would change. The shift to a national arena of conflict would make it difficult for a challenger to a sitting president to concentrate his efforts and other resources in a small state like New Hampshire in order to gain credibility for other challenges elsewhere, as

McCarthy did in the 1968 New Hampshire primary. On the other hand, the president's ability to gain an advantage by redistributing federal grant and contract monies to key states would disappear if there were no key states.

The influence of the press in the nominating process would diminish. A national primary offers its own scoreboard, which the present system does not. Polls provide relatively objective measures of how the candidates are faring before voting day. Reporters no longer would be called on to create, as well as report, the shape of the race.

Historically, opposition to the national primary has come from those who feel that it "would be the final nail in the coffin of the party system." But it is by no means clear that a national primary would destroy the parties. Direct primary nomination of candidates, far from being a bizarre, untested idea whose consequences are beyond anticipation, is the practice for virtually all other elected offices at all other levels of government in all states and regions of the United States. As Scammon points out, "many of the strongest party machines in the country thrived in primary systems—Boss Crump in Memphis, Harry Byrd in Virginia, and Dick Daley in Chicago, among others."[15]

Would national party conventions become extinct if candidates for president were not chosen there? Not necessarily; there still would be the need to nominate vice-presidential candidates, make party rules, and potentially most important, write the platforms. F. Christopher Arterton (1977:671) suggests that these latter activities, so central to the health of the party as an enduring organization, are submerged in the nomination politics of present-day "candidate-centered conventions." If, as Barber (1980:322) has suggested, "Purpose comes first, then party," if what is needed are "themes of unity so compelling that they will attract allies whose allegiance might survive the selection" of this year's candidate, then divorcing the conventions from the nominating process well might free them to become idea and theme-setting forums whose products the parties now seem to need.

Another common objection to a national primary system is that it would limit the field of contenders to the already famous and close out the possibility of a less well-known candidate's ever gaining the resources to mount an effective campaign. Just as the present system seems biased toward out-of-office politicians with unlimited time to campaign, the prereform system leaned too heavily toward Washington politicians, and a national primary system might swing the pendulum back too far in their favor. An ideal system would not place handicaps on any reasonable candidate.

To help approach this ideal, preprimary debates could be conducted among all candidates who qualify for the ballot. Debates already are nearly a routine practice in the present nominating system—the Democrats held several in 1976, as did the Republicans in 1980—and their track record for bringing outsider candidates before the public on equal footing with their opponents is well established. John Anderson, for example, rose to public prominence largely on the strength of his performances in a pre-Iowa caucus debate where he alone endorsed a tax on gasoline and a pre-New Hampshire primary debate in which he spoke out for gun control. At the same time, the presidential candidacies of incumbent office-holders, who can spare time for debates but not for daily campaigning, would not be at a disadvantage.

A lesson from the experience of Australia could help us counter another objection that has been made to the national primary proposal. A primary, writes Ranney (1978a:20), "has no way of identifying, let alone aggregating, [voters'] second and third choices so as to discover the candidate with the broadest—as well as the most intense—support." Since 1918 Australian voters have been called upon to number their candidate preferences on the election ballot—first choice, second choice, and so on. If no candidate receives a majority of first-choice votes, the lowest ranking candidate is dropped, and voters' second and, if need be, third and fourth choices are tallied until someone has a total of 50 percent or more. Thus, the extreme candidate who leads on the first count because he has the support of an intense but relatively small minority, but who gets few second-choice votes, will be beaten by a candidate with more broadly based support. No runoff is needed.

Steven Brams (1978) advocates a variation of the Australian method that he calls "approval voting." Brams's proposal would allow primary participants to vote for as many candidates as they liked in a given field, though not more than once for each candidate. Brams, who campaigned strenuously but unsuccessfully to persuade the New Hampshire legislature to adopt his system for the 1980 primary, argues that approval voting has all the purported advantages of the Australian system, yet is more likely to select the candidate acceptable to most voters than either the Australian or the runoff system.[16] He offers the following hypothetical example (Brams, 1979:550, 553):

> It is entirely possible in a three-candidate plurality race in which A wins 25 percent of the vote, B 35 percent and C 40 percent that the loser, A, is the strongest candidate who would beat B in a separate two-way contest (because C supporters would vote for A), and would beat C in a separate two-way contest (because B supporters would vote for A). Even a runoff election between the two top vote getters (B and C) would not show up this fact. On the other hand, approval voting in all likelihood would reveal A to be the strongest candidate because some B and C supporters—who liked A as much or almost as much—would cast second approval votes for A, who would thereby become the winner. . . .
>
> [The Australian system] has a major drawback: it may eliminate the candidate acceptable to the most voters. . . . [Candidate] A would have been eliminated at the outset.

Approval voting also has the advantage over the Australian system of being easily comprehended by voters. They do not have to express a preference—even a fourth-place preference—for a candidate they despise. And the candidate with the most votes wins.

Prospects for Change

Admittedly, approval voting is an idea whose time has not yet come. A more achievable task is to get a national primary law enacted, one that will not only simplify and clarify the nominating process for voters but make it more responsive to them as well.[17] The national primary has the kind of popular support among voters that may win it serious consideration in Congress eventually. The Gallup poll, which has been asking people what they think of the idea every election year since 1952, has discovered bipartisan support ranging from 2 to 1 to almost 6 to 1; its January 1980 survey found 66 percent supporting the national primary—62 percent of all Republicans, 65 percent of Democrats, and 72 percent of the Independents—and only 24 percent opposed. The level of support also was almost uniform across educational, regional, sexual, occupational, and religious lines, as well as those of age, income, and place of residence (*Gallup Opinion Index,* 1980:19–20). George Gallup included the national primary in a recent article on the "Six Political Reforms Americans Want Most" (Gallup, 1978). With even doubters like Austin Ranney conceding that a national primary "certainly would be better than what we have now," Americans someday may get it.

But the American political system remains a perfect illustration of Newton's First Law of Motion: When it comes to existing programs and policies, American government tends to stay in motion; almost nothing is fully undone, even in conservative periods (Hargrove and Nelson, 1981). In treating new proposals for action, American government tends to stay at rest, except in crisis times. Thus, there are any number of ideas circulating in Washington that, although supported for some time by an overwhelming majority of the public, show little sign of becoming law. Sometimes the reason is that only a few of the many people who favor these ideas have a strong enough personal commitment to push fervently for their enactment. Although the number of people ardently opposed is equally small, they can prevail because of the built-in inertia of our checked and balanced constitutional system of separated powers (Dahl, 1956). In other cases strong advocates of change disagree on the precise nature or method of change, and so they "hang separately." One thinks of gun control, national health insurance, direct election of the president—and the national primary.

A reasonable forecast, then, is for more of the same; the nostalgic counter-reformationists have as little reason for hope as national primary advocates. Nothing is likely to change unless some significant segment of the presently apathetic, pro–national primary majority becomes active on behalf of its cause. Given the history of nominating politics in the United States, this seems likely to occur as an outgrowth of some decisive intraparty factional clash resembling those that produced our previous nominating systems.

3. Morality, Democracy, and the Intimate Contest

Joel L. Fleishman

Abstract

In response to a perceived decline in the morals of Americans, a group that calls itself the moral majority has embarked on a campaign to elect politicians who will enact and enforce strict laws governing behavior. Such an attempt to coerce morality is questioned. Although the abandonment of traditional values is, in many cases, lamentable, it is contended that a proper response to this problem is to strive to heighten Americans' sense of ethical behavior and moral obligation. It is argued that while morality constitutes an important dimension of social life, morality and legality are most appropriately kept separate and recognized as applying to different aspects of human conduct. Americans are entitled to relative freedom from coercion, but the corollary to the insistence on this freedom is "the intimate contest for self-command." We must learn to regulate ourselves.

We have heard a great deal recently about the political activities of those who call themselves the Moral Majority. Their goal appears to be to elect public officials who will enact and enforce laws that embody the moral majoritarians' sense of right conduct. It is not clear exactly what has provoked them to frenzy, but their list of complaints includes pornography, sexual laxity, tolerance of unconventional sexual activity, the growing crime rate, the growing number of abortions, governmental support for abortions, growing equality of opportunity for women in all realms of life, and the Equal Rights Amendment, to name only a few. A recent cartoon in the *Philadelphia Inquirer* shows a sound truck emblazoned with "Moral Majority" blaring the message "Rise Up, Fellow Christians . . . stop the big-spending, bra-burning, sex-crazed, homosexual lesbian abortionist commie weaklings and givers-up of the Panama Canal . . . . And, oh, yes, love thy neighbor." On the back of the sound truck we are advised to "honk if you hate" and "cast a stone."

It is hard to know exactly what the moral majoritarians would do about most of these problems if they succeeded in electing the candidates whom they support. If they believe that passing stricter laws with harsher penalties will restore what they regard as morality to the world, they are surely mistaken.

Their entire purpose suggests that they are mistaken in an even more profound sense. Those who would make such moral questions, perhaps any moral questions involving individual behavior, the sole or principal determinants of political choice understand neither democracy nor morality. In fact, as a speaker to a recent conference of Protestants and Others United for the Separation of Church and State pointed out, these moral majoritarians are committed not to democracy but to theocracy. The only trouble is that each member of that alleged majority wants to be theo! As the top of that sound truck says, "We are the *only* way."

Democracy denies that there is only one way on matters of morals and values. The genius of our democracy is precisely that it cleanly and clearly separates all individual and social behavior into two realms, one that may be coerced by the power of a majority and another that may not. While some forms of behavior with moral consequences are indeed coerced on pain of fine, prison sentence, or even death, they are limited mainly to actions that tangibly and causally harm another individual or an institution to which one owes a special responsibility. Most behavior that would be considered a matter of morality—including most of the moral majoritarians' concerns—we choose not to coerce by the power of a majority.

There are three principal reasons for this noninterference. In the first place, even if some of us are fairly confident that we know what right conduct is, we are doubtful that our fellow human beings have the same access to divine instruction. Most of us, however, have enough humility to understand that there is almost always substantial room for disagreement about what is right and wrong. We recognize that to compel what we regard as the right inevitably exposes us to the risk that we may in fact be compelling the wrong, as well as prohibiting what some regard, and what may eventually be seen by many, as the right.

Once one begins coercing matters of morality in one realm, it is very difficult, as the Communists, the Fascists, and the medieval Church all proved, to know where to stop. The inevitable tendency is to broaden the sweep of coercion until one has imposed universal orthodox behavior and belief in all matters of morality.

Our founding fathers, heeding their own common sense as well as the social philosophers whom they admired, well understood the social dangers that might flow from coerced morality and coerced opinions, the stifling of the search for truth, the burdening of the pursuit of beauty, and the frustration of each individual's capacity to define the good for himself. Hence the First Amendment's rigid separation of church and state and its guarantee of freedoms of speech and the press.

Our reluctance to coerce the moral behavior of others also involves a bit of self-defense. While others may be willing to join with us today in denying what someone else regards as his freedom to engage in some kind of conduct, how do we know that tomorrow we may not find ourselves in the place of today's victim?

A second and equally important reason for not coercing morality is the wish to maintain flexibility. Even if we could agree for a substantial period of time on a definition of morality and in fact made all immorality coterminous with illegality, there would be no room for morality to evolve once the majority's underlying view of its content began to change. And one must be pessimistic indeed to believe that morality in human affairs must always get worse, never better. Despite all too frequent retrogressions, such as the Holocaust in Europe, the slaughter in Cambodia, and continued widespread starvation in many parts of the developing world, one can convincingly argue that individual and group behavior today is more moral across the world than it was 500 or 1,000 years ago.

So, if we were to freeze all immorality into illegality at any given point, we would make it much more difficult for it to improve. And there is very little reason to suppose that legal steps could have the desired effect of keeping morality from getting worse. Indeed, the periods of greatest immorality in the past appear to have been times when legal coercion of behavior was greatest.

The third and perhaps most important reason for keeping a sharp division between matters of morality and coercible behavior is to maintain a space in which virtue can be said to exist. The person who obeys the law principally to avoid going to jail shows more self-interest than virtue. Virtue consists of doing those things that morality, one's conscience, or one's sense of duty commands, not what a government compels. If there is no room for virtue in a society, there is no room for the exercise of conscience. And if there were no room for conscience, humankind would be denied perhaps the greatest satisfaction that we know, the intrinsic satisfaction of freely choosing what we think to be the right over the wrong.

So, for all three reasons, our democracy coerces the behavior of its citizens only to the minimal extent necessary to achieve social peace, and only with respect to those matters which large majorities can agree are absolutely essential.

There is a corollary to this insistence on freedom from coercion: each of us must undertake what Tom Schelling has called "the intimate contest for self-command."[1] If those who would legislate morality constitute a great danger to democratic freedom, those who shirk personal responsibility for measuring their own morality by historically tested standards pose an equally great danger to the survival of democracy itself. As Sir Isaiah Berlin reminds us repeatedly, "the tolerance and pluralism of democracy must not be mistaken for total moral relativism or lead to a loss of conviction!"

It is all too easy in any society as free as ours for many to conclude that what is not made illegal is therefore not immoral. It is all too easy for unthinking people in open societies like ours to succumb to the belief that whatever is permitted can be indulged in with moral impunity. If something can be legally sold, no stigma attaches to its purchase. If pornographic books or films are permitted, it does no harm to read or view them. If an idea can be advanced freely, there is no shame in adhering to it, no matter how outrageous it may be.

I do not think that deep down most of us believe that whatever is not illegal is morally permissible, but many of us act from time to time as if we did. The matter goes much deeper than the apparent chief concern of the moral majoritarians, namely, sexual mores. It is as broad as the entire area of relationships in personal, social, commercial, and political life. It involves a weakening sense of fidelity to standards of excellence, pride in our work, duty to our employers, loyalty to institutions from which we benefit. And it has also to do with the entire range of aesthetic values. There is a kind of laxity, of permissiveness, of toleration, of suspension of judgment about many matters of morality and values. Do we really believe that all values are relative, that none can be said to be better or worse than any other, that exemplary conduct is no better than conduct of the basest self-interested kind, that historically validated great art or literature is no better than spur-of-the-moment outpourings?

Democracies can survive only if both citizens and leaders understand that a personal, individual commitment to excellence, however defined, is at least as important in its proper realm—the realm of uncoerced values—as deference to transitory quantitative measures of preference, e.g., a majority vote, is in the coercible realm. *Vox populi* is not *vox Dei*, at least not in the realm of values and not in any way that matters over time. That we do not prohibit certain kinds of conduct is no license to engage in them. That we are free to believe whatever we wish and to express ourselves as we like does not discharge us of the obligation to choose as wisely as our intelligence permits that which will most conduce to our own long-run welfare and that of our family and friends.

Moreover, it is imperative that we articulate and advocate those values to which we are personally committed. If we believe that some values are better than others, then we should have the courage of our convictions about those judgments. If the marketplace of ideas, of morality, of values is to yield better outcomes, then it is imperative that we be less diffident about urging what we view as superior, enduring values. Those who subscribe to the transient values have no such diffidence. Moreover, because it intersects so greatly with the marketplace of goods and services, the marketplace of values has a built-in bias toward the here-and-now, the transient, those salable values that become obsolete and are replaced by other equally ephemeral values. Parents should recognize the value contest for what it is and not lose the battle for their children's loyalties by default. Teachers must not shy away from expressing their views and, to the fullest extent possible, exemplifying their values.

If we fail to instill that sense of personal responsibility for moral and value judgments in our citizens and to assert them ourselves, we run two very serious risks. One was precisely described two centuries ago by Edmund Burke: "Men are qualified for civil liberty in exact proportion to their disposition to put moral chains upon their appetites. . . . Society cannot exist unless a controlling power upon will and appetite be placed somewhere, and the less of it there is within, the more there must be without. It is ordained in the eternal constitution of things, that men of intemperate minds cannot be free. Their passions forge their fetters." A failure to assert personal responsibility for morality and values is likely to produce ever more intense demands, from larger numbers of people, for imposing those fetters from without, for coercing morality.

Moreover, as we know all too well, these issues of morality are highly charged and inherently divisive. More than almost any other public issues, they lend themselves to exploitation by power-seeking demagogues. And that is, of course, the second danger, the danger that our democracy might degenerate, as Aristotle predicted, into government by mob.

Unless we learn to cultivate, as Frank Porter Graham described it, "democracy without vulgarity and excellence without arrogance," our moral majority or some equally misguided successor may succeed someday in fatally undermining this greatest incarnation of the least objectionable form of government ever tried.

"There is nothing worth dying for," read a sign at a recent Princeton anti-registration rally. I know that most of our generation does not believe that, but if there are even a few who do, it is a few too many. That is indeed a seductive slogan to idealistic young people faced by what seem to some to be hopelessly corrupt institutions. But the truth is as it has always been. Despite our national shortcomings, the qualities that made this nation great, unique, and worth fighting for in the beginning still prevail. As William Lee Miller put it in the title of his book, "Of Thee Nevertheless I Sing."

Nowhere in history has there been as much individual freedom of expression and freedom from arbitrary governmental action. Nowhere in history has there been greater personal economic freedom for an overwhelming preponderance of the population. Nowhere in history has there been greater opportunity for every citizen to improve his or her educational attainments. Nowhere in history has an entire ethnic or racial group within a nation moved from slavery to full political freedom. Nowhere in history has a nation so committed itself to the full participation in governmental decisions of those affected by those decisions. And I could go on. Then why are so many unhappy?

Because of that same preference for short-run satisfaction that has led us increasingly to be impatient with our lives and with our institutions, bringing some of us perilously close to personal disaster and our nation as a whole to repeated bouts of racking turbulence. Short-run gratification is always based on a "what-have-you-done-for-me-lately" mentality. Human lives and social institutions—be they governments, universities, or families—prove themselves over the long run. From time to time, they falter. But over the long run, they provide many more benefits to us than they exact in cost. Yet the short-run perspective blinds us to those benefits and tempts us again and again in times of crisis to throw out the baby with the bathwater, to junk the old reliable because it is sputtering a bit, because it does not do instantly for us what we think it ought to do. We fail to understand that it may very well be right, rather than we, and that if something *is* wrong this time, a minor repair is all that is required, not a major overhaul.

In the last twenty years, the short-run instinct has soured us on institution after institution. Because we did not like the Vietnam War, down with the military. Because we did not like parietal rules and required curricula, down with the colleges and universities. Because we did not like environmental pollution, down with the corporations. Because we did not like energy prices, down with free enterprise in oil. Nationalize. Because we did not like Watergate and Vietnam, down with the powerful presidency, the so-called imperial presidency. Because we did not like FBI spying and CIA covert actions, down with the intelligence agencies. Because some politicians are thieves and faithless to the public trust, down with politics and government itself.

If all we care about, and talk about, are the short-run shortcomings, we will never see the long-run strengths clearly enough to have them sustain us. And if we do not appreciate the long-run strengths, there will be neither stability in our personal and institutional lives, nor any possibility of personal or institutional improvement from one generation to the next.

One of the main reasons that our short-run dissatisfactions have led to disillusionment with our institutions is that, for some time, we have been afflicted, in a variety of ways, with the "patriotism is the last refuge of a scoundrel" syndrome. If we hear a politician or a businessman or a professor urge, or even talk about, the love of country, many of us think that he or she is old-fashioned at best, and perhaps a fraud at worst. If the businessman praises the free enterprise system or suggests that government regulation of business is not all good, we are inclined to dismiss him as self-interested at best, and an immoral defender of reaction and inequality at worst. If a scholar talks about the mission of universities and schools as one of instilling love of learning, many will dismiss his views as pious, sententious "Mr. Chipsism" at best, or intentional camouflage of what any "intelligent" person knows to be a system of training and credentialing to serve business, professional, and class elites. The sophisticates, skeptics, and radicals have indeed begun to achieve their aim of undermining the faith of Americans in their institutions. Without that faith, we will lack the determination to carry on. And I think the time has now come to fight back.

We must not be afraid of believing in the virtue of our society and its institutions, even while we know they are imperfect. We must not be embarrassed to feel deeply and articulate openly and vigorously the ideals that have animated our institutions, even while we confess that we have not yet measured up fully to what they require.

Those who adhere to ancient, enduring values such as patriotism, freedom, love, religion, learning, excellence, reason, discipline, and sacrifice have retreated from public discourse and, therefore, from the battle for this generation's loyalties, under the onslaught of modernism, know-nothingism, and short-runism.

These time-honored values give meaning to our lives, sustain us when shortcomings create doubt. If, as Thomas Jefferson declared, the tree of liberty must be watered by the blood of patriots in every generation, so must the values that give meaning to liberty be affirmed in every generation by the convictions of our hearts and the words of our mouths.

I think that the time has now come to put off our embarrassment, to be unashamed, perhaps even to be proud, as we are put down as old-fashioned, to take our stand for values that we know give meaning, as well as strength, over the long haul of our personal and institutional lives. Make no mistake, history is with us. Civilization has been through such periods of ascendancy of short-run gratification and consumerism before, in ancient Rome, in Babylon, in Assyria, in Egypt, and such times have always proved to be dead ends. It is our urgent responsibility today to insure that this genuinely extraordinary nation in which we live—a nation dedicated to political, personal, and economic freedom, to human equality of opportunity, to justice—along with the civilization which it tries from time to time to lead continues to thrive. If it is to do so, however, the long-run values, which can never be compelled by law, need to be bred again in our own hearts and in the hearts of our young people. They are the values that give meaning to freedom; indeed, in the most profound sense they justify freedom. Without them, freedom can never long survive.

We must learn to be loving critics—capable of affirming the value of an institution, a form of government, a style of life, and fighting to defend it from others at the same time we are fighting to make it better than it already is. Our government is not perfect, but no one has ever claimed that it was. All that has been claimed is that it is the least bad form of government ever devised. It has far more good than bad, but its critics rarely point that out, choosing to lambaste it for every conceivable kind of wrong.

The consequence is that we are losing faith in our institutions—the frameworks that hold us together, the symbols that have the potential of infusing our lives with values and meaning. Too few of us understand our democratic form of government or appreciate why it is the least bad alternative. Too few of us understand the essential purpose of higher education or appreciate the special opportunity it affords us. Too few of us understand the central meaning of our civilization and feel any obligation to incorporate some of it into our lives and help carry it onward to the next generation. Too many of us live increasingly for our private selves and quest for the easy gratification, discovering much too late that easy gratification leads nowhere but to an increased appetite for a more easy gratification and never to genuine satisfaction.

The nation is strong. Our wavering is not yet fatal. This is only the first or second generation afflicted. We still have time to prevail, but only if we reassert our enduring values.

"I shall tell you a great secret, my friend," Albert Camus confided. "Do not wait for the last judgment, it takes place every day."

Part II. Economic Well-Being

4. Transfer Recipients and the Poor during the 1970s

Richard A. Kasten and John E. Todd

Abstract

During the 1970s, there was very little change in the number of persons below the official poverty threshold, despite a near doubling in federal social welfare spending. Several explanations are advanced that shed light on this apparent paradox. Demographic shifts and the poor performance of the economy tended to push the poverty rate upward. Moreover, in-kind transfers are a growing share of total welfare spending, but they are not counted in determining whether an individual is above or below the poverty line. Participants in the Aid to Families with Dependent Children (AFDC) program fared particularly poorly in the inflationary 1970s. The average real benefit level fell by 19 percent between 1969 and 1979. A number of strategies for dealing with this problem are discussed. Designing federal policies that could reverse this trend is difficult. States now set benefit levels and do not want to give up this responsibility. Providing states with incentives to raise their benefit levels can be expensive, and the program must be carefully designed so the states will use the additional funds to raise benefit levels.

At the beginning of the 1980s, analysts looking back at the previous decade found that, despite the near doubling of the real value of federal social welfare spending, virtually no progress had been made in reducing the fraction of the population with incomes below the official poverty threshold. It is important for those who will be planning social welfare programs in the austere 1980s to understand this apparent paradox.

Official poverty statistics for the 1970s show a small drop in the proportion of people who are poor, from 12.1 percent to 11.6 percent. In the same decade federal social welfare spending increased by 92 percent in constant dollars. Three explanations are advanced to reconcile these facts. First, the demographic groups most likely to need assistance represent an increasing share of the population. Both the elderly population and the number of female-headed families with children are growing much more rapidly than the total population. Without substantial increases in transfer programs the poverty rate would have grown. Second, a relatively small part of the growth in transfers has been in income-tested cash assistance programs (i.e. those for which eligibility depends on income). Transfers of goods and services (in-kind assistance) are not counted as income when determining poverty. Programs that are not income-tested are less efficient per dollar in fighting poverty. Third, the economy was in much worse condition in the 1970s than it was in the 1960s. If there had been as much growth in real wages in the 1970s as there was in the 1960s and if the unemployment rate had been as low in 1979 as it was in 1969, the poverty rate in 1979 would have been nearly 2.5 percentage points lower.

Participants in Aid to Families with Dependent Children (AFDC) have been hit particularly hard by the inflation of the 1970s. Average real benefit levels for AFDC recipients fell by 19 percent during the decade. Many other programs have indexed their benefit levels to the Consumer Price Index (CPI), but AFDC remains unindexed except in California.

The current period of fiscal austerity is not the time to try to raise benefit levels, but this study suggests a number of alternative policy measures that may be considered in the future. Designing federal policies to reverse the deterioration in benefit levels is a complex problem. States want to preserve their responsibility for setting AFDC benefit levels. Providing states with incentives to encourage them to raise benefit levels can be expensive, and it is difficult to insure that new federal money will go to raise benefits rather than provide fiscal relief.

Poverty Statistics versus Expenditure Growth

The Poverty Population During the 1970s

During the 1970s very little progress was made in reducing the percentage of people whose income fell below the official poverty threshold. The proportion fell from 12.1 percent in 1969 to 11.6 percent in 1979. In 1973, 1974, and 1978 the poverty rates were lower than in 1979. The lack of progress contrasts sharply with the 1960s, when the poverty rate fell from 22.4 percent in 1959 to 12.1 percent in 1969.

Table 4.1 shows the change in the number of poor people and the poverty rate for a number of different demographic groups. Considerable progress was made in reducing poverty among the elderly. Because of the increasing proportion of children living in female-headed families, the fraction of all children living in poverty rose even though the poverty rates for children in male- and in female-headed families both fell. The fraction of the poor who are black increased over the decade. Because of a 68-percent increase in the number of individuals living alone, the number of poor unrelated individuals rose even though the poverty rate for the group dropped substantially.

Growth in Social Welfare Expenditures

Although little progress has been made in reducing poverty, the total cost of social welfare expenditures has grown enormously in real terms over the last

Table 4.1. Millions of poor people and poverty rates, 1969 and 1979

	1969		1979	
	Poor people	Poverty rate	Poor people	Poverty rate
All persons	24.1	12.1%	25.2	11.6%
Persons 65 or older	4.8	25.3	3.6	15.1
Children under 18	9.5	13.8	9.7	15.9
Persons in female-headed families	6.9	38.2	9.1	34.7
Blacks	7.1	32.2	7.8	30.9
Unrelated individuals	5.0	34.0	5.6	21.8

decade. Table 4.2 shows the increase in federal expenditures for the major programs for 1970 and 1980. The second column shows the 1970 costs in 1980 dollars. The CPI was used to inflate 1970 expenditures. By any standard, the costs have grown dramatically. State and local expenditures for the same sorts of programs have also been growing, although at a somewhat lower rate.

Table 4.3 divides federal expenditures into income-tested and in-kind programs. Although income-tested programs grew faster than the others, only 29 percent of the increase in real spending is accounted for by income-tested programs because of their relatively small size. The two non-income-tested programs that serve primarily the elderly, Old-Age, Survivors, and Disability Insurance (OASDI) and Medicare, together account for over half of the increase in total spending. Despite the decrease in AFDC benefit levels discussed below, real spending on AFDC has grown by 69 percent, although that increase masks the fact that real total spending in 1979 was the same as in 1971.

Reconciling These Two Findings

How can we reconcile the lack of appreciable progress in reducing the official poverty statistics with these dramatic increases in social welfare expenditures? Three explanations dominate.

Growth in the need for transfers. The 1970s saw a significant increase in the percentage of the population in demographic groups that are traditionally more dependent on transfers. Between 1970 and 1979, the elderly population, for example, grew by 22 percent (compared with 8 percent for the total population), and the percentage of the population that is over 65 rose from 9.5 percent to 10.7 percent. The number of elderly receiving Social Security benefits increased from 17.3 million in 1970 to 22.8 million in 1979. The number of female-headed families with children grew from 3.5 million in 1970 to 5.8 million in 1979. This was reflected in the increase in the number of families receiving AFDC benefits from 2.2 million in 1970 to 3.5 million in 1980. The growth of female-headed families might have been smaller if transfer programs

Table 4.2. Growth in federal social welfare expenditures, 1970–1980 (billions of dollars)

Program	1970	1970 in 1980 dollars	1980	Real growth	In-kind benefit	Income tested
I. Entitlement						
Indexed by law						
OASDI	29.7	62.9	117.9	87%		
Civil Service Retirement	2.6	5.5	14.6	165		
Food Stamps	.6	1.3	8.7	569	X	X
SSI (formerly Adult Asst.)	2.3	4.9	6.4	31		X
Railroad Retirement	1.6	3.4	4.7	38		
Black Lung	0	0	2.0	—		
Total indexed	36.8	78.0	154.3	98		
Not indexed by law						
Medicare	7.1	15.0	33.5	123%	X	
Unemployment Compensation	3.4	7.2	15.6	117		
Medicaid	2.7	5.7	14.2	149	X	X
Veterans Pensions, compensation & life ins.	5.8	12.3	12.2	−1		X
Veterans health & medical	1.8	3.8	6.4	68	X	
AFDC	2.0	4.2	7.1	69		X
Veterans education	1.0	2.1	2.2	5	X	
Earned income tax credit	0	0	1.7	—		X
Total not indexed	23.8	50.3	92.9	85		
II. Discretionary						
General health & medicine	3.2	6.8	8.8	29%	X	
Elementary & secondary ed.	3.0	6.4	7.3	14	X	
CETA	0	0	6.7	—		X
Higher education	1.4	3.0	5.5	50	X	X
Housing assistance	1.3	2.8	5.3	89	X	X
Child nutrition & WIC	.4	.8	4.7	488	X	X
Other Manpower	1.8	3.8	4.3	13	X	
Social services (including child care)	.7	1.5	3.1	107	X	X
Low Income Energy Asst.	0	0	1.7	—	X	X
Vocational rehabilitation	.4	.8	1.1	38	X	
Total of discretionary programs	12.2	25.9	48.5	87		
TOTAL	72.8	154.9	295.7	92%		

Note: OASDI = Old Age, Survivors, and Disability Insurance; SSI = Supplemental Security Income; AFDC = Aid to Families with Dependent Children; CETA = Comprehensive Employment and Training Act; WIC = Women, Infants, and Children.

Table 4.3. Federal expenditures by type, 1970–1980 (billions of dollars)

	Expenditures		
	1970 in 1980 Dollars	1980	Percentage growth
Income tested			
In kind	15.1	43.2	186
Not in kind	21.4	34.1	59
Total	36.5	77.3	112
Not income tested			
In kind	38.7	63.6	64
Not in kind	79.0	154.8	96
Total	117.7	218.4	86

Table 4.4. Persons in poverty (in millions)

	1969	1977	Change
Before transfers			
In families with children	17.7	20.4	15%
Other with aged or disabled	9.1	12.0	32
Other with no aged or disabled	7.6	11.0	45
	34.4	43.5	26
After transfers			
In families with children	14.7	16.0	9
Other with aged or disabled	4.0	3.1	−23
Other with no aged or disabled	5.4	5.9	9
	24.2	24.9	3

were less generous, but this growth came in a decade in which AFDC benefit levels fell.

Perhaps the most straightforward way to demonstrate this shift is to compare the change in the pretransfer poverty counts to the change in the posttransfer poverty counts, as shown in table 4.4. We were able to do this only for the years 1969–1977, but the trend is clear enough even without the last few years.

It is clear that, without the growth in income-assistance programs, the number of poor persons in the United States would have increased substantially during this period. Poverty would not have grown as fast as the pretransfer poor population, because with lower transfers some families would have worked more or relied on relatives, but an increase in benefits was necessary to offset the growth in the transfer-dependent poor populations.

Growth in in-kind programs.   The past decade has seen a considerable growth in the costs of in-kind programs, which finance particular types of purchases or provide services directly to the recipient. These programs have no impact on the poverty rate, since in-kind benefits are not included in income when determining if a family is poor. The two largest in-kind programs are the medical programs, Medicaid and Medicare, which grew by 130 percent in real terms. Taken together, in-kind benefits grew by 99 percent from 1970 to 1980 while benefits received as cash grew by 88 percent. The set of programs best able to reduce poverty, those that are both income tested and received in cash, grew by only 59 percent.

This is not the place for a complete discussion of the merits of including in-kind benefits in the determination of poverty status, but a few points should be kept in mind in assessing the total picture.

(*a*) In-kind benefits were not counted when the practice of collecting poverty statistics was begun. A look at all social welfare expenditures since that time shows that in-kind programs have grown only slightly faster than cash programs (although, as we saw in table 4.3, among income-tested programs they have grown considerably faster). Including in-kind benefits now would produce a statistic that could not be used legitimately for comparisons over time.

(*b*) In-kind benefits are excluded from income in most other measures as well. For example, fringe benefits are excluded when the income of the middle class is measured. We should be careful, again for comparison purposes, to be consistent in our treatment of in-kind benefits.

(*c*) If the amount of the in-kind benefit is less than the person would have spent for that good if he had total discretion over all of his income, the case for counting that benefit as income is stronger. For example, for most Food Stamp recipients, the coupons serve to release money for other purchases and therefore have consumption value (if we exclude stigma and administrative burden) very close to cash. Medical benefits are quite different, however. Most of the growth in medical benefits is either a replacement for free or subsidized service previously received, e.g., at charity hospitals, or it is a net addition to medical services. The cost of these benefits far exceeds the amount those families would actually spend for medical care if they had all of their income as cash, so these medical programs free up a relatively small amount of resources that are needed for other purchases. In terms of consumption, these benefits are worth far less than the same amount of cash. While program beneficiaries may not be medically poor, they may remain shelter poor, clothing poor, food poor, and the like, since the medical benefits do not serve to free up resources for these other essential items.

(*d*) Over 43 percent of Medicaid spending goes to provide long-term care, mostly in nursing homes, to institutionalized persons. These persons are not counted by the Current Population Survey and are not included in the poverty statistics. Any attempt to attribute medical benefits to the poor must be careful to exclude benefits to the institutionalized.

The state of the economy. The state of the economy influences both transfers and poverty rates. The unemployment rate rose from 3.5 percent in 1969 to 5.8 percent in 1979. In general, a 1-percent increase in the unemployment rate tends to increase the poverty rate by 0.3 percentage points. If the unemployment rate in 1979 had been as low as it was in 1969, the poverty rate would have been about 0.7 percent lower.

The level of real wages is also an important determinant of the poverty rate. About half of all poor families in 1979 were headed by a person who worked. Between 1959 and 1969 real wages grew by 16 percent and the poverty rate of families with a working head dropped from 15 to 7 percent. Between 1969 and 1979 real wages dropped by 3 percent and the poverty rate of workers dropped only slightly, to 6 percent. If wage growth during the 1970s had made wages 20 percent higher in 1979, the poverty rate would have been about 1.7 points lower.

Variations by Demographic Group and Program

In assessing the economic well-being of the poor and the role that transfer programs have played in ameliorating their poverty, we need to look separately at demographic groups and programs. The coverage and the generosity of some programs have increased far more than others. As a result, the incomes of the groups served by those programs have grown at very different rates.

The Panel Study of Income Dynamics shows striking differences between families receiving AFDC and families receiving Social Security. The average ratio of income to the poverty line for families receiving most of their income from AFDC fell by 24 percent between 1969 and 1977 (table 4.5). For families receiving Social Security, the same ratio increased by 13 percent. For all families, for all poor families, and for all families with earnings, there was virtually no change in this measure.

AFDC Benefit Levels

The AFDC program is of particular interest among transfer programs because (*a*) it is not indexed; (*b*) its recipients have been particularly hard-hit over this past decade; and (*c*) it is amenable to federal legislation (unlike the general assistance program, which has also deteriorated in real terms).

Table 4.5. Changes in income-to-poverty ratio (from Panel Study on Income Dynamics)

	1969	1977	Change
All families	3.83	3.78	− 1%
Poor families	0.69	0.69	0
Families receiving Social Security	2.48	2.81	+13
Families receiving income from AFDC	0.99	0.76	−24
Families with earnings	3.97	4.09	3

AFDC Benefits: 1969-1979

Between 1969 and 1979 the cost of living doubled. Average hourly wages also doubled, however, leaving most salaried workers with about the same real income in 1979 as they had had a decade earlier. Other people also have been protected against inflation, at least partially, by cost-of-living increases built into their incomes: many retirement plans, including Social Security, federal pensions, and some private pensions are adjusted—or "indexed"—by the Consumer Price Index (CPI). Benefits from some income-transfer programs, notably Supplemental Security Income (SSI) and Food Stamps, also are indexed, but AFDC benefits are not.

The unique structure of the AFDC program in large part explains why it is the only federally funded cash transfer program that is not indexed for inflation. In the other major transfer programs, SSI (federal portion) and Food Stamps, the benefit levels are set by and the costs are borne by the federal government. AFDC benefits, on the other hand, are determined by state governments. AFDC costs, then, are shared by the state and federal governments, with the federal government paying an average of 54 percent.[1] Because the states control benefit levels, there are wide variations in AFDC payments: In July 1979, Hawaii, the most generous, paid $6,552 per year to a family of four with no other income, while Mississippi paid $1,440. Further, in the absence of a mandate from Congress, indexing state AFDC benefits to keep pace with inflation would require action by 51 different governments. Today, only California has chosen to index its benefits automatically; in the other states increases must be legislated on an ad hoc basis.

Between 1969 and 1979 the average maximum AFDC benefit[2] paid to a family of four with no other income increased 61 percent, from $225 to $361 per month. The cost of living rose much faster, however. In constant 1979 dollars, AFDC benefits declined 19 percent, from $445 to $361, as shown in table 4.6. The greatest drops in real benefits occurred in the years 1973–1975 and in 1978 and 1979. Incidentally, these (except 1978) were the only years in the decade in

Table 4.6. AFDC and AFDC plus Food Stamp benefit levels in 1979 dollars

State	AFDC			AFDC + FS	
	1969	1974	1979	1974	1979
Alabama	160	183	148	358	329
Alaska	366	589	450	705	609
Arizona	350	271	240	422	393
Arkansas	198	184	188	359	357
California	438	458	487	548	566
Colorado	378	386	327	502	454
Connecticut	543	489	517	570	587
Delaware	370	339	287	464	426
Dist. of Col.	412	411	349	518	470
Florida	267	222	230	383	386
Georgia	263	236	170	396	344
Hawaii	517	587	546	695	659
Idaho	475	439	367	537	482
Illinois	533	424	333	531	459
Indiana	297	368	275	484	418
Iowa	483	436	419	534	519
Kansas	469	489	375	570	488
Kentucky	370	252	235	403	390
Louisiana	236	180	187	355	356
Maine	414	247	332	408	458
Maryland	362	333	294	467	431
Massachusetts	594	447	396	546	503
Michigan	521	589	470	643	554
Minnesota	572	545	454	612	543
Mississippi	137	88	120	290	309
Missouri	257	269	270	421	414
Montana	444	403	331	511	457
Nebraska	396	412	370	520	484
Nevada	283	296	297	439	433
New Hampshire	509	509	392	590	500
New Jersey	687	524	386	605	496
New Mexico	362	303	242	446	395
New York	620	577	476	631	559
North Carolina	297	271	210	422	372
North Dakota	519	464	389	553	498
Ohio	382	296	327	439	454
Oklahoma	366	347	349	472	470
Oregon	445	498	464	578	550
Pennsylvania	546	514	373	595	487
Rhode Island	588	458	389	548	498
South Carolina	184	172	142	352	325
South Dakota	483	483	361	573	478
Tennessee	255	194	148	365	329
Texas	255	206	140	372	323
Utah	384	403	389	511	498

Table 4.6. (Continued)

State	AFDC			AFDC + FS	
	1969	1974	1979	1974	1979
Vermont	527	530	503	598	578
Virginia	471	458	335	548	460
Washington	602	495	483	576	564
West Virginia	273	319	249	453	400
Wisconsin	438	593	458	648	546
Wyoming	396	334	340	468	463
Average	406	383	334	501	461
Wt. average	445	414	361	520	478

which real wages fell. It is not surprising that in the years of decreasing real wages taxpayers and politicians allowed benefits to decline more than in years of economic growth.

Table 4.7 shows the changes in AFDC benefits over the decade by region. The West is the only region in which benefits have not declined. Over the decade its average benefit level passed those of the Northeast and the North Central states. Of the eight states that show real benefit increases from 1969 to 1979 (Alaska, California, Hawaii, Missouri, Nevada, Oregon, Utah, and Wisconsin), six are in the West. Table 4.7 also shows the growth rates for states ranked by their 1969 benefit levels. The lowest states grew more slowly than the average. Fifteen of the 17 lowest benefit states in 1969 remained in the bottom third in 1979. None of the economic variables we examined, including changes in income and per capita income, were related to changes in benefit levels.

At the same time that the real level of AFDC benefits has declined, inflation has also made it more difficult to qualify for the program. Eligibility is judged according to a need standard set by each state. During the past ten years, the average income cutoff point has declined, in real terms, by 23 percent. A real income that could have qualified for the program ten years ago may be above the eligibility ceiling today.

Most AFDC recipients are also eligible to receive Food Stamps. Since 1974, when all the various Food Stamp programs were consolidated into one uniform program, the federal government has set the benefit levels and borne the full cost of the program. Because some states did not have a Food Stamp program until 1974, we examine here the trends in Food Stamp benefits that have occurred between that year and 1979.

When benefits from the Food Stamp program, which are indexed to food prices, are added to AFDC benefits, the fall in real benefits is mitigated somewhat. Nationally, real AFDC benefits fell 13 percent between 1974 and 1979; AFDC plus Food Stamps fell 9 percent. These delines in benefits varied among states. The fourth and fifth columns of table 4.6 show the change in benefits by

Table 4.7. Changes in AFDC benefits by region and benefit level, 1969 to 1979

	1969 Average benefit in 1979 dollars	1979 Average benefit	Change
National	445	361	−19%
Northeast	600	425	−29
North Central	458	377	−18
West	444	461	+ 4
South	280	209	−25
States[a]			
Top third	576	423	−27
Middle third	421	411	− 2
Bottom third	255	199	−22

a. Ranked by 1969 benefit levels.

Table 4.8. Percent change in AFDC and AFDC plus Food Stamp benefits: 1974–1979, in constant dollars

	AFDC	AFDC+ Food Stamps
National	−13%	− 9%
Northeast	−19	−13
North Central	−16	−10
West	+ 2	− 0
South	−15	− 8

state. Table 4.8 shows that the combined AFDC and Food Stamp benefit actually stayed the same in real terms over this period in the West, whereas it decreased by 13 percent in the Northeast.

The Food Stamp program has had two effects on how well AFDC families' incomes have kept pace with inflation. Their Food Stamp benefits are automatically adjusted for increases in food prices, with the federal government paying the full cost. On the other hand, the Food Stamp program has made it more costly for states to raise incomes by raising AFDC benefit levels. The Food Stamp benefit for an AFDC family is reduced by 30 percent of any AFDC increase. Without Food Stamps, a state with a 50 percent match in AFDC could pay 50 cents to raise benefits by a dollar. With Food Stamps, a state must pay $1.42 more in the AFDC benefits for a $1.00 increase in income, which costs the state 71 cents and the federal government only 29 cents.

Figure 4.1 summarizes trends in average AFDC and Food Stamp benefit levels for the period 1970−1979. The Food Stamp program caused a large increase in real incomes when it was introduced and has moderated but not prevented the loss in real incomes since its complete implementation in 1974.

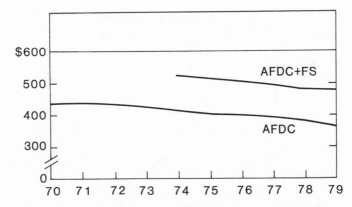

Figure 4.1. AFDC and Food Stamp benefits in 1979 dollars

Three further points should be made. First, the benefits from some other programs serving AFDC families have increased over this period, but not enough to compensate for the decline in AFDC benefits. Benefits from housing and social service programs have stayed about constant in real terms, but many recipients are excluded from these programs because of their limited budgets. Expenditures for Medicaid have increased, but to some degree this has sub-stituted a full-fee cash payment for free or reduced-fee care, and in any case the greater medical services cannot be translated into resources for food, clothing, and shelter. Energy assistance payments have increased but by far less than energy expenses have risen. In fact, the Consumer Price data used to calculate the constant dollar benefit levels in the above tables may understate the actual rise in prices for the poor since direct energy expenditures are only 7 percent of the market basket used to calculate the CPI but represent over 20 percent of the expenditures of the average poor family. Second, the figures shown above are national averages. Many states have seen an even larger deterioration in real benefits. In fact, in 16 states, AFDC benefits in 1979 dollars have declined by more than 25 percent since 1969. Third, these figures take us only through mid-1979. Real AFDC benefit levels declined another 6 percent between mid-1979 and mid-1980.

Why Have Benefit Levels Deteriorated?

Several factors are responsible for the deterioration in benefit levels.

First, the total state spending in all areas has fallen in real terms in every year since 1976. Real 1979 expenditures were no higher than they were in 1973. In order to reduce real expenditures on AFDC recipients, states must allow benefit levels to deteriorate since the number of single-parent families is growing and the cost of providing AFDC families with medical coverage through Medicaid is rising.

Second, as discussed above, the Food Stamp program has reduced the need for cash assistance and made it more expensive for states to increase benefit levels. Even with the deterioration of AFDC benefit levels since 1969, the average benefit from AFDC plus Food Stamps in 1979 was 10 percent higher than the real value of AFDC in 1969, when relatively few families participated in the Food Stamp program.

Finally, deterioration varies regionally. Of the four regions examined, the South has had the second largest decrease in real benefit levels despite its relative prosperity. One explanation is that the Food Stamp program has had its largest impact on southern families, since their AFDC benefits, which are included in income when determining Food Stamps eligibility, are lowest. A typical AFDC family gets 24 percent of its AFDC plus Food Stamp income as Food Stamps. In the South, Food Stamps represent 45 percent of the total. Because of the large Food Stamp benefits, the average southern family received 33 percent more from AFDC plus Food Stamps in 1979 than it got from AFDC alone in 1969, despite the deterioration in AFDC benefit levels.

Benefit Levels in Other Programs

Benefits of the two major federally administered cash assistance programs, Social Security and Supplementary Security Income (SSI), have been indexed by inflation since 1974. Real benefit levels in SSI, even with the inclusion of nonindexed state supplements, have been nearly flat since 1974, when the program began. Real benefit levels in Social Security have actually risen about 10 percent, since the covered earnings of each year's cohort of retirees is higher than that of the previous year. For the period 1969 to 1979 average Social Security benefits rose in real terms by 52 percent. About half of the increase was due to increased covered earnings; the remainder was caused by pre-1974 legislative changes that made the program more generous. In July 1980, Social Security and SSI recipients received a 14.3 percent increase in their payments that fully adjusted for the previous year's inflation.

Federal Policy Options

There are a number of options available to policymakers who think that the deterioration in AFDC benefit levels is a problem and are willing to commit federal funds to deal with it. Even in 1980, when these options were developed, there was little support in the Senate for increasing federal spending or for placing any additional requirements on the states. In 1981, only the reforms that save money by taking AFDC away from families with earnings or other sources of income are being considered.

Offsetting or reversing the decline of AFDC benefits is both difficult and complex because, under present law, the states set AFDC benefit levels, and the federal and state governments share the costs. A number of different approaches are possible, however. Some mandate higher benefit levels; others encourage them. The first two listed below are primarily directed at raising the lowest benefit levels to some minimum standard; the remainder aim to maintain real benefit levels in all states. Some of these options would decrease state costs (and so are usually labeled "fiscal relief"), and others would increase state costs. Some would treat all states alike; others would vary the treatment of a state on the basis of its benefit level at some time in the past. Most would require legislation; Options 7B and 8 could probably be accomplished through regulation. The options are not mutually exclusive; they could be combined in a variety of ways.

Require One National Minimum Benefit

The federal government could legislate that states must pay some minimum benefit in order to receive matching funds. H.R. 4904, the welfare reform bill passed by the House in 1979 but never considered by the Senate, set such a minimum standard, requiring that AFDC plus Food Stamps equal at least 65 percent of the poverty level. (An alternative would be to set up a direct federal entitlement, with the uniform basic benefit fully financed and administered by the federal government, which the states could supplement, as in the SSI program.) In 1979 this would have raised benefits in fourteen states. If the minimum were indexed to the CPI, as it was in H.R. 4904, more states would probably be affected eventually since experience suggests that states are not likely to keep pace with the CPI. Such a minimum would increase state costs, but this increase could be offset with a hold-harmless provision, which assures no increase in state costs, that could either be permanent or for a transitional period as in H.R. 4904. The major drawbacks to this approach have been the strong opposition of the states whose benefits would be increased and the fact that a national minimum would do nothing to protect recipients in higher-benefit states from inflation.

Raise Matching Rates to National Minimum

An alternative approach would be to raise matching rates to perhaps 90 percent of the national minimum benefit level. This would make it very attractive financially for a state to raise its benefit level up to the minimum standard, but it would not insure that all states would reach that standard. The major difficulty with this approach is that if matching rates above the minimum benefit are set at current levels, the fiscal relief, almost all of which would go to the states having the higher benefits, would be very expensive (nearly $3 billion). If instead the matching rates above the minimum were set lower than current levels with an option for states to use current law, then the fiscal relief would be reduced, but the matching rate at the margin for all states that used the new rules and were at or above the national minimum would be reduced from current law. This would increase the cost to the state of raising benefits to keep up with inflation.

Require Indexing of Benefits

This approach was proposed by the Johnson administration in 1967, but Congress agreed only to a one-time requirement that by 1969 a state's need standard (which determines eligibility but not necessarily benefit levels) be adjusted to reflect price increases through 1969. (The option of adjusting needs standards is discussed below; see G.)

The principal difficulty with this approach is again the likely opposition by states to federal legislation that takes away state discretion and requires higher state costs. In this case, all states, not just those with the lowest benefits, are likely to balk. The cost problem could be offset by some sort of hold-harmless provision, but this would be particularly hard to design. It is difficult to determine what states would do without this provision and thus difficult to know the extra costs this provision would incur. The federal government would probably end up absorbing costs that the states otherwise would have picked up.

Another difficulty of mandatory indexing is that high-benefit states would always be required to make larger increases than those that have been less generous. Recipients would be protected from inflation, but this option would do nothing to equalize benefit levels across states or to bring the lowest benefit levels up to some national minimum standard.

Raise All Matching Rates

Encouraging higher benefit levels may be politically more acceptable than requiring them is. H.R. 4904 contained a provision that would have lowered by 10 percent the share of AFDC costs paid by the states. By freeing up state revenues and by reducing the state's share of the cost of increasing benefits, the provision was intended to encourage states to do a better job of keeping pace with inflation. We do not have a very good idea of how states respond to such incentives, however. This approach might provide considerable fiscal relief to states without having much effect on their benefit levels.

The cost of this approach could be reduced somewhat by applying the higher matching rates only above some benefit level. This would reduce the federal cost (by about two-thirds if the matching rate were changed only for payments above 65 percent of the poverty line) while retaining the same incentives at the margin for most states. Note that this is nearly the opposite of option B, discussed above.

Raise Matching Rates for Benefit Increases

Another matching rate option uses incentives to achieve the aims of mandatory indexing. A state's share of the cost of AFDC benefit level increases would be only half of its current share. (We might want to limit the size of the increases that the federal government would match at the higher rate.) In other words, each state's matching rate would depend on the extent to which it had raised its benefit above the level it paid in some base year. This would minimize the fiscal relief in the short run while providing strong incentives at the margin to increase benefit levels. Over many years, as all states increased their benefit levels, the federal share of AFDC benefits would increase. States that have high benefit levels in the base year would consider this proposal unfair, since they would have lower matching rates than other states. In addition, if states would have raised their benefit levels in any case, the change in the matching rate would provide fiscal relief without benefiting recipients.

To increase leverage, these matching-rate increases could be made conditional on a state's willingness to index its benefits over time and/or to pay at least some minimum benefit. The difficulty here is that the increases would have to be quite large in order to avoid increases in state costs. Otherwise, the states would very likely be able to defeat any such proposal. This difficulty reflects the basic problem: indexing AFDC benefits during a time of high inflation is expensive. Raising AFDC benefit levels even by 10 percent would cost over a billion dollars. To provide fiscal relief for the states as well would clearly represent a substantial federal commitment, no matter how the matching rates were arranged.

Award a One-time Block Grant for Benefit Increases

The federal government could make a one-time payment to states, to be passed on to recipients in the form of higher benefit levels. In order to assure that the payments were used to increase benefits, the government would give payments only to states that used the funds to increase benefits above some baseline figure. The difficulty is that we would have no precise idea of what states would have done without the payment. If our assumed baseline is high, more than states would have provided, then the states will either have to share in the cost of raising benefits up to the baseline level or forgo the payment. If, in order to increase state support for the proposal, the assumed baseline level is lowered, then in some states the payment will produce only fiscal relief.

Increase Need Standards

A state's need standard determines the eligibility cutoff for applicants but it does not determine actual payments. Some states (27) pay their full need standard, but many pay only a fraction of that standard. Louisiana, for example, pays only 42 percent of its need standard.

In 1969 the federal government required all states to update their need standards. Even though there was no requirement to increase their benefit levels, an analysis of that experience conducted by Urban Systems under contract to the Social Security Administration indicates that the requirement appears to have raised benefit levels, presumably because the higher need standards exerted a pressure on state legislatures to bring benefits closer to the standard of need that the state itself had set.

Policies related to need standards could influence benefit levels. Either of two approaches could be used:[3]

Requiring states to index their need standards. Need standards have deteriorated badly in the last decade. Only eight states have maintained the real value of their need standards during the 10-year period, and only eight have maintained their payment standards. Only four states have preserved the value of both standards. In 1969, 30 states had need standards in excess of 80 percent of the poverty line; by 1979 that number had declined to 10. In 1969, only one state had a standard lower than 50 percent of the poverty line; now 13 are below that level. Indexing would repair some of the damage. The federal government could require a one-time "catch-up" increase and thereafter require year-by-year indexing. States would continue to set their own benefit levels, but experience suggests that payments will follow the need standard as states try to close, or at least maintain, the gap between the two standards. The imposition of an indexing provision requires congressional action, but there are precedents, in AFDC and other assistance programs.

Requiring states to set their need standards by an approved methodology. A one-time adjustment followed by annual updates would get standards back to their (real) 1969 levels, but some of them would remain unrealistically low. Moreover, freezing standards that reflect substantial inequities across states is somewhat unfair to the states that in 1969 happened to have relatively high standards, to say nothing of the injustice to the families in the states with relatively low standards. If each state were required to develop an approved methodology as the basis for its need standard, the resulting standards would be both more realistic and more consistent. The regulation need not apply to the levels of the standards, but rather to the method by which states derive those levels. States are already required to submit, as part of their state plans, the methods they use to derive their standards. But for the most part, they submit a brief description of their methods of consolidation ("statistical fair averaging" or "pre-added schedule"), which fails to shed any light on the methodological basis for the preconsolidation standard.

Either or both of these approaches could be combined with any of the first five options discussed above. Needless to say, states—that is, the representatives of the governors and the state legislatures—would oppose both need standard measures, and state welfare officials might oppose the second.

Use More Modest Approaches

In combination with any of the above approaches, the Department of Health and Human Services could play a more active role in support of higher benefit levels, particularly in the areas of information, technical assistance, and advocacy. The Social Security administration could distribute information to the states on approaches to standard-setting. It could provide technical assistance to states that are interested in developing more normative standards but lack the expertise or resources to invest in the process. In regard to advocacy, SSA could urge states to reconsider their current practices and adopt more systematically derived standards, perhaps according to one or more preferred methods.

Postscript

These approaches to increasing benefits are not being considered in 1983, since the major legislative emphasis is on budget reduction. However, some of the proposals now being considered may have the effect of raising benefit levels for at least some recipients. For example, the reduction of payments for working families and other changes in the rules of eligibility will decrease state costs. Some states may use these savings to restore real benefit levels. In addition, allowing states to require recipients to work for their grants may increase the political support for the AFDC program. More direct approaches to increasing benefit levels may become politically more possible at some future time. In any event, an examination of the various means of influencing AFDC benefit levels provides an interesting case study of the difficulties of achieving federal objectives in a joint federal-state program.

5. Labor Supply Response to a Negative Income Tax

Philip K. Robins, Richard W. West,
and Gary L. Stieger

Abstract

Over the past decade, four major social experiments have been conducted in the United States to test various forms of a negative income tax (NIT) as an alternative to the present welfare system. A great deal of empirical research has been conducted using the data generated from these experiments to determine how labor supply would be affected by an NIT. The typical study generates such estimates by comparing average labor supply of persons in the experimental group with average labor supply of persons in the control group. In this paper, it is argued that, because of the income cutoff used in the experiments, such an approach does not provide useful information about the likely effects of a nationwide NIT program. Instead, the analysis should focus on the response of persons actually receiving benefits (i.e., participants) as opposed to the response of persons eligible to receive benefits. In this chapter, a statistical methodology is developed for obtaining unbiased estimates of the response of participants in an NIT program. The methodology is tested using data from the Seattle and Denver Income Maintenance Experiments. The statistical procedure presented in the chapter is quite general and is applicable to a wide variety of evaluation problems.

Over the past decade, government expenditures on income security have been absorbing an ever-increasing share of the federal budget, growing from 22 percent of total outlays in 1970 to 34 percent in 1980 (Economic Report of the President, 1980). Social welfare expenditure, primarily Aid to Families with Dependent Children (AFDC) and Food Stamps, are two of the more rapidly growing segments of this component of the federal budget. Between 1970 and 1979 expenditures on these programs increased more than threefold, from $5.4 billion to $17.6 billion, a rise of 75 percent in real terms. In 1979, 17.7 million persons received Food Stamps and 11.1 million persons received AFDC benefits.

Despite the rapid growth in welfare expenditures, a significant number of persons remain in poverty. According to one of the most conservative estimates (one that includes the value of in-kind benefits and accounts for the tax system), about 4.1 percent of the U.S. population, or more than 9 million persons, had incomes below the poverty level in 1980 (Danziger & Haveman, 1981). One important reason why so many families continue to live in poverty is that public assistance programs do not provide adequate benefits to two-parent families.

The lack of adequate benefits to two-parent families under the current welfare system has led policymakers to consider alternative approaches to distributing welfare payments to low-income families and to evaluate the proper role of the federal government in providing these payments. One of the most frequently debated alternatives is the negative income tax (NIT), a program that would, in principle, consolidate all existing programs and would be administered by the federal government.

During the late 1960s and early 1970s, congressional attempts to implement a national NIT were thwarted partly because definitive empirical evidence regarding the size of its probable impact on the labor supply was not available. Knowledge of the labor supply impacts of an NIT is of enormous interest to policymakers because such impacts are likely to have a major effect on program costs. Moreover, there is great political concern that a NIT would create a sizable dependent population by inducing large-scale withdrawals from the labor force.

In response to this void in knowledge, researchers conducted many empirical studies in an attempt to estimate the labor supply effects of a NIT. These studies, which were generally based on nonexperimental cross-sectional data, concluded that labor supply reductions in response to a NIT would not be large enough to cause massive withdrawals from the labor force (see Cain & Watts, 1973). However, the wide variance of these nonexperimental estimates and the methodological problems associated with the various studies that produced them (see the survey by Keeley, 1981) led to proposals for experimental research in which a NIT would be imposed exogenously on a random sample of low-income families. Since 1968, four major social experiments have been conducted in the United States to test various forms of a NIT: the New Jersey Experiment (1968–1972), the Rural Experiment (1969–1973), the Gary Experiment (1971–1974), and the Seattle-Denver Experiment (1971–1978).

To determine the effects of a NIT on labor supply, much empirical research has been performed using the data generated from these experiments.[1] The typical study produces such estimates by comparing average labor supply of persons in the experimental group with average labor supply of persons in the control group. While useful for some purposes, this approach has limited relevance for policy. An alternative approach, taken in several studies, makes a distinction between two groups of eligible families: those participating in the NIT program (families below the breakeven level) and those not participating in the NIT program (families above the breakeven level).[2] Distinguishing participants from nonparticipants is important for several reasons.

First, the average labor supply response in the experimental population (i.e., the response of those eligible to participate) will be different from the average labor supply response in the U.S. population. The difference arises because the participation rates in the two populations are different (as a result of the income cutoff used in selecting the experimental samples). In order to generalize the experimental results to the national population, either the response of participants or the fraction of the experimental population that participates must be identified.[3]

A second reason for distinguishing participants from nonparticipants is that doing so may permit a more precise identification of experimental response. For example, if only a small proportion of the experimental sample participates or if the experimental sample as a whole is small, then it may not be possible to detect a significant response if the focus is on eligibles, but it may be possible if the focus is on participants. This appears to have occurred in evaluation of the New Jersey Experiment, where Watts and Rees (1977) generally find no significant effects on eligibles while Cogan (1978) finds significant effects on participants.

A third reason for distinguishing participants from nonparticipants is to focus attention on the group directly affected by the program (i.e., the group receiving benefits). By determining the size and response of the participating population, one can more easily evaluate the merits of competing programs. For example, two nationwide NIT programs with the same aggregate labor supply response and cost (i.e., the same effect on eligibles) may have very different effects on certain groups within the economy. By focusing on participants, we can more easily identify these differences.[4]

Empirically, it is not easy to distinguish the responses of participants and nonparticipants. Unlike an ordinary regression model, in which the treatment variable is eligibility (which is randomly assigned[5]), a model with participation as the treatment variable generally yields biased estimates. The bias arises for two distinct reasons. First, when the treatment variable is current participation,[6] the procedure does not account for the fact that participation is affected by the experimental treatments (i.e., participation is endogenous). Second, the procedure inappropriately compares average labor supply of participants (or nonparticipants) to average labor supply of the entire control group. Since average labor supply of participants (nonparticipants) tends to be lower (higher) than average labor supply of the entire control group,[7] an artificial experimental-control differential is created that may be wrongly attributed to the experimental treatments. This is the classic case of selection bias that plagues so much of evaluation research. It differs from the first source of bias because there need not be causation between the experimental treatments and participation.

In this study, we compare a variety of different empirical models in an attempt to distinguish the labor-supply response of participants and nonparticipants in the Seattle and Denver Income Maintenance Experiments (SIME/DIME), the largest of the NIT experiments.[8] Our approach follows suggestions by Garfinkel (1976), Burtless (1979), and Burtless and Greenberg (1979) to create matched control groups by hypothetically assigning control families to a set of experimental treatments. Our statistical procedure to correct for the bias represents a combination of techniques developed by Heckman (1976, 1978, 1979) and Maddala and Lee (1976). To account for selectivity bias we include participation variables, defined over both experimentals and controls, on the right-hand side of the response equations. To account for the endogeneity of current participation, we create an instrumental variable for current participation, based on the experience of the experimental group, and use this variable in place of actual participation.

The Models

The Eligibility Model

The first model we consider utilizes a single dummy variable to measure the effects of the financial treatments on labor supply. The dummy variable takes on the value of one if the person is eligible to receive NIT payments (i.e., is assigned to a NIT treatment), and zero otherwise. This is the model most commonly used to estimate experimental effects (Robins & West, 1980b, 1980d; West & Stieger, 1980; Moffitt, 1979; portions of Watts & Rees, 1977; Pechman & Timpane, 1975; Palmer & Pechman, 1978), and all the subsequent models are extensions of it. The eligibility model yields answers to two important questions: (a) Does the experiment have any effect on labor supply? (b) What is the average effect of the financial treatments on labor supply for all persons eligible to receive NIT payments, regardless of whether or not they actually received them? The eligibility model yields efficient answers to these questions because it measures the effects of the financial treatments on labor supply by a single parameter.

In the eligibility model, the dependent variable (actual hours worked in the second year of the experiments[9]) is assumed to be generated in the following fashion:

$$H_0 = C_0 + \mu + e_0 , \tag{5.1}$$

$$H_2 = C_2 + \gamma F + \mu + e_2 , \tag{5.2}$$

where

H_0 = hours of work in the pre-experimental period,

H_2 = hours of work in the second year of the experiments,

C_0, C_2 = constant terms,

μ = permanent component of labor supply that persists over time (assumed to have a mean of zero),

F = a dummy variable for NIT treatment (1 for experimentals, 0 for controls),

γ = the experimental effect on hours of work in the second year,

e_0, e_2 = random error terms, assumed to be uncorrelated.

In this model, equation (5.1) indicates that labor supply before the experiment is the sum of a permanent and a transitory component plus a constant term. Equation (5.2) indicates that during the experiment, there is also an experimental effect, γ, for persons eligible to receive NIT benefits.

If assignment to treatment in SIME/DIME were not stratified, an unbiased estimate of γ could be obtained by regressing H_2 on F. However, as indicated by Robins and West (1980d) and Keeley and Robins (1980), such a procedure yields a biased estimate of γ when assignment depends on strata that are related to μ. In SIME/DIME (and to some extent in the other experiments), families were assigned to the experimental treatments (including control status) on the basis of a variable called "normal income," which is supposed to represent expected pre-experimental income adjusted for family size. In practice, normal income was determined primarily on the basis of pre-experimental labor supply.

Because of the assignment model, the least squares estimate of γ in equation (5.2) has the following expected value:

$$E(\gamma) \;=\; \gamma + \frac{\bar{\mu}_F}{1 - \dfrac{N_F}{N}} \;=\; \gamma + \bar{\mu}_F - \bar{\mu}_C, \qquad (5.3)$$

using the fact that $N\bar{\mu} = N_F\bar{\mu}_F + (N-N_F)\bar{\mu}_C = 0$, and where

$\bar{\mu}_F$ = the mean of μ for experimentals,

$\bar{\mu}_C$ = the mean of μ for controls,

N_F = the number of experimentals, and

N = the total sample size ($N_C + N_F$).

The means $\bar{\mu}_F$ and $\bar{\mu}_C$ are not zero because the permanent component of the error term determining labor supply (μ) is correlated with the treatment variable (F). Consequently, $\hat{\gamma}$ is biased with the bias equal to the difference in the means of μ for experimentals and controls.

Although estimation of equation (5.2) yields biased results, it can be shown (see Robins & West, 1980d, or Keeley & Robins, 1980) that the bias can be removed by including normal income in the regression equation. This result holds because μ is correlated with F only through normal income. After correcting for the assignment $\bar{\mu}_F = \bar{\mu}_C = 0$. The actual equation estimated is

$$H_2 = C_2 + \alpha E + \gamma F + \mu + e_2, \qquad (5.4)$$

where E is a vector of dummy variables representing normal income. In all the models estimated in this paper, E is included in the equation.[10]

The eligibility model is a parsimonious representation of the experimental treatments and as such provides a useful summary of the overall effect of the experiments. However, the eligibility model suffers from the weakness that it does not identify the response of persons directly affected by the program (i.e., those below the breakeven level). In addition, because of the income cutoff used in the experiments, it is difficult to extrapolate the results from the eligibility model to the national population.

The Initial Status Model

The second model we consider is designed to generate separate responses for persons above and below the breakeven level at the beginning of the experiment. This model, which we call the initial status model, bears close resemblance to the model estimated in Keeley et al. (1978a, 1978b). The initial status model, unlike the eligibility model, can be extrapolated to the national population. In our application of this model, we represent initial status by two dummy variables, one for initial participation and one for initial nonparticipation.[11] Initial status is determined on the basis of family income in the year before the beginning of the experiment.

A natural way to write a model that expresses labor supply response as a function of initial participation status is given by:

$$H_2 = C_2 + B_0 F b_0 + A_0 F a_0 + \mu + e_2 , \qquad (5.5)$$

where

B_0 = a dummy variable for being initially below the breakeven level,

b_0 = the response of persons initially below the breakeven level,

A_0 = a dummy variable for being initially above the breakeven level,

and

a_0 = the response of persons initially above the breakeven level.

This model can be estimated by ordinary least squares (OLS). However, OLS estimates may suffer from a potentially serious bias that arises because initial participation status is a complicated function of the financial treatments and pre-experimental income. Since similar functions of income are not allowed to affect hours of work for control families, OLS estimates could confound the experimental effects with the direct effects of these functions of income. In essence, this problem arises because we are comparing the two groups of experimentals with a noncomparable control group. Rather than comparing each experimental group with a group of controls with similar pre-experimental incomes, OLS estimates of equation (5.5) compare each group of experimentals with all controls.

The nature of the problem can be seen by examining a simplified version of equation (5.5) in which it is assumed that a_0 is zero (i.e., that persons above the breakeven level do not respond to the experiment and behave like controls):

$$H_2 = C_0 + B_0 F b_0 + \mu + e_2 \ . \tag{5.6}$$

We can also write a linear approximation for the equation determining B_0:

$$B_0 = C_B + c H_0 + d T + w_0 \ , \tag{5.7}$$

where

   $T =$ a vector of variables indicating the actual treatment to which an individual is assigned,

   $C_B =$ a constant term, and

   $w_0 =$ a random error term assumed uncorrelated with e_2.

Equation (5.7) indicates that initial breakeven status depends on pre-experimental hours of work and the particular NIT treatment to which an individual is assigned.[12]

   If we estimate equation (5.6) by OLS, then the expected value of the estimator of b_0 is given by

$$E(\hat{b}_0) = b_0 + \frac{\bar{\mu}_{BOF}}{1 - \dfrac{N_{BOF}}{N}} = b_0 + \bar{\mu}_{BOF}$$

$$- (\bar{\mu}_C N_C + \bar{\mu}_{AOF} N_{AOF})/(N_C + N_{AOF}) \ , \tag{5.8}$$

using the fact that $N\bar{\mu} = N_{BOF} \bar{\mu}_{BOF} + N_{AOF} \bar{\mu}_{AOF} + N_C \bar{\mu}_C = 0$, and where

   $\bar{\mu}_{BOF} =$ the mean of μ for experimentals initially below the breakeven level,

   $\bar{\mu}_{AOF} =$ the mean of μ for experimentals initially above the breakeven level,

   $N_{BOF} =$ the number of experimentals initially below the breakeven level,

   $N_{AOF} =$ the number of experimentals initially above the breakeven level,

   $N_C =$ the number of controls, and

   $N =$ total sample size ($N_{BOF} + N_{AOF} + N_C$) .

Thus, OLS estimation of b_0 is biased unless $\bar{\mu}_{BOF} = 0$, which is not guaranteed to be true since, according to equation (5.9), B_0 depends on μ through H_0, and B_0 depends on w_0, which may be correlated with μ. The bias is equal to the difference between the mean of μ for experimentals below the breakeven and the mean of μ for all others.[13] Since it is likely that $\bar{\mu}_{BOF} < 0$ (i.e., persons with lower hours of work are likely to be below the breakeven level), $\hat{b}_0$ will be an overestimate (in absolute value) of b_0.

A natural way to correct for the bias is to adopt a procedure similar to that used to correct for the bias caused by the assignment process in the eligibility model—that is, to include B_0 in the regression equation. The model to be estimated then becomes

$$H_2 = C_2 + B_0 b_0' + B_0 F b_0 + \mu + e_2 , \qquad (5.9)$$

where B_0 is defined for both experimentals and controls. If we regress H_2 on $B_0 F$ and B_0, the expected values of the estimated coefficients of $B_0 F$ and B_0 are given by

$$E \begin{bmatrix} \hat{C}_2 \\ \hat{b}_0' \\ \hat{b}_0 \end{bmatrix} = \begin{bmatrix} C_2 - \bar{\mu}_{B0} N_{B0} N_{B0F}(N_{B0} - N_{B0F})/D \\ \bar{\mu}_{B0} N_{B0} N_{B0F}(N - N_{B0F})/D - \bar{\mu}_{B0F} N_{B0F}^2(N - N_{B0})/D \\ b_0 + (\bar{\mu}_{B0F} - \bar{\mu}_{B0}) N_{B0} N_{B0F}(N - N_{B0})/D \end{bmatrix}, \quad (5.10)$$

where

N_{B0} = the number of experimentals and controls initially below the break-even level,

$\bar{\mu}_{B_0}$ = the mean of μ for experimentals and controls initially below the breakeven level, and

$D = N_{B0F} N_{B0}(N - N_{B0}) - N_{B0F}^2(N - N_{B0}).$

Under the assumption that $\bar{\mu}_{B0} = \bar{\mu}_{B0F}$ and using the fact that $N_{A0} \bar{\mu}_{A0} + N_{B0} \bar{\mu}_B = 0$, we have

$$E \begin{bmatrix} \hat{C}_2 \\ \hat{b}_0' \\ \hat{b}_0 \end{bmatrix} = \begin{bmatrix} C_2 + \bar{\mu}_{A0} \\ \bar{\mu}_{B0} - \bar{\mu}_{A0} \\ b_0 \end{bmatrix}, \qquad (5.11)$$

where

N_{A0} = the number of experimentals and controls initially above the break-even level, and

$\bar{\mu}_{A0}$ = the mean of μ for experimentals and controls above the breakeven level.

Hence, inclusion of B_0 in the equation leads to an unbiased estimate of the experimental effect b_0.

If only one NIT treatment were being tested in SIME/DIME, it would be straightforward to calculate B_0 for control families. However, more than one NIT treatment is being tested, and these treatments were assigned in a stratified fashion to the experimental population. One way of approximating the procedure when there is more than one treatment is to "hypothetically" assign control families to the same set of treatments as experimental families and then to calculate the relevant variables on the basis of this hypothetical assignment. To account for the stratified assignment, the probability of obtaining a given treatment can be set equal to the proportion of experimentals within the same normal income level, ethnic group, and family status.

One drawback to this procedure, however, is that the estimated experimental effect will vary depending on the outcome of the hypothetical assignment of controls. Alternative procedures, such as repeatedly assigning controls (using a Monte Carlo procedure) or assigning each control to all the treatments and taking the weighted average of the calculated breakeven status variables (where the weights represent the probability of an equivalent experimental being assigned to the particular treatment), would probably yield estimates of the experimental effect that have more desirable properties.

Rather than conducting a series of hypothetical assignments or assigning each control to all the treatments, we adopt the simplest procedure of performing only one assignment, which is described in an appendix to this paper that is available from the authors upon request. We then calculate the simulated breakeven status variables on the basis of income reported in the pre-experimental year with the same formulas used to construct breakeven status for experimental families. These simulated breakeven status variables (defined for everybody) are then included in the regression equation. The actual equation estimated is

$$H_2 = C_2 + B_0 b_0' + B_0 F b_0 + A_0 F a_0 + \mu + e_2 . \qquad (5.12)$$

The Current Status Model

The third model we present is designed to estimate separate responses for persons above and below the breakeven level during the second year of the experiment. Thus, instead of breaking down response on the basis of initial participation status, we break down response on the basis of participation at the time the dependent variable is measured. This is the model considered by Cogan (1978) and Robins and West (1980a). Such a model gives a better picture of the response of persons affected by the program.[14] Current breakeven status is measured in two different ways. First, it is calculated on the basis of second-year incomes reported in the interviews; second, it is derived from NIT payments reported in the interviews.

The basic model of response based on current breakeven status is given by:

$$H_2 = C_2 + B_2 F b_2 + A_2 F a_2 + \mu + e_2 , \qquad (5.13)$$

where

   B_2 = a dummy variable for being below the breakeven level in the second year,

A_2 = a dummy variable for being above the breakeven level in the second year,

b_2 = the response of persons below the breakeven level in the second year, and

a_2 = the response of persons above the breakeven level in the second year.

In the current status model, problems of bias are much more severe than in the initial status model, for two reasons. First, current breakeven status is correlated with both the individual specific component (μ) and the random component (e_2) of the error term, whereas in the initial status model it is correlated only with the individual specific component. Second, participation status is likely to be affected by the experimental treatments (because of the labor supply response). We refer to the first type of bias as "selectivity bias." This is the same bias that exists in the initial status model, except that it is more severe in the current status model. We refer to the second type of bias as "endogeneity bias." Endogeneity bias does not exist in the initial status model because initial labor supply (by definition) is not affected by the experimental treatments.

To get a clearer picture of the nature of these two types of biases in the current status model, consider a simplified version of equation (5.13) in which it is again assumed there is no above-breakeven response:

$$H_2 = C_2 + B_2 F b_2 + \mu + e_2 . \tag{5.14}$$

We can also write a linear approximation for the equation determining B_2:

$$B_2 = e H_2 + FT + w_2 , \tag{5.15}$$

where w_2 is a random error term assumed uncorrelated with e_2. Equation (5.15) indicates that current breakeven status depends on current hours of work and the particular NIT treatment to which an individual is assigned. For the moment, we assume that B_2 is not affected by the experimental treatments.[15]

If we estimate equation (5.14) by OLS, then the expected value of the estimator is given by:

$$E(\hat{b}_2) = b_2 + \frac{\bar{\mu}_{B2F}}{1 - \dfrac{N_{B2F}}{N}} + \frac{\bar{e}_{B2F}}{1 - \dfrac{N_{B2F}}{N}} , \tag{5.16}$$

where

$\bar{\mu}_{B2F}$ = the mean of μ for experimentals currently below the breakeven level,

N_{B2F} = the number of experimentals currently below the breakeven level, and

$\bar{e}_{B2F}$ = the mean of e_2 for experimentals currently below the breakeven level.

A comparison of equations (5.16) and (5.8) indicates that there is an additional source of selectivity bias in the current status model. Not only is B_2 correlated with the individual specific component μ, it is also correlated with the random component e_2, since B_2 (unlike B_0) depends on current period labor supply. Since $\bar{e}_{B2F} < 0$, the bias in the current status model is likely to be greater than the bias in the initial status model.

As long as B_2 is not affected by the experiment, including B_2 for control families (i.e., including the simulated treatment variables) will remove the bias; that is, estimation of

$$H_2 = C_2 + B_2 b_2' + B_2 F b_2 + \mu + e_2 \tag{5.17}$$

will yield unbiased estimates of b_2. The proof, given in an expanded version of this paper available from the authors, is similar to the proof for the initial status model presented earlier.

Use of the simulated breakeven status variable B_2, however, insures the comparison of comparable groups only under the fairly restrictive assumption that the probabilities of being in the two groups are not affected by experimental-control status. For instance, if some experimentals are induced by the experiment to drop below the breakeven level, some experimentals below the breakeven level would be most appropriately compared with controls above with the breakeven level. This problem arises because current breakeven status is endogenous. Thus, in the presence of an experimental effect on current breakeven status, the means of μ and e_2 are different for experimentals and controls currently above the breakeven level and OLS estimation of equation (5.17) will be biased.

One way of generating consistent estimates of b_2 is to use the technique of instrumental variables (IV). The IV technique deals with the endogeneity of breakeven status by replacing it with the predicted probability of being in the current breakeven status.

The probability of currently being below the breakeven level is calculated using a model similar to that presented in Robins and West (1980a). A logit model of participation is estimated on the sample of experimentals using predetermined characteristics as the explanatory variables. The predicted probabilities from this model are then used in place of the actual breakeven status variables in the regression equation.[16] As in the previous models, a simulated probability for both experimentals and controls is also included so that experimentals are compared with controls with the same participation probability rather than with all controls. The same formula is used for controls as for experimentals.[17]

The full model estimated is

$$H_2 = C_2 + \hat{B}_2 b_2' + \hat{B}_2 F b_2 + \hat{A}_2 F a_2 + \mu + e_2 , \tag{5.18}$$

where

$\hat{B}_2$ = the predicted probability of being below the breakeven level, and

$\hat{A}_2$ = the predicted probability of being above the breakeven level ($\hat{A}_2 = 1 - \hat{B}_2$).

For purposes of comparison, we also estimate equation (5.18) using actual status in the second year (B_2 and A_2).

Data and Variables

The sample used to estimate the empirical models is a subset of originally enrolled families in SIME/DIME. SIME/DIME tested 11 NIT programs with an average guarantee level of about 115 percent of the poverty level and an average tax rate of about 50 percent. These programs are considerably more generous than most NIT programs that have been considered for actual implementation. In addition, unlike most existing and proposed welfare programs, SIME/DIME did not impose work requirements as a condition for eligibility. Separate samples of husbands (1,682) are constructed for the second experimental year.[18] A discussion of the sample selection procedure appears in an expanded version of this paper available from the authors.

Two definitions of participation are used in this paper. One definition relies on reports elicited from experimental families about the monthly payments they receive; the payment they report is used to determine their participation status in the second experimental year. Under this definition, a person participates if he or she reports receiving a payment greater than the minimum payment ($20 per month) in *any* month during the second experimental year. The other definition, based on a calculation of the annual NIT grant to which a family is entitled, is used to determine simulated or actual participation status in both pre-experimental and second experimental years for control and experimental persons, respectively. Under this definition, a person participates if he or she is in a family in which the calculated annual payment based on income reported in interviews is greater than the minimum annual payment ($240 per year).[19] Again, a detailed description of the construction of the participation variables is given in a longer version of this paper.[20]

Table 5.1 shows how participation status changes during the first two years of the experiments for the second-year sample of experimental husbands, wives, and single female heads of families. Roughly 70 percent of all experimental families are calculated to be participants at the beginning of the experiment. During the second year of the experiment, participation based on the calculated payment definition drops to 56 percent for husbands, 62 percent for wives, and 68 percent for single female heads. Several reasons can account for this drop: initial truncation of the sample by income, growth in income due to both general and life-cycle increases in real wage rates, and increases in labor force participation rates of women (see Robins & West, 1980a, 1980b). Of those

Table 5.1. Movements of experimental families between participation and non-participation during the first two years of the experiments

	Proportion participating during second year	
	Reported payment	Calculated payment
Husbands ($N = 1,211$)		
Initial participants (71%)	77%	68%
Initial nonparticipants (29%)	33	26
All	64	56
Wives ($N = 1,248$)		
Initial participants (71%)	80	76
Initial nonparticipants (29%)	36	30
All	67	62
Single female heads ($N = 1,049$)		
Initial participants (70%)	79	80
Initial nonparticipants (30%)	43	40
All	68	68

initially participating, 68 percent of the husbands, 76 percent of the wives, and 80 percent of the single female heads were participating during the second year. Of those initially not participating, 26 percent of the husbands, 30 percent of the wives, and 40 percent of the single female heads were participating during the second year. Clearly, there are substantial movements between participation and nonparticipation during the first two years of the experiments.

As indicated earlier, in order to account for the stratified assignment to experimental treatments, we included variables representing the assignment strata in the estimated equation. These variables are dummy variables for the normal income category of the family, dummy variables for racial-ethnic group, a dummy variable for those in Denver, and a dummy variable for those controls who file an income report form.[21] Several additional variables are included in the equation to increase the efficiency of the estimates. These additional variables consist of hours worked in the pre-experimental year, the amount of AFDC received in the pre-experimental year, the number of family members at enrollment, the number of family members aged 0 to 5 at enrollment, and the age at enrollment. Three dummy variables are used to represent eligibility for the SIME/DIME manpower treatments:[22] one for counseling only, one for counseling plus a 50 percent training and education subsidy, and one for counseling plus a 100 percent subsidy. Separate equations are estimated for husbands, wives, and single female heads of families.

Empirical Results

In this section, we present the estimation results for the three models we have described. Each of these models answers a somewhat different question about

Table 5.2. Average hours of work for comparable control groups during the second experimental year

	Husbands	Wives	Single female heads
(1) Eligibility model	1,828	712	1,071
(2) Initial status model			
Participants	1,881	680	1,110
Nonparticipants	1,717	780	997
(3) Current status model			
Participants	1,785	569	1,052
Nonparticipants	1,862	844	1,087

response to SIME/DIME. First, we will discuss differences in average hours of work of control families among the various categories of participation to provide a general picture of the noncomparability of the various groups considered in the models and to give a rough indication of the importance of including the simulated treatment variables in the equations.

Table 5.2 presents average hours of work of control families in the current period (second experimental year), by the various categories of participation. The one surprise in this table is that, for husbands and single female heads of families, average hours of work of initial participants exceeds average hours of work of initial nonparticipants. This perplexing result is undoubtedly a reflection of the assignment model, the initial truncation of the sample by income, and factors other than labor supply that determine participation status (such as nonwage income received).

The other figures in table 5.2 are more obviously plausible. In particular, current participants tend to have lower average hours of work than current nonparticipants. In general, the numbers illustrate the importance of correcting for selection bias when estimating experimental effects for the various groups.

Table 5.3 presents the estimated experimental effects for the three models. Also presented in this table are the results of tests for differences in the models. The purpose of the tests is to determine whether breakeven status makes a difference in estimating labor supply response in the SIME/DIME sample.[23]

Results for the Eligibility Model

The results for the eligibility model are remarkably close for all three types of family heads, ranging from −154 hours per year for single female heads of families to −161 hours per year for husbands. In percentage terms, however, the effects are quite different for the three groups because of differences in hours of work of comparable control families. The percentage effects are −8.8 percent for husbands, −22.3 percent for wives, and −14.4 percent for single female heads of families. The results indicate a substantial disincentive effect for families eligible to receive payments.

Results for the Initial Status Model

The results for the initial status model indicate that for husbands and single female heads of families, breakeven status makes a difference. As one would expect, the response of initial participants is larger than the response of all eligible families. The similarity between the results when the simulated break-even status variables are excluded and included indicates that for husbands and wives, selection bias is not an important problem. For single female heads of families, the response is 28 percent *greater* (in absolute value) when the simulated breakeven status variables are included in the equation. Hence, contrary to prior expectations, the initial status model that excludes the simulated break-even status variables tends to underestimate the true labor supply response.[24] In percentage terms, the responses of initial participants are −12.6 percent for husbands, −23.6 percent for wives, and −20.5 percent for single female heads of families.[25] These results are roughly consistent with the results from the eligibility model if they are weighted by the proportions in each of the initial statuses.

Economic theory suggests that some initial nonparticipants will reduce their labor supply and become participants (see Robins & West, 1980a). The results indicate that for husbands and single female heads of families there is no evidence of an above-breakeven response. The results for wives indicate that the response of initial nonparticipants is about the same as the response of initial participants. Hence, for wives, there is evidence of an above-breakeven response.

Results for the Current Status Model

The current status model is estimated using two different definitions of participation—one calculated on the basis of second-year incomes reported in the interviews and the other derived from interview-reported payments. In general, the two definitions yield roughly comparable estimates of labor supply response. The only possible exception is for husbands, for whom the estimated responses using the interview-reported payments definition tend to be a bit smaller (in absolute value). In the remainder of this section we focus on the results obtained using the calculated payments definition.

Two versions of the current status model are presented. The first version consists of ordinary least squares (OLS) regressions with and without the simulated breakeven status variables. As indicated earlier, the simulated breakeven status variables correct for selectivity bias but not for endogeneity of current participation status. The second version of the model attempts to correct for endogeneity of current participation, in addition to selectivity bias, by using the technique of instrumental variables (IV). In general, we expect that ignoring selectivity bias will lead to an overestimate of the response of current partici-pants and ignoring endogeneity of participation will lead to an underestimate of the response of current participants. Response is overestimated when selectivity

Table 5.3. Estimated experimental effects on annual hours of work by breakeven status (standard errors in parentheses)

	Husbands ($N=2,135$)			
	-161.0^{***}			
	(33.7)			
(1) Eligibility model F	Simulated treatment variables excluded		Simulated treatment variables included	
	Calculated payments	Interview-reported payments	Calculated payments	Interview-reported payments
(2) Initial status model (*OLS*)				
$B_0 F$	-211.6^{***}	—	-236.9^{***}	—
	(36.0)	—	(39.5)	—
$A_0 F$	-41.3	—	64.6	—
	(45.8)	—	(55.1)	—
(3a) Current status model (*OLS*)				
$B_2 F$	-345.4^{***}	-282.1^{***}	-273.1^{***}	-207.7^{***}
	(37.2)	(36.3)	(44.3)	(37.5)
$A_2 F$	64.9^{*}	50.9	6.0	-16.3
	(39.2)	(42.0)	(43.8)	(42.7)
(3b) Current status model (*IV*)				
$\hat{B}_2 F$	-316.9^{***}	-286.8^{***}	-382.7^{***}	-330.1^{***}
	(50.3)	(44.9)	(65.3)	(54.8)
$\hat{A}_2 F$	31.2	59.9	102.7	132.4
	(57.1)	(62.1)	(72.8)	(81.4)
F-test for differences between models:				
1 and 2	14.8^{***}	—	14.2^{***}	—
1 and 3a	111.7^{***}	67.3^{***}	22.8^{***}	18.0^{***}

Key:

OLS = ordinary least squares.
IV = instrumental variables.
$F = 1$, if eligible for NIT payment.
$B_0 = 1$, if initial participant.
$A_0 = 1$, if initial nonparticipant.
$B_2 = 1$, if current participant.
$A_2 = 1$, if current nonparticipant.

* Significant at the 10% level.
** Significant at the 5% level.
*** Significant at the 1% level.

bias is ignored because the noncomparable control group has higher average labor supply than the comparable control group; response is underestimated when endogeneity of participation is ignored because the noncomparable control group has lower average labor supply than the comparable control group.

The results for the model using OLS suggest that there is a substantial selectivity bias in the labor supply response of current participants. When the simulated breakeven status variables are included in the equation, the responses

Table 5.3. (Continued)

(1) Eligibility model	Wives ($N=2,206$)			
	-159.4^{***}			
	(31.7)			
F	Simulated treatment variables excluded		Simulated treatment variables included	
	Calculated payments	Interview-reported payments	Calculated payments	Interview-reported payments
(2) Initial status model (OLS)				
B_0F	-164.1^{***}	$--$	-160.4^{***}	$--$
	(34.2)	$--$	(37.2)	$--$
A_0F	-148.7^{***}	$--$	-156.0^{***}	$--$
	(43.3)	$--$	(52.4)	$--$
(3a) Current status model (OLS)				
B_2F	-231.0^{***}	-232.3^{***}	-119.7^{***}	-177.9^{***}
	(35.0)	(34.2)	(40.9)	(35.7)
A_2F	-49.4	-13.8	-152.6^{***}	-63.1
	(39.3)	(41.1)	(43.8)	(42.1)
(3b) Current status model (IV)				
$\hat{B}_2F$	-168.2^{***}	-178.5^{***}	-168.1^{***}	-177.9^{***}
	(43.4)	(41.2)	(53.5)	(49.2)
$\hat{A}_2F$	-145.8^{**}	-121.2^{**}	-145.9^{**}	-122.1
	(55.5)	(61.5)	(71.4)	(81.4)
F-test for differences between models:				
1 and 2	0.1	$--$	0.0	$--$
1 and 3a	22.1^{***}	30.5^{***}	0.3	6.7^{***}

are reduced by 21 percent for husbands, by 48 percent for wives, and by 10 percent for single female heads of families. A comparison of the results for the current status model using OLS and IV when the simulated breakeven status variables are included in the equation also suggests that there is a substantial bias due to the endogeneity of current participation. When the IV technique is used, the response of current participants rises by 30 percent for husbands, by 40 percent for wives, and by 36 percent for single female heads of families.[26] Overall, the results suggest a substantial disincentive effect for current participants. The IV results suggest that current participants reduce their labor supply in response to the experiments by 21 percent for husbands, by 30 percent for wives, and by 33 percent for single female heads of families. Such reductions are substantially larger than the reductions of initial participants because many initial participants are above the breakeven level during the current period.

Table 5.3. (Continued)

	Single female heads ($N=1{,}682$)			
	-154.3^{***}			
	(39.4)			
(1) Eligibility model F	Simulated treatment variables excluded		Simulated treatment variables included	
	Calculated payments	Interview-reported payments	Calculated payments	Interview-reported payments
(2) Initial status model (*OLS*)				
B_0F	-177.6^{***}	$--$	-228.1^{***}	$--$
	(51.5)	$--$	(46.2)	$--$
A_0F	103.2^{***}	$--$	-4.0	$--$
	(51.5)	$--$	(63.4)	$--$
(3a) Current status model (*OLS*)				
B_2F	-282.8^{***}	-256.4^{***}	-254.5^{**}	-185.7^{***}
	(41.6)	(41.8)	(50.8)	(45.5)
A_2F	95.8^{*}	49.4	72.1	6.5
	(49.1)	(49.3)	(54.8)	(50.4)
(3b) Current status model (*IV*)				
$\hat{B}_2F$	-268.4^{***}	-276.7^{***}	-345.7^{***}	-375.6^{***}
	(50.4)	(51.9)	(60.7)	(64.1)
$\hat{A}_2F$	75.5	94.7	244.1^{**}	312.8^{***}
	(74.8)	(79.6)	(105.3)	(114.9)
F-test for differences between models:				
1 and 2	2.4	$--$	9.2^{***}	$--$
1 and 3a	68.5^{***}	45.2^{***}	20.5^{***}	12.6^{***}

Key:

OLS = ordinary least squares.
IV = instrumental variables.
$F = 1$, if eligible for NIT payment.
$B_0 = 1$, if initial participant.
$A_0 = 1$, if initial nonparticipant.
$B_2 = 1$, if current participant.
$A_2 = 1$, if current nonparticipant.

* Significant at the 10% level.
** Significant at the 5% level.
*** Significant at the 1% level.

Conclusion

We have examined a variety of different models in an attempt to determine the labor supply response of SIME/DIME families. We have argued that participation (or breakeven) status is an important concept that must be considered if one wishes to use the experimental results to make inferences about

Table 5.4. Average labor supply responses for three groups (in percent)

	Husbands	Wives	Single female heads
Eligibles	− 8.8	−22.4	−14.4
Initial participants[a]	−12.6	−23.6	−20.6
Current participants[b]	−21.4	−29.5	−32.9

a. Results for the initial status model with simulated treatment variables in the equation.
b. Results for the current status model using the instrumental variables technique, with the simulated treatment variables in the equation and using the calculated payment.

the likely effects of a national program. Several previous studies, including those by Robins and West (1980a), Robins (1978), Keeley et al. (1978a, 1978b), and Cogan (1978), also make the same point, but none has been able to deal adequately with the statistical problems associated with estimating the response of participants. In this chapter we have drawn on the work of Burtless (1979) and Burtless and Greenberg (1979) to develop a method of obtaining unbiased estimates of the response of participants. We find that the response of participants is substantially larger than the response of eligibles. We also find that the response of current participants is substantially larger than the response of initial participants.

Table 5.4 summarizes the major findings of this paper. The response of husbands and single female heads of families varies considerably over the three definitions of treatment status, ranging from −9 percent to −21 percent for husbands and from −14 percent to −33 percent for single female heads. The response of wives is much more stable, ranging from −22 percent to −30 percent.

These findings suggest that a universal NIT program without any work requirements, as a replacement for the current welfare system, would lead to significant reductions in labor supply. However, it is important to recognize that the SIME/DIME programs were considerably more generous than most feasible welfare reform alternatives and, hence, probably overstate the size of the response to a NIT for the various groups in table 5.4. Nevertheless, regardless of which definition of treatment status is used, it is evident that implementation of a NIT in the United States would create significant work disincentives that are likely to limit the antipoverty effectiveness of such a program. As the debate on welfare reform continues through the 1980s, work disincentive effects of alternative proposals such as the NIT must be taken into account.

6. Measuring the Distribution of Personal Taxes

Marcus C. Berliant and Robert P. Strauss

Abstract

The chapter develops a set of index numbers that compare and aggregate each individual's relative income and tax position with the income and tax position of other individuals. The index numbers, which are directly viewed as social welfare functions, are then applied to U.S. Treasury Department samples of individual income tax returns to characterize the vertical and horizontal distributions of tax liability. The empirical analysis is performed for 1973, 1975, 1978, and for several widely discussed tax reform proposals. Vertical progressivity is found to increase modestly through time; however, horizontal equity is found to decrease.

A multiperiod index is also developed which keeps track of each person's relative tax position before and after a tax change, unlike most index numbers. Empirical analysis of this new index indicates significant changes in relative positions of individuals under alternative policies which are not captured by conventional measures. It is suggested that the multiperiod index number be used for policy analysis since before and after relative positions of individuals are of inherent policy interest.

Evaluation of the effects of public policy on distribution or allocation typically requires summarizing large amounts of information. Such aggregation to obtain a "single number" for a busy policymaker usually entails the use of common statistics such as the mean or standard deviation of a critical variable. The normative content of these statistics is usually inferred from their size vis-à-vis that of a current law base case. The prior matter of the *choice* of the particular aggregation rule or statistic is rarely discussed but rather asserted without comment, even though the particular index chosen may be insensitive to wide variations in policy and therefore may not be informative to policymakers.

The use of such aggregation rules or index numbers is quite common in the analysis of taxation and the distribution of income. Although we focus on how to properly characterize the impact of alternative tax policies on the distribution of tax liability, we also raise quite general concerns about how to choose an index number. The indices we have developed can be applied to aggregations of data about a wide range of socioeconomic behavior.

The difference between indices used by policymakers and academic researchers is apparent in the contrast between the measures they use in the area of taxation. The U.S. Treasury Department routinely makes available to the tax committees of the Congress the following indicators: (*a*) the number of taxpayers by income class whose tax liability decreases and the number of taxpayers whose tax liability increases as a result of the policy proposal; (*b*) the average dollar amount of the tax increase or tax decrease by income class; and (*c*) the change in tax burden on representative taxpayers, such as families with various incomes and exemption levels. Such an analysis does not determine whether the tax proposal makes the distribution of after-tax income more equal (regardless of whether more equality is normatively desirable), whether it makes the tax system more progressive vertically, or whether it makes the tax system more horizontally equitable.[1] Another limitation of this type of analysis is that it deals with average effects, although the within-income class variation in tax rates is quite large. For example, the coefficient of variation in effective federal tax rates in 1979 for rather narrowly defined economic income classes ranged from 20 percent to 180 percent.

On the other hand, statisticians and students of income distributions have long used a variety of summary index numbers, such as the Gini coefficient, which are generally more informative than the above qualitative indicators. These index numbers, however, are often computationally burdensome and do not always convey intuitively to policymakers the effects of proposed tax policy changes. For example, a 2 percent change in the after-tax Gini may not be as informative to a policymaker as the statement that 5 percent of all taxpayers experienced tax increases while 35 percent experienced tax decreases, and the remainder experienced no appreciable change.

With regard to the issue of which index number to use, there has been academic interest in deriving index numbers that characterize income distributions from social welfare functions (Atkinson, 1970); Blackorby & Donaldson, 1976), or in finding axioms that are consistent with various index numbers (Kondor, 1975; Fields & Fei, 1978; Sen, 1973; Bourguignon, 1979; and Shorrocks, 1980). Both of these recent approaches attempt to identify more carefully the normative content of various index numbers, although neither approach specifically considers their utilization for public policy analysis.

In choosing among alternative index numbers, one must make several decisions explicitly or implicitly. First, is after-tax income the only variable of interest, or are additional variables significant in determining the equity under scrutiny? If in fact additional variables are of interest, then the index numbers we develop here must be employed because they are naturally *multivariate* in construction in contrast to most conventionally used index numbers, which are *univariate* in construction. On the other hand, if equity is defined in terms of a single variable, one can choose from the usual artillery of index numbers. These univariate index numbers are of several types; however, some are not supported by an axiomatic characterization and are arbitrary in the sense that judgments concerning social welfare are unclear; other univariate index numbers have been at least partially characterized in terms of their axiomatic underpinnings. For example, Kondor (1975) and Fields and Fei (1978) provide conditions that reasonable (univariate) index numbers should satisfy and indicate which index numbers indeed satisfy these axioms. Blackorby and Donaldson (1976), Atkinson (1970), Bourguignon (1979), and Shorrocks (1980) generate certain univariate index numbers axiomatically. The index numbers in this study are also generated by known axioms and are also multivariate in construction.

We seek to develop several new index measures of the horizontal and vertical distributions of income and taxes which are computationally feasible, conceptually complete, and intuitively attractive for policy purposes. To summarize: our principal contributions are: (*a*) the concept that an index number can be viewed directly as an empirical social welfare function, thus obviating the need to deduce it from a social welfare function; (*b*) the creation of a broad class of index numbers, which are based on *relative* comparisons among persons and whose axiomatic underpinnings are completely characterized; (*c*) within this broad class of index numbers, the creation of certain intertemporal index numbers that permit the analysis of equity over time; and (*d*) the extensive empirical implementation of these index numbers for various U.S. tax laws and a variety of widely debated tax reform proposals, using data from the Treasury Department's Individual Income Tax Model. For example, we found an *increase* in the vertical progressivity of U.S. taxes over the period 1973–1979, which is consistent with Bridges (1978) and Okner (1979); however, this was accompanied by significant *decreases* in horizontal equity, which had not been measured previously. Also, the inflation adjustment, usually viewed as proportional in effect, was found to be significantly regressive.

The chapter is organized as follows: section II discusses the choice of an index number; section III develops in detail certain index numbers of vertical and horizontal equity; section IV develops the various tax policy proposals and presents the empirical results; and section V presents conclusions.

On the Choice of Alternative Index Numbers for Evaluation Purposes

Atkinson's Social Welfare Function Approach to Choosing Index Numbers

Sixty years ago, Dalton (1920) pointed out that underlying the choice of one inequality index over another (e.g., choosing the Gini coefficient rather than the variance of income) is some notion of social welfare that would be achieved were an index to reach its limit as a result of incomes' being altered in a particular way. More recently, Atkinson (1970) reiterated this and argued that an index number summarizing the income distribution should be derived from a well-defined social welfare function. Since Atkinson's approach has been the starting point for several recent contributions and differs materially from our approach, we review briefly his line of argument and indicate certain difficulties with it to motivate our justified class of index numbers.

Following Dalton, Atkinson puts certain limitations on the form of social welfare function (SWF) from which he seeks to derive an index number. In particular, he assumes that the SWF is an additively separable and symmetric function of individual income (y). Moreover, Atkinson argues that the reference point in his index number, I, against which the empirical distribution of income should be gauged or compared, is a per capita income or equally distributed income, Y_{EDE}, such that the utility level to society from Y_{EDE} is equal in total to that of the observed distribution of income. The index measure, I, is then stated as:

$$I = 1 - \frac{Y_{EDE}}{\Sigma y / n} = 1 - \frac{Y_{EDE}}{\mu}. \tag{6.1}$$

Based on the work of Pratt (1964) and Arrow (1965), Atkinson indicates that if one assumes that I is invariant to proportional shifts in y, e.g., $I(y) = I(ky)$, $k \neq 0$, then one may deduce that the SWF or $U(y)$ is

$$U(y) = A + B \frac{y^{1-\epsilon}}{1-\epsilon}, \quad \epsilon \neq 1 \tag{6.2}$$

$$U(y) = \log_e(y), \quad \epsilon = 0,$$

where ϵ is parametric and represents the degree of aversion to inequality. Atkinson shows that I in discrete terms is

$$I = 1 - \frac{Y_{EDE}}{\mu} = 1 - \left[\sum_i \frac{(y_i^{1-\epsilon})}{\mu} f(y_i) \right]^{\frac{1}{1-\epsilon}}, \tag{6.3}$$

where $f(y)$ is the density of income.

We note five limitations to the approach suggested by Atkinson. First, Atkinson puts certain mathematical limitations on the SWF and, second, certain *other* mathematical limitations on I. That is, he does not solely derive I from a SWF, but deduces I and then imposes certain limitations on I which are imposed on the SWF. From a theoretical point of view, this may be unsatisfactory, for the limitations on I may have implications for the form of the SWF and thereby cancel out a presumed advantage of the approach, namely, that one deduces I solely, and therefore consistently, from a set of initial assumptions or axioms. If I is not solely derived from the SWF, then it is not clear how one decides which axioms are to be placed on the SWF and which are to be placed on I.

For example, the limitation imposed on I which Atkinson needs to obtain equation (6.3) leads to an inconsistent ranking of alternatives as viewed by the SWF, as opposed to I. If the y's increase by $k \cdot y$, $k > 1$, throughout society, then it is apparent from equation (6.1) that social welfare is enhanced. However, I, because it is invariant to proportional shifts, will be indifferent as a measure of well-offness between $I(y)$ and $I(ky)$. Further counter-examples may be developed.

Third, because the axioms on the SWF and I are different, and because they are fundamental value judgments, it is not clear what is being assumed. This blurs the normative underpinnings of the index number and complicates evaluation of it and the normative interpretation of empirical results.

Fourth, the type of derivation Atkinson entertains would appear to limit his derived index numbers to only one variable. This occurs because he derives his index number from the inverse of U, where $SWF = \int U$; the inverse can only be unique for one variable. This is a limitation if one wishes to characterize social welfare in terms of several variables.

A fifth limitation of his derivation of I from SWF is that it is appropriate only for a variable for which U is monotone. For a variable such as income this is, of course, quite reasonable; however, for other variables whose inequality may be of interest,[2] the monotonicity restriction may not be reasonable.

We may also note that while Atkinson requires additive separability of the SWF, I itself is not additively separable. For equation (6.3) to be additively separable in individual utilities, we must be able to separate it so that the social welfare from y_i does not depend on y_j. However, unless $1 - \epsilon$ equals 1 or 0, interaction terms will occur in the expansion of equation (6.3) as the expression is raised to $1 - \epsilon$. Moreover, each y_i is compared in ratio form to μ, which is of course equal to $1/n \Sigma_i y_i$ and therefore contains all other persons' incomes. To be sure, Atkinson does not claim that equation (6.3) is or should be additively separable in individual utilities. However, if the resultant I does not have the property of the parent SWF, we question what is gained by placing the restriction on the SWF to begin with.

These considerations raise a question about the proper relationship between social welfare functions and implied index numbers. To the extent that the two are considered separate—the social welfare function reflects abstract concerns while the index number operationalizes these concerns or is more practical in nature—one must place axioms on both, justify each, and relate them to each other.

An alternative approach, which is attractive to the authors, is to consider an empirical index number to be a social welfare function in and of itself. Then only one set of axioms is involved: those that generate the index number. Conversely, one set of axioms may generate an index number directly, rather than relying on one set of axioms for SWF and other axioms on I.

Beyond simplicity and convenience, another reason for viewing an index number as a social welfare function derives from the role such indices can play in public policy. It is common, for example, to measure the degree of progressivity in the tax system through the use of an index number, even though there is no widely accepted concept of progressivity. Higher scores of progressivity, however measured, are often considered more socially desirable. Just as there is no widely accepted view of how to characterize social welfare in its abstract sense, there is frequently no widely accepted view of how to measure empirically such concepts as vertical or horizontal equity. In our opinion, then, social welfare functions and empirical index numbers are similar in that they both refer to subjective notions. Moreover, both social welfare functions and index numbers seek to characterize and rank subjective states of the world. When a concept such as horizontal equity is formalized by a specific mathematical form, subjective judgments are implicitly made which are similar if not identical in form to those made when formalizing a social welfare function.

For these reasons (simplicity and convenience, similarity of normative content, and formal similarity), we treat index numbers as social welfare functions.[3] Below, we describe two general forms of index numbers that meet the five concerns raised with regard to Atkinson's social welfare function approach to index numbers.

A New Class of Group-utility Index Numbers

There are two separate conceptual parts to any index number or social welfare function that one may wish to construct: (*a*) a set of rules that compares values of variable(s) for individuals in the society and as a result creates a "score" or initial index-number value, and (*b*) a set of aggregation rules that combine these individual-level scores to obtain an overall score or level of social utility for the entire society.

Consider, for example, the variance, σ^2, of a distribution of income, y, to be a social welfare function or index number of interest:

$$\sigma^2 = \frac{1}{n} \sum_i (y_i - \bar{y})^2, \text{ where } \bar{y} = \frac{1}{n} \sum_i y_i. \tag{6.4}$$

The comparison rule is $(y_i - \bar{y})^2$, and the aggregation rule is $1/n \sum$ (i.e., normalized addition). For each ith observation, one creates a comparison or value $(y_i - \bar{y})^2$ and then adds these scores up for all persons in society. Of course, the comparison rule contained in σ^2 is not the only one we might entertain; there are an infinite number of algebraic statements that could be written down.

This characterization of index numbers may be elaborated by examining more closely the nature of the comparison function. In the case of the variance, the comparison is made once for each person's y vis-à-vis $\bar{y}$, and the *form* of the comparison is the squared difference. A more general treatment of the comparison value might be to consider more persons in the comparison, and more variables (e.g., the income and age of each person).

It may appear somewhat unusual to have more than one person in the initial comparison which is then added up; however, Kendall (1947) showed that equation (6.4) can be algebraically transformed so that $(y_i - \bar{y})^2$ becomes

$\frac{1}{2}(|y_i - y_j|)^2$. That is, the accumulation of comparisons contained in the variance between a person's income and the overall mean is equivalent to the accumulation of absolute differences between *pairs* of persons in society. This equivalent statement of the variance must be accumulated across *all possible* pairs of persons in society, whereas the initial statement in equation (6.4) contains an accumulation of individuals vis-à-vis the mean only once. Thus, equation (6.4) tells us that there are n comparisons, whereas the transformed version contains n^2 comparisons.

This equivalent relationship observed between a comparison of all possible pairs of persons' incomes in society and a more traditional statement of an index number suggests that there may be a much richer class of index numbers than is usually considered. Thus, one might argue for expanding the size of the comparison group from two to three, or for choosing a functional form other than squared differences.

In the case of comparisons of pairs of persons in society, a general form of an index number or social welfare function, S, is then

$$S = G\left[C(\underline{y}_1, \underline{y}_2), \, C(\underline{y}_1, \underline{y}_3), \, \ldots \, C(\underline{y}_{n-1}, \underline{y}_n)\right], \tag{6.5}$$

where:

$\underline{y}$ is the vector of variable(s) of interest for person 1; it could be the income of a person in a n-person society;

C is a comparison function; it could be $\frac{1}{2}|y_1 - y_2|^2$

G is an aggregation function; it could be $\sum_i \sum_j$, $i \neq j$

It is apparent from equation (6.5) that the value of S increases with the value of each group's scores. That is, S is monotone in C. This property of monotonicity may not be desirable in all applications because the value of S is dependent on the initial distribution of y. In other words, S is dependent on the mean of the income distribution, a trait not necessarily desirable in an index number. A more general way of stating this is that the index number has a unit description associated with it (e.g., income). This is not desirable, since units are, in most social science contexts, arbitrary. For this reason and to make the index measure independent of the (mean) level of income, we desire a unitless measure. This leads us to normalize S:

$$S^* = \sigma / \Delta \, ,$$

where σ and Δ are index numbers of form S with the same units.

The treatment of the S-index number as an empirical social welfare function meets all of the concerns raised with respect to Atkinson's derivative approach to obtaining I. First, any initial conditions need only be placed on one object, and the question of consistency in ranking of alternatives between the SWF and *I* cannot occur. Value judgments that need to be entertained are thus more clearly apparent in the group-utility index approach than in the social welfare function approach. Second, it is obvious that S or S^* can be generalized to more than one variable and variables other than income, whereas I or most variants of it cannot.

Also, in current, related work (Berliant & Strauss, 1980), we have shown that S and S^* may be characterized by a set of consistent initial axioms, and that the axioms are generally sufficient to generate S or S^*.[4] We have already indicated that Atkinson's approach is deficient by contrast, because certain axioms are placed on the SWF, which are not placed on I, and vice versa.

Application of *S*-index Numbers to the Distribution of Income and Taxes

We now apply the general index numbers developed above to characterize the distribution of taxes for a sample of persons in society. To keep subsequent computations tractable, we compare all possible *pairs* of persons' variable values, and thus fix the group size at 2. Also, because we are interested in the usual subjective notions of vertical and horizontal tax equity, we consider two variables per person in our development below: the pretax, economic income of the ith person, y_i, and the effective tax rate of the person, t_i (the ratio of net taxes to y). We take up first the single time-period case, and then the important two time-period case.

One-period *S*-index Measure of Taxes and Income

To describe the vertical characteristics of the tax system, we follow Wertz (1978) and partition taxpayers into three groups: The fraction of taxpayers whose liability vis-à-vis others is progressively distributed, ϕ; the fraction of taxpayers whose liability is proportionately distributed vis-à-vis others, θ; and the fraction of taxpayers whose liability is regressively distributed vis-à-vis others, γ, ($\phi + \theta + \gamma = 1$). A comparison of two taxpayers shows progressivity when both the income and the effective tax rate of one are greater than the income and effective tax rate of the other. Proportionality occurs when the incomes of the two taxpayers are different but the effective tax rates are the same. Regressivity is said to occur when one taxpayer has a larger income but a lower effective tax rate than the other.

To ascertain the extent to which taxes are distributed progressively, proportionately, and regressively, we take into account not only the number for each comparison, but also the degree of the income and tax rate disparity. Our subjective judgment was that it matters whether person A with tax rate of 28 percent and person B with tax rate of 20 percent have similar or very different incomes. Accordingly, we weight each comparison by the absolute difference in income of each pair of taxpayers.

Similarly, it would seem to matter whether the tax rates of A and B are similar or very different. If A had an income of $30,000 and B had an income of $15,000, it would seem important to observe whether their respective tax rates were 28 percent and 20 percent, or 32 percent and 18 percent. The former would appear to be a "less progressive" comparison than the latter. When we account for the disparity in tax rates, we weight by the ratio of tax rates rather than the difference in tax rates for two reasons. First, using the ratio effectively distinguishes between a paired comparison of 14 percent and 10 percent vis-à-vis 54 percent and 50 percent, whereas using (absolute) differences in tax rates would not.[5] Second, using a ratio is more effective mathematically for dealing with proportional comparisons. That is, if $t_i = t_j$ and $y_i \neq y_j$, then $t_i/t_j = 1$ and $|t_i - t_j| = 0$. In the latter case, such weighting would yield an index score of 0 for that comparison, which would be misleading.

Our analysis of tax rates is in terms of effective rates of taxation. Another approach would be to compare individuals in terms of how much income they retain after taxation, or their "after-tax income rate." The two approaches are obviously related. If the effective tax rate is t, then the after-tax income approach to measuring vertical equity involves comparisons of $1 - t$ among taxpayers. The scoring of comparisons in terms of progressivity, regressivity, and proportionality would be the same in both instances, except that progressivity would be deemed to occur when the fraction of retained or after-tax income declined as income rose. Mathematically, *Max* $(t_1/t_2, t_2/t_1)$ and *Max* $(1 - t_1/1 - t_2, 1 - t_2/1 - t_1)$ are monotonically related. Note, however, that the second expression is not invariant to scalar multiplication and thus does not have all the desired properties discussed earlier.

The three fractions (progressive, proportional, and regressive) are obtained essentially by making all possible comparisons among taxpayers, weighting each comparison by the income and tax-rate disparities, and dividing the weighted count of these progressive, proportional, and regressive comparisons by the total number of weighted comparisons.

Horizontal equity, unlike vertical equity, does not admit of progressive, proportional, or regressive distinctions. Usually, horizontal equity denotes identical tax treatment of persons in the same economic circumstances. Measuring horizontal equity thus requires a plausible criterion for testing whether two people's economic circumstances are the same. Whether the absence of the same effective tax rates for persons in the same income class is in a sense "good" or "bad" becomes problematical.[6] Accordingly, we shall measure the extent to which effective rates are *different*, instances of inequity, among all paired comparison of taxpayers, and the extent to which effective tax rates are the same, instances of equity, within each income class. As with the measure of vertical equity, we weight by the ratio of the rank of effective tax rate classes to account for the extent to which horizontal inequity occurs.

A complete, mathematical development of these one-period vertical and horizontal, group-utility index numbers is provided in the appendix (below).

Two-period S-Index Measures of Taxes and Income

The vertical and horizontal index numbers developed above, like other index numbers used for distributional analysis (e.g., the Gini or variance), are static portrayals of the distribution of income and tax burdens among individuals. The group-utility index numbers developed do have the desirable property that each is bounded by 0 and 1, so that one could compare, for example, θ for current law and θ under the proposal. However, both the traditional vertical measure, such as the Gini, or θ, developed above, presume anonymity; that is, the switching of ownership of high and low incomes will not affect the value of the index number when recomputed. For policy purposes this property of anonymity is unsatisfactory, because the policymaker is usually interested in "how different" in distributional impact a tax change will be when compared with current law. These considerations suggest that it would be useful to characterize the relative tax positions of all pairs of taxpayers in society before and after the tax change, and therefore eliminate the anonymity property usually associated with index numbers. Below, we give an intuitive statement of how one may achieve this.

To permit an intertemporal comparison of the relative vertical tax status among pairs of taxpayers, we need to characterize the vertical distribution of taxes in the second period relative to that of the first for each pair of taxpayers in society. "No change" is said to occur if the same *relative* vertical distribution of taxes in the first period is maintained in the second period after the tax change. For example, if initially $y_1 = \$30{,}000$, $y_2 = \$10{,}000$, $t_1 = 0.15$, and $t_2 = 0.05$, we would score that as a progressive comparison in the first period. If t_1 and t_2 remain the same in the second period, then the policy is said to result in "no change" because the *relative* tax rates for the particular individuals did not change. Note that economic income is defined to be independent of tax schemes. We thus characterize as "no change" any maintenance of relative tax position in the second period vis-à-vis the first period, be it progressive, as above, regressive, or proportional.

The characterization of intertemporal progressive and regressive tax changes then follows immediately. If the relative tax position of a pair of taxpayers is more progressive, less regressive, or involves movement from proportionality to progressivity, then the comparison in the second period is said to be more progressive. Similarly, if the relative tax position of a pair of taxpayers in the second time period is less progressive, more regressive, or moves from proportionality to regressivity, then the comparison in the second period is characterized as more regressive.

Table 6.1 displays the various possibilities in period 1 and period 2 and identifies which movements in relative tax position are classed as more progressive, as no change, and as more regressive. Note that every comparison must fit into exactly one category. Once we have decided which comparisons are pro-

Table 6.1. Definition of two-period index number values

Period 1—Initial comparison is		Period 2		
		More progressive	No change	More regressive
Progressive	$y_1 > y_2$ $t_1 > t_2$	$\dfrac{t'_1}{t_1} > \dfrac{t'_2}{t_2}$	$\dfrac{t'_1}{t_1} = \dfrac{t'_2}{t_2}$	$\dfrac{t'_1}{t_1} < \dfrac{t'_2}{t_2}$
Proportional	$y_1 \neq y_2$ $t_1 = t_2$	$t'_1 < t'_2$ for $y_2 < y_1$	$\dfrac{t'_1}{t_1} = \dfrac{t'_2}{t_2}$	$t'_1 < t'_2$ for $y_1 > y_2$
Regressive	$y_1 < y_2$ $t_1 > t_2$	$\dfrac{t'_1}{t_1} < \dfrac{t'_2}{t_2}$	$\dfrac{t'_1}{t_1} = \dfrac{t'_2}{t_2}$	$\dfrac{t'_1}{t_1} > \dfrac{t'_2}{t_2}$

Note: y is income, persons 1, 2; t is effective tax rate in period 1; and t' is effective tax rate in period 2.

gressive, proportional, and regressive, we can compute the index numbers simply by counting the number of comparisons of each type and dividing the three counts by the total number of comparisons. To see that these index numbers are of form S^*, note that each numerator consists of the sum of paired comparisons: the comparison value is 1 if the comparison is of the proper type and 0 otherwise. Note that the determination of comparison type depends only on three variable values of each member of the pair. Thus, the numerators are of the form S. If every vertical comparison is given a score of 1 irrespective of the variable values, the sum of all comparisons, or the denominator, is of form S. Hence the index number is of the form S^*.

Application of Index Numbers to Alternative Tax Policy Proposals

Data and Policy Proposals

The data bases used for the empirical application of the various index numbers are: 1975 tax data extrapolated to 1978 levels, 1975 tax data, and 1973 tax data; data were supplied by the U.S. Treasury Department.[7] The effective tax rates in our analysis are computed by dividing net taxes due after credits and refunds by our concept of economic income.[8] The empirical results reported here are based on a 112×25 matrix of effective tax rates by economic income classes. The tax rates were more finely divided than income to characterize more accurately the vertical aspects of the distribution of income taxes. The 25 economic income classes were chosen so that each class contained roughly 4 percent of all returns.

Five different policy proposals are analyzed in addition to 1978 law at 1978 levels, 1975 law at 1975 levels, and 1973 law at 1973 levels. The proposals analyzed at 1978 levels are: (*a*) 50 percent maximum tax rate on all sources of income; (*b*) taxation of capital gains at ordinary tax rates; (*c*) partial integration

Table 6.2. S-index number analysis of 1973, 1975, and 1978 federal tax law (overall)

	1973[a]	1975[b]	1978[c]
Vertical measure			
Progressive	0.882	0.891	0.913
Regressive	0.097	0.095	0.076
Proportional	0.021	0.014	0.011
Horizontal measures			
Equity	0.251	0.166	0.176
Inequity	0.749	0.834	0.824

a. 1973 tax law at 1973 income levels.
b. 1975 tax law at 1975 income levels.
c. 1978 tax law at 1978 income levels.
Source: Computer analysis of Treasury data tapes.

of the corporate and individual income taxes through a flat 133 percent gross-up, 25 percent refundable credit, and repeal of the dividend exclusion; (d) a combined package of (a)−(c); (e) a 15 percent inflation adjustment of all nominal tax amounts (exemptions, brackets, etc.).

Empirical Results

Our empirical results are provided first in terms of 1973, 1975, and 1978 tax law, and then in terms of the five policy proposals at 1978 income levels.

Tables 6.2, 6.3, and 6.4 display the one-period vertical and horizontal group-utility index measures for 1973, 1975 and 1978 tax law at their respective income levels. Table 6.2 shows the overall results. In 1973, 88.2 percent of all weighted vertical comparisons among pairs of taxpayers could be characterized as being progressive in character; 9.7 percent of the weighted comparisons were regressive in character, and 2.1 percent of the comparisons were proportional. By 1978, 91.3 percent of all weighted comparisons were progressive (an increase of 3.1 percentage points), and 7.5 percent of the weighted comparisons were regressive. In terms of the vertical characteristics of the distribution of tax liability, 1978 and 1973 are thus rather similar, and the results for 1975 fall between the two.

The horizontal measures, by contrast, reveal substantial differences between 1973 and 1978. In 1973, 25.1 percent of the weighted comparisons were horizontally equitable in character, and 74.9 percent were inequitable. Put another way, within each of the 25 economic income classes, there were three times as many taxpayers with different effective tax rates as there were taxpayers with the same effective tax rates. In 1978 the fraction of taxpayers experiencing horizontal equity dipped to 17.6 percent, or a reduction of 7.5 percentage points—a one-third decline in horizontal equity.

Table 6.3 stratifies the analysis by whether or not the individual taxpayer itemized deductions. Between 1973 and 1978 it is clear that progressivity in-

Table 6.3. S-index number analysis of 1973, 1975, and 1978 federal tax law (standard vs. itemized returns)

	1973		1975		1978	
	Itemizers	Standard	Itemizers	Standard	Itemizers	Standard
Vertical						
Progressive	0.837	0.907	0.825	0.901	0.835	0.931
Regressive	0.146	0.064	0.161	0.079	0.153	0.050
Proportional	0.017	0.029	0.014	0.019	0.011	0.019
Horizontal						
Equity	0.082	0.384	0.072	0.217	0.067	0.239
Inequity	0.918	0.616	0.928	0.783	0.933	0.761

creased for those who took the standard deduction and remained about the same for itemizers. Similarly, the decrease in horizontal equity was experienced primarily by those who took the standard deduction. Also of interest is the fact that for any year, horizontal equity was greater for those who took the standard deduction than for those who itemized their deductions.

Table 6.4 stratifies the results by filing status and then by standard or itemized deduction. The general pattern of increased progressivity over time, apparent in table 6.3, is also apparent in table 6.4 for married filing jointly and head of household returns. On the other hand, married filing separately and single returns displayed some decrease in progressivity over time.

Perhaps the most striking result of stratifying by filing status involves the varying degrees of horizontal equity among types of filers. In all three years, single nonitemizers displayed horizontal equity in 64 percent (or more) of the comparisons. In contrast, married filing jointly comparisons were horizontally equitable 19.5 percent of the time in 1973 and 14.5 percent in 1978. The most remarkable increase in horizontal equity occurred for married filing separately returns between 1973 and 1975. In 1973, 29.2 percent of the comparisons displayed horizontal equity, while in 1975, 48.2 percent of the comparisons displayed horizontal equity. This increase in horizontal equity, however, was countered by dramatic decreases for head of household comparisons. Nonitemizers in 1973 displayed equity 23.7 percent of the time; in 1978, only 11.2 percent of the comparisons displayed horizontal equity.[9]

Table 6.5 displays the results for the various proposals at 1978 levels. Several general observations about these results may be made immediately. First, none of the proposals appreciably changes the static vertical measures. The static progressive score hovers around 0.913 to 0.935. It would appear that the progressive structure of the rate schedules, coupled with a high density of taxpayers below the 50 percent marginal rate, ensures that progressivity is maintained. Second, horizontal equity is also reasonably stable among proposals although the refundable, partial integration proposal does substantially decrease horizontal equity.

Table 6.4. S-index number analysis of 1973, 1975, and 1978 federal tax law (stratified by filing status and by standard vs. itemized deductions)

	Married filing jointly			Married filing separately			Single			Head of household		
	Total	Itemizers	Non-itemizers	Total	Itemizers	Non-itemizers	Total	Itemizers	Non-itemizers	Total	Itemizers	Non-itemizers
1973 Vertical												
Progressive	0.872	0.855	0.890	0.890	0.805	0.924	0.931	0.772	0.961	0.888	0.830	0.931
Regressive	0.110	0.129	0.086	0.088	0.179	0.047	0.048	0.214	0.014	0.088	0.152	0.042
Proportional	0.018	0.016	0.024	0.022	0.016	0.029	0.022	0.014	0.025	0.024	0.018	0.027
1973 Horizontal												
Equity	0.112	0.093	0.197	0.235	0.118	0.292	0.601	0.106	0.642	0.178	0.109	0.237
Inequity	0.888	0.907	0.803	0.765	0.882	0.708	0.399	0.894	0.358	0.822	0.891	0.763
1975 Vertical												
Progressive	0.908	0.844	0.943	0.861	0.673	0.922	0.890	0.775	0.905	0.944	0.833	0.974
Regressive	0.083	0.143	0.046	0.112	0.313	0.027	0.089	0.213	0.070	0.051	0.155	0.022
Proportional	0.010	0.013	0.010	0.027	0.014	0.051	0.021	0.011	0.025	0.005	0.013	0.004
1975 Horizontal												
Equity	0.085	0.082	0.110	0.372	0.142	0.482	0.599	0.127	0.646	0.084	0.101	0.095
Inequity	0.915	0.918	0.890	0.628	0.858	0.518	0.401	0.873	0.354	0.916	0.899	0.905
1978 Vertical												
Progressive	0.926	0.868	0.953	0.888	0.751	0.937	0.900	0.720	0.957	0.954	0.844	0.977
Regressive	0.067	0.122	0.038	0.093	0.240	0.020	0.080	0.272	0.015	0.042	0.143	0.019
Proportional	0.007	0.010	0.009	0.019	0.009	0.043	0.019	0.008	0.028	0.004	0.013	0.004
1978 Horizontal												
Equity	0.096	0.077	0.145	0.374	0.154	0.486	0.612	0.109	0.665	0.102	0.104	0.112
Inequity	0.904	0.923	0.855	0.626	0.846	0.514	0.338	0.891	0.335	0.898	0.896	0.888

Table 6.5. Vertical and horizontal index numbers at 1978 income levels for alternative tax policies

Index number	1978 law	50 percent max rate	Capital gains as ordinary income	Partial integration	Combined package	15 percent inflation adjustment
			Proposal[a]			
Vertical						
Progressive	0.913	0.911	0.955	0.906	0.931	0.909
Regressive	0.076	0.077	0.033	0.084	0.059	0.078
Proportional	0.011	0.012	0.012	0.010	0.010	0.013
Horizontal						
Equity	0.176	0.176	0.180	0.144	0.145	0.187
Inequity	0.824	0.824	0.820	0.856	0.855	0.613
Vertical two-period						
Progressive	0.000	0.000	0.054	0.081	0.113	0.132
Regressive	0.000	0.021	0.048	0.206	0.207	0.472
No change	1.000	0.979	0.898	0.713	0.680	0.396

a. See text for a full description of each proposal.

If we examine the two-period index numbers, a somewhat stronger pattern of changes may be observed and requires some amendments to the above. For example, as a result of partial integration, 8.1 percent of the comparisons became *more* progressive, and 20.6 percent of the comparisons became *more* regressive than under 1978 current law. Note also that an inflation adjustment, usually viewed as quite neutral, is regressive for better than 47 percent of the weighted comparisons. The reason why the intertemporal results can be so different from the static results is that the static vertical index number is unaltered if a rich taxpayer changes place with a poor taxpayer, while the intertemporal index number will be markedly affected because effective tax rates will change. Such significant changes in the intertemporal, vertical measure under an integration or inflation adjustment regime means that these proposals move significant numbers of taxpayers relative to one another. The results also indicate the utility of keeping track of initial and subsequent positions in the vertical distribution of taxes.

Conclusion

We have found it reasonable to view index numbers as empirical social welfare functions. Such a direct approach to index number construction permits a much more consistent development of the theoretical underpinnings of the index number than the approach suggested by Atkinson (1970). A broad class of index numbers has been developed; they have a variety of desirable theoretical properties.

With these index numbers we have examined the vertical and horizontal characteristics of the distribution of federal individual income tax liability for a number of years. We note here some of our major empirical observations: (*a*) over the period 1973–1975 there was a modest increase in the vertical progressivity of the federal individual income tax. It would appear, however, that this was accompanied by significant deteriorations in horizontal equity; (*b*) examination of a variety of tax proposals, often considered quite radical in their distributional impact, revealed that they did not have significant overall effects on the vertical or horizontal characteristics of the distribution of tax liability; (*c*) a 15 percent inflation adjustment did not affect the vertical and horizontal index measures in any material way; and (*d*) single nonitemizers appear to be subject to the most equitable taxation; (*e*) conclusions (*b*) and (*c*) were overturned (that is, strong vertical effects were found) when the index number accounted for the change in relative tax position of taxpayers under current law and then under the proposal. This measure of before-and-after tax position appears to be quite sensitive to various tax policy changes and may be a useful guide to the effects of complicated tax proposals.

Appendix. Mathematical Development of One-Period Group Utility Index Numbers to Measure Vertical and Horizontal Equity

To facilitate the algebraic development of the index numbers, let there be $i = 1, \ldots m$ ordered, effective tax-rate classes and $j = 1, \ldots n$ ordered, economic income classes for the first group of taxpayers, and let there be $h = 1, \ldots m$ effective tax-rate classes and $k = 1, \ldots n$ ordered, economic classes of the second group of taxpayers ($i \neq h$, and $j \neq k$, so we do not compare taxpayers to themselves). Further, let N_{ij} be the number of taxpayers in the ijth tax rate–economic income group which is to be compared to N_{hk}, the number of taxpayers in the hkth tax rate–economic income group. Note that increasing subscripts denote higher income and higher effective tax-rate classes, and that $j = k = 1$ is the lowest effective tax-rate class, which empirically will be the lowest-*negative* tax-rate class (among other reasons, because of the refundable earned income tax credit). To deal with a comparison between a positive and negative tax rate, we take a ratio of the tax-rate class *ranks* (or subscripts) rather than the ratio of the average tax rates in the classes themselves.

Of course, any monotone, increasing transformation of tax rates, such as the rank, may be used in lieu of the rates themselves. Thus, negative tax rates may be handled in many ways; how the tax variable enters the index number determines the trade-offs associated with different comparisons. The same reasoning applies to the handling of negative incomes and the manner in which incomes enter into the index number.

We obtain our measure of the extent to which taxes are proportionately distributed, θ, by making all possible comparisons among groups of taxpayers in the same effective tax rate class but with different economic income classes ($j \neq k$), and then add up these proportional comparisons from different effective tax rate classes to get the total number of proportional comparisons. Normalization by the sum of all weighted comparisons, Δ, provides the fraction of weighted comparisons in which tax liability is proportionately distributed:

$$\theta = \frac{1}{\Delta} \sum_{i=1}^{m} \sum_{j=1}^{n} \sum_{\substack{k=1 \\ k \neq j}}^{n} \left[N_{ij} \cdot N_{ik} \cdot | Y_{ij} - Y_{ik} | \right] \tag{6.i}$$

Note that since tax rates are the same in these proportional comparisons, we do not weight by the ratio of rates, since that ratio always equals one.

The fraction of taxpayers whose tax liability is progressively distributed, ϕ, is obtained by accumulating across comparisons in which the effective tax rate and economic income classes of the second group of taxpayers are smaller than those of the first group of taxpayers ($h < i, k < j$), and by accumulating across comparisons in which the effective tax rate and economic income of the second group of taxpayers are greater than the first group of taxpayers ($h > i, k > j$). Since tax rates vary now in these progressive comparisons, we weight by the ratio of the ranks of tax rate classes discussed earlier. Note that in forming the weight for the tax-rate ratio, we always divide the larger rank by the smaller rank of effective tax rates to insure that comparisons are treated symmetrically. Since the first group of progressive comparisons always entails $h < i$, we form the weight as i/h; similarly, since the second group of progressive comparisons always entails $h > i$, we form the weight as h/i:

$$\phi = \frac{1}{\Delta} \sum_{i=1}^{m} \sum_{j=1}^{n} \sum_{h<1}^{m} \sum_{k<j}^{n} \left[N_{ij} \cdot \frac{i}{h} \cdot | Y_{ij} - Y_{hk}| \right] +$$

$$\frac{1}{\Delta} \sum_{i=1}^{m} \sum_{j=1}^{n} \sum_{h>i}^{m} \sum_{k>j}^{n} \left[N_{ij} \cdot N_{hk} \cdot \frac{h}{i} \cdot | Y_{ij} - Y_{hk}| \right]. \quad (6.\text{ii})$$

The fraction of taxpayers whose tax liability is regressively distributed, γ, is obtained in the same manner as the fraction of taxpayers whose tax liability is progressively distributed, except now $h < i$ and $k > j$ in the first accumulation, and $h > i$ and $k < j$ in the second accumulation. For the comparisons to be regressive, the second group of taxpayers either has lower effective tax rates and greater economic income or higher effective tax rates and lower economic income than the first group of taxpayers. Since in the first accumulation the effective tax rate of the second is lower than the first group of taxpayers, our tax-rate weight for regressivity is formed by i/h. Similarly, our tax-rate weight for the second accumulation is γ. We then have for γ:

$$\gamma = \frac{1}{\Delta} \sum_{i=1}^{m} \sum_{j=1}^{n} \sum_{h>i}^{m} \sum_{k<j}^{n} \left\{ [N_{ij} \cdot N_{hk}] \cdot \frac{i}{h} \cdot | Y_{ij} - Y_{hk}| \right\} +$$

$$\frac{1}{\Delta} \sum_{i=1}^{m} \sum_{j=1}^{n} \sum_{h>i}^{m} \sum_{k<j}^{n} [N_{ij} \cdot N_{hk}] \cdot \frac{h}{i} | Y_{ij} - Y_{hk}|. \quad (6.\text{iii})$$

As may be evident, Δ can be obtained from summing the right hand sides of (6.i)–(6.iii) (without the initial $1/\Delta$ terms), or more compactly:

$$\Delta = \sum_{i=1}^{m} \sum_{j=1}^{n} \sum_{h=1}^{m} \sum_{\substack{k=1 \\ k \neq j}}^{n} \left\{ N_{ij} \cdot N_{hk} \cdot \max \left\{ \frac{i}{h}, \frac{h}{i} \right\} \cdot | Y_{ij} - Y_{hk}| \right\}. \quad (6.\text{iv})$$

If one obtains Δ from equation (6.iv), then γ may be obtained as $1 - \theta - \phi$.

Several comments about the index of vertical tax equity reflected in equations (6.i)–(6.iv) are in order. First, it is invariant to linear transformations of income or tax rates, and is invariant with respect to multiplication or division by a constant of the number of taxpayers. This means that the index is independent of the units of measure. Second, all variations of the numerator and denominator of the index are symmetric and additively separable with respect to comparisons of each of the three types. The index as a whole is invariant with respect to proportional shifts in any factor or factors. Thus, our empirical social welfare function/index number displays variants of the axioms Atkinson recommends for I and SWF.

Recall that the measurement of horizontal equity entails tax-rate comparisons of taxpayers with the same incomes. Thus, since analysis is done within each income class ($j = k$), there are no income differences to weight by. More precisely, we compactly define the fraction of taxpayers with the same income, but whose tax liability is different from other taxpayers with the same income, or the index of horizontal inequity, β, as:

$$\beta = \frac{1}{\delta} \sum_{i=1}^{m} \sum_{j=1}^{n} \sum_{\substack{h=1 \\ h \neq 1}}^{m} \left\{ N_{ij} \cdot N_{hj} \cdot \max\left(\frac{i}{h}, \frac{h}{i}\right) \right\}, \tag{6.v}$$

where the sum of the inequity and equity comparisons, δ, is:

$$\delta = \sum_{i=1}^{m} \sum_{j=1}^{n} \sum_{\substack{h=1 \\ h \neq 1}}^{m} \left\{ N_{ij} \cdot N_{hj} \cdot \max\left(\frac{i}{h}, \frac{h}{i}\right) \right\} +$$

$$\sum_{i=1}^{m} \sum_{j=1}^{n} \left\{ N_{ij} \cdot (N_{ij}-1) \right\}. \tag{6.vi}$$

The second term in equation (6.vi) represents the number of comparisons in which the effective tax rates and income classes are the same ($i=h$), ($j=k$). A total of N_{ij}^2 comparisons are possible; however, this would involve N_{ij} inappropriate comparisons of taxpayers with themselves. Eliminating these cases results in $N_{ij}(N_{ij}-1)$ comparisons. The complement of β is our measure of horizontal equity. The fractions β and $1-\beta$ differ from those developed by Wertz (1975), in that the extent of effective tax-rate differences are accounted for in equations (6.v) and (6.vi).

7. Private Sector Unions in the Political Arena: Public Policy versus Employee Preference

James T. Bennett and Manuel H. Johnson

Abstract

Since the 1950s, membership in private sector unions has declined, both in absolute numbers and in relative terms, as a percentage of the nonagricultural work force. Unless reversed, this trend portends a steady erosion of the economic and political power of unions. The causes of membership losses are numerous and are related to changes in the structure and composition of the labor force, so that the problem of obtaining members is one of long-term duration. Unions are failing to attract and retain members; certification and decertification election defeats are at record levels. Thus unions must develop organizing tactics that minimize the role of workers in the decision to initiate or retain collective bargaining. This study discusses three techniques: the use of pension fund leverage on employers; union-management cooperation in the political arena to obtain government favors, with unionization as the price of union support of management positions; and indirect pressures exerted by unions through government to encourage collective bargaining.

Although unionism in the public sector has developed very rapidly during the past decade, private sector unions have continued a secular decline whose origins can be traced at least as far back as the 1950s. This paper explores briefly the dimensions and root causes of this deterioration in the absolute and relative standing of labor unions in the private sector, to show that the problems they face in organizing workers are not transitory but, rather, systemic and long-lasting. Labor unions will not react passively to the steady erosion of their economic and political power, but such erosion is inevitable unless the tide of declining membership can be turned. The techniques that private sector unions will use to obtain members without organizing workers provide the central focus of this paper: political power, public policy and employers will, we predict, become the primary vehicles for the revival of private sector unionism.

Membership in the Maelstrom: The Decline of Private Sector Unions

If trends in membership are used as a measure of the viability of labor unions, vastly different assessments must be made of these organizations in the private and public sectors. Among local, state, and even federal employees, unionization has expanded rapidly since 1960. For example, between 1968 and 1974, the number of state, county, and municipal workers who joined unions increased by 75 percent (Marshall, King, & Briggs, 1980:99). In contrast, union membership in the private sector declined in absolute numbers and also in relative terms: as a percentage of nonfarm employment, the total union membership declined from about one worker in three in 1955 to approximately one in four in 1976 (Mitchell, 1980:3). Because total membership data include the flourishing public sector union membership, it is clear that membership in the private sector has declined dramatically.

There is little to be gained from speculation about the exact number of union members in the private sector. At least six sets of conflicting figures exist (Heldman, 1979:76–77); one investigator (Thieblot, 1978) has convincingly argued that reported data overestimate membership by at least 10 percent. For our purposes, it is enough to note that membership in the private sector has declined sufficiently to reduce the importance of unionized labor in the economy; on this point, there is wide agreement.

Membership has declined because labor unions are failing to attract new members and to retain old members. Data from the *Annual Reports* of the National Labor Relations Board clearly indicate that unions are now winning a smaller proportion of certification and decertification elections than previously. In 1956 unions won almost two-thirds (65.3 percent) of all certification elections; by 1966, however, the victory rate had diminished to 60 percent and, by 1976, less than half (48.1 percent) of the certification elections produced a union victory. As a result, the uncertainties and costs of unions' organizing activity have increased. A similar trend is also apparent in the data on decertification elections. By 1977 labor unions were losing three-fourths of all decertification elections, the highest loss percentage ever reported. Moreover, the number of decertification elections has also increased substantially. Between 1977 and 1979, 2,433 decertification elections were held; between 1967 and 1979 only 766 were conducted. More decertification elections were lost by unions in the three-year period 1977–1979 (a total of 1,822) than in the decade 1960–1969, when only 1,628 union defeats were recorded. The record shows that employees are much less inclined to join unions or to remain unionized now than they were only a few years ago.

Many explanations have been offered to account for the decline in union membership in the private sector. Among the most widely accepted interpretations are those that emphasize changes in the structure and composition of the labor force and the economy, the geographical distribution of employment, and the attitudes of employers and union leaders. These demographic and economic changes are interrelated, as is discussed briefly below.[1]

Among the most notable changes in the post–World War II labor force is the greater participation of women. In 1950 only about one-third of the women over 16 years of age worked; by 1976 almost one-half did so. Millions of women have actively entered the job market (Kochan, 1980:73). The female worker has always presented problems for union organizers in the private sector. In spite of the growing number of women in the labor force, the percentage who are union members declined from about 15 percent in 1956 to 11 percent in 1976 (Marshall, King & Briggs, 1980:100).

Two reasons may be offered for the increasing role of women in the world of work. Many women have sought employment to offset the rapid erosion in purchasing power of family income caused by inflation. In addition, because of changes in the structure of the economy, employment opportunities have increased for women. The service sector of the economy has grown more rapidly and now dominates the U.S. economy in terms of total employment. Employees in the service sector are now concentrated in white-collar rather than blue-collar occupations, and work for smaller firms that are more dispersed geographically; they are, therefore, more difficult to organize. In smaller firms and in white-collar occupations work is more personalized, and workers are more likely to identify with "management" than with "labor."

Employment opportunities have increased more rapidly in the South and West (the "Sunbelt"), where attitudes toward unions have historically been less favorable than in the Northeast and Midwest (the "Frostbelt"), the traditional stronghold of private sector unions.

The attitudes of workers have also changed; the average employee today is better educated than ever before and, consequently, is better able to judge and evaluate the often conflicting claims made by unions and managers. To attract and retain highly qualified workers, companies have increasingly emphasized positive labor relations by taking steps that reduce the need for union representation. Today, under the terms of the Landrum-Griffin Act of 1959, labor unions are pressuring the Department of Labor to monitor the activities of labor relations consultants who are sometimes used to dissuade employees from organizing. The unions' concern about these activities indicates that they are damaging to organizing efforts.

Some workers may believe that unions, in the long run, could threaten the survival of their jobs. A number of major industries in the U.S. economy, e.g., automobiles, rubber, and steel, have suffered badly from foreign competition. Plants have closed and thousands of unionized workers have been displaced. In such circumstances, workers may conclude that unionization is a mixed blessing, for the unions were largely powerless to stem the massive retrenchments. Highly publicized strikes of long duration (as in the coal industry) and acrimonious relations between labor and management may also tarnish the image of unionism among workers.

Ironically, labor unions themselves have contributed to a reduction in the importance of collective bargaining and the need for unions. For years, unions have used their political power and lobbying activity to support regulatory and social legislation. The Occupational Safety and Health Act was vigorously supported by labor unions. As administered, this act not only eliminates the "sweatshop," once fertile ground for the union organizer, but governs virtually every other physical aspect of the work environment. Employees are now far less dependent upon labor unions to bargain for better "working conditions." To the extent that government has mandated better working conditions, the role of unions in negotiating these improvements for workers has been reduced.

All the factors mentioned above, as well as others, have contributed to the decline of unions in the private sector as measured by membership. Although it is unreasonable to expect further large increases in the female labor force participation rate—most of the women who are able to work and desire to do so have already entered the work force—the other factors portend a bleak future for private sector union membership: educational levels cannot be expected to decrease; manufacturing, mining, and construction are likely to decline in importance in the economy relative to the service sector; the Sunbelt is likely to prosper relative to the Frostbelt; and regulatory fervor appears to be on the increase. Unions have learned from experience that organizing workers at the factory gate is no longer as productive an activity as it was in the past. The diminished zeal for organizing is a predictable economic response in terms of costs and benefits. If private sector unions are to thrive or even survive in the long run, new tactics for obtaining members must be developed in response to changing economic and demographic conditions and attitudes.

Private Sector Unions in the Political Arena: Public Policy versus Employee Preference

No intelligent observer of industrial relations can expect American labor unions in the private sector passively to permit the gradual loss of their economic and political power, which is directly related to their membership. Even the disturbing decline in the number of members does not fully capture the extent of the problem, for tens of thousands of workers are still counted as members even though they are on indefinite layoff in such industries as autos and steel, have little prospect of returning to work, and pay no union dues. Even the unions have not attempted to institute the checkoff in unemployment compensation payments. Because the workers no longer seem to respond enthusiastically to the union organizer at the factory gate and are showing increasing disenchantment with union representation, the unions in the private sector must devise some means of obtaining members that minimizes the role of the workers in the decision to initiate or retain collective bargaining. The evidence clearly shows that worker choice is no longer a reliable source of support for unionism in the private sector.

Many workers apparently believe that their self-interest is not enhanced by unionization. This in itself is a very interesting statement, for it has long been axiomatic that a union is an organization of workers formed for the purpose of advancing its members' interests. Yet the fact remains that private sector unions, if they are to prosper, must obtain members without relying upon the support of workers themselves. As we have noted elsewhere (Bennett & Johnson, 1980:10–11), it is not only possible but also perfectly legal for an employer to agree unilaterally to recognize a union as the exclusive bargaining agent for employees—without an election or, indeed, without any input whatever from the workers, who must (in states without right-to-work laws) financially support the union. This practice of unionism by fiat is becoming more common and is ideally suited to the unions' difficulty. The private sector union seeking members may have far more success in the boardroom than on the factory floor. This is the direction that unionism must take during the 1980s.

The assertion that employers will be a major source of union members seems, on the surface, nonsensical if not totally ridiculous. After all, the notion that management and labor are adversaries has existed for decades: the foundation of the union movement is rooted in the idea that individual employees, whose self-interest conflicts with that of employers, must organize to offset the vastly greater economic power of employers. Given this adversarial relationship, why should employers acquiesce to the unionization of their work force?

This question has several answers. An employer may, for example, accept one union to avoid pressures from another that is thought to be far less desirable. We believe, however, that there is a more basic and pervasive reason, related to the role of government in the economy. In the 1960s and 1970s, the operations of firms in the U.S. economy were greatly constrained by all types of regulation, related not just to employment (such as equal employment opportunity and affirmative action requirements) but to the environment, production processes, product restrictions, and practices in the work place as well. Indeed, regulation appears to have reached the point at which everything that is not strictly forbidden is mandated. These public policy actions have raised the costs of production, made the output of the private sector less competitive with the output of unregulated foreign producers, and threatened the financial viability of U.S. firms. Government at all levels has contributed to the difficulties that plague the economy and its workers.

Because government is seen as the cause of economic problems, it is also perceived as the cure. Companies and industries are actively working in Washington to obtain special exemptions and assistance. For political reasons, however, success is less likely if employers alone seek federal largesse, for it then appears that profit-seeking capitalists are asking for favors at taxpayer and consumer expense. If corporate executives and labor union leaders together request federal assistance, an entirely different picture is presented to the politician. Any politician who strongly opposes a labor union position runs the risk of being labeled "anti-labor," an anathema to most members of Congress. Labor unions are politically active and well-financed, and they have a record of attempting to aid friends and punish enemies. Further, there are far more votes to be gained from workers than from managers.

It is not surprising, then, that Chrysler and the United Auto Workers (UAW) jointly sought financial aid for the ailing corporation. Similarly, the organized truckers and the Teamsters worked as a unit in vociferous opposition to the deregulation of trucking, and Ford Motor Company and the UAW together petitioned the U.S. International Trade Commission for protection against imported foreign cars. Labor unions, then, can be useful to companies and industries in seeking special treatment from government. The price of union support in the political arena may be union membership of an industry's employees. As the effects of regulation become more apparent and as foreign competition intensifies, more labor-management efforts to obtain exemptions, protections, and assistance from government can be expected.

The political clout of unions is being used to advance unionization in other ways. Federal grants for various purposes have been conditional upon the existence of satisfactory labor relations in the grantee's organization. As administered, such grants require the presence of a collective bargaining agreement with a compulsory unionism clause (see Bennett & Johnson, 1980:18). For the most part, grants are made to state and local governments, but political moves can be expected from the unions to encourage the award of contracts to private firms that are unionized. Certainly, in those industries where labor unions and employers work together to obtain government favors, a natural step is for the union to insist that, when subcontracts are awarded by the firm, preference be given to unionized suppliers.

One of the most recent initiatives by labor unions to induce unionization through the boardroom is the employee pension fund issue. It has been estimated that employee pension funds now control about $0.5 trillion in assets; about half of these funds have been set up and are controlled in part by unions. The assets of pension funds are also growing rapidly (Rifkin & Barber, 1978). Labor union leaders have announced their intention to obtain voting rights for the stocks in fund portfolios and to obtain control of investment decisions. Financial capital is the lifeblood of commerce. By withholding funds from nonunion firms, unions can force capitulation regardless of the desires of the workers. If the alternatives are unionization or extinction, most firms will prefer the former to the latter. In any case, if unions control the voting of massive amounts of stock, they can have a direct influence on the composition of corporate boards and on corporate policy and management. In a number of cases, the pension fund weapon has already been used successfully, e.g., to influence a bank board of directors by threatening to withdraw the pension funds from the bank's trust department.[2]

Summary and Conclusion

Economic and demographic changes have resulted in relative and absolute declines in union membership in the private sector. The traditional method of obtaining members is no longer as effective as it once was. Workers appear less likely to join or to remain as members of labor unions in private firms. To offset this decline in membership, unions must use new tactics that minimize the role of the reluctant employee. These tactics will emphasize pressure on the employer through pension fund issues and the political process. Employers, in turn, may find unionization advantageous in obtaining special favors from the government.

The increasing politicization of the labor union movement in both the public and private sectors has ominous implications. It remains to be seen whether the U.S. will follow Britain, where the labor union movement is synonymous with a political party, and where the nationalization of industry, sweeping socialism, and an enormous public sector have led to massive inefficiencies, falling productivity, and social, political, and economic disruption.

8. The Davis-Bacon Act

Arnold H. Raphaelson

Abstract

The Davis-Bacon Act of 1931 requires the payment of local prevailing wage rates for federally financed construction projects. This is consistent with the efficiency criterion for optimal intersector resource allocation—that the government should pay market prices—and with other uses of the prevailing wage concept for federal wage board workers and employees of service contractors. The act has been the subject of substantial controversy and of recent bills that would repeal it. Some of the literature on the act concludes that the administration of prevailing wage rates results in requiring wages at union levels (or at levels substantially above competitive market rates) and hence in inflating the dollar costs of federal projects. Other analyses conclude that restrictive wage and other effects may be offset by higher labor productivity and by management differences between union and nonunion firms. Benefits of the act include the protection of local construction wage rates and employment from the instability and external competition that may be induced by federal projects, while disadvantages of the act include reduced competition in government bidding because some nonunion employers object to levels of wage rate determinations and to the job classifications used. The study reviews the arguments and the literature and concludes that the decision on repeal of the act is more likely to be based on a determination of who will benefit (or suffer) than on an assessment of costs and benefits or on a criterion for efficiency in achieving optimal intersector allocation.

For optimal efficiency in intersector resource allocation, the prices paid by government should equal those paid by the private sector. The requirement for competitive bidding for most government purchases of goods and services represents an effort to assure that market prices will be paid. Moreover, for reasons of equity as well as efficiency, federal policy (e.g., the Federal Salary Reform Act of 1962) provides that government wage and salary levels be comparable to market rates for similar work. The provisions for achieving comparability vary from program to program, but they are generally based on the notion that the prevailing wage rates in a locality or an industry should be paid.

If all prevailing wage rates were set under perfectly competitive conditions in labor markets, the government would have to pay those rates in order to attract labor even in the absence of prevailing wage laws. But labor markets are not perfectly competitive; a number of institutional factors, such as the existence of large employers, labor unions, and various sets of regulations, limit competition within and among local labor markets.[1] Prevailing wage rates may be viewed by some as too high in comparison with competitive levels if union influences dominate, and by others as too low if employer influences dominate in market negotiations or transactions. Moreover, market wage rates are rarely expected to decline, even in markets with unemployed workers.

It is not realistic, under these market conditions, to expect wage rates to be competitively set. It has been argued, however, that government procurement activity should not interfere in local labor markets. Efficiency is one basis for such an argument; if, for example, workers with a given skill and productivity were offered a higher wage rate by public sector than by private sector employers, the result would be greater than optimal public sector production and less than optimal private sector production. For reasons of allocative efficiency as well as of equity (Building Construction Trades Department, 1977), then, the government has required that contractors pay prevailing wage rates.

The Davis-Bacon Act is the oldest element in the current structure of programs for wage rate comparability. The general principle of wage rate comparability has not been attacked, and the effects of the act have been repeatedly endorsed by its adoption (by reference) in many federal grant programs and in a number of state laws with similar provisions. Yet it remains controversial. Several bills have been proposed in Congress to amend or to repeal this act, and hearings on its effects have been held. A number of analyses have reached conflicting conclusions concerning the costs and benefits of the act.

The Act and the Arguments

The Davis-Bacon Act of 1931 requires that locally prevailing rates serve as the minimum wage rates for various classes of workers employed in virtually all federally funded contract construction. The history of the act is described concisely by Fulton (1978), whose work is the principal source for this section. The act was the first of several protective labor laws enacted during the Depression, and it was also the first federal law to regulate minimum wages for private sector workers. The act covers both negotiated and bid contracts, but it does not apply to construction work done by government workers. The act requires, specifically, that minimum wage rates under federal construction contracts should be the same as those prevailing for corresponding classes of laborers and mechanics on similar nonfederal projects in the "city, town, village or other civil subdivision of the State" in which work is to be done. The secretary of labor is charged with developing regulations and with implementing these and other provisions of the act. To the president is given the authority to suspend the act in national emergencies, and this authority has been used twice: in 1934 there was a 25-day suspension to end administrative confusion related to the National

Industrial Recovery Act, and in 1971 the act was suspended for about a month to reduce wage inflation in construction before the procedures of the Cost of Living Council were established.

Hence the act has been in force for most of the past 50 years. It was amended in 1935 to require predetermination of prevailing wage rates by the secretary of labor, so that contract bidders would know the minimum wage rates in advance. The scope of the act has been expanded to include public works and additional types of construction, to reduce the minimum amounts for covered contracts to $2,000, to require that workers be paid at least once a week, and to add a number of enforcement provisions. Later amendments made few substantive changes in the act except for the addition, in 1941, of coverage of negotiated as well as bid contracts, and the inclusion in 1964 of fringe benefits (as well as wages) as elements that must be figured into locally prevailing wage rates.

The effects of the act extend beyond its application to construction bought directly by the federal government. Some 60 federal programs that involve federal grants, loans, or other financing provisions have incorporated the Davis-Bacon provisions. In addition, more than 40 states have "little Davis-Bacon Acts" with similar prevailing wage requirements. While no estimate is available of the amount of construction covered by state laws, it has been estimated that 20 to 25 percent of all construction in recent years has been carried out under federally funded contracts—a minimum of $34 billion of the 1977 total construction value of $171 billion. Most of that $34 billion has been attributed to federally assisted (rather than direct federal) contracts.

The construction industry, with some 500,000 firms and more than 30 crafts, employs some 4.5 million workers—just under 5 percent of the nonagricultural work force. The act thus directly affects about 1 percent of the total nonagricultural labor force. Though its indirect effects are undoubtedly greater, our research has not identified any substantial spillover effects of the act on the rest of the labor force.

In accordance with the initial provisions of the act, the Labor Department developed criteria for determining the locally prevailing wage rate for each category of project and classification of worker. The criteria are:

(a) The 50 percent rule: When the majority of workers in a classification who are employed in construction of similar projects in an area are paid at the same wage rate, that rate shall be used for federal contracts.

(b) The 30 percent rule: When a majority of comparable workers are not paid at a single rate, then federal contracts shall use the rate paid to the highest number of workers if that number is at least 30 percent of such workers.

(c) The average rate: When less than 30 percent of such workers are paid at the same rate, the prevailing rate is declared to be the average rate.

Criticisms of the act's effects have focused on these criteria and on other administrative elements; Fulton (1978) has identified three principal issues in the arguments surrounding the act. The first issue is whether the initial intent of the act remains applicable. Opponents of the act note that the original purpose of the measure was to protect local workers, and pay levels, from itinerant contractors who would pay substandard wages to migratory workers on federal projects; these opponents deny the current need for such protection, pointing out that construction wage rates are high compared with those in other industries. On the other hand, those who support the act, including union sources, claim that such protection is still needed and note that the instability of industry employment serves as a basis for protecting wage rates at a level higher than the minimum levels for other employment.

The second objection to the act is that it interferes with market competition by limiting wage competition and by inhibiting competition from nonlocal contractors. To this objection the act's supporters reply that it only prevents competition where there are many small firms that would compete by wage cutting—a method closed to union firms under a labor contract. A major element in this argument, then, concerns competition between union and open-shop employers. Opponents of the act argue that union employers are given an unfair advantage in bidding against nonunion firms—that nonunion firms with pay scales below union levels lose much of the competitive advantages of those scales, and encounter special problems if they pay higher wages to workers on projects subject to the act. But to counter this objection supporters of the act note its consistency in policies requiring payment of prevailing wages in other industries and programs.

Opponents of the act also cite the increased cost and inflationary effects of requiring payment of prevailing wages when they are higher than those in competitive labor markets, and when they are often set at union wage levels under the Labor Department's criteria. But others hold that the act helps to reduce construction costs in several ways—by limiting awards to incompetent contractors, by reducing strife in the labor market through maintaining standards, and by permitting employment of more productive workers on federally funded projects.

Finally, opponents of the act argue that minority employment in construction is impeded because minority workers are more likely to find jobs in nonunion firms and because the Labor Department follows union job classifications. These classifications omit some entry-level jobs, and thus may require higher than market wage rates for, and reduce the number of openings in, the helper or informal trainee positions open to minority workers. Supporters of the act, however, respond that minority workers realize offsetting gains from the formal training provided by union firms' apprentice programs, which would be more limited in the absence of the act.

Most of these arguments can be supported by some data or evidence. But there have been many more position papers related to value of the act than analytical studies of its effects. Most of the analytical studies have been concerned with wage rate differentials and cost implications; these are reviewed in the next section.

Review of the Literature

A number of recent studies of the construction industry generally, and of the Davis-Bacon Act specifically, have been cited as evidence of the need for revision or repeal of the act. Some studies have dealt primarily with particular elements in the act and in the Labor Department's regulations and methods of administration. One objective review, with a more comprehensive economic analysis, is a 1979 report prepared for the U.S. Department of Housing and Urban Development (HUD) (Solomon & Bourdon, 1979); it does not attempt to estimate the costs or benefits of the act. Some studies do try to estimate costs of the act and problems in its administration, or rely on the estimates from other studies (Gujarati, 1967; Gould, 1971; Mills, 1972; Northrup & Foster, 1975; Thieblot, 1975; Goldfarb & Morrall, 1976; and U.S. Comptroller General, 1979), while others deny that there are appropriate data to demonstrate any undue nonadministrative costs or any inflationary effects (Bourdon & Levitt, 1978; Building and Construction Trades Department, 1977).

Gujarati's (1967) study of Davis-Bacon Act administration of prevailing wage rate determinations was based on a sample of 372 wage rate determinations in 300 counties in 1960 and 1961. A number of reports of the Comptroller General on the same subject had concluded that administrative changes should be made. Gujarati's study, however, was the first to subject such a large sample to statistical analysis; no similar study has since been published. He found that determinations of the prevailing wage rate were based on surveys in a small proportion of his sample (8 of the 372), and that a very large proportion of determinations were based on union wage rates. Moreover, he found that a high proportion of prevailing wage rate determinations were "imported," or based on rates from other counties—counties which were often not contiguous with the one in which construction was to occur, and which were beyond a normal average of commuting distances. He concluded that union wage rates were determined as prevailing wage rates more frequently than the extent of union membership would suggest.

Gould's study (1971) accepted the conclusions of the Gujarati study. Solomon and Bourdon (1979), however, noted that Gujarati's data on the extent of unionization were neither current nor related specifically to construction, so that his analysis could not demonstrate that the wage determinations did not reflect prevailing wages. No recent studies with a similarly large sample have been carried out, either to confirm or to deny the conclusions of Gujarati's study, though the U.S. Comptroller General (1979) and Bourdon and Levitt (1978) dealt with some similar issues.

The econometric analysis by Ehrenberg, Kosters, and Moskow (1971) tried to determine the act's effects on union construction wages relative to the wages of local workers in manufacturing. But problems with the data used were significant; no attempt was made to standardize for differences among areas in levels of unionization or in activities in the construction and other sectors, and the authors were unable to separate the effects of Davis-Bacon provisions from the effects of changes in demand for construction financed by public funds. As a result, their conclusions on the wage rate effects of Davis-Bacon provisions were, at best, tentative.

Nevertheless, the Gould study (1971), published later in the same year, accepted the implications of the Ehrenberg-Kosters-Moskow study that the effect of Davis-Bacon provisions was to increase construction wages. Gould also relied on the Gujarati study and on several reports of the U.S. Comptroller General. These cost studies concluded that reform was needed in the administration of Davis-Bacon provisions. Gould went further and urged considering repeal (rather than reform) of the act. He designed an algebraic model to isolate the effects of Davis-Bacon provisions on related wage rates and construction costs but did not attempt to test that model empirically.

In his more general 1972 work, Mills found that the Davis-Bacon Act did require higher wages and fringe benefits, but this was not seen as a very strong effect. He believed the act provided a benefit by reducing labor strife. However, any higher level of wages might be expected to have that effect.

The most comprehensive study of the act was carried out by Thieblot (1975): it covers the history and administration of the act, the relevant literature, and the results of a survey of contractors. It emphasizes the view that the act causes considerable increases in construction wage rates and costs because of the use and administration of prevailing wage rates and comparable work (occupation) concepts. Thieblot's cost estimates are drawn either from prior studies or from data from his survey, or represent extrapolations from particular situations. In one analysis, differences in bid prices as a result of the suspension of the act (from February 23 to March 29, 1971) are used to estimate the costs of the Davis-Bacon provisions. Thieblot failed, however, to account for changes in the bidding process and their effects, and offers his estimate only with some appropriate disclaimers. (Nevertheless, his estimate has been widely cited.) Thieblot estimates the possible annual savings from repealing the Davis-Bacon Act at from $150 million to $1 billion. His study, however, assumes a direct link between wage rates and construction costs, and fails to account for labor productivity elements. Thieblot favored repeal of the act, or at least (in the absence of repeal) a number of changes in the general administration of the act and in its appeals procedure.

Northrup and Foster (1975), relying mainly on the Thieblot study, also discuss the act in a study of open-shop construction. In their view, the purpose of the act was to prevent federal construction projects from contributing to unfair competition by producing "downward pressure on wage rates." They feel that most students of the act agree, however, that it has brought about an unintended "upward pressure on wages" instead. After a brief review of some of the issues involved in the administration of the act, they cite Gould's estimates of "excessive costs." Northrup and Foster found Gould's (1971) assumption about the union-nonunion wage differential to be a reasonable one but termed "speculative" his assumption that there would be a shift of construction job demand to the nonunion sector if the act were repealed. They concluded that Gould failed to "account for the possibility of a general downward pressure on union wage rates resulting from repeal."[2]

Northrup and Foster also noted that, even if open-shop contractors lose some advantages of lower wage rates because of the act, they retain the advantages of greater flexibility in the use of labor, of "freedom from costly disputes," and of the inapplicability of some union contract provisions. Many open-shop contractors indicated that they had lower labor costs than union contractors, even though they were paying union-negotiated wage rates and benefits. A principal problem cited by some open-shop contractors who were working on both public and private sector projects was the difference in wage rates between projects, since they did not use the act's prevailing wage scale on private sector projects.[3] Furthermore, Northrup and Foster (1975) observed, "the large wage differential in private commercial work, where open shops have far from completely displaced unionized contractors, itself attests to the fact that wages are not the only terrain on which union and nonunion firms compete." The act has helped unions to organize and to maintain their hold on some segments of the industry during an upsurge of open shop activity in others. Their conclusion, however, is that the impact of prevailing wage rate laws upon open shop construction is not clear.

In a study for the Council on Wage and Price Stability (COWPS), Goldfarb and Morrall (1976) attempted a cost-benefit study of the act. Citing estimates of costs in the studies described above, they argued that most of the benefit from proposed changes in administration or from repeal of the act would lie in a redistribution of income from construction workers to other taxpayers. "Savings" would come principally from the use of different concepts and methods for calculation of the prevailing wage rate, which would result in more government construction and more employment in construction at lower wage rates. Using data from a special survey (with which they encountered some problems), they estimated the "savings" obtainable from changing the methods of determining the prevailing wage rate, and extrapolated, from the amount of wages reduced, a "savings" in construction costs of \$222 to \$571 million in 1972. Productivity elements were not considered in their analysis, and they indicated a need for separate treatment of occupations and cities to derive more sophisticated estimates.

A more extensive study by Bourdon and Levitt (1978) was completed for HUD. Their sample survey of construction firms in eight metropolitan areas focused upon wages and labor-management issues in union and nonunion sectors of the industry. They reported problems in comparing union and nonunion wages for similar jobs because of variations within both sectors in the labeling of workers' skill levels and productivity. They found more flexibility and innovation in labor practices among the open-shop firms, but they also discovered that such firms employed more foremen than were required in union shops.

Bourdon and Levitt found the informal impact of a union, when related to individual attitudes, more important than union work rules or the technology-related effects of unions, especially for larger firms. On the basis of these and other findings on the expansion of open-shop construction activity, they suggested that use of a wider range of occupational skill levels under the act might permit a "better fit between mandated and market wages." And while they found that open-shop contractors resented having to pay prevailing wage rates set at union levels and having to follow the mandated skill and occupational definitions, they also admitted that neither past studies nor their own analysis "effectively established that such laws do in fact raise wages or actually raise the final costs of construction."

In general, then, while surveys of contractors do yield some valuable insights on these issues, they fail to provide comparable hard data on wage or total project costs. Such surveys do, however, lend support to arguments that wage rates may be higher because of the act, though differences may be offset by other factors.

The most recent in a series of reports on the act was issued by the U.S. Comptroller General (1979); unlike earlier reports that urged changes in administration, it urged repeal of the act. Its recommendations were based on cost estimates derived from a study of a sample of public construction situations. The study itself, however, was criticized for the representativeness of its sample, the conceptual models implicit in its analysis, the statistical techniques employed, and the validity of the inferences drawn. The report was explained, attacked, and defended in hearings in 1979. But beyond adding more cost studies to the literature, the report contributed little to the analysis of issues. Like the 1977 publication on Davis-Bacon by the Building and Construction Trades Department of the AFL-CIO, the Comptroller General's report was stronger on argument than on analysis.

However, another report prepared for HUD by Solomon and Bourdon (1979) provided an analytical framework for examining the possible cost impacts of the Davis-Bacon provisions. The authors found evidence of higher wage rates on some projects as a result of Davis-Bacon provisions, but they noted that the samples used were not adequate to permit similar, valid conclusions for all federally assisted projects. Moreover, the numbers of manhours used had not been related to wage rates for similar projects in open-shop and union-shop sectors of the industry. As a result, it was not possible to draw valid inferences about any differences in total wage costs from evidence on wage rate differences. Further, differences in wage costs can arise from differences in the mix of occupations and skill levels employed on different types of projects; differences in productivity of labor and in management practices must be considered in assessing the effect of wage rate differences on final construction costs. Solomon and Bourdon discovered that past studies did not include those factors in any estimates of costs or inflationary effects. They also found no evidence that any Davis-Bacon inflationary effects went beyond the construction industry and into the general economy.

Little analytical work has been devoted to any such productivity analysis. More recent studies described by Lehner (1979), however, associate unionization with higher labor productivity. A study by the National Bureau of Economic Research found higher labor productivity among several union cement plants, which was attributed to better management methods. It is not clear that this conclusion would be generally applicable in construction. Another study for the Building and Construction Trades Department of the AFL-CIO found that average output per worker was 29 percent higher in union construction firms than in nonunion firms. This study indicated skill and training levels of workers as the likely causes of the productivity differences, but it is not clear that such productivity measures are cost effective in the absence of labor cost (rather than output per worker) relationships.

These studies suggest that an increase in construction wage rates, relative to union rates, may be offset (totally or in part) by productivity differences. Even where the prevailing wage rates for government construction are higher than nonunion wage rates, the contractor may be able to screen for the most productive workers available and will have a greater incentive to manage carefully the use of a more expensive input. If this were the case, Davis-Bacon wage rate determinations might have no net effect on total wage costs. More definitive studies would also attempt to relate wage rate, productivity, and other cost effects to the process of bidding by contractors for government projects.

Alan G. King (1979), in an unpublished paper, attempted to identify the act's benefits by its labor market effects. He found two bases to support prevailing wage levels in federally funded construction projects. The first is that such projects are likely to be among the larger ones in most local areas, and the associated increase in demand for construction labor will probably induce a separate rise in labor costs. Ignoring this likely effect by failing to specify an adequate prevailing wage level could lead contractors to underbid and thus could cause quality control problems. One benefit of the act, King suggested, would be to minimize such quality control problems for government. Moreover, to the extent that such projects are "volatile and unpredictable," local workers could expect a "risk premium" for such work unless the local labor force were supplemented by mobile workers, including illegal aliens; King saw the protection of local jobs and risk premiums as appropriate benefits because of the nature of federal construction jobs. King also viewed the provisions of the act as a means of allocating projects to union and nonunion firms, with the effects of stabilizing employment for both groups and increasing the training opportunities in the industry.

Other studies have emphasized cost effects of the act and reached varied estimates and conclusions. King's study is the only one in the recent literature to emphasize the act's benefits. It approaches the problem through analytical models of labor market effects, without presenting empirical evidence or dollar evaluations of the benefits cited, and thus (like Gould's work) it presents models of reasoning that are separate from empirical results. King appropriately titles his paper "A Brief in Support of the Davis-Bacon Act."

Other Prevailing Wage Provisions

The use of prevailing wage rate levels is not limited to procurement in federally funded construction projects. The Walsh-Healey Act of 1935 sets minimum wage standards for all contracts over $10,000 for materials and equipment purchased by the federal government. The secretary of labor is given the authority to determine the industry-wide prevailing wage rate. There is no reference to local areas, since the procurement contracts can be placed in any area. Currently little effort is made to administer or enforce this act.

Firms performing work for the federal government under service contracts are required to observe special minimum pay standards by the McNamara-O'Hara Service Contract Act of 1965 (Employment Standards Administration, 1978). This act covers contracts in excess of $2,500 for services such as laundry, mail transport, custodial and grounds services, food, survey, inventory, lodging, computer services, warehousing, repairs and maintenance of equipment, and other support services for federal installations. All workers who are not in executive, administrative, or professional positions are considered service employees of the covered contractors and must receive the minimum wages specified.

As under the Davis-Bacon Act, the minimum levels of wages and fringe benefits are those determined by the secretary of labor to be prevailing in the locality where the service work is performed. Further, if a previous contractor had a union agreement covering his service workers, the minimum wage levels are the union rates for current or prospective periods under the agreement, and these levels must be specified in any bid or services contract. The minimum wage levels of the Fair Labor Standards Act apply only in the absence of a prevailing wage rate determination or in the absence of a prior union agreement covering service workers. A contractor is also required to furnish any prevailing fringe benefits or to make equivalent or differential cash payments. If a wage determination fails to provide a wage rate or fringe benefits for a particular classification of workers, the contractor must provide a "reasonably conforming" wage rate for that classification, and that rate must be approved by the workers and by the contract officer of the government.

Overtime pay standards are not specified in the Service Contract Act, but they are specified under other laws, such as the Fair Labor Standards Act. The Service Contract Act does not apply to work done under the Davis-Bacon or Walsh-Healey acts or to contracts for utility services, for freight services where there are published tariff rates, or for services furnished outside the United States. There is no current estimate of the number of workers covered by the Service Contract Act. Generally, however, it covers those workers on government contracts who are not covered by the other acts.

The principle that federal government salaries should be comparable with private salary rates for similar work was declared as policy in the Federal Salary Reform Act of 1962 and was applied to white collar employment. Procedures for annual reports on this comparability were established. The general schedule (GS) salary ratings for more than half of the federal workers were established on the basis of national scales.

Nearly 20 percent of the federal government's employees are blue collar workers covered by the wage board system, with minimum wages based on locally prevailing rates (Federal Personnel Manual System, 1978). Most of the wage board workers are employed in crafts-oriented occupations in Navy yards, arsenals, and other installations, but some classes of workers are widely distributed among the agencies of the government. The wage rates for these employees are determined on the basis of surveys of wage rates paid by private sector employers in local areas. The Federal Wage System defines and groups the occupations into 15 grades, and there are 39 key ranking jobs for the framework of the system. One department is defined as the lead agency in each survey including a metropolitan area or major city. The wage rates established in such a survey are often applied to a broader area, including additional contiguous or nearby counties; if some key jobs cannot be surveyed in the private sector of a particular area, the rates of the nearest similar wage survey area may be applied. The surveys of wage rates are conducted annually. Union representatives of federal employees are often consulted on the sample design and implementation of the survey process. Among the 22 occupations that must be surveyed in each area are truck drivers, carpenters, electricians, and pipefitters. Once a survey is scheduled, the resulting prevailing wage rates are to be applied for the first pay period starting after 45 days from that date, in order to minimize delay between the determination of the prevailing wage rate and its implementation for federal employees.

Thus the wage rates for nonsupervisory federal workers reflect the current prevailing levels paid in the same area for the same work in the private sector. Rates for supervisory staff are based on the rates of nonsupervisory workers but are adjusted by established schedules for differentials, which must also correspond reasonably with those found in the private sector. These rates are applied uniformly within each area unless exceptional conditions warrant the use of special schedules. Regulations for the wage board employees include premium pay for overtime, differentials for night shifts and physical or environmental hazards, and provisions for pay retention in transfers. Several agencies and government-controlled corporations are not part of this system. For the Tennessee Valley Authority, for example, union wage rates negotiated in the private sector may be adopted as the relevant prevailing wage rates for certain occupations.

Comparability with private sector wage rates is thus the basis for pay determinations for more than 2.5 million federal employees. National wage comparability is established for 1.4 million general schedule employees. Moreover, 470,000 wage board employees receive wages based on local prevailing wage levels in the private sector. Locally prevailing wages and benefits are the bases for determining the compensation of most workers under federal service contracts, as is the case for construction workers under the Davis-Bacon Act. Thus federal prevailing wage provisions cover most federal employees and most workers under federal procurement contracts. Local prevailing wage determinations affect private sector construction and service contract workers as well as federal board employees. In addition, local prevailing wage determinations are required under 41 state "little Davis-Bacon Acts" (Fulton, 1978); in 16 of these states all public contract construction is covered. The determination of wage rates to be paid by local governments is also often based on locally prevailing rates in the private sector. Thus the application of the prevailing wage concepts, including locally prevailing wage rates, is much broader than the construction employment covered under the Davis-Bacon Act.

Summary and Conclusion

A policy providing that government wage, salary, and fringe benefit levels should be comparable with those prevailing in the private sector is consistent with the efficiency criterion that requires public sector purchases of goods and services to match market prices. Moreover, the use of locally prevailing rates, rather than of industry or national levels for wage board employees, has been justified by some on the basis of fixed locations of agency offices and installations and geographic differentials in living costs and wage rates. Providing similar work for similar pay has been held to be both equitable and efficient in attracting productive workers.

There has, however, been significant disagreement about the appropriateness of using the prevailing wage rates as the minimum wage rates for federal contracts. For several reasons, disagreement has focused on the coverage by the Davis-Bacon Act of federally financed contract construction, rather than on the greater numbers of industries covered by the Walsh-Healey Act for purchase of manufactured goods or by the Service Contract acts.

While the Davis-Bacon Act does not restrict the competitive bidding process that should assure government of market prices for construction, it effectively prevents wage rates from being elements in the bidding competition by specifying minimum rates. The effect may be analogous to the result of requiring millers, who must all pay the same support prices for wheat, to submit competing bids for government flour contracts. Requiring payment of minimum input prices or wage rates will act as a constraint on the range and nature of the bidding. Such a requirement may be justified on equity or efficiency grounds.[4]

A second reason for opposition to the Davis-Bacon Act is that it affects a single industry rather than many; moreover, there are other sources of controversy within that industry. Though many small firms are in the business of contract construction, there are few associations of such firms to represent their interests. In addition, a sharp division exists between union and nonunion firms and interests. Hence much of the opposition to the act has centered on the 30 percent rule and on the importation of prevailing wage rates from areas far from proposed construction. These administrative elements of the act have led to the adoption of union pay and benefit levels as the minimum rates to be paid under federally funded contracts, have classified construction jobs primarily in relation to union categories, and have thus introduced some wage rate constraints that open-shop firms might not encounter in private sector projects. Yet it is impossible to estimate wage rates that might be set in competitive labor markets that do not exist. As the act is currently administered, prevailing wage rates may exceed the average wage rates in many cases; hence it has been argued that union contractors and union workers gain an advantage under the act, and that this advantage is passed on as an increase in government contract construction costs.

Analytical literature on the Davis-Bacon Act has failed to provide unambiguous support for those conclusions. Since the act has been in effect for almost 50 years, realistic comparisons to periods without it are impossible. Some authors have identified situations where the prevailing wage rate, set at union levels, was higher than in nonunion firms and have concluded that this resulted in more contracts for union firms. No one, however, has demonstrated why nonunion firms are less able than union firms to compete for government contracts with higher minimum wage requirements, or how union firms with higher wage rates can compete with open shops in the private sector.

More recent studies also conclude that the evidence on wage differentials alone offers an inadequate basis for estimating any costs resulting from the act. Some argue that differences in labor skills and productivity and in management practices may offset any wage differentials that result from the use of prevailing wage determinations. Thus it is not clear whether the act has in fact raised government contract construction costs. Certain benefits have been attributed to the act, but these have not been evaluated in dollar terms for purposes of comparison with the costs (if any) of the act.

Cost-benefit analysis, however, has not been the real problem. Instead, the act has become part of a political controversy between open-shop forces, which generally oppose it, and union construction firms and labor organizations, which generally favor it. Much of the controversy involves the decision rules and the administration of local prevailing wage rates in contract construction. But controversy has not arisen over the applicability of local prevailing wage rates set for wage board employees or for employees of service contractors. No private sector employers are directly involved in the case of wage board workers. Seldom does a split between union and nonunion employers and workers arise in the service industries as it does in the construction industry. It may be impossible to define and administer a local prevailing wage rate that would satisfy both the union and nonunion sectors of the construction industry. Any determination may be too high for open-shop contractors, who may use less productive workers at lower rates, or too low for union firms, whose current contracts may call for higher rates than were paid at the time the prevailing rate was determined.

The benefits of the act are that it has accomplished its original purposes by protecting local construction wage rates and employment from external competition and thus by reducing labor strife. The instability of construction employment and the special local impact of federal projects may justify such benefits for this industry (as compared, for example, with manufacturing, where products themselves are mobile). There is, however, a cost for these benefits. Some nonunion contractors exclude themselves from bidding for government contracts because of the Davis-Bacon wage constraints and thus limit the effective competition for government projects. The dollar cost of this and other effects has not been clearly quantified in the analytical literature, since the effects of wage rate differences cannot, without accounting for total wage cost effects, be extended to indicate clear differences in project costs. As a result, the judgment on whether to repeal the Davis-Bacon Act is likely to be made on the basis of who benefits from the act, and who would benefit from its repeal, rather than on the basis of any dollar cost differences in assessing the benefits and costs of the act, or on the basis of an attempt to attain optimal intersector resource allocation.

9. OPEC II and the Wage-Price Spiral

Stephen G. Cecchetti, David S. McClain,
Michael J. McKee, and Daniel H. Saks

Abstract

The 1979 oil price shock reopened the debate about the proper response of aggregate demand policy to supply shocks. In the wake of the 1973 oil price increase, monetary policy turned restrictive in an attempt to "extinguish" the flare-up in inflation. Inflation was reduced, but the U.S. economy experienced its worst recession since World War II. The optimal policy response to any supply shock depends not only on social preferences about inflation and unemployment, but also on the institutional framework in which wages and prices are set. In particular, the scope for maintaining output and employment in the face of an oil price disturbance ("accommodating" instead of extinguishing the disturbance) depends on the flexibility of real wages and real non-oil prices—that is, on the degree to which the oil price increase is built into the trend rate of increase of industrial costs and prices. To assess this flexibility, a small econometric model of wage and price behavior during the last fifteen years is estimated. The model includes some minor refinements to conventional techniques used to assess both the manner in which expectations of inflation are formed and the degree to which temporary oil price increases are incorporated into expectations of inflation. Simulations of the model suggest the existence of real non-oil price flexibility. The 1979 oil price increase will not raise the trend rate of inflation, though it may appear to do so because of the long lags involved in pricing behavior, expectations formation, and wage determination. The model is also used to assess the impact on the incomes policies of the Carter administration, which were designed to promote real wage and price flexibility; simulations suggest that the pay and price standards had a modest effect on wages during the first program year. The authors conclude that the appropriate response to an oil price shock is an aggregate demand policy that aims at keeping the GNP gap relatively constant on its preshock trajectory. In the process of performing their analyses, they identify some of the major problems in addressing these important policy issues with the standard techniques.

> We expect everything and are prepared for nothing.
> —found by one of the authors in a fortune cookie

The year 1979 saw a doubling of oil prices followed by a one-third rise in the implicit price deflator for personal consumption expenditures. It was as if a sequel had been made to a 1973 disaster film. In the wake of this second oil-price shock, much of the macroeconomic policy discussion was centered on the question of whether the oil price increases would be incorporated into the trend rate of increase in industrial costs and prices.

If such an incorporation were to occur (suggesting the inflexibility of real wages and non-oil prices in the economy), it would severely impair the case for an expansive or accommodating aggregate-demand policy response, designed to minimize the loss in real output and employment caused by this supply shock. In this situation, such a stimulative policy would cause extra inflation with little benefit in the form of real output. The case would be strengthened for a restrictive policy to extinguish the shock-induced flare-up in inflation, despite the attendant costs in lost output. A similar policy, followed by the Federal Reserve after the 1973 oil-price shock, did help to cool off inflationary pressures but contributed to the worst recession since World War II.

If this incorporation were not to occur, or if it were to take several years to materialize (so that real wages and non-oil prices exhibited some flexibility, at least for an extended period), then the scope for an accommodating monetary and fiscal policy response would be enlarged.[1]

This question of an eventual embedding of the oil-price shock into the core or underlying rate of inflation is intimately related to the hypothesis that there is a "natural" rate of unemployment—that is, a rate of unemployment to which an economy in long-run equilibrium will converge, and which is independent of the rate of inflation. Such a rate of unemployment will exist if past rates of change of prices get fully built into expectations about inflation, if wages and other costs of factors of production fully reflect changes in inflation expectations, and if firms set prices on a full percentage markup basis over cost— precisely the set of circumstances that guarantee the incorporation of an oil-price shock into the trend rate of increase in industrial costs and prices. This description of the inflation process is often termed "accelerationist" because it implies that any attempt by government policymakers to lower permanently the unemployment rate below the natural rate will only lead to a steady increase in the rate of change of prices.[2]

In this short study, we use some minor refinements of conventional techniques to trace the transmission of inflationary pressures to other sectors following an oil-price shock. One major line of inquiry relates to the impact of such a shock on expectations of inflation. An oil-price shock will raise the price level and the rate of inflation in the short run. It may increase expectations of future inflation and thus contribute to an increase in the rate of change of wages. We examine two questions central to this process. First, how should one measure the manner in which past price changes affect inflation expectations, assuming that expectations are what properly belong in the wage equation? Second, given this measurement approach, are all components of the price-index increase passed through to wage increases in the same way?

Our econometric results lend weight to the view that aggregate-demand policy need not feel quite so pressured to tighten in response to a shock, in that they suggest the existence of a measure of real non-oil price flexibility in the economy.

To the extent that our estimated model of a damped wage-price spiral has captured the relationship between prices and wages in recent times, we can then use it to analyze the effectiveness of the recent incomes policies that were designed in part to limit the consequences of major price shocks by temporarily increasing the flexibility of real wages and real non-oil prices. Our analysis suggests that, during the first program year, the pay and price standards of the Carter administration had a modest impact on wage behavior.

We conclude by identifying some of the major problems which arise in trying to answer these important policy questions with the standard techniques, and we discuss the implications of these problems for the design of an appropriate aggregate-demand policy response to an external supply shock. We suggest that a sensible policy response should aim at holding the gap between actual and potential Gross National Product (GNP) roughly at its expected preshock trajectory (recognizing that the shock will have an effect, it is hoped small in magnitude, on the level of potential GNP). If policymakers are to deviate from this path, it is probably better for an economy in which expectations of inflation are entrenched if they do so on the side of extra restraint—as long as any such deviations are slight. Adoption of sharply restrictive policies during the period of the shock wastes output without altering the path of the trend rate of increase of industrial costs and prices.

Model Specification

Following the earlier work of Gordon (1971, 1975), we estimate both a wage Phillips curve augmented with price expectations and a model of price determination, which consists of two equations. The first equation is an elaboration of the specification of the price equation used in the basic accelerationist model. The rate of change of output prices is assumed to depend on the rates of change of standard unit labor costs, on import and farm prices, on deviations in productivity change from trend, and on the change in the gap between actual and potential GNP. The second price equation is merely an accounting relationship between output prices and consumer prices. We discuss each of these three equations separately, although the behavioral equations are part of a simultaneous system. All the equations use two dummy variables to represent, respectively, Phases I and II and Phases III and IV of the Nixon Economic Stabilization Program.[3]

The Wage Equation: General Structure

The wage equation is traditional in structure, in that the rate of change of wages is explained by excess demand in the labor market and the expected rate of change of prices.[4] The dependent variable (following Gordon, 1971) is the one-quarter change in the log of the hourly earnings index for the private nonagricultural sector (adjusted for overtime and interindustry shift) multiplied by the ratio of total labor compensation to wages and salaries. It is an earnings index inflated to represent compensation using the necessary (but unrealistic) assumption that the ratio of compensation to wages is independent of industrial mix. This hybrid is better for our purposes than available series on compensation or hourly earnings alone, since the former does not adjust for overtime and interindustry shift, and the latter does not include all the considerations involved in wage bargaining.

The measure used to represent labor market slack is the unemployment rate for males 25 years and older. This measure attempts to control for the problem of demographic changes in the labor force causing a given overall unemployment rate to represent shifting degrees of labor-market tightness. The extreme assumption here is that other groups are not substitutes in production. We tried using the inverse of the unemployment rate to capture the supposed convexity of Phillips curves, but the linear approximation gave a slightly better fit and was simpler to interpret. The quit rate is a more appropriate measure of labor-market tightness, but we rejected it in favor of the unemployment rate on statistical grounds. We also examined the change in our unemployment rate variable on the grounds that the speed of adjustment in the labor market would be important, as suggested in a recent annual report of the President's Council of Economic Advisers (CEA, 1979). This "speed limit" variable was statistically insignificant.

Since compensation includes social insurance tax receipts, the choice of hourly compensation as the dependent variable in the wage equation requires the inclusion of a measure of social insurance tax on the righthand side. The formulation of the variable is again based on Gordon (1971). It is the percentage change in the inverse of one minus the total effective social insurance tax rate. An attempt was made to separate the tax into Social Security and other taxes, but this did not prove fruitful. The coefficient of this variable reflects the short-run incidence of Social Security or unemployment insurance taxes. Efforts to allow for a lagged response were quite sensitive to the specifications of the lag and were not pursued for the work here.[5]

Measurement of price expectations in the wage equation.   Finally, there is the specification of the price term—a principal issue for this paper. It is now generally agreed that current and past rates of change of prices have a place as independent variables in a Phillips curve model even though this changes the original Phillips relation into one dealing with real rather than nominal wages. Whether or not the price term represents the expectation of future price changes or an attempt to regain a real-wage position lost through past price changes is problematical. What is certain is that the estimates of a wage equation are quite sensitive to the exact specification of the price term and to the period over which the equation is estimated. In keeping with a general recognition of the problems associated with the Consumer Price Index (CPI)—that it treats the purchase of a house as a purchase of a consumption good, when in fact such a purchase has significant investment characteristics—we avoid using it to measure inflation. We have used instead the implicit deflator for Personal Consumption Expenditures (PCE), which includes a measure of the value of the housing services consumed by households. This deflator is not without its limitations for our purposes; it ignores the welfare losses associated with substitution by consumers, and the weights as well as the prices of individual categories of consumption expenditures change from period to period. In future work, we can avoid this second shortcoming by using the chain-weighted PCE deflator.[6]

Expectations about the future are reflected in efficient markets for longer-term contracts. Gordon (1971) generated price expectations from Treasury bill rates using a reduced form of an IS-LM model. We found the structure of that model too unstable over the last 20 years and instead tried a term structure of interest rates equation to generate price expectations. Our equation mirrored that of Modigliani and Stutch (1966). The long-term (3-year Treasury note) rate was equal to a 16-quarter polynominal distributed lag on the real rate of interest on 3-month Treasury bills plus expected inflation (estimated as a 12-quarter polynominal lag on changes in the PCE deflator).[7]

We attempted one refinement to this approach. The usual way of generating such expectations is to estimate the parameters of the expectations-generating equation over the full sample period and then to use those parameters to generate the expectations for each sample point in estimating the wage equation. If the structure of the expectations equation is quite stable, that is reasonable. But if people are adjusting the way they form their expectations (as, say, when the economy moves to a regime of high and variable inflation), then it seems reasonable to have them estimate their expectations-generating function from information of the recent previous years only. In order to implement such a scheme, we generated inflation expectations for each quarter from 1964:2 by estimating a term-structure equation using data from the seven years prior to that quarter. That equation was then used to generate expected inflation for that quarter. This refinement made very little difference in the expectations series generated because the parameters of the term structure equation were so stable. As figure 9.1 shows, the fixed[8] and varying structure yielded quite similar expected inflation estimates.

In the end, we found that we could explain more variance in hourly compensation by putting the distributed lag on changes in the PCE directly into the wage equation than by using our constructed expectations variable. Further, the coefficient on our constructed expectations variable in the wage equation was significantly less than one and the coefficient on the unemployment rate became zero when this constructed variable was used. This result for the coeffi-

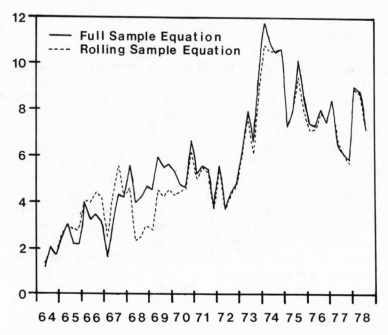

Figure 9.1. Expectations of inflation based on a term structure of interest rates equation

cient on the constructed expectations variable may reflect measurement errors that arise from using expectations among those who set bond prices as a proxy for expectations among those who set wages. In addition, past prices may be serving the additional role in the equation of representing the encouragement of catch-up (i.e., wealth effects) by past declines in real wages.[9]

Decomposition of expected price changes.   The other major issue with respect to prices in the wage equation is decomposition of the PCE deflator into energy and other components in order to determine whether all sources of expected price increase have the same impact on wage inflation. There are several rationales for why components of a price index might enter a wage equation with coefficients unequal to their weights in the index. Since the wage equation is a reduced form of a supply-and-demand equation system for the labor market, it is helpful to divide the arguments into supply-and-demand side effects. If expected real wages enter the labor supply equation, then the expected total PCE should be in the nominal wage equation. Yet workers may worry only about permanent real wages and they may feel that certain movements of the PCE are so erratic and transitory that they ignore those movements. To test this hypothesis, "permanent" and "temporary" PCE series could be constructed (with the property that temporary deviations between actual and permanent prices sum to zero over the sample period) and used in the wage equation. [10] The coefficient on the temporary rate of inflation should be zero if workers are concerned only with permanent real wages.

Firms also may be concerned with only permanent real wages in assessing their demand for labor, in the same spirit as they are thought to use "standardized" unit labor costs in setting prices. In this case a permanent private nonfarm deflator series should enter the wage equation; a temporary series, based on deviations of the actual series from the permanent series, should get a coefficient of zero in such an equation if firms are concerned with only permanent real wages in their hiring decisions. Further, if permanent profit margins influence firms' behavior in wage negotiations, a measure of permanent or standardized costs of materials (supplied from sectors other than the private nonfarm sector) should be considered.

An alternative approach to the permanent/transitory price issue, perhaps more efficient in terms of information cost considerations, is the assumption that workers and firms treat as transitory the behavior of certain *components* of the relevant price index that have behaved erratically in the past. Energy and food are two elements of the PCE whose movements in the past have been quite noisy; the coefficient on those items might be small.

We have elected to address this decomposition question employing this simple approach of estimating the wage equation using the total PCE and, as an alternative specification, a division of the PCE into two components. The interpretation of the results is complicated by the fact that, as noted, while the PCE (or its components) is (are) the relevant variable(s) for the labor supply equation from which our reduced form specification is derived, it is not an ideal measure for firms to use in assessing the value of the marginal product of labor. The mix of private nonfarm output is not the same as the mix of consumer expenditures, though they are likely to be highly correlated.

A further complication occurs because some consumption falls on imports and some of the raw materials used by firms are imported. A rise in the price of an imported commodity such as oil—that is both used as a raw material by firms and purchased for final demand by households—will have different effects on the wage demanded and wage offered. The wage demanded will rise, while the wage offered will not (unless there are domestically produced substitutes for the imported commodity) since the value of the marginal product of labor will not rise in any industry. This problem does not occur in the case of a rise in the price of a domestically produced good, such as autos. In that situation, the value of the marginal product of labor in the auto industry rises, as does the wage offered; whether they raise wages to hold their workers or to react to demonstration effects, firms in other industries will have to follow suit.

One other mechanism through which a rise in the price of imported oil can add to the nominal wage offered operates when such a price rise "lubricates" the price inflation mechanisms in other sectors by exacerbating firms' (and households') expectations of inflation. If, perhaps because of political considerations, the monetary authorities are expected to accommodate an oil price rise, that could, of course, trigger this mechanism.

Thus, not all consumer price increases need result in a higher derived demand for labor and higher wage offered. However, we need not exaggerate the distinction; most of our energy derives from domestic sources.

In our estimations to test the decomposition issue, we did not include current price changes so that the need to use simultaneous equation-estimation techniques is not present. The coefficient using changes in the total PCE to measure expected inflation was approximately 1.0, a result suggesting no long-run flexibility in real wages, consistent with our prior beliefs. When the equation was reestimated with the energy component broken out, the PCE less energy variable had a coefficient of 1.28 and the coefficient on energy was slightly negative (because foreign oil prices squeezed domestic employer margins in the short run?). The fit of the equation was slightly better. When both food and energy were broken out, the coefficient was not significantly different from the component weights in the PCE, though the total for all components was 1.19. Coefficients greater than 1 may reflect wage bargaining on an after-tax basis, given a tax system in which marginal tax rates increase with inflation.

These experiments were, in short, inconclusive. We decided to use the total PCE for several reasons. The energy component of the PCE is relatively small, and it is difficult to assess its role in a wage equation since its major variance comes during the period of decontrol of wages and prices. On the basis of essentially one observation, it is hard to tell whether the wage explosion following the end of controls (a) represented post-controls catch-up and had nothing to do with energy prices, or (b) represented a reaction to an energy price increase (perceived as temporary). In addition, we felt the values of the estimated parameters and the lag structure were implausible for the equation with energy broken out. Finally, the food-plus-energy results reinforced our feelings that the energy estimates were extremely imprecise, in that the ratio of the coefficient on food and energy to the sum of the coefficients on both PCE components was not significantly different from the food and energy weight in the PCE.

The Price Equations

The price equations complete the model of wage-price dynamics. The principal price equation used is in the spirit of the analysis of optimal pricing behavior by Nordhaus (1972). The dependent variable is the change in the log of the implicit deflator for nonfarm output, excluding housing. This is a function of the change in the logarithms of standard unit labor costs, the deviation in labor productivity from its trend, the exogenous prices of farm products and imports (representing materials costs external to the nonfarm sector), and the GNP gap. Capital costs are not included under the assumption that capital and

Table 9.1. Sum of coefficients on distributed lags[a] for *PCE* and components in alternative wage equations (standard errors in parentheses)

Component	Coefficients for alternative specifications		
Total *PCE*	1.05 (0.10)		
PCE less energy		1.28 (0.16)	
Energy component of *PCE*		−0.04 (0.07)	
PCE less food and energy			0.95 (14)
Food and energy component of *PCE*			0.24 (0.10)
Coefficient of determination adjusted for degrees of freedom	0.80	0.82	0.80

a. A 13-quarter third-degree polynominal constrained to zero for the last quarter.

labor cannot be substituted for each other in the short run. Early estimation results led to the acceptance of the hypothesis that only bottlenecks in product markets measured by the change in the GNP gap affect the markup and hence prices and not the level of excess demand or supply itself. One estimate showed that when the current and lagged values of the level of the GNP gap were included in the price equation, the coefficient estimates were of equal magnitude and opposite sign. Some experimentation was done with straight-line productivity trends for use in the standardized unit labor cost variable before we chose (on statistical grounds) an 8-quarter moving average.

To close the wage-price model, we needed an equation relating the output price in the price equation to the consumption price in the wage equation. Since inclusion of a constant term in a specification where variables are measured as percentage changes, or changes in the log, forces one to interpret the coefficient estimates on the independent variables as effects which result from deviations from trend, we decided to remove the constant term. It made little sense to have a trend in this relation. In addition, the specification included the deflator for housing services, which is basically a trend itself. To improve our results, we constrained the coefficient on housing prices to be a fixed weight equal to the average weight housing had in personal consumption over the sample period.

Because we use our model for simulation, it is useful at this point to discuss the expected magnitudes of the sum of the coefficients on the labor and materials cost variables. Nordhaus (1972) has demonstrated that, in a long-run price equation for a firm using a technology characterized by a Cobb-Douglas production function with constant returns to scale and neutral technical progress, the sum of the coefficients on the factor prices (wages, the price of capital, and the price of materials) should be one. We intuited its occurrence in the competitive case because, with constant returns to scale, the long-run industry supply curve is horizontal. In this circumstance, doubling all factor prices doubles the equilibrium output price, whatever the elasticity of demand.

Gordon (1975) has shown that, if technical progress is labor-augmenting, the sum of the coefficients on unit labor costs, the price of capital services, and the price of materials should be one. However, he notes that, by rearranging the terms of this long-run price equation, one can obtain an equation in which (a) the coefficient on unit labor costs itself is one and (b) the sum of the coefficients on unit labor costs, the price of capital services relative to the price of output, and the price of materials relative to the price of output is equal to $1/a_2$, where a_2 is the elasticity of output with respect to labor input from the production function. As Gordon indicates, the choice between the two specifications is contingent upon whether one believes the relative price of capital services and materials is diminished when the wage rate increases (as Nordhaus implicitly assumes), or whether the two relative prices are independent of changes in the wage rate.

Our price equation is a short-run specification, and, by not using as explanatory variables relative prices of farm output and of imports, we have implicitly assumed that the relative price of materials is reduced when the wage rate increases. In the short run, since our wage and price equations represent a reduced form of a more elaborate structural system, the sum of the coefficients on labor and materials costs in general will be less than one if the long-run production function exhibits constant returns to scale. Again, we intuited its occurrence (in a competitive industry) because with an upward sloping short-run industry supply curve, a doubling of the prices of variable inputs will not double the equilibrium industry price unless the industry demand curve is completely inelastic. Similarly, a monopolist with an upward sloping marginal cost curve would not double the price of output if prices of variable inputs doubled.

In this context it is also important to note that the price equation is estimated over a period in which domestic crude oil prices were controlled. The extent to which decontrol of those prices will alter the structure of aggregate price formation is uncertain. Any econometric analysis at an economy-wide level must inevitably ignore imperfections in the markets for the thousands of goods subsumed in the aggregate totals used. Certainly, with decontrol, domestic crude oil prices will become more responsive to increases in the price of imported oil. One can hope that, over the sample period, final goods prices have not been unduly constrained by crude oil price controls, and that decontrol will simply result in the reallocation of value-added among producers as the rent to scarce oil is taken by owners of crude oil. If price controls on domestic oil were viewed as permanent, however, the coefficient on the import price variable in the equation for the nonfarm deflator would be biased downward. In the longer run, the increased cost of domestic crude oil will alter the structure and composition of the capital stock and will therefore alter the properties of the price equation that we estimate.

Estimates

Since prices and wages are simultaneously determined in this model, estimation of the model requires the use of simultaneous equation estimation procedures. The two-stage least-squares technique was employed.

The equations were estimated using quarterly data from 1964:3 to 1978:3. We do not use data beyond 1978:3 because we wish to use postsample simulation to evaluate the impact of the Carter wage and price standards program administered by the Council on Wage and Price Stability (COWPS). There is a general recognition that the structure of the wage equation has been changing over the 1970s (the coefficient on prices has been approaching 1.0 from below and the coefficient on unemployment has been declining in absolute value). The recent paper by Perry (1980) (which uses a sample that extends back to 1954) provides empirical evidence that in the wage equation the intercept and the coefficient on the unemployment rate have changed in the 1970s from earlier periods. Nevertheless, a test of the broader joint hypothesis that the coefficients on *all* variables in the wage equation are the same in the pre- and post-1970 period fails to reject this hypothesis. Hence we use the earlier data to enlarge our degrees of freedom and to improve the precision of the estimates.

The estimated equations are presented in table 9.3. Several items are noteworthy:

(*a*) The sum of the coefficients on the lags in the price expectations variable is not significantly different from 1.0. Thus all expected price changes eventually pass through to hourly compensation. The average lag is 5.6 quarters.

(*b*) The coefficient on the unemployment rate is small, implying that a one-percentage-point increase in the rate of unemployment for males 25 years and older that lasts one year lowers wage inflation by one-half of a percentage point.

(*c*) The coefficient on the social insurance tax variable suggests no shifting of that tax in the short run.

(*d*) The price equation is not accelerationist. The coefficient on standard unit labor costs is 0.69 and is significantly different from 1.0. Further, the sum of the coefficients on unit labor costs, the farm deflator, and import deflator is 0.77, and this sum is also significantly different from 1.[11] This suggests some flexibility of real non-oil prices, even in the long run.

As noted, there is no presumption that the sum of the coefficients on factor prices need be one in a short-run price equation. Yet this sum may be biased downward, for several reasons. Domestic oil price controls may have been perceived as permanent, as discussed above. The import deflator is an imperfect measure of the cost of imported materials, since it reflects the prices of imports

Table 9.2. Definition of variables

Variable	Definition
$DL(X)$	the one-quarter change in the log of X.
$AHEG$	the average hourly earnings index adjusted for overtime and interindustry shift multiplied by the ratio of total compensation to wages and salaries. The index is from the Bureau of Labor Statistics (BLS) establishment survey while compensation and wages and salaries are on a National Income Accounts (NIA) basis from the Bureau of Economic Analysis (BEA).
GAP	the ratio of actual to potential real Gross National Product (GNP).
GTS	the change in the log of the inverse of 1 minus the effective social insurance tax rate, measured as the ratio of total federal, state, and local receipts for social insurance to total compensation: $DL(1/(1-\text{Receipts/Compensation}))$.
$ND12$	1 for 1971:4 to 1972:4, 0 otherwise.
$ND34$	1 for 1973:1 to 1974:1, 0 otherwise.
PC	the implicit deflator for personal consumption expenditure.
PF	the implicit deflator for gross domestic product originating in the agricultural sector.
$PHOUS$	the implicit deflator for housing services in personal consumption expenditures.
PM	the implicit deflator for imports from the NIA.
$PNFXH$	the implicit deflator for nonfarm gross domestic product excluding housing.
$TPROD8$	the ratio of actual output per hour in the private nonfarm sector, all persons, to an 8-quarter moving average in output per hour: $$Q_t \Big/ \left(\frac{1}{8} \sum_{i=0,7} Q_{t-i} \right)$$
$ULC8$	the ratio of $AHEG$ to the 8-quarter moving average in output per hour defined above.
U	the unemployment rate for males 25 years and older.

of consumption goods (some of which, such as oil, are also used as material inputs), expenditures on capital account, and government expenditures. Both of these problems would bias the coefficient on the import deflator downward. The lag distribution on standard unit labor costs has been truncated after the first lag; however, including values of standard unit labor costs lagged two or more periods did not increase the sum of the coefficients on current and lagged standard unit labor costs.

On the other hand, some part of capital costs may in fact be variable in the short run. Excluding them from the equation would tend to bias the sum of the coefficients on factor prices upward.[12]

(e) If we assume that productivity growth is on trend, the GNP gap is fixed, the implicit social insurance tax rate is unchanging, and all prices rise at the same rate, we can calculate the steady state properties of the model. On those assumptions, our two price equations become

Table 9.3. Two-stage least-squares estimates of wage and price equations: quarterly data from 1964:3 to 1978:3

Dependent variable	Coefficients (standard errors)		
	$DL(AHEG)$	$DL(PNFXH)$	$DL(PC) - 0.155$ $\times DL(PHOUS)$
Constant	0.0092 (0.0011)	0.0025 (0.0011)	
$DL(PC)$	0.40 (0.13)		
Sum of coefficients on lagged $DL(PC)$	0.62 (0.16)		
$ND12$	0.0013 (0.00097)	−0.0021 (0.0017)	−0.0015 (0.0012)
$ND34$	−0.0048 (0.0012)	0.0013 (0.002)	−0.00075 (0.0017)
U	−0.0013 (0.0005)		
GTS	0.59 (0.084)		
$DL(ULC8)$		0.44 (0.15)[a]	
$DL(ULC8)_{t-1}$		0.25 (0.12)	
$DL(PF)$		−0.033 (0.0086)	0.033 (0.0064)
$DL(PM)$			0.076 (0.018)
$DL(PM)_{t-1}$		0.064 (0.025)	
$DL(PM)_{t-2}$		0.048 (0.026)	
$DL(TPROD8)$		−0.24 (0.073)	
$DL(GAP)$		0.12 (0.061)	
$DL(PNFXH)$			0.62 (0.061)[a]
$DL(PNFXH)_{t-1}$			0.054 (0.057)
$\bar{R}^2$	0.82	0.82	0.82
Durbin-Watson statistic	1.99	2.19	2.37

a. Endogenous variable.

$$PN\dot{F}XH = .00245 + .684\,(A\dot{H}EG - \dot{Q}^*) + .078\,PN\dot{F}XH \text{ and} \qquad (9.1)$$

$$\dot{P}C = .942\,PN\dot{F}XH, \qquad (9.2)$$

where $\dot{Q}^*$ is trend quarterly growth in labor productivity. By substituting equation (7) into (8), we get

$$\dot{P}C = .0025 + .699\,(A\dot{H}EG - \dot{Q}^*), \qquad (9.3)$$

which can in turn be substituted into the wage equation to get:

$$A\dot{H}EG = .0412 - .00448\,U - 2.50\,\dot{Q}^*. \qquad (9.4)$$

If, for example, we assume a growth in labor productivity of 1.25 percent per year, we can calculate that when the unemployment rate for males 25 years and older is 3.6 percent (and the total unemployment rate is about 6 percent), the annual rate of increase of wages would be about 7.1 percent; of output prices, about 5.4 percent; and of consumer prices, about 5.1 percent.

(f) The model estimated is a damped wage-price spiral. Figure 9.2 shows this rather dramatically. It shows the time path of the change in the dependent

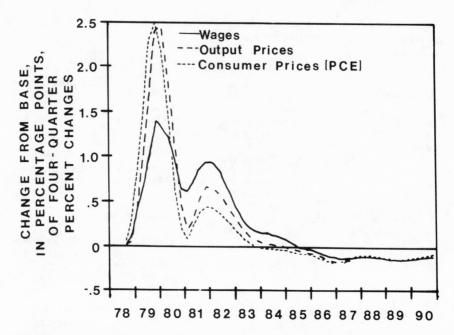

Figure 9.2. Simulated consequences for wages and consumer and output prices of increases in imported oil prices of 100% from 78:4 to 79:4 and of 9% per year thereafter

variables that would follow a 100-percent rise in oil prices over a 1-year period from 1978:4. It assumes the monetary authorities accommodate and then restrict so as to keep the GNP gap and unemployment rate constant; that is, in setting the monetary aggregates, the authorities are assumed to allow for any lowering of productivity and potential GNP due to the oil-price shock.[13] These simulations suggest that, though it may take three or four years, the impact of the shock would eventually die out once the preshock growth rate of oil prices was reestablished and that the inflation rate would not be ratcheted upward. This may appear to have happened only because of the frequency of the shocks and the length of the lags.

To be sure, this result is derived from a short-run equation, and this equation comes from a structure that does not include a reaction function for OPEC pricing based on expected inflation in industrial countries. However, given that the sum of the estimated coefficients on the variable factor prices is less than one, incorporation of this feature would not alter the basic result that an oil-price shock would have no ultimate effect on the inflation rate; only the length of time needed for dampening out the effect of the shock would change. Similarly, inclusion of a direct impact of monetary growth on expected inflation in the model would lengthen the time needed for dampening the effect of the shock, as long as any accommodation were only temporary. A definitive assessment of the effects of an oil shock on the inflation rate involves the estimation of a structure that specifies not only the determination of materials prices, but also the determination of the price of capital services.

Such an assessment also requires consideration of the insights of the "credibility" and "rational expectations" views of the inflation process.[14] The simulation of a model with unchanging coefficients under an assumption of monetary accommodation to an oil-price shock inevitably suffers from ignoring the impact of the policy-response assumption on coefficients of the model, an effect emphasized by both hypotheses. As Gramlich (1979:156) notes, however, "going from this view (that likely policy responses to external shocks are potentially important in influencing price and wage equations) to a knowledge of exactly how standard models of the inflationary process must be modified to deal with the phenomena is a far more difficult step."

Gramlich also concludes that the considerations determining the optimal policy response to an external shock in a rational-expectations model are broadly similar to those in a standard model—unless the Federal Reserve's inside information lag is long relative to the contract period, in which case it should do nothing.[15] The principal difference between the two models lies in the difference in the length of time that shock-induced inflation or unemployment persists. This time period, substantial in standard models, is brief in rational-expectations models—though even in the latter models (Taylor, 1980), the more accommodative the monetary policy, the longer inflation pressures persist.

Evaluation of Carter Wage and Price Standards

To the extent that our model has captured the structure of wage-price dynamics and that structure remains unchanged, our model can be simulated forward to see whether events like the imposition of President Carter's voluntary pay and price standards[16] have had any impact. A number of problems exist with such procedures and we refer the reader to Blinder and Newton (1978) for an excellent discussion of the issues. As figures 9.3 and 9.4 show, our equations overpredict wages but not prices and, if taken by themselves, might suggest that the program had no effect on prices and some effect in suppressing wages. Figure 9.4 hints that during the first program year the price standard may have permitted firms to increase prices faster than in the absence of the standard, so it allowed them to pass through "uncontrollable" cost increases more rapidly than they otherwise would have. But the difference between actual and predicted values is slight, and one might expect firms to exert more effort today to pass on materials costs than they did on average during the entire sample period.

We would expect the wage effect to have been mostly in the nonunion sector. Though COWPS monitored union wage settlements more closely, its prospective evaluations of cost-of-living escalators at an unrealistically (in retrospect)

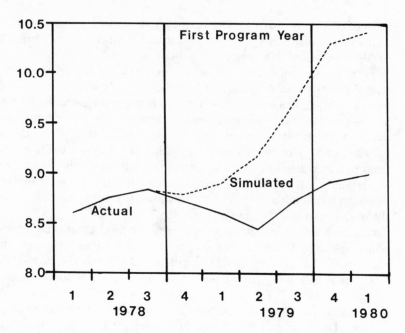

Figure 9.3. Four-quarter percent changes in wages: actual and simulated

low level let union members have substantially larger increases than nonunion members. COWPS has estimated that something like three-fourths of the slippage from the wage standards in the covered sector was due to the COLA, cost-of-living adjustment, problem.

Our finding that, by the beginning of the second program year, COWPS may have kept the increase in wages (measured from the same quarter in the previous year) almost 1.5 percentage points lower than predicted is likely an upper limit on the effect of the program for at least two reasons. First, there was a large influx of youth and women into the labor market; because of their limited experience, in part, these groups tend to have low wages. Their entry into the labor market changed the implicit demographic weights of the index. That could account for perhaps one-third of the overprediction.[17] Second, if energy price expectations really should have a smaller weight in the wage equation (see the discussion above), that would also cause the equation to overpredict.

Though our simulations do not extend through the end of the second program year (and the dissolution of COWPS by the Reagan administration), it is clear that the impact of the program diminished over time. Such is the fate of all attempts to control incomes: emerging distortions require relaxation of the controls—or less compliance, in a voluntary program—if efficiency is not to be adversely affected. Indeed, it is possible that incomes lost due to the program

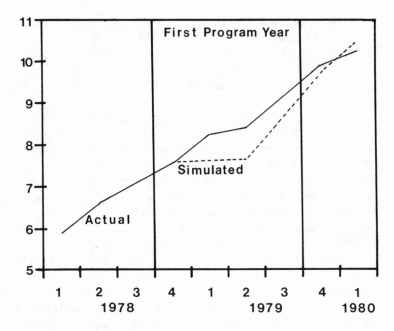

Figure 9.4. Four-quarter percent changes in the PCE deflator: actual and simulated

were recouped in 1980 and 1981; Blinder and Newton (1978) reported such a result for the Nixon Economic Stabilization Program.

Conclusion

Our model allows us to put some bounds on the effect of the pay and price standards in the first 18 months of their operation. The estimation results also suggest that a feasible policy response to an OPEC shock may be to attempt to wait out its effects on the inflation rate, which are ultimately likely to be transitory. Because an external price shock does not ratchet upward the trend rate of inflation, economic policy need not attempt to offset the effects of the shock by squeezing wages and profit margins. Rather, it can aim, as in our simulations, at holding the GNP gap on its expected trajectory before the shock occurred.

Several caveats to this prescription are appropriate. Economic policy is not made in the absence of political pressures, and it would be difficult for policy-makers to sustain an unchanged policy stance for the apparently long period of time needed for the bubble in the general inflation rate caused by an oil-price shock to dissipate. The maintenance of a neutral or accommodating stance for an extended period could damage policymakers' credibility as inflation fighters. Further, as with all empirical estimates, these results are subject to some degree of imprecision; the bubble in the inflation rate may dissipate more quickly than suggested here. Conceivably, it may not dissipate at all.

Given these warnings, policymakers who are averse to risking higher inflation may well shift the stance of aggregate demand policy slightly toward restraint. However, the proper timing and magnitude of such shifts will be complicated by data and recognition lags in the process of formulating policy, as the experience with the implementation of the credit control program in the spring of 1980 suggests (CEA, 1981: 160). Whatever the short-run problems that confront the design of aggregate demand policy are, policy officials will certainly work to reduce adjustment lags in the determination of wages and prices and to limit the vulnerability of the economy to future shocks.

The recent glut in world oil markets confirms the transitory character of the 1979 oil shock, and the consequent slowdown in inflation suggests the appropriateness of an "even keel" aggregate-demand policy. However, this sunnier turn of events does not imply that inflation will continue to slow, or that the 1980s will be free of further oil shocks. Political uncertainties in the Middle East together with the pivotal role of Saudi Arabia in the OPEC cartel raise the specter of future oil market disruptions. A steady aggregate-demand policy response to future shocks can avoid unnecessary losses in output and employment. Indeed, by reacting in a measured fashion, policymakers can improve popular support for a longer, sustained effort to lower the trend rate of inflation.

10. The Political Economy of Wage and Price Regulation: The Case of the Carter Pay-Price Standards

W. Kip Viscusi

Abstract

During the final two years of the Carter administration, the Council on Wage and Price Stability (COWPS) administered President Carter's incomes policy, which took the form of a "voluntary" pay-price standards program. Unlike the Nixon Economic Stabilization Program, the standards program was not enforced with legal sanctions. Moreover, the standards did not serve primarily as the basis for a high-level jawboning effort, as in the case of the Kennedy-Johnson guideposts. Instead, the emphasis was on identifying the firms violating the standards, using the sanction of adverse publicity to promote restraint. The effectiveness of the publicity sanction deteriorated the more frequently it was used, thus affecting the stringency of the standards and their enforcement. Econometric evidence based on fairly conventional wage and price models fails to indicate any direct effect of the program on prices, although wage increases may have been dampened. The dampening of the rate of wage increases coincided with the impact of the energy price shock on the economy, which suggests that it may have been the energy price shock, not the standards, which restrained wage increases. This explanation is consistent with firm-specific data submitted to the council. Although it is difficult to disentangle these influences reliably, there appears to be no clear-cut evidence of any substantial anti-inflationary effect.

The weakness of the program derived in part from the absence of an effective enforcement sanction. The more fundamental problem, however, was that the standards were never fully integrated into an effective anti-inflation strategy, but were initiated in part simply to serve a political role as "the president's anti-inflation program."

The chief domestic policy problem faced by President Jimmy Carter during his term and in his bid for reelection was inflation. The severity of this problem was reflected in the escalation of inflation rates throughout his administration, with monthly rates of increase reaching levels unprecedented in the post–World War II economy. Whereas double-digit inflation rates had long been regarded as politically unacceptable, Carter administration officials frequently expressed the hope that inflation would eventually return to a double-digit threshold of about 10 percent.

President Carter pursued two methods for reducing inflation—an incomes policy without legal sanctions and a program of fiscal and credit restraint. The Carter pay-price standards program was established in the fourth quarter of 1978 to establish voluntary limits on wage and price increase and to serve as "the president's anti-inflation program." When inflation continued to accelerate, Carter augmented this policy with a program of budgetary and credit restraint in early 1980. I shall focus my remarks here on the design of the pay-price standards program, its relation to the other economic policies, and its effect on inflation.

Differences in views regarding the efficacy of incomes policies are more sharply defined than are opinions on most economic policies. Critics of wage and price restraint maintain that these efforts can only produce an illusory, temporary dampening of wage and price increases, and that the cost of this restraint is a distortion in market-determined wages and prices. Advocates of controls note that inflation also produces inefficiencies, and that incomes policies can augment the decelerating effect of fiscal and monetary policies by overcoming downward rigidity in wages and prices. The most enthusiastic incomes policy proponents maintain, somewhat implausibly, that controls can permanently reduce inflation irrespective of the presence of more fundamental changes in fiscal and monetary policy. This optimistic view has obvious political appeal, since it frees policymakers from the need for budgetary restraint or tight money policies.

Throughout the duration of the Carter pay-price standards program, the viability of this voluntary effort was questioned. Indeed, shortly after Carter lost the 1980 election, the administration's own tripartite Pay Advisory Committee urged that the standards program be abolished: "The present 'voluntary program' has lost its capacity to command effective support. Inflation has been too high and enduring and the regulations too complex and artificial. The guidelines do not deal with many of the factors which have been responsible for the current inflation, including food, housing, interest rates, energy, medical, and other costs. Moreover, the program has done little to focus the imagination and creativity of business and labor on genuine problems of individual sectors."[1]

This chapter examines both the structure and performance of the Carter incomes policy. I begin with an overview of the design and structure of the program, since these factors largely determined its effectiveness and the kinds of inadequacies cited by the Pay Advisory Committee. The question whether the program actually reduced inflation can best be addressed with an econometric model that assesses the discrepancy between actual rates of inflation and those that would have been predicted in the absence of the program. This question provides the focus for the latter half of the chapter.

Although our subject here is the anti-inflationary policies of the Carter administration, many of the economic policy issues it raises have been confronted throughout the past decade. The Nixon administration also attempted to limit the overall inflationary impact of an energy price shock through a formal incomes policy. In each case, the price standards made some allowance for the direct, uncontrollable impact of energy price increases, while at the same time they attempted to moderate the indirect effect of the shock on prices and wages.

More recently, the Reagan administration has abandoned the incomes policy approach and has coupled substantial inflationary tax cuts with restrictive monetary policies and budgetary restraint. The latter anti-inflationary components of the Reagan policy are reminiscent of the budget cut–credit control policy adopted by Carter in early 1980. To the extent that a deceleration in inflation has occurred during 1982, it has been caused by a dissipation of the impact of the energy price shock, as petroleum prices have remained stable. Various measures of the underlying rate of inflation, which will be the focus of my analysis, have remained around the double-digit level. The deceleration in the rate of increase in the Consumer Price Index (CPI) has been due to transitory influences and significantly overstates the extent to which there has been progress in reducing inflation. The public's deeply embedded inflationary expectations are reflected in the extremely high level of interest rates (20 percent prime rate in September 1981) and in the skepticism that greeted the Reagan economic package.

There is now widespread belief that historically high levels of inflation will continue and that, given our long-run susceptibility to energy price shocks, there are likely to be future repetitions of the recent inflation experience. Since incomes policies represent a targeted anti-inflation strategy and may arouse less political opposition than additional budget cuts or monetary restraint, it is likely that they will remain an important policy instrument. Indeed, the Reagan administration, which has forsworn the use of controls, has adopted a limited incomes policy through its decision to fire the striking air traffic controllers and to limit federal pay increases to 4.8 percent. Each of these actions will affect inflationary expectations and other wage increases.

The intent of my analysis is to address the issues raised by more formal incomes policies. Many aspects of the design of the Carter effort were quite innovative but, as I shall indicate, the fundamental aspects of the approach were so seriously flawed that there was little economic benefit from the program. Nevertheless, the standards policy may have served a short-term political purpose, and it is this political motivation for incomes policies which will shape their overall structure.

An Overview of the Standards Program

From the fourth quarter of 1978 through 1980, the Carter administration had a formal incomes policy. The program consisted of a set of voluntary pay and price standards issued and administered by the Council on Wage and Price Stability (COWPS). Operationally, this effort closely resembled the Nixon mandatory controls program.[2] Formal standards were issued; companies were required to report their actual and allowable wage and price increases on the basis of complex provisions for determining increases that were chargeable against the standards; firms with special problems had to negotiate formal exceptions from the council; the exceptions granted and adjustments made to the standards became the basis for future interpretation of the standards within this legalistic system; and finally, noncompliers were subjected to sanctions—principally, adverse publicity. In short, the program had all the trappings of a rigid mandatory controls program, save one. It had no legal sanction to promote compliance. Moreover, unlike the Kennedy-Johnson guideposts, this voluntary standards program did not serve as the basis for a high-level jawboning effort.[3]

A major weakness of this approach, as the Pay Advisory Committee observed, was that restraint of wages and prices was not linked to other economic policies targeted at specific sectors. The administration's other economic policies often had a sectoral focus—for example, the bailout of the Chrysler Corporation, relief efforts for the auto and steel industries, various import restrictions, and the planned revitalization program for American industry. The purpose of these initiatives, however, was not to restrain inflation, but to aid depressed industries. Since one objective of these policies was to secure the support of organized labor in the 1980 election, efforts to secure wage rollbacks or other meaningful restraints were not consistent with the political spirit of these undertakings.

A notable exception was the success of Alfred E. Kahn, inflation advisor to the president and chairman of COWPS, in the Chrysler bailout case. At Kahn's insistence the administration modified its bailout provisions to include $250 million in wage reductions for Chrysler workers, whose wages had risen much faster than the industrial average, in both relative and in absolute terms. Kahn effected the wage rollback provisions after he publicly diverged from what Secretary of the Treasury Miller regarded as the consensus administration position, which called for no wage restraint. The difficulties Kahn encountered in achieving wage restraint as part of the bailout action reflected the general unwillingness of the administration to integrate the anti-inflation effort into its broader economic program.

Beginning in the second quarter of 1980, a sustained attempt was made to establish an industry-based focus for the anti-inflation program through a series of bi-weekly White House meetings with industry leaders. Organized and run by Alfred Kahn, these sessions included a brief appearance by President Carter and participation of two cabinet officials (including Kahn). The initial meetings received substantial press coverage and thus provided additional support for an incomes policy that relied almost exclusively on the sanction of adverse publicity. While these sessions were often linked to regulatory policies, the political environment before the election made it infeasible to link the standards program with sectoral economic policies, thus limiting their potential impact. After the brunt of the recession had made the council's price standards unconstraining for virtually all firms, the industry meetings were terminated in the summer of 1980.

An institutional mechanism that might have been used to integrate the incomes policy with sectoral economic policies was the Pay Advisory Committee, which was established in 1979. This tripartite group was chaired by John Dunlop and included leading representatives of business, labor, and the general public. The committee's principal task was to recommend changes in the council's pay standard and to review all council actions regarding the standard. Unlike the Price Advisory Committee, which consisted only of public representatives, the Pay Advisory Committee exerted a powerful influence over the design and operation of the standards. From the outset the COWPS staff, then headed by council director R. Robert Russell, viewed the Pay Advisory Committee as a threat to the standards program and, as a result, resisted all efforts by the committee to modify the pay standard.[4] Almost invariably, the council's attempts to oppose the changes in the standard were unsuccessful.

The prevailing emphasis on specific aspects of the standards, rather than on ways in which the influence of the Pay Advisory Committee could be integrated into the anti-inflation effort, represents a major shortcoming of the Carter program. Cooperative efforts between COWPS and the committee were rare, the principal exception being John Dunlop's intervention in construction industry wage settlements. The dominant view among the COWPS staff was that any cooperative venture was inconceivable, since they assumed that the committee's sole purpose was to dismantle the program. Whether these fears were warranted or were simply a reaction to the threat the committee posed to their own influence is unclear. Since the pay standard that resulted from the protracted conflicts was not a restraining influence after the shift in fiscal and credit policies in 1980:1, it seems clear in retrospect that the failure to use the committee in a more constructive fashion was a major foregone opportunity.

Conflicts between the COWPS staff and the committee also may have undermined the council's effectiveness within the administration. Problems were typically resolved (in the committee's favor) by the cabinet-level Economic Policy Group, a pattern which weakened the council's credibility and diverted attention from more fundamental issues of program design.

A second critical determinant of the success of the program was its enforcement mechanism—principally the use of adverse publicity for noncompliers. In many respects this sanction is analogous to quality-grading schemes for consumer goods; the difference is that certification of noncompliance is intended to communicate a relatively high price for the product rather than a relatively low quality for the price. Similarly, the pay standard strengthens employers' bargaining power by providing an objective index against which to measure wage demands.

Firms will comply with the standards if the gains from doing so exceed the possible losses, when the effect of the enforcement sanction is taken into account. Since the degree of noncompliance could not be precisely conveyed without disclosing confidential information, the magnitude of the publicity threat tended not to depend on the extent of the violation.[5] When the magnitude of the sanction does not increase with the size of the violation, the sanction will be most effective when the extent of noncompliance is small. But during the initial stages of the program, the legal staff responsible for negotiating settlements disregarded small violations of the standards in order to focus on large violations. As a result, the emphasis fell on cases where little progress could be made, and cases where a modest sanction could have been effective were ignored.[6]

This difficulty arose in part from the administrative structure of the council. Unlike the Office of Price Administration in World War II, the program failed to integrate its legal and technical staffs.[7] Negotiations with companies found to be out of compliance were the responsibility of a staff unit composed entirely of lawyers, while the policy staff that designed and evaluated the program, and the technical staff that evaluated a firm's compliance status, were not involved in the negotiations once companies were found to be out of compliance. This decentralization, combined with the autonomy of the legal staff, prevented the misplaced emphasis of the enforcement effort from being identified earlier.

The publicity sanction has an additional limitation, since its value deteriorates the more frequently it is used. In the extreme case in which all firms are out of compliance, the publicity sanction becomes completely ineffective because noncompliance is the norm. To prevent unraveling of this type, officials kept the number of cited noncompliers relatively small, with fewer than 20 firms listed as noncompliers for either the pay standard or the price standard.[8] As the number of noncompliers increased, an effort was made to prevent further deterioration of the publicity sanction by encouraging companies to take corrective actions, which the council would regard as a substitute for price restraint in the period of price violations. Companies could thus avoid being cited for noncompliance by promising additional future price restraint, without having to roll back past price increases that had violated the standards. A quantitative summary of these actions involving noncompliers is provided in table 10.1; for both the pay and price standards most noncompliance decisions were issued in the three-quarter period 1979:3–1980:1.

Since compliance with the standards clearly provides a binding constraint during periods of noncompliance and may not be binding during the subsequent period in which the corrective action is taken, corrective actions will usually produce less restraint than compliance in the violation period will. The flurry of corrective pricing actions during 1980:2 pushed this general principle to its extreme. Since firms could avoid making amends for price violations in earlier quarters by adopting more stringent standards in a major recessionary period (in which price standard was not binding), the incentive for firms to undertake corrective actions was enhanced. The press, however, widely portrayed these

Table 10.1. Noncompliance decisions and corrective actions for pay/price standards

	Noncompliance decisions		Corrective actions	
	Pay	Price[a]	Pay	Price
1978:4	0	0	0	0
1979:1	0	0	0	0
1979:2	0	1	0	1
1979:3	4	4	1	0
1979:4	6	3	3	2
1980:1	5	5	3	2
1980:2	0	3	1	9
1980:3[b]	2	2	0	3

a. Noncompliance decisions for the price standard include only listed noncompliers since many of the preliminary decisions were reversed.
b. These data are preliminary and pertain to only part of the quarter.

corrective actions as meaningless, and thereby diminished the credibility of the program and undermined its publicity sanction.

The final sanction against noncompliers was the requirement for all firms bidding on federal contracts of $5 million or more to certify that they were in compliance with the standards. But this condition was waived when it could not be met, so that no contracts were ever denied on this basis; noncomplying firms were awarded these contracts because of alleged overriding national needs. The pressure to grant these contracts was often so great that this sanction may actually have given more leverage in the noncompliance negotiations to noncomplying firms than to the council.

The inadequacies of these sanctions were well known and, in 1980:1, the council proposed to the Economic Policy Group that it be given the authority to suspend and delay wage and price increases. This proposal, like all other suggestions that resembled mandatory controls, was ruled out, since Senator Edward Kennedy's campaign against Carter was based in part on advocacy of a controls program. For its anti-inflation policy, the Carter administration opted instead for a program of credit restraint and budget cutbacks, which contributed to the 1980 recession.

Further, the council's reliance on a weak publicity sanction dictated the stringency of the standards. Both the basic level of the standard and the subsequent adjustments made by the council were designed to be constraining, but not to be so strict that rampant noncompliance would result. If the number of noncompliers had become quite large, the value of the publicity sanction would have been eroded.

The standards were issued in program years, with the first program year beginning in 1978:4, the second in 1979:4, and the ninth and final quarter of the program taking effect in 1980:4. The pay standard differed little from a simple numerical limit on rates of wage and salary increase. During the first program year, average rates of pay increase, excluding overtime and Social Security taxes, were not to exceed 7 percent. This standard was raised to a 7.5–9.5 percent range in the second program year and in the ninth quarter of the program. Allowance for the valuation of cost-of-living adjustments, the costing out of fringe benefits, and various exceptions led to considerable variation in the effective standard. In the first program year, for example, workers with average rates of pay increase above 14 percent received adjustments of 8.05 percent, which were sufficient to bring their firms into compliance with the pay standard.

The price standard was considerably more complex. Although the council had overall price increase objectives—6.5 percent in the first program year—there was no simple numerical limitation of prices. In addition to a basic price standard, there were also special standards for certain sectors (e.g., a gross-margin standard for petroleum refiners) as well as a variety of exceptions for unusual economic conditions. Chief among these exceptions was an alternative profit-margin limitation available to firms with uncontrollable costs. Exogenous price shocks, principally energy costs, could be passed through in most instances.

The design of the standards had many innovative features. The focus on average pay and price increases rather than on individual increases provided leeway for relative price and wage adjustment. In addition, the profit-margin exception under the price standard provided for dollar-for-dollar cost pass-through (in certain ranges) rather than percentage-cost pass-through as under the Nixon program, and thus avoided supplying the perverse incentives for a firm to increase its costs in order to raise its total allowable profits.

Despite these advances, shortcomings endemic to all incomes policies remained. One problem that grew worse over time was that of firms with unrepresentative base periods. When the base period used for compliance purpose (i.e., for calculating average rates of pay and price change) resulted in major inequities, it was often modified on an ad hoc basis. More fundamental was the problem of granting exceptions to firms for which the standards had created major inefficiencies. Since all controls programs induce market distortions, policymakers need a much stronger conceptual basis than now exists for selecting which inefficiencies to generate in the pursuit of price restraint.[9]

Some judgments along these lines were made as part of the monitoring strategy. Prices set in auction markets, for example, were exempted from coverage. In particular, there was no monitoring of prices of food at the farm, crude oil, raw materials with prices set in open markets, forestry and fishery products, interest rates, medical care, or individual home sales. In addition, to limit the reporting burdens, during most of the program only firms with $250 million or more in revenues and employee units of more than 5,000 employees were required to report to the council.

Even with such exemptions, it is not clear whether a formalistic program

Table 10.2. Rates of change in wages and prices (annualized quarterly increases)

Period	CPI	PCE	PCE'	PAY	Ave. hourly earnings index
1978:1	7.7	7.7	6.5	10.4	8.7
1978:2	9.5	9.6	7.3	8.4	8.7
1978:3	9.2	7.1	6.9	8.0	7.9
1978:4	9.5	7.5	6.7	8.2	8.3
1979:1	11.2	10.9	7.8	9.9	8.2
1979:2	12.8	10.1	6.8	7.8	7.1
1979:3	13.4	11.4	7.8	8.9	8.4
1979:4	13.6	10.4	8.4	8.9	8.5
1980:1	16.9	13.9	10.7	10.2	9.4
1980:2	13.7	11.0	10.4	11.0	9.9

without effective sanctions can serve as much more than a form of systematic harassment of the private sector. The pervasive attitude at the council was that it was essential to make firms "jump through hoops" in order to make them aware of the consequences of their wage and price decisions. This view is compelling only if the required paperwork and formal company meeting do in fact increase companies' assessment of the effectiveness of the monitoring and enforcement process, and do raise the expected cost of noncompliance. Whether the council standards actually created more awareness and different outcomes than would have been achieved through the powerful forces of the market is an issue that can be tested empirically, as is discussed below.

Empirical Evidence: The Model and the Variables

The context in which the Carter administration's pay and price standards operated can best be understood by analyzing the data in table 10.2.[10] The first three columns present alternative measures of the rate of price increase: the Consumer Price Index (CPI), the fixed-weighted personal consumption expenditures index (PCE), and the PCE underlying rate (PCE'). The PCE is constructed from the CPI after excluding the home purchase and mortgage interest component. The PCE', which will be the focus of the empirical analysis, removes from the PCE the costs of food and energy. Thus PCE and PCE' focus on narrower sectors of the economy than does the CPI. The final two columns of table 10.2 provide measures of rates of pay increase. The first measure is an index of total compensation (PAY), which will be described in detail below, while the second is the average hourly earnings index.

The advent of the pay-price standards program did not produce a discontinuous decline in any of the rates of pay or price increase. Rates of price increase accelerated sharply, particularly for the CPI and PCE, as the energy price shock and rising costs of home purchase and interest resulted in sharply higher prices. The underlying rate of inflation, as reflected in PCE′, did not show this rapid acceleration until 1980, when effects of the energy price shocks began to spread to other sectors of the economy. The wage data are more difficult to interpret since the quarterly fluctuations are so irregular. For the total compensation variable PAY, rates of increase were identical in 1978 and 1979—8.7 percent. The more rapid rates of increase in 1980 represent a marked acceleration of pay increases.

The fundamental issue is whether these wage and price increases were dampened by the standards program. One index of the possible effectiveness of the program is the degree of noncompliance. If violations were rampant, one could conclude that the program was not successful. Over the course of the program, however, the number of noncompliers remained relatively modest. Moreover, actual rates of wage and price increase were concentrated just below the rates of increase permitted under the standards.[11] Evidence such as this, however, is not a particularly powerful test of the program's effectiveness, since compliance with the standards does not imply that the standards were binding. Compliance might be observed even if the standards were too lenient to have any restraining effect.

The clustering of firms' rates just below the allowable rates of pay and price increase is in part a statistical artifact, attributable to the manner in which the standard was set and to the endogeneity of the amount of adjustments and exceptions. Since the council designed and administered the standards so as to result in only a modest degree of noncompliance, the actions of the COWPS staff tended to produce a clustering of adjusted rates of pay and price increase near their allowable levels. Firms seeking exceptions from the council generally bargained for sufficient adjustments to bring them into compliance. Those firms that were in compliance without taking advantage of the exceptions and adjustments to which they were entitled seldom bothered to calculate the full increases that were allowable under the standards; as a result, the observed discrepancies between actual and allowable increases understate the actual difference.

Finally, even if the noncompliance patterns were meaningful, one could not rule out the possibility that the standards had a floor effect; e.g., workers might bargain for larger wage increases than they would have if the pay standard had not set a high wage increase target. Mayor Edward Koch, for example, feared that the floor effect might influence the wage demands of municipal workers in New York City.

A more meaningful test of the program's effectiveness compares the actual rates of pay and price increase with what one would predict on the basis of an econometric model. Two principal approaches are possible—the simulation approach and the use of some explicit measure to estimate the program's effectiveness directly. With a simulation technique, pre-COWPS equations are used to predict pay and price increases, and the impact of the standards is measured by the discrepancy between these predicted values and their actual levels. The net effect of the shifts in the constant term and in the regression coefficients is then attributed to the role of the standards.

The alternative approach is to add a proxy for the standards—usually some form of dummy variable—into equations estimated for the program period. This technique is useful if the impact of the program is indicated by a shift term rather than by changes in other coefficients of the model. If the coefficients in the model change for reasons other than the impact of the standards, both these techniques may yield inaccurate results. In view of the unusual economic conditions that have prevailed since the program's inception, one should be cautious in evaluating the resulting estimates of program effectiveness.

The basic wage and price equations used were formed in the general spirit of other analyses in this area.[12] Most previously estimated equations differ by relatively inconsequential types of product differentiation (such as the particular variable selected to reflect labor market tightness). The most important difference between the equations considered here and those in the literature is that I have included the influence of energy prices as exogenously determined explanatory variables; in the absence of these energy variables, one cannot distinguish the effect of the energy price shock from the contemporaneous effect of the standards. In addition, I have introduced a variety of policy variables to reflect the impact of the standards, instead of relying on a simple dummy variable, in those equations in which the effect of the program is estimated explicitly.

The analysis below estimates wage and price equations by using quarterly data from 1964:2 to 1980:2.[13] The dependent variable for the wage equation is the rate of increase in total compensation (PAY), including fringe benefits and employers' Social Security tax payments.[14]

Explanatory variables were included to reflect the influence of price inflation, labor market disequilibrium, Social Security taxes, and incomes policies. The first of these variables is past inflation rates, which affect inflationary expectations and the real value of any nominal wage increase. The price variable used was the rate of increase in the fixed-weighted personal consumption expenditures index (PCE), which was constructed from the CPI after excluding the home purchase and mortgage interest component (a misleading index of the current price of housing services). The long-term nature of the formation of price expectations was captured by including a PCE price variable for the current quarter and for each quarter of the previous three years.[15]

Labor market disequilibrium is reflected by the inverse of the unemployment rate for males aged 25–54 (1/UE). This demographic component of unemployment is a more reliable index of labor market conditions than are broader indices, which are distorted by shifts in the composition of the unemployment (notably the increase in black youth unemployment). An increase in 1/UE, or equivalently a decrease in the unemployment rate, reflects a tighter labor market and should lead to more rapid rates of wage increase.

The pay increase equation also included a Social Security tax variable (SSTAX), since Social Security tax payments have become an increasingly important wage component. The SSTAX variable has been constructed so that a coefficient of 1.0 will indicate that, in the short run, the employer bears all of the employer's payroll tax share.[16] The long-run incidence of the tax may, of course, be quite different.

The role of the Nixon Economic Stabilization Program from 1971:3 to 1974:2 is captured by a weighted dummy variable for phases I and II (ESP1) and by a similar variable for phases III and IV (ESP2).[17] During phase II the Pay Board was established, its members walked off, and the board was reconstituted. During phase III the Pay Board was merged with the Cost of Living Council. To reflect a possible wage rebound after the program, a dummy variable for the year following controls (CATCHUP) has been included.

With the simulation technique, no explicit COWPS variable is included, because the equation is estimated for the preprogram period only. For direct estimation of program effects, one would wish ideally to construct a variable reflecting the expected cost of noncompliance, since that will determine firms' behavior. Here I have used a simple 0–1 dummy variable (COWPS) to capture the program's effectiveness. Later I shall explore the implications of alternative measures.

The price equation did not focus on the entire CPI, since many components of the CPI were not covered by the program or were only partially monitored. Whereas most price equations in the literature focus on the PCE, I have excluded food and energy costs from the PCE (which already excludes home purchase costs) to create a PCE underlying rate (PCE') that would more adequately reflect program coverage. The PCE' variable, then, serves as a more meaningful measure of the prices directly influenced by the program. But if the standards program did restrain these prices, one must then ascertain whether prices in the excluded components rose more than they would have in the absence of the program. Since all experiments using the PCE variable rather than the PCE' variable failed to indicate any program affect, the results below should be viewed as the most favorable case for the program.

Firms' markup of prices by a fraction of unit labor costs is a fundamental determinant of price trends in most price models. This study uses the current change in unit labor cost (ULCOST) and its value lagged in one quarter (ULCOST1). The wage component of the unit labor cost increase is based on the PAY variable, while the productivity component is a trend productivity measure.[18]

The role of energy price increases was entered explicitly into the equation, since energy price shocks were principal contributors to overall price behavior during the program period. More specifically, the equation included the energy price component of the CPI lagged two and three quarters (ENERGY2, ENERGY3.)[19] The inclusion of these variables represents a departure from traditional price equations estimated for earlier periods in which energy price shocks were not prevalent.

Table 10.3. PAY regression results* coefficients and *t* statistics

Independent variables	OLS		TSLS	
	1	2	3	4
Constant	+1.81 (2.49)	+1.91 (2.66)	+1.79 (2.43)	+1.88 (2.57)
PCE	+0.84 (4.02)	+0.83 (4.34)	+0.84 (3.67)	+0.83 (3.91)
1/UE	+3.08 (2.34)	+2.89 (2.23)	+3.20 (2.40)	+3.07 (2.32)
SSTAX	+1.10 (7.55)	+1.10 (7.77)	+1.13 (7.58)	+1.14 (7.85)
ESP1	+0.64 (1.54)	+0.61 (1.49)	+0.59 (1.40)	+0.55 (1.32)
ESP2	−1.95 (−3.52)	−1.82 (−3.39)	−1.64 (−2.87)	−1.46 (−2.62)
CATCHUP	−0.02 (−0.03)	−0.18 (−0.24)	−0.22 (−0.29)	−0.39 (−0.52)
CWPS	—	−1.13 (−2.22)	—	−0.95 (−1.82)
$\bar{R}^2$	0.82	0.83	0.82	0.83
SEE	0.87	0.86	0.88	0.88
D-W	1.95	1.93	1.93	1.93

* The PCE coefficients pertain to the sum of values for the distributed lag, and the *t* statistics for PCE pertain to the ratio of the sum of the coefficients to the sum of the standard errors.

Finally, product market disequilibrium was reflected by the ratio of unfilled orders to capacity (UFOCAP), and the incomes policy variables were the same as those in the PAY equation.

Empirical Results

The wage and price equations were estimated using ordinary least squares (OLS) and two-stage least squares (TSLS) techniques. The TSLS technique was employed since the pay equation includes a contemporaneous price variable and the price equation includes a contemporaneous pay variable (ULCOST); pay and price increases are consequently jointly determined, which leads to a simultaneity bias in the OLS results.[20]

Both the ordinary least squares and two-stage least squares results have similar implications for both the pay and price equations (see tables 10.3 and 10.4). An increase in the PCE is transmitted into subsequent pay increases on nearly a one-to-one basis; tighter labor markets increase the rate of pay increase, and employers bear their Social Security contribution in the short run. For the

Table 10.4. PCE′ regression results coefficients and *t* statistics

	OLS		TSLS	
	1	2	3	4
CONSTANT	−1.54	−2.10	−1.55	−2.08
	(−1.58)	(−2.16)	(−1.56)	(−2.10)
ULCOST	+0.38	+0.42	+0.38	+0.42
	(6.73)	(7.61)	(5.59)	(6.21)
ULCOST1	+0.37	+0.36	+0.37	+0.36
	(6.71)	(6.67)	(6.24)	(6.26)
UFOCAP	+1.13	+1.41	+1.13	+1.41
	(2.23)	(2.79)	(2.21)	(2.75)
ENERGY1	+0.03	+0.02	+0.03	+0.02
	(3.57)	(3.33)	(3.55)	(3.32)
ENERGY2	+0.03	+0.02	+0.02	+0.02
	(2.50)	(2.24)	(2.46)	(2.22)
ENERGY3	+0.01	+0.01	+0.01	+0.01
	(1.29)	(1.93)	(1.29)	(1.92)
ESP1	−1.33	−1.35	−1.33	−1.35
	(−3.95)	(−3.87)	(−3.95)	(−3.87)
ESP2	−0.46	−0.36	−0.46	−0.36
	(−1.23)	(−0.93)	(−1.23)	(−0.93)
CATCHUP	+0.44	+0.57	+0.44	+0.57
	(0.78)	(1.15)	(0.78)	(1.16)
CWPS	—	−0.48	—	−0.48
	—	(−1.17)	—	(−1.17)
$\bar{R}^2$	0.92	0.92	0.92	0.92
SEE	0.71	0.73	0.71	0.73
D-W	1.86	1.76	1.86	1.76

price equation, roughly 80 percent of unit-labor cost increases are transmitted into price increases, with rising energy costs contributing an additional 4–6 percent.[21]

Perhaps the most surprising result is that the Nixon controls program reduced both wage and price increases. The wage effect occurs during phases III and IV, while the price effect occurs during phases I and II. The CATCHUP variable is not significant in either equation. The absence of a post-control price catchup such as that found in other studies seems largely due to the inclusion of energy price increases in the price equation, coupled with the exclusion of food and energy costs from the price variable PCE′.[22] As Kosters has discussed (1975), much of the ESP effort was concentrated in these two sectors. The inclusion of energy prices as exogenous variables is particularly misleading, since the most important case of post-control price catchup was for energy costs that could not be fully passed through until the controls had been lifted.

Table 10.5. Wage increase (PAY) simulations

		OLS results		TSLS results	
	Actual	Predicted	Actual−predicted	Predicted	Actual−predicted
1978:4	8.2	8.3	−0.1	8.3	−0.1
1979:1	9.9	11.3	−1.4	11.0	−1.1
1979:2	7.8	9.9	−2.1	9.8	−2.0
1979:3	8.9	10.2	−1.3	10.0	−1.1
1979:4	8.9	10.5	−1.6	10.5	−1.6
1980:1	10.2	11.8	−1.6	11.4	−1.2
1980:2	11.0	11.0	−0.0	11.1	−0.1

While the price equation is not wellsuited to assessing the overall price effect of the Nixon program, it does include the sectors that were the focus of the COWPS effort. If, however, there is evidence of a price effect in these sectors, one must then ascertain whether shifts in the composition of aggregate demand led to price increases elsewhere. As the results below will indicate, there is little reason to explore the possibility of such broader price effects.

The matter of central interest is the influence of the council's standards. The COWPS dummy variable indicates a statistically significant direct reduction of pay increases of about 1 percent, as does the simulation of pay increases using the preprogram PAY equation (see table 10.5).[23]

The wage increase simulations indicate a restraining effect of the standards through 1979:2, after which such effect declines. The apparently large effect in 1979:2 and the continued effectiveness of the pay standard through the second program year are difficult to reconcile with indices of program performance based on company reports.

The results for the price equations show no comparable effect on prices. The COWPS standards dummy variable has statistically insignificant coefficients of rather small magnitude—about half a percentage point. The quarterly simulation results in table 10.6 show somewhat larger effects—about 0.9 percent— that seem due largely to a failure of the equation to track the price performance in 1979:4 accurately. Even if these results were taken at face value, they would imply a decrease in the CPI of only 0.4 points. This estimate is likely to provide an upper limit for any direct price effect of the program.

Sensitivity Tests

There are two principal ways to assess the robustness of these results. First, different measures of program activity can be used to reflect changes in the standards and their enforcement. Second, other variables in the equations can

Table 10.6. Price increase (PCE′) simulations

		OLS results		TSLS results	
	Actual	Predicted	Actual−predicted	Predicted	Actual−predicted
1978:4	6.7	6.7	0.0	6.7	0.0
1979:1	7.8	7.6	+0.2	7.6	+0.2
1979:2	6.8	7.3	−0.5	7.3	−0.5
1979:3	7.8	8.8	−1.0	8.8	−1.0
1979:4	8.4	11.6	−3.2	11.6	−3.2
1980:1	10.7	11.4	−0.7	11.4	−0.7
1980:2	10.4	11.4	−1.0	11.4	−1.0

be altered to see whether the presence of the program effect is sensitive to the specification used. Here I shall only explore variations in the wage equation, since the price effects remained small or zero for all reasonable alternatives.

The direct estimates of program effectiveness can be calculated by using five different measures of program activity. The first measure is the COWPS dummy variable used earlier. The second technique creates separate variables for each program year. The pay standard was (nominally) relaxed in the second program year, and the price standard was tightened relative to the pay standard. The third technique creates separate dummy variables for three different price-monitoring periods—firms with sales above $100 million (period 3), firms with sales above $250 million (period 2), and the earlier limited monitoring efforts (period 1).[24]

These measures also serve as good proxies for the level of program activity and for the administration's differing levels of commitment to the standards program. The program was a relatively informal effort during period 1; it represented the principal anti-inflation policy tool during period 2; it was subordinated to the administration's other economic initiatives in period 3, as the standards began to be phased out of Carter's economic program.

The fourth measure is the number of noncompliance decisions, and the fifth is the number of noncompliance decisions and corrective actions for each standard. In the case of the pay standards, these measures indicate that almost the entire program weight was felt during three quarters, 1979:3–1980:1. For the price standard, there is a substantial number of noncompliance decisions beginning in 1979:3 and a similar increase in corrective actions by noncompliers beginning in 1979:4 (see table 10.1).

Since the number of noncompliance decisions remained relatively low (under 20 for each standard), this number may be a better measure of program activity than of disregard for the program. (To the extent that it reflects ineffectiveness of the standards, it does so for an earlier quarter because of the long processing lag.) Inclusion of the number of corrective actions in the fifth test is less mean-

Table 10.7. Results with alternative program measures*

	PAY equation		PCE' equation	
	Coefficient (t statistic)	Mean effect	Coefficient (t statistic)	Mean effect
Total program (CWPS)	−1.13 (−2.22)	−1.13	−0.48 (−1.17)	−0.48
First program year	−1.18 (2.11)	−1.11	−0.22 (−0.52)	−0.89
Second program year	−1.03 (−1.48)		−1.77 (−2.32)	
Monitoring period 1	−0.69 (−1.02)	−1.13	+0.11 (0.20)	−0.70
Monitoring period 2	−1.64 (−2.76)		−1.05 (−1.92)	
Monitoring period 3	−0.01 (−0.01)		−0.93 (−0.78)	
Noncompliance decisions	−0.21 (−1.74)	−1.80	−0.25 (−1.57)	−2.28
Noncompliance decisions & corrective actions	−0.14 (−1.66)	−1.84	−0.14 (−1.46)	−2.39

* All results are based on OLS estimates so that the implications of the program measure variables for each equation could be distinguished. The TSLS results are quite similar.

ingful, since these alternatives to noncompliance decisions represent a weakening of the program rather than more vigorous enforcement of standards.[25]

The most striking aspect of the results in table 10.7 is that the mean effect of the standards on pay increases is almost identical for the first three measures. Although the effect is about 50 percent larger for the last two noncompliance measures, these variables are less meaningful since 11 of the 15 pay noncompliance actions were issued in the second program year for first-year violations. In contrast, the price results indicate widely varying magnitudes of influence that are generally not statistically significant. Those coefficients that are significant are for variables that place substantial weight on 1979:4, the period in which there is a large unexplained overprediction of inflation. Since there is no firm-specific evidence to indicate that the standards were unusually constraining in that quarter, it is doubtful whether the overprediction of price increases in that

There is no firm evidence at this point to indicate that the program had any direct effect on prices. Reductions in the rate of pay increase will, however, be transmitted into rates of price increase through the effect on unit labor costs. The price reduction in turn has a feedback effect on wages.

Since the impact on pay increases appears to be the principal direct impact of

Table 10.8. Alternative PAY equations*

	1	2	3	4
PCE	+0.83	0.84	+0.89	+0.65
	(4.34)	(4.20)	(4.68)	(3.25)
1/UE	+2.89	+2.86	+2.37	+5.18
	(2.23)	(2.18)	(1.97)	(3.47)
1/UE-1/UE1	—	+1.30	—	—
		(0.35)		
ENERGY	—	—	−0.03	—
			(−3.30)	
1970–80	—	—	—	+1.51
				(2.69)
ESP2	−1.82	−1.83	−1.45	−2.31
	(−3.39)	(−3.38)	(−2.86)	(−4.28)
CWPS	−1.13	−1.15	−0.65	−0.89
	(−2.22)	(−2.22)	(−1.32)	(−1.81)
$\bar{R}^2$	0.83	0.83	0.86	0.85
SEE	0.86	0.86	0.79	0.81
D-W	1.93	1.88	2.10	2.24

* Each equation also includes all other variables present in the PAY equations
reported in table 10.2.

the program, it is instructive to analyze the robustness of the result. Table 10.8
presents the earlier COWPS dummy variable equation (OLS) and three alternatives. In the first, the change in the inverse of the unemployment rate is
added. The influence of changes in labor market tightness is statistically insignificant (though with a large coefficient), and it has little effect on the rest of the
equation.

The next variation is more fundamental. Both the Nixon controls and the
COWPS standards had their greatest wage effect during periods of energy price
shocks, and most of the COWPS effect occurs during the energy price shock
period. Energy price increases rose to an annualized quarterly rate of increase
of 78 percent in 1979:2, the period in which the discrepancy between actual and
predicted wage increases was greatest. Similarly, the last three quarters of phase
IV of the Nixon program were the period in which the earlier oil shock was
transmitted to the retail level—the period in which ESP2 had its restraining
effect.

A current energy price increase variable should enter the pay equation nega-
tively if energy price shocks do not influence longer term price expectations, or
if, as we would expect, they reduce the demand for labor and consequently
dampen wage increases.[26] Inclusion of energy prices not only raises the effect of
overall price increases on pay increases to 0.89, but also diminishes the effect of
the Nixon controls and the council's standards by about half a percentage
point. In the case of the COWPS program, the program effect is −0.65, but this

value is not statistically significant. It is quite likely that the pay equations overpredict rates of pay increase more because energy price shocks are not transmitted into subsequent wage increases than because of any effect of the standards.

The final variant includes a dummy variable for the post-1960s period (1970–80) to capture any possible shift in the Phillips curve. This variable, originated by Perry (1980), reduces the effect of price increases on wage increases and, in effect, captures the recent high inflation experience by a positive shift term. Although the desirability of this formulation is questionable, the most important observation for our purposes is that this variable has little effect on the estimate of the impact of the COWPS standards.

Modifications of the analysis by including different measures of program activity, a variable to reflect changes in labor market tightness, and a dummy variable for shifts in the Phillips curve do not appear to be consequential. If, however, the influence of energy price shocks on wage growth is included in the analysis, the impact of the COWPS standards on wages is all but eliminated. The more conventional wage equation may overpredict wage increases after energy price shocks wholly apart from any influence of the standards program. The plausibility of this interpretation is enhanced by the inconsistency of the evidence based on company reports to COWPS and on the simulations using standard wage equations. Once energy prices are included as an explicit determinant of wages, this inconsistency is eliminated.

Conclusion

The Carter pay-price standards program had no independent effect on prices. Such an effect, however, is not necessary or even desirable if the objective of the program is to restrain inflation without shifting aggregate income shares from profits to wages and salaries. Wage restraint will be reflected in lower prices if markets are competitive.

Most important, the rate of pay increase was reduced by about 1 percent annually since the advent of the standards. The quarterly pattern, however, is difficult to reconcile with the absence of any firm-specific evidence that the standard was binding in the second program year. Moreover, the coincidence of these effects with the energy price shocks suggests that it was not the standards program that restrained wage increases; instead, the energy price shock may have depressed the demand for labor. Moreover, if workers regarded the price shock as an aberration, the usual models of price expectations will overstate the extent to which these price increases affect wages.

It is doubtful whether the program would have been more effective if COWPS had tightened the standards, changed the monitoring procedures, or manipulated other policy parameters. The program's critical weakness was the overall structure of the voluntary standards effort. It is likely, but by no means certain, that greater collaboration with the Pay Advisory Committee would have enhanced the effectiveness of the standards.

Ultimately, the program was hindered by the failure of the Carter administration to strengthen the publicity sanction—perhaps by integrating the incomes policy into its sectoral economic policies or by instituting some form of mandatory controls. The fundamental weakness of the voluntary standards approach is that the effectiveness of the publicity sanction deteriorates quite rapidly, particularly once some firms refuse to comply with the standards after being identified as noncompliers. But the strengthening program needed was not undertaken, largely because of the political vulnerability of the Carter administration in the 1980 election year.

Whether incomes policies can ever be a productive component of an economic program is a more difficult issue to resolve. The most convincing case for the efficacy of incomes policies is that they may augment fiscal and monetary restraint by overcoming the downward wage and price rigidities that impede the price deceleration achievable with such policies. Even in this instance, however, control of prices and wages is likely to induce some inefficiencies and distortions which may outweigh the benefits from more rapid price deceleration.

Perhaps a greater concern than these economic dislocations is the political danger. Instead of augmenting a meaningful program of restraint, politicians may utilize incomes policies as a substitute for a substantive economic program. During the first year of the Carter program, the pay-price standards were widely touted as "the president's anti-inflation program." The standards, in effect, served primarily as a concrete policy that could be identified as the anti-inflation strategy and thus muted criticism and diverted attention from the need for fundamental changes in economic policy. Once the dramatic shift in monetary and fiscal policies occurred in the second year of the program, the standards became unconstraining and irrelevant to the overall economic program. At no time did the standards program augment a broader policy of economic restraint. So long as the enthusiasm for incomes policies stems from the misguided hope that they will eliminate the need for fiscal and monetary restraint, any possible efficacy of incomes policies will be jeopardized.

Part III. Health

II. The Value of a Life: What Difference Does It Make?

John D. Graham and James W. Vaupel

Abstract

A survey of 35 benefit-cost analyses of lifesaving programs finds significant variability in assumptions about the monetary value of lifesaving. The foregone earnings method continues to be used by analysts even though it is feasible to use the theoretically more attractive concept of willingness-to-pay for safety. Because of their reliance on the foregone earnings measure, many studies have underestimated the dollar value of lifesaving policies. Nonetheless, sensitivity analysis reveals that large changes in the monetary value assigned to lifesaving do not alter the policy implications of most studies. In addition, cost-effectiveness calculations using life-years preserved (instead of lives saved) do not change the rank order of policy options. This suggests that the question of lives saved versus life-years saved may be of little operational significance, at least in setting health, safety, and environmental priorities. Finally, the survey reveals striking disparities across agencies and programs in cost per life saved and even greater disparities in cost per life-year saved. Larger-scale efforts aimed at quantifying the cost-effectiveness of lifesaving opportunities could help us think more systematically about lifesaving policy.

Benefit-cost analyses of lifesaving programs are sometimes dismissed with the query, "But how can you put a dollar value on a life?" Some believe that it is "morally and intellectually deficient" to attempt to monetize mortality (Baram, 1979:27). Other critics have observed that there are, at least currently, no generally agreed-upon estimates of the so-called value of a life and consequently, as Nicholas Ashford of M.I.T. has argued, "until society better understands this value, current analytic valuations of life must always be inadequate, and cannot be directly compared with the monetary costs or benefits of a regulation" (1980:19).

It is certainly true that no consensus exists about how to express in dollars the benefits of averting deaths. Although the advocates of "willingness-to-pay" measures have gained the offensive against defenders of the "foregone earnings" (or "human capital") approach, the internecine battle is by no means over.[1] Within the willingness-to-pay community, a subdued and often unacknowledged disagreement divides those who value lives from a smaller—but persuasive—group who value life-years; in a second debate, the psychologists and decision analysts who ask individuals their preferences question the methods of the economists who impute safety preferences on the basis of wage premiums for hazardous occupations. Surveys of expressed willingness-to-pay for small reductions in the probability of death have yielded values of a life from $500,000 to $8 million (in 1978 dollars).[2] Nine recent labor market studies of wage premiums have produced a somewhat narrower range of values spread roughly evenly from $300,000 to $3.5 million.[3]

We have scrutinized some 35 studies of the costs and benefits of health, safety, and environmental programs. Given the disarray among both the theorists who attempt to define the value of a life and the empiricists who attempt to measure it, it is not surprising that these policy analyses differed considerably in how they valued lives. Of the 35 studies, 24 were benefit-cost analyses that explicitly assigned dollar values to lives saved, while 11 were cost-effectiveness analyses that estimated the cost per life saved. Of the 24 studies that valued lives, 15 used a foregone-earnings value, 7 used a willingness-to-pay value, and 2 used values that were claimed to be consistent with both the foregone-earnings and the willingness-to-pay approaches. Four of these analyses used ranges of values; the other 20 picked point estimates ranging from $55,000 to $7 million.

In the 7 studies that relied on willingness-to-pay estimates, the median value of a life was $625,000; in the 15 foregone-earnings studies, it was $217,000, only about a third as much.[4]

The predominant reliance on the foregone earnings method is somewhat unsettling since this method is not a logical extension of the principles of benefit-cost analysis.[5] Given that reasonable estimates of people's willingness to pay for safety are available, there is little justification for continued use of the foregone-earnings method. Our review of studies suggests that reliance on foregone-earnings studies has caused many analysts to underestimate the monetary benefits of lifesaving programs.

Given the uncertainties about how to define, let alone measure, the value of a life, it might be expected that the authors of the benefit-cost studies would include—and the reviewers and editors would demand—very careful sensitivity analyses of how robust their conclusions were in comparison with alternative assumptions about the monetary value of lifesaving. Only 7 of the 24 benefit-cost studies, however, contain any sensitivity analysis at all, and only 2 studies identify the "switch point" or "breakeven" value that determines when a policy option should be favored over the contending alternative. Frequently, the estimates of mortality risks used in these studies are even more uncertain than the valuation of lifesaving, making the absence of sensitivity analysis even more inexplicable—and inexcusable. Beyond this, most of the studies are afflicted with a variety of sins of omission and commission that we intend to detail in another paper. Even those who in principle favor analysis have to admit that analysis in practice is so devilishly demanding that the most diligent, intelligent, and well-intentioned practitioners often go astray.

Comparison of the 35 analyses of lifesaving programs leads to some intriguing, if broad-brush, conclusions. To facilitate comparisons across studies, we calculated the "additional cost per additional life saved" of going from one policy option (usually, but not always, the status quo) to some alternative. Since some of the 35 studies considered several policy alternatives, we were able to compute a cost per life saved for 57 policy pairs. In each instance, we computed a net cost by subtracting from total costs any nonmortality benefits that the authors of the studies estimated. We made no attempt to correct for omitted costs or benefits.

A number of analysts have cogently argued that since lives are never saved but merely prolonged, it is also informative to consider cost per life-year saved. Consequently, we estimated this figure for each of the 57 policy pairs as the quotient of the cost per life saved and the average life expectancy gained by individuals whose lives were saved.[6]

For illustrative purposes, consider the example of governmental policy toward residential smoke detectors. One team of analysts, after an assessment of benefits and costs, found that a policy of mandatory installation of smoke detectors in sleeping rooms of residential buildings would cost society an additional $40,000 per life saved compared with the status quo policy of purely voluntary purchases of smoke detectors. Since fire victims lose, on average, about thirty years of remaining life, this policy would cost about $1,300 per life-year saved. We went further and considered the cost-effectiveness of installing smoke detectors in all rooms of residential buildings, not just those that are used for sleeping. As one might expect, the extra cost per unit of safety for the "all rooms" policy increases to about $1 million per life saved, or about $32,000 per life-year saved, compared with the base case of "sleeping rooms only."

Table 11.1 summarizes the cost-effectiveness estimates for all 57 policy pairs. A number of interesting patterns and conclusions emerge.

First, for almost a quarter of the policy pairs (13 of 57), the net costs are less than zero even when the benefits of saving lives are ignored. These lifesaving programs are justified by various morbidity and nonhealth gains alone; the mortality reductions achieved can be viewed as a generous bonus.

For many of the remaining policy pairs, the cost per life saved is low. Two judicious students of benefit-cost analysis have surveyed the theoretical and empirical literature to estimate a reasonable range of the value of a life: Bailey's "low" estimate is $170,000 (1980:52-66); and Smith's plausible lower bound is $300,000 (1979). For 60 percent (34 of 57) of the policy pairs in table 11.1, the cost per life saved is under $170,000 and for 65 percent (37 of 57) it is no more than $300,000. Thus, although benefit-cost analysis is sometimes charged with a bias against health, safety, and environmental policy, for some three-fifths of the policy pairs examined benefit-cost analysis strongly supported lifesaving programs.

Bailey's high estimate of the value of a life is $715,000, while Smith's plausible upper bound is $3 million. In 16 cases (28 percent), the cost per life saved

Table 11.1. Cost-effectiveness estimates for 57 policy pairs

Problem area	Agency concerned	Author	Base case policy option	Alternative policy option	Net additional cost of alternative policy option	
					Per life saved	Per life year saved
Highway safety	NHTSA	Warner, et al. (1975)	Status quo	Mandatory air bags	$ 0	$ 0
"	"	Coleman (1976)	Status quo	Mandatory passive belts	0	0
"	"	COWPS (1977b)	Status quo	Compulsory belt usage law	0	0
"	"	Clotfelter & Hahn (1978)	Status quo prior to 55 mph limit	55 mph speed limit	0	0
"	"	U.S. DOT (1976)	Status quo	Roadside hazard removal	0	0
"	"	"	Status quo	Traffic enforcement	0	0
"	"	"	Status quo	Vehicle inspection	0	0
"	"	Muller (1980)	Voluntary motorcycle helmet usage	Compulsory helmet usage law	0	0
Genetic screening	HHS	Swint et al. (1979)	Status quo	Community screening program	0	0
Clothing	CPSC	Dardis et al. (1978)	No law	Clothing flammability law	0	0
Smoke detectors	CPSC	Waterman et al. (1978)	Status quo	Mandatory smoke detectors	0	0
Stationary source air pollution	EPA	Koshal & Koshal (1973)	Pre-1970 conditions	1970 Clean Air Act standards	0	0

Table 11.1. (Continued)

Problem area	Agency concerned	Author	Base case policy option	Alternative policy option	Net additional cost of alternative policy option	
					Per life saved	Per life year saved
Stationary source air pollution	EPA	Crocker et al. (1979); CEQ (1980)*	Pre-1970 conditions	1970 Clean Air Act standards	$ 0	$ 0
Highway safety	NHTSA	COWPS (1977b)	Status quo	Mandatory passive belts	3,600	88
"	"	Zeckhauser & Shephard (1976)	"	Mandatory air bags	13,000	538
Heart disease policy	HHS	"	"	Mobile coronary heart disease unit	15,000	1,800
Highway safety	NHTSA	Gates (1975)	Status quo	Active lap/shoulder belts	21,000	516
Stationary source air pollution	EPA	Lave & Seskin (1977)	Pre-1970 conditions	1970 Clean Air Act standards	30,000	2,300
Smoke detectors	CPSC	Potter et al. (1976)	Status quo	Mandatory, in sleeping rooms only	40,000	1,300
Highway safety	NHTSA	Arnould & Grabowski (1980)	Status quo	Mandatory passive belts	40,700	1,000
"	NHTSA	U.S. DOT (1976)	Status quo	Emerging medical services program	41,000	1,000
Stationary source air pollution	EPA	Freeman (1979) CEQ (1979)	Pre-1970 conditions	1970 Clean Air Act	50,000	3,800
Highway safety	NHTSA	Zeckhauser & Shephard (1976)	Status quo prior to 55 mph limit	55 mph limit with full adherence	59,000	2,500

Table 11.1. (Continued)

Problem area	Agency concerned	Author	Base case policy option	Alternative policy option	Net additional cost of alternative policy option	
					Per life saved	Per life year saved
Furniture fires	CPSC	SRI (1979)	Status quo	Mandatory smoke detectors	$ 60,000	$1,900
Highway safety	NHTSA	Zeckhauser & Shephard (1976)	Status quo prior to 55 mph limit	55 mph limit with partial adherence	64,000	1,900
"	"	Coleman (1976)	Status quo	Mandatory air bags	78,000	1,900
"	"	U.S. DOT (1976)	Status quo	Alcohol Safety Action Projects	81,500	2,000
"	"	COWPS (1977b)	Status quo	Mandatory air bags	94,000	2,300
"	"	Coleman (1976)	No restraint	Active lap/shoulder belt system	94,000	2,300
Heart disease policy	HHS	Zeckhauser & Shephard (1976)	Status quo	Diet program	102,000	6,500
Highway safety	NHTSA	Robertson (1977)	Status quo	Mandatory air bags	117,000	2,800
Saccharin	HHS	COWPS (1977a)	Status quo	Ban	136,000	8,500
Highway safety	NHTSA	Zeckhauser & Shephard (1976)	Mandatory air bags	Mandatory air bags plus 55 mph limit with full adherence	148,000	6,000
"	"	Gates (1975)	No restraint	Mandatory air bags with active lap belts	162,000	4,000

Table 11.1. (Continued)

Problem area	Agency concerned	Author	Base case policy option	Alternative policy option	Net additional cost of alternative policy option	
					Per life saved	Per life year saved
Highway safety	NHTSA	GAO (1976)	Pre-1966 conditions	1966 Motor Vehicle Safety Act	$ 255,000	$ 6,300
"	NHTSA	Gates (1975)	Status quo	Mandatory air bags	300,000	7,300
Pertussis vaccine	HHS	Kaplan et al. (1979)[b]	Immunize	No program	300,000	4,200
Furniture fires	CPSA	SRI (1979)	Mandatory smoke detectors	CPSC flammability standard	400,000	12,900
Highway safety	NHTSA	Arnould & Grabowski (1980)	Status quo	Mandatory air bags	408,000	10,000
"	"	Castle (1976)	65 mph limit	55 mph limit	500,000	12,000
"	"	Ford (1979)	Unsafe fuel tank	Safer fuel tank	686,000	17,000
Smoke detectors	CPSC	Potter et al. (1976)	Mandatory, in sleeping rooms only	Mandatory in all rooms	1,000,000	32,000
Highway safety	NHTSA	Lave (1979)	Status quo prior to 55 mph speed limit	55 mph speed limit	1,200,000	29,000
Mobile source air pollution	EPA	NAS (1974)	Pre-1970 conditions	1970 Clean Air Act	1,350,000	105,000
Highway safety	NHTSA	Arnould & Grabowski (1980)	Mandatory passive belts	Mandatory passive belts and air bags	1,400,000	34,000
Acrylonitrile	OSHA	COWPS (1978b)	Status quo	2.0 ppm	3,520,000	230,000

Table 11.1. (Continued)

Problem area	Agency concerned	Author	Base case policy option	Alternative policy option	Net additional cost of alternative policy option	
					Per life saved	Per life year saved
Carcinogens in water	EPA	COWPS (1978a)	150 mcl rule	100 mcl rule	$ 3,800,000	$ 240,000
"	"	COWPS (1978a)	Status quo	150 mcl rule	3,900,000	240,000
Arsenic	OSHA	COWPS (1976b)	5 mcl rule	.004 mcl rule	5,000,000	390,000
Carcinogens in water	EPA	COWPS (1978a)	100 mcl rule	50 mcl rule	6,300,000	390,000
Vinyl chloride	OSHA	Perry & Outlaw (1978)	50 ppm	1 ppm	7,500,000	490,000
Benzene emissions	EPA	Nichols (1980)	No control	97% control	7,600,000	480,000
Coke ovens	OSHA	COWPS (1976a)	Status quo	Proposed OSHA standard	12,100,000	790,000
Acrylonitrile	"	COWPS (1978b)	2.0 ppm	1.0 ppm	28,800,000	1,900,000
Benzene emissions	EPA	Nichols (1980)	97% control	99% control	51,000,000	3,200,000
Benzene	OSHA	Wilson (1979)	10 ppm rule	1 ppm rule	102,000,000	6,600,000
Acrylonitrile	"	COWPS (1978b)	1.0 ppm	0.2 ppm	169,200,000	11,000,000

a. This report estimates incremental costs of stationary source cleanup at $7 billion.
** "No program" is desirable at high values of a life because more deaths will be caused by reactions to a vaccine than will be prevented.

exceeds Bailey's value and in 12 cases (21 percent) it exceeds Smith's. Thus, in roughly a quarter of the policy pairs we compared, the additional benefits of a lifesaving program would not appear, at least to a benefit-cost analyst, to be worth the additional costs. That leaves relatively few cases in the middle. In only 7 cases (12 percent) does the cost per life saved fall within Bailey's range ($170,000 to $715,000); similarly, in only eight cases does it fall within Smith's order of magnitude range ($300,000 to $3 million). Furthermore, in only 11 cases does the cost per life saved fall within the wide combined range from $170,000 to $3 million.

This is an encouraging finding, since it implies that in something like four-fifths or five-sixths of the cases, the specific value of a life used in a benefit-cost analysis does not alter the policy implications of a study.[7] Given the confusion in the theory and practice of valuing lives, it is reassuring that precise estimates of the value of a life were usually not needed. In a prescient observation made before the recent spate of benefit-cost studies of lifesaving programs, Richard Zeckhauser argued: "there are conceptual and philosophical difficulties inherent in any procedure that attempts to attach a value to life, though conducting assessments with the aid of such procedures may nevertheless be helpful. In many circumstances policy choices may not change substantially if estimates of the value of life vary by a factor of ten. Getting a valuation that is accurate within a factor of three might be very useful" (1975). Our results support Zeckhauser's optimism.

Beyond this, the results suggest that it is usually not necessary to value lives explicitly: Instead of a benefit-cost analysis, a cost-effectiveness analysis that calculates cost per life saved may often be sufficient. Given the controversy about assigning monetary values to the benefits of saving lives—and many people's distaste for doing so—it would seem judicious to rely on cost-effectiveness analysis where possible (for further discussion, see Raiffa, Schwartz, and Weinstein, 1978). Indeed, decisionmakers and other readers of these studies may be at least as interested in knowing that the cost per life saved by some program is $10,000—or $10 million—as in knowing that estimated net benefits amount to $35 million or that the estimated benefit/cost ratio is 1.7.[8]

Table 11.2 cross-tabulates the 57 policy pairs in table 11.1 by the agency concerned and by three ranges of cost per life saved. Since the studies we surveyed may not be representative and since they suffer from various empirical and theoretical flaws, great caution should be used in drawing implications from table 11.2. Nonetheless, the table does suggest that the costs of saving lives differ greatly across agencies or at least that the policy options being weighed by different agencies vary considerably in cost-effectiveness.

Another rough indication of interagency disparities is given by the median values of the cost per life saved for each agency's range of policy options. For the National Highway Traffic Safety Administration (NHTSA), the Department of Health and Human Services (HHS), and the Consumer Product Safety Commission (CPSC), the medians are comparable: $64,000, $102,000, and

Table 11.2. Breakdown of policy options by agency and by net cost per life saved

Agency	Number of cases where net cost per life saved is			
	Under $170,000	Between $170,000 and $3,000,000	Above $3,000,000	Total
NHTSA	22	7	0	29
HHS	4	1	0	5
CPSC	4	2	0	6
EPA	4	1	5	10
OSHA	0	0	7	7
Total	34	11	12	57

$50,000, respectively. For the Environmental Protection Agency (EPA), however, the median is $2.6 million and for the Occupational Safety and Health Administration (OSHA) it is $12.1 million.

In addition to data on cost per life saved, table 11.1 also presents estimates of cost per life-year saved. The policies that are most cost-effective in terms of saving lives also tend to be ones that, by preventing accidents and acute diseases, save the lives of younger people. Conversely, the least cost-effective policies are those that focus on preventing various kinds of chronic diseases with long latency periods, conditions that largely afflict the elderly. For example, the victims of motor vehicle accidents lose, on average, 41 years of life expectancy, while the victims of cancer lose 16 years.[9] Measuring performance in this manner does not substantially alter the rank order of the programs. The policies that cost the least per life saved tend to be the same policies that save the most years of life per life saved. Hence, the question whether safety should be measured in terms of life-years or lives saved may be of greater theoretical interest than operational significance, at least in setting priorities.

Measuring performance in cost per life-year saved does, however, further widen the large differences among the various types of lifesaving programs. The *least* expensive OSHA program is seven times more expensive per life-year saved than the *most* expensive NHTSA program; the median OSHA program is more than 400 times more expensive per life-year saved than the median NHTSA program.[10] Again, these findings are merely suggestive, since they are based on a crude comparison of a set of disparate studies. The primary studies of cost and risk estimation that lead to these cost-effectiveness comparisons are subject to potentially large scientific uncertainties. For example, both economic and risk assessments of regulations that control carcinogens are based on very limited evidence and highly questionable types of extrapolation. Nonetheless, it seems unlikely that these uncertainties could account for the persistently huge disparities between, say, OSHA and NHTSA investments.[11]

These cost-effective comparisons suggest some intriguing topics of investigation that extend beyond the scope of this short paper. First, not all of the policy options summarized in table 11.1 have been implemented by policymakers. Some options are in effect today (e.g., the 55 mph speed limit with partial adherence), others were considered but rejected (the ban on saccharin), still others are currently under consideration (mandatory passive restraints), and a few are being repealed (compulsory motorcycle helmet laws). It would be possible to compare the cost-effectiveness of those that have been adopted with those that have been considered but rejected. Moreover, it would be interesting to compare how the cost-effectiveness of lifesaving policies changes over time. Do policymakers tend to save cheapest lives first? We have not yet considered these issues.

A second topic of interest concerns the bureaucratic, statutory, and behavioral correlates of lifesaving investments. What factors explain why some programs with high costs per life saved are adopted while opportunities for saving lives inexpensively are neglected? Are there any systematic explanations for interagency disparities in lifesaving investments? We do not propose, of course, that marginal lifesaving investments in all agencies should be equalized or even that the disparities we have documented are clear cases of "irrationality" in the political process. Policymakers may consider decision-making criteria that are not captured by simple cost-effectiveness calculations. Such criteria might include: (a) the degree to which risks to life and limb are known and subject to control by potential victims; (b) the various statutory demands placed upon agencies by the Congress; (c) society's desire to provide extra protection to those victims who are identifiable before or after lifesaving policies are implemented; (d) the distribution of the costs and benefits of lifesaving policies within the population. Other criteria could be added to this list but it is clear that a more detailed analysis would be necessary to draw firm conclusions about the rationales for existing lifesaving investments.

Our admittedly roughhewn study has uncovered some striking discrepancies across agencies and programs in cost per life saved and even greater discrepancies in cost per life-year saved. The controversy about whether and how to quantify the monetary value of lifesaving does not imply that thoughtful quantitative analysis cannot help us sort out our confusion about how best to save lives. More careful, larger scale efforts at comparing opportunities for saving lives should make a constructive contribution to the political process of setting priorities among lifesaving policies.

12. The Formation of Health-Related Habits

Gerard F. Anderson, Anthony E. Boardman,
and Robert P. Inman

Abstract

*Recently, health professionals have begun to agree that the greatest poten-
tial for improving health status lies in improving personal habits. This chapter
examines the formation of four health-related habits: dieting, regular physical
examinations, regular physical exercise, and stopping smoking. We review
the health belief and health maintenance models of health-related habit
formation. These models form the basis of a statistical model estimated by
the use of a panel dataset of 3,756 white male twins. The equations are
estimated by logit analysis. We examine the effects of over 30 exogenous
variables and find that age, income, education, health insurance, and cues to
action (such as a heart attack) increase the probability that an individual will
engage in one or more health-beneficial actions.*

The health of the U.S. population, as measured by most available standards
of mortality and morbidity, has improved steadily over the past century. Historically, the major contributors to our increased physical well-being have been
improvements in preventive health policies—e.g., better sanitation and extensive public vaccinations—and some impressive advancements in the technology
of medical care. A growing list of recent epidemiological studies suggests that
we may be on the frontier of yet another breakthrough in the promotion of our
population's health. The evidence is mounting that how we as individuals
behave towards our bodies, what we eat and drink and how we live, can have a
significant effect on the incidence and severity of illness. In the face of such
evidence, the policy question inevitably arises: what, if anything, should be
done by those concerned with national health care policies to promote the
adoption of health lifestyles? To answer this question, it is necessary, first, to
examine the possible determinants of individual health care behavior. If policies
capable of altering health behavior can be identified, then we must push our
analysis to the next step and decide how and if these potential instruments
should be applied. In this study we shall only step near the edges of the hardest
questions. We shall pursue that first level of analysis and seek to determine the
possible policies for encouraging the adoption of a healthy lifestyle.

That there is a significant relationship between personal health habits and
health states has long been recognized. The ancient Greeks stressed the importance of physical exercise and weight control. Scientists and physicians continue

to warn the public about the role of cigarette smoking in causing cancer and heart disease. Numerous studies have stressed the importance of regular physical examinations. While better access to medical care and new medical technologies will also improve health status, changes in smoking, dietary, athletic, and other habits are potentially more significant. Fuchs (1974), for instance, attributes differences in the mortality rates of Nevada and Utah to differences in alcohol and cigarette consumption and in levels of stress. Belloc (1973) finds that poor health practices (smoking, poor weight control, drinking, reduced hours of sleep, irregular meals, inadequate physical exercise) are highly correlated with higher mortality rates. Studies by Berry and Bowland (1977) and Abt (1977) on the economic cost of "premature" deaths have found that changes in lifestyle could save billions of dollars per year. Lalonde (1974), in a white paper on Canadian health policy, emphasized the importance of the research on health and lifestyle.

This study presents a preliminary examination of the formation of health-related habits. We examine four decisions: to stop smoking, to control weight, to have regular physical examinations, and to take regular exercise. These behaviors are representative of good health habits, have a significant potential for improving health status, can be easily monitored, and represent a conscious long-term commitment to better health.

The association between cigarette smoking and excess mortality and morbidity is well known. In 1964 the surgeon general issued the report declaring that cigarette smoking is hazardous to health. The report climaxed years of study of the effects of cigarette smoking and echoed the warnings of physicians and scientists. Cigarette smoking is most commonly associated with increased incidence of cerebrovascular diseases, cancer, and respiratory diseases.

For many years obesity has been associated with a number of diseases, most importantly cardiovascular disease (Society of Actuaries, 1959). Many studies show that obesity is a determining factor of disease even when other risk factors are independently controlled (Gordon & Kannel, 1973).

Physical activity is associated with good physical and mental health. It has been associated with lower cardiovascular morbidity (Kannel et al., 1962), less coronary heart disease (Mann et al., 1969), myocardial infarction (Wilhelmsen et al., 1976), and greater emotional health (Folkins, Lynch, & Gardner, 1972).

Recently the economic value of comprehensive preventive examinations has been questioned (Knox, 1974; Delbanco & Noble, 1975). Because comprehensive exams might not be cost-beneficial, physicians have been urged to substitute more selective examinations. Nevertheless, preventive examinations have a positive value and demonstrate a general concern for health status and early treatment. They are still commonly viewed as promoting good health.

The formation of health-related habits has been approached from two major perspectives. The prevalent approach adopted by health care analysts is the health belief model, which focuses on the psychological and sociological determinants of behavior. Economists have developed utility-maximizing models, the best known of which is Grossman's (1972) health maintenance model. These two models are reviewed in section II. While the approaches are quite different, empirical formulations of these models are similar and differ only with respect to the emphasis placed on different explanatory variables.

Our empirical analyses are based on a sample of 3,756 white male twins who were born between 1917 and 1927. They are part of the National Academy of Science–National Research Council panel dataset. These twins served in World War II, were alive in 1974, and responded to two questionnaires in 1971 and 1974. While inferences made in this chapter pertain specifically to approximately fifty-year-old, relatively healthy, white male twins, they may also be appropriate for other individuals.

Model of Health-related Behavior

This section reviews two models of individual health-related behavior.[1] The health belief model emphasizes subjective perceptions of health and disease and is based on psychological and behavioral theory, particularly Lewin's (1948) field theory. The utility-maximizing or health maintenance model is based on human capital theory.

Health Belief Models

Health belief models have been formulated in a variety of ways (Becker et al., 1977; Maiman & Becker, 1974; Nelson et al., 1978; Rosenstock, 1974). Rosenstock (1966) first used the model to predict the use of health services. Subsequently, researchers have studied different health-related actions and have used different explanatory variables. Despite their differences, all health belief models share certain common aspects. Our particular formulation allows a useful comparison with the utility-maximizing model.

Before taking any specific health-related action, the individual must be in a psychological state of readiness to take action. This state of readiness, R, depends on the individual's perceived susceptibility to a particular health condition, SUS, and the extent to which he feels contracting that condition would have severe consequences, SEV.

$$R = R(SUS, SEV) \tag{12.1}$$

Once the individual is in a state of readiness to take action, he engages in a specific health-beneficial action, y, when the perceived health benefits of that action, B, exceed the perceived costs, C. If $P(y)$ denotes the probability of engaging in a specific health-beneficial action, we can write

$$P(y) = F(B, C | R) . \tag{12.2}$$

The perceived benefits reflect the efficacy of the health-beneficial action; that is, they depend on the difference between the severity of a health condition, with and without the action, and the susceptibility to that condition, with and without the action:

$$B = B(SEV|y - SEV|\bar{y}, SUS|y - SUS|\bar{y}) \,. \qquad (12.3)$$

Since "severity" refers both to physical (clinical) and to personal consequences, the concept of individual utility is implicit in the health belief model. If the health-related habit has a negligible perceived effect on severity and susceptibility, the perceived benefits of the action are small.

Perceived severity and susceptibility to disease are jointly determined variables; they depend on the individual's demographic (D), socioeconomic (SES), and sociopsychological (PSY) characteristics and attitudes, the health related habit (y), and cues to action (CUE).

$$SEV = SEV(D, SES, PSY, y, CUE) \,. \qquad (12.4a)$$

$$SUS = SUS(D, SES, PSY, y, CUE) \,. \qquad (12.4b)$$

Cues to action are an essential concept in health belief models. If an individual is to engage in certain health-related behaviors, some external influence must trigger the appropriate behavior. Some cues are provided by the health state of an individual and are evidenced by certain symptoms of disease; others may result from information provided by physicians, friends, relatives, or the mass media.

The costs of engaging in a particular health-related action, C, are a function of monetary, opportunity, and pyschological costs. Monetary costs are denoted by P. Opportunity costs depend on the individual's income and on other variables that are elements of the vector of socioeconomic characteristics, SES. Psychological costs depend on the individual's demographic, socioeconomic, and sociopsychological attitudes and characteristics.

$$C = C(P, D, SES, PSY) \,. \qquad (12.5)$$

These relationships are represented diagramatically in figure 12.1.

We are interested in the effects of the explanatory variables on a health-related action. Substituting equations (12.1) and (12.3) through (12.5) into (12.2) gives the reduced form equation:

$$P(y) = f(P, D, SES, PSY, CUE) \,. \qquad (12.6)$$

Thus the probability of taking action depends directly or indirectly on potentially manipulable variables.

Health Maintenance Model

The health maintenance model was developed by Grossman (1972). He postulates the following intertemporal utility function for a typical consumer:

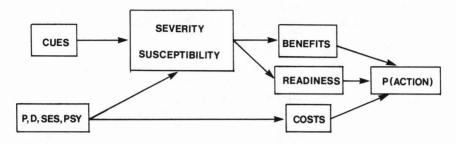

Figure 12.1. The health benefit model

$$U = U(\phi_0 H_0, \ldots, \phi_n H_n, Z_0, \ldots, Z_n) , \tag{12.7}$$

where H_0 is the inherited stock of health, H_i is the stock of health in period i, $h_i = \phi_i H_i$ denotes the consumption of "health services," and Z_i measures the total consumption of other commodities in the ith period. Individuals inherit an initial stock of health which depreciates over time, although investments in health mitigate this depreciation:

$$H_{i+1} = H_i - \delta_i H_i + I_i , \tag{12.8}$$

where I_i is gross investment at age i and δ_i is the depreciation rate at age i.[2] When the stock of health reaches some minimum level, death occurs; thus n becomes an endogenous variable and individuals "choose" their length of life.

Gross investments in health capital and other commodities in the utility function depend on the time a consumer spends on each function, on certain market goods, and on environmental variables:

$$I_i = I_i(M_i, TH_i; E_i) , \tag{12.9}$$

$$Z_i = Z_i(X_i, T_i; E_i) . \tag{12.10}$$

While Grossman lets M_i represent medical care, he recognizes that housing, diet, exercise, recreation, cigarette smoking, and alcohol consumption also influence health.[3] Some of these health-related commodities are the focus of our study. Consequently we will treat M_i as a vector and will refer to it as the vector of health-related habits. TH_i and T_i denote the amount of time an individual spends to produce investments in health and other commodities, respectively. X_i is a vector of market good inputs to Z_i, and E_i reflects certain environmental variables, including level of education, which influence the efficiency of the production process.

The utility function is subject both to an income constraint and to a time constraint. The present value of total income from work and nonearned income equals the present value of total expenditures on medical care, health-related goods, and other goods:

$$A_0 + \sum_{i=0}^{n} \frac{W_i TW_i}{(1+r)^i} = \sum_{i=0}^{n} \frac{P_i M_i + V_i X_i}{(1+r)^i} , \qquad (12.11)$$

where P_i and V_i denote the prices of M_i and X_i, respectively, W_i is the wage rate, TW_i is time worked, A_0 is the discounted value of nonearned income, and r is the interest rate. The total time spent on all activities equals Ω. Therefore,

$$TW_i + TL_i + TH_i + T_i = \Omega , \qquad (12.12)$$

where TL_i is amount of time lost in a year because of sickness.

Health is regarded both as a consumption commodity (it is unpleasant to be sick) and as an investment (health determines the total amount of time an individual can spend producing more earnings and commodities). In this latter respect, health capital differs from other forms of human capital, E, which affect an individual's market and nonmarket productivities and, consequently, his wage rate.

Individuals behave as if they maximize their utility function (equation 12.7) subject to the production function and resource constraints (equations 12.8 through 12.12). Conceptually, the first-order conditions may be solved to yield reduced-form demand equations for health and, using equation 12.9, to yield derived-demand equations for health-related habits, of which the following equation is a simplified form:

$$M_i = M_i(c_i, \pi_i, v_i, w_i, E_i, \delta_i, A_i, r, H_0) . \qquad (12.13)$$

In his paper Grossman ignores the consumption aspects of health and works through several implications of his model under specific assumptions. The effects of age, education, and income are of particular interest and will be discussed in the results section.

Comparison of the Two Models

While the derivations of the health belief model and the health maintenance model differ considerably, empirical estimation of both models will be quite similar. Consequently, it is impossible to test empirically whether one model is superior to another. Comparison of equations (12.6) and (12.13) illustrates the differences and similarities. Both models include the price of the habit. The health belief model includes a vector of socioeconomic characteristics and the health maintenance model includes the individual's wage rate, the discounted value of nonearned income, and certain human capital variables, including level of education, all of which are indicators of socioeconomic status. The health belief model includes demographic variables and the health maintenance model includes environmental variables such as race and sex. The health maintenance model also includes a depreciation rate which, as we shall discuss later, depends on demographic variables such as age. The health belief model includes cues to action, some of which are provided by the health status of the individual, and the health maintenance model also recognizes the importance of at least the initial stock of health. The major difference between the two models is the inclusion in the health belief model of psychological variables, which are difficult to measure accurately.

Data Description and Preliminary Analyses

The analyses are based on a sample of white male twins from the panel dataset maintained by the National Academy of Science–National Research Council. These twins were born between 1917 and 1927 and served in World War II; none suffered from serious debilities prior to induction. They underwent extensive medical examinations upon induction and discharge and were surveyed many times. The original sample consisted of over 16,000 twins, but some died, others failed to respond to all questionnaires, and for some, information on critical variables was missing. Our dataset consists of 3,756 individuals who responded to all questionnaires and provided complete information about their health, health-related habits, occupational earnings, and home background, and whose twin brothers provided similar information. At the time of the last questionnaire in 1974 the twins were about 50 years old. Taubman (1976) provides more information about the data.

The empirical section examines four health-related habits: the decision to stop smoking, to be on a diet to control weight, to have regular physical examinations, and to have regular physical exercise. Suppose these decisions are denoted as $y_j(j = 1, \ldots, 4)$. Our model of these health-related habits is a composite of the health habit and health maintenance models. Specifically, it takes the following form:

$$P(y_j) = g(P_j, D, SES, CUES, H25, Y25, \tilde{y}_j) \qquad j=1,\ldots,4 , \qquad (12.14)$$

where P_j is the price of habit j, and D and SES include variables that affect Grossman's depreciation rate and environmental variables. Education, income, and age are included in all equations. Health insurance is included in all equations because it is an important policy variable and reduces the out-of-pocket costs of some health-related behaviors, particularly regular physical exams.

The variables $H25$ reflect the individual's health at age 25. Proponents of the health belief model may consider them as cues. Motivation is also provided by Grossman's model. Formally, equation (12.13) should include all prior measures of the exogenous variables; in practice, however, this is impossible. The variable, H_0 is unobserved; as a compromise, we include as explanatory variables $H25$, health at age 25, and $Y25$, individual habits at or before age 25. Examples of habits practiced at or before age 25 include smoking and checkup exams as a child.

It appears that we have included or controlled for most variables suggested by both models. We believe, however, that health-related habits are likely also to depend on unobserved home environmental factors and, possibly, on unobserved genetic factors. It has been argued, for example, that the alleged causal relationship between lung cancer and smoking may be overemphasized or even spurious; rather, it may be a consequence of a latent genetic variable that causes increased propensities for both lung cancer and smoking. In order to control for the influences of such latent variables, we include in each equation a variable, $\tilde{y}_j$, that indicates whether the individual's twin brother engages in the same health-related habit.

Little is known about the effects of many control variables. Consequently, different specifications of each equation were estimated using the ordinary least-squares technique. Variables with significant coefficients were retained while variables with insignificant coefficients were eliminated unless they were of particular interest.[4] The set of dependent and independent variables is shown in table 12.1.

Because of the dichotomous dependent variables, these specifications were estimated subsequently by logit analysis; the results are reported in table 12.2. Before this analysis, however, we estimated the correlations among the error terms. A high correlation might indicate the presence of an important omitted variable that has a similar effect on two habits. For example, the desire for good health, which is unobserved, may have similar effects on the decisions to take regular exercise and to have regular physical examinations. Estimation methods that take account of high correlations are more efficient than other methods. Since the estimated correlations are all very small, less than 0.06 in absolute value, the logit analysis results, which ignore correlations across equations, are likely to be efficient.

Results

Grossman (1972) focuses on the investment aspects of health and ignores the consumption aspects of demand. He also makes a number of other simplifying assumptions that should be considered. Specifically, he discusses the effects of age, the wage rate, and human capital (education). As age increases, the depreciation rate, δ_i, increases. As δ_i increases, the horizontal supply curve of health capital shifts upward and the equilibrium stock of health decreases. Grossman shows that if the elasticity of the demand schedule for health capital is less than unity, gross investments in health increase with age: "given a relatively inelastic demand curve for health, individuals would desire to offset part of the reduction in health capital caused by increase in the rate of depreciation by increasing their gross investments" (1972:239). Consequently, we would expect age to have a positive coefficient in all equations, as it does. In three equations, the coefficient is significant at the 0.05 level for a one-sided alternative.

Table 12.1. Descriptions, means, and standard deviations of variables

Description[a]	Mean	Standard deviation
Stopped smoking	0.207	0.405
Have been on a diet to control weight	0.239	0.427
Have regular physical examinations	0.527	0.499
Take regular physical exercise	0.860	0.347
Age (in years)	50.119	2.940
Family income (in thousands)	19.483	14.850
Education (years)	13.260	3.119
Health insurance	0.266	0.442
Heart attack	0.020	0.140
Chest pain	0.243	0.429
Overweight	−0.008	0.124
Infective disease (ICDA[b] Codes 000-136) before age 25	0.269	0.444
Cancer (ICDA Codes 140-239) before age 25	0.060	0.237
Respiratory disease (ICDA Codes 461-500, 509-520) before age 25	0.198	0.398
Digestive system (ICDA Codes 530-577) diseases before age 25	0.292	0.455
Congenital anomalies (ICDA Codes 740-759) before age 25	0.037	0.189
Physical exam as child	0.019	0.135
Began smoking before age 15	0.023	0.150
Began smoking age 15-19	0.145	0.352
Began smoking age 20-24	0.456	0.498
Population of childhood home city (in millions)	0.357	0.620
Reside on East Coast	0.294	0.456
Number of children	2.662	1.719
Never married	0.155	0.362
Attend religious services (occasions per month)	2.469	2.448
Unsocial leisure activities (3=frequent social activities, . . . , 15= very seldom engage in social activities)	6.994	2.286
Inactive leisure activities (3=frequent active leisure activities, . . . , 15=seldom engage in active leisure activities)	8.259	3.242
Occupation physically active (1=sedentary, 3=moderately active, 5=physically strenuous)	2.981	1.290
Overtime work (0=none, 1=from time to time, 2=regularly)	0.720	0.449
Ever smoked	0.752	0.432
Overweight at age 25= (actual weight−ideal weight)/ideal weight[c]	0.0002	0.126
Twin has stopped smoking	0.207	0.405
Twin has been on a diet	0.239	0.427
Twin has regular physical examinations	0.527	0.499
Twin takes regular physical exercise	0.860	0.347
Twin ever smoked	0.752	0.432

a. Unless indicated to the contrary, all variables are dichotomous; affirmative responses are coded as unity, other responses are zero.
b. International classification of Diseases Adopted (for use in the United States).
c. Ideal weight is taken from the *World Almanac* (1977), p. 956.

Table 12.2. Logit analysis estimates of four health habit equations[a]

	Stop smoking[b]	Diet	Physical examination	Physical exercise
Age	0.084 (4.23)	0.028 (1.92)	0.035 (2.88)	0.021 (1.25)
Family income	0.005 (1.14)	0.021 (7.12)	0.015 (5.52)	−0.004 (−1.15)
Education	0.030 (1.41)	0.075 (4.64)	0.015 (1.23)	0.114 (6.80)
Health insurance	0.229 (1.79)	0.123 (1.27)	1.231 (14.53)	0.313 (2.65)
Heart attack	0.612 (1.65)	1.316 (4.82)	1.361 (4.38)	−0.362 (−1.17)
Chest pain		0.257 (2.54)		
Overweight		7.985 (17.32)		
Infective before 25				−0.162 (−1.47)
Cancer before 25	−0.029 (−0.12)			
Respiratory before 25	−0.044 (−0.31)			
Digestive before 25	0.299 (2.38)			0.131 (1.18)
Anomaly before 25			0.425 (2.25)	
Exam as child			2.113 (4.79)	
Smoke before age 15	3.104 (9.78)	0.028 (0.09)		−0.312 (−1.12)
Smoke 15–19	2.885 (16.49)	0.344 (2.98)		−0.009 (−0.06)
Smoke 20–24	−0.407 (−2.57)			
Childhood pop.	−0.407 (−3.99)	0.205 (3.09)	−0.072 (−1.24)	−0.0007 (−0.009)
East Coast			0.318 (4.10)	
Number children			−0.054 (−2.52)	
Never married		0.150 (1.26)	0.104 (1.03)	−0.436 (−3.49)

As the wage rate increases, the value of healthy time increases and the benefits associated with less time lost because of illness increase. As the wage rate increases, the demand for health capital shifts to the right and the stock of health capital demanded increases. Since the wage rate has no assumed effect

Table 12.2. (Continued)

	Stop smoking[b]	Diet	Physical examination	Physical exercise
Religious attendance	0.129	−0.015	0.015	−0.002
	(5.34)	(−0.85)	(1.01)	(−0.09)
Unsocial leisure		0.0004	−0.089	−0.266
		(0.019)	(−5.70)	(−10.76)
Inactive leisure		−0.038		
		(−2.64)		
Work active		−0.115		
		(−3.17)		
Overtime work			−0.147	−0.144
			(−1.86)	(−1.31)
Ever smoke	10.636			
	(0.84)			
Overweight at 25			0.359	−1.096
			(1.28)	(−2.85)
Twin stop smoke	13.581			
	(0.38)			
Twin diet		0.853		
		(9.19)		
Twin exam			0.503	
			(7.17)	
Twin exercise				0.479
				(3.90)
Twin ever smoke	−0.636			
	(−4.19)			
Constant	−16.993	−4.621	−2.007	1.588
	(−1.33)	(−5.52)	(−3.03)	(−1.71)
Log likelihood function	−999.0	−1677.0	−2351.0	−1384.0
R^2 (OLS)[c]	0.48	0.18	0.13	0.07

a. Asymptotic t-statistics in parentheses.
b. These results did not converge after 10 iterations to within 10^{-4}.
c. To provide a measure of predictive power we include the R^2 of the ordinary least-squares regressions.

on the amount of gross investment supplied by a given input of a health-related habit, the demand for that commodity will rise with the wage. In our estimations the wage rate is unavailable, but we believe that salary should behave similarly, although it is technically an endogenous variable. Despite this, we expect income to have positive coefficients in all equations. In fact, it is positive in three equations and is significant in two of these. In the physical exercise equation it is negative but insignificant.

High wage rates also cause individuals to substitute health-related commodities for their own time and to substitute quick and easy health-related behaviors for more time-consuming behaviors. Consequently, we would expect the wage

Table 12.3. Logit analysis of four health habits: partial derivatives

	Stop smoking	Diet	Physical examination	Physical exercise
Age	0.014	0.005	0.009	0.003
Family income	0.0008	0.004	0.004	−0.0005
Education	0.005	0.014	0.004	0.014
Health insurance	0.038	0.022	0.307	0.038
Heart attack	0.100	0.239	0.339	−0.044
Chest pain		0.047		
Overweight		1.453		
Infective before 25				−0.019
Cancer before 25	−0.005			
Respiratory before 25	−0.007			
Digestive before 25	0.049			0.016
Anomaly before 25			0.106	
Exam as child			0.527	
Smoke before age 15	0.509	0.005		−0.038
Smoke 15–19	0.473	0.063		−0.001
Smoke 20–24	−0.067			
Childhood pop.	−0.067	0.037	−0.018	−0.00008
East Coast			0.079	
Number children			−0.013	
Never married		0.027	0.026	−0.053
Religious attendance	0.021	−0.003	0.004	−0.0002
Unsocial leisure		0.00007	−0.022	−0.032
Inactive leisure		−0.007		
Work active		−0.021		
Overtime work			−0.037	−0.017
Ever smoke	1.743			
Overweight at 25			0.089	−0.132
Twin stop smoke	2.226			
Twin diet		0.155		
Twin exam			0.125	
Twin exercise				0.058
Twin ever smoke	−0.104			

rate to have a greater effect on non-time-consuming health care practices, such as annual physical checkups, than on time-consuming activities, such as regular physical exercise. The large positive coefficient for income in the physical checkup equation and the insignificant coefficient for income in the physical exercise equation support this argument.

Environmental variables are assumed to affect the productivity of the production function inputs. If education, for example, increases the productivity of health-related behaviors, it reduces the quantity of those investments required to produce a given amount of gross investment. Under certain conditions it shifts the demand for health capital to the right, thereby increasing the optimal stock of health (Grossman, 1972:245). If the elasticity of the demand schedule for health capital is less than unity, the demand for health-related commodities would decline as education increases. This is the converse of the age effect discussed above: individuals with higher education levels will have higher stocks of health, which they may partially offset by reducing their demand for health-related commodities.

The conclusion that, given a relatively inelastic demand curve, education will lead to reduced consumption of health-related habits is no doubt surprising to health professionals and would not be predicted by the health belief model. Auster, Leveson, and Sarachek (1969) claim that education increases compliance with the advice of physicians, and Silver (1972) argues that education influences the level of health education. In fact, the coefficients of education are positive in all equations and are significant in the diet and physical exercise equations. Perhaps education is positively correlated with an individual's taste for health or with his taste for certain health habits, physical exercise in particular.

Health insurance, which is an important policy variable, is positive in all equations and significant in three of them. The partial derivatives (which appear in table 12.3) indicate that, controlling for other variables, individuals with health insurance are 30 percent more likely than others to have regular physical examinations. While this large coefficient may be due partially to a price effect, it may also reflect the fact that some health insurance policies require participants to have regular physical examinations.

Of special interest to proponents of the health belief model are cues to action. The results show that an individual who has had a heart attack is more likely to stop smoking, go on a diet, and to have a regular physical examination than an individual who has not had a heart attack, and these coefficients are significant at the 0.05 level for a one-sided alternative. This variable is negative but insignificant in the physical exercise equation, which is understandable since a heart attack may severely limit a person's ability to engage in physical exercise. The chest pain variable is significant and positive only in the diet equation. Being overweight is likely to increase the cues to go on a diet, and this variable is very significant in the diet equation.

One might think that the presence of cancer before age 25 or a heart attack before age 25 would increase the probability of giving up smoking or having regular physical examinations. Only two of the prior disease variables, however, are significant: the results suggest that a person who had a disease of the digestive system is more likely to stop smoking than one who has not, and that a person who had a congenital anomaly before 25 is more likely to have a regular physical examination than one who has not.

Whether a person had physical exams as a child has an important effect on whether he has regular physical exams as an adult. The results suggest that men exposed to regular physical examinations in their childhood are about 53 percent more likely to have regular physical examinations as adults than those who did not have regular childhood examinations. Clearly, certain behaviors practiced in childhood, whether they are voluntary or imposed, are maintained throughout life.

Since one of the dependent variables is the decision to stop smoking, we included a variable that indicated whether the individual had ever smoked; it was, however, insignificant. More important is the age at which a person started to smoke. We had thought that those who started earlier might find it harder to stop smoking, but the results indicate that people who started before age 24, particularly those who started between the ages of 15 and 24, are more likely to stop smoking than those who started later. Perhaps the decision to start smoking at a relatively young age depends more on social pressures than does a later decision. As people age, the social pressures to smoke decline, and those who smoke for social reasons are more likely to stop than those who smoke for other reasons.

A number of variables to measure an individual's demographic, social, and psychological background were included. One background variable is size of the town or city in which the person grew up. This variable has a significant negative effect on the probability that the person stops smoking and a significant positive effect on the decision to be on a diet. Individuals who live on the East Coast are significantly more likely than others to have regular physical examinations, perhaps because of the relative oversupply of physicians in that region. A highly significant background variable is attendance at religious services, which has a positive effect on the decision to stop smoking. Previous research by Breslow and Klein (1971) found that this variable is correlated with health habits.

The results suggest that married males take significantly more physical exercise than do single males and that, as the number of children increases, the probability of having a regular physical exam decreases. Two variables, "unsocial" and "inactive," reflect how individuals spend their leisure time. Individuals who frequently engage in social activities (including entertaining at home with friends and family, visiting friends, and engaging in club activities) are significantly more likely to take regular physical exercise and to have a regular physical examination than are individuals who do not engage in social activities. These coefficients are two of the most statistically significant. Individuals who frequently engage in active leisure activities (including home improvements and gardening, outdoor activities, and participation in sports) are less likely to be on a diet than are individuals who do not frequently engage in these activities. Similarly, individuals whose work is physically strenuous are less likely to be on a diet than those whose work is sedentary.

The remaining variables measure characteristics of each individual's twin brother. Over 90 percent of the individuals in our sample spent at least fifteen years with their twin brothers. To control for omitted home background, genetic, and other factors, we include in each equation a variable that indicates whether the twin engages in the same health-related habit. While theoretical justification for this technique has not been developed, it makes intuitive sense. Of course, these variables are endogenous, and the estimation procedure should consider this (although one does not). In any case, these variables are significant in all equations, except that the decision to quit smoking is not significantly related to the twin's decision to stop smoking. An individual, however, is more likely to stop smoking if his twin never smoked.

Conclusion

This study has drawn upon the health belief model and health maintenance model to study the formation of certain health-related habits. While these models are based on completely different theories, empirical specification of the health-related habit equations are similar. Consequently, it has proved more useful at this stage to find out empirically which variables are important than to evaluate the theoretical merits of these models. Fortunately, we have utilized a particularly rich dataset. Considering the salient aspects of both models and accounting for the unique features of our dataset, we have developed a statistical model to study the decision to stop smoking, to go on a diet to control weight, to have regular physical examinations, and to take regular physical exercise. These health-related habits were chosen because they have significant potential for improving health.

There are a number of problems with our analysis that future research will overcome. One problem is that the decision to stop smoking equation is estimated using all observations rather than using only those who had ever smoked. This problem arose because we treated all habits as health-beneficial so that the tables would be easy to read. In future research we shall examine health-harmful habits, such as the decision to start smoking, duration and quantity of smoking, and excessive alcohol consumption. Another problem is that some variables, such as income, are really endogenous. A model in which health-related habits, the twin's health-related habits, income, and health are endogenous variables would be a major advance. (Of course, any future model should give more attention to interaction effects.) Finally, since we have so much information about each individual's twin brother and we know their zygosity, we should be able to obtain better parameter estimates—including, for example, those of the relative importance of genetic and environmental effects.

Despite these problems and considerations for future research, the current results provide us with some tentative conclusions for health care policy. The first major conclusion is that people can and do change their health-related habits. While over 75 percent of the individuals in our sample have smoked at one time or another, almost 30 percent of them have stopped smoking. Second, while some variables, such as age, education, and health insurance, have beneficial effects on all health-related habits, most explanatory variables are habit-specific. Third, the economic constraints of time and money have substantial and statistically significant effects on the probability of regular physical exam-inations. Relaxing these constraints through health insurance or less demanding home or work environments (fewer children, less overtime) increases this type of preventive medical care. Fourth, evidence suggests that some health-benefi-cial actions, such as having checkups as a child, are habit-forming. Fifth, poor early life habits can be overcome: for example, those who started smoking at an early age are more likely to quit than those who started after 20. Sixth, bad adult health habits can be altered if one is frightened enough. While diseases before the age of 25 do not have significant, systematic effects on health habits, recent indicators of current health (heart attack, overweight) are important cues. Perhaps the same shock value can be achieved through adult health programs. Finally, the effects of religious attendance, engagement in social leisure activities, and the twin brother's behavior suggest that programs oriented toward the family, friends, church, or community will be more effective than those that are not.

While our results require considerable refinement before one can move into the policy forum with confidence, they suggest hypotheses that should be ex-amined further in controlled, behaviorally based experiments. Economic and social-environmental variables do influence a person's decision to adopt a healthy lifestyle. Identifying exactly which policy programs will work best to encourage healthy behavior is the next item on the research agenda. Our work suggests that price and time subsidies for preventive medical care, checkups, and childhood and adult health education are productive topics for further study.

13. The Effect of Liquor Taxes on Drinking, Cirrhosis, and Auto Fatalities

Philip J. Cook

Abstract

The real price of liquor fell by almost 50 percent between 1960 and 1980, in part because the federal liquor tax remained constant in nominal terms during this period. This revolutionary change in the affordability of liquor over a relatively short period may have stimulated a substantial increase in liquor consumption and in the incidence of alcohol-related problems.

The hypotheses that liquor taxes influence apparent consumption, cirrhosis deaths, and auto fatalities are tested using a quasi-experimental, nonparametric technique. In 39 instances between 1960 and 1975, a state raised its liquor tax. The state-specific rates of change in the criterion variables in these instances tended to be lower than in other states during the years when the tax changes occurred. Rough estimates of the price elasticities suggest that all three criterion variables are quite responsive to liquor prices. Thus an increase in the federal tax might have some beneficial public health effects. Such a tax is probably regressive but may nonetheless benefit some poor households; a liquor tax can also be justified as a sort of user fee, since heavy drinkers make heavy use of government-financed health care and income maintenance programs.

Alcoholic beverages have been taxed at a relatively high rate throughout U.S. history. During the last 20 years, however, taxes on beer, wine, and liquor have increased more slowly than the overall price level has. The result has been a substantial reduction in the price of alcoholic beverages relative to the prices of other commodities. Federal and state alcohol tax policies during this period have thus had the effect of providing an economic incentive for increased drinking. Since alcohol consumption is a contributing factor in the etiology of highway and other accidents, violent crime, suicide, cirrhosis, and a number of other causes of injury and death, it is possible that the downward trend in the relative price of alcoholic beverages has reduced Americans' life expectancy and increased morbidity.

The social science literature contains almost no direct evidence that would enable us to test whether the rate of alcohol taxation has an important influence on rates of morbidity and mortality, although the potential importance of alcohol taxation as a public health policy instrument has been discussed in several recent scholarly presentations.[1] The most controversial aspect of this question is whether changes in the price of alcohol influence the drinking habits of heavy drinkers; this group accounts for the bulk of alcohol-related problems, and it is widely believed that the drinking habits of this group are insensitive to the price of alcohol.

This study presents a new statistical analysis that indicates that liquor consumption in the United States is moderately responsive to price. More important, there is evidence that increases in the tax rate on spirits reduce both the auto fatality rate and the cirrhosis mortality rate, suggesting that the demand for alcohol by heavy drinkers is responsive to price.

The following section presents a brief history of alcohol taxation, prices, and consumption in the United States since 1950. Then I present new results for the 1960–1975 period using quasi-experimental technique, review available results relating alcohol consumption levels to mortality from certain causes and present new findings on the impact of alcohol prices on cirrhosis and auto fatalities. The next to last section discusses the use of excise taxes on alcoholic beverages as part of a public health strategy for reducing alcohol abuse, and the final section presents concluding observations.

Prices and Taxes

While the average prices of beer, wine, and distilled spirits have been increasing during the last two decades, the rates of increase are less than the overall inflation rate. The statistics in table 13.1 demonstrate that the price of spirits, relative to the average price of all other consumer goods as measured by the Consumer Price Index (CPI), has declined 48 percent since 1960. During the same period, the relative price of beer has declined by 27 percent and the price of wine by about 20 percent.

We would expect that price reductions of this magnitude, especially when coupled with the substantial increases in average real disposable income during this period, would result in increased consumption. In fact, average consumption of ethanol per person (aged 15 and over) increased 29 percent between 1960 and 1971; since then, average consumption has remained roughly constant at about 2.7 gallons of ethanol per year. Figure 13.1 depicts the recent history of consumption rates for beer, wine, and spirits.

Nominal consumer expenditures for alcoholic beverages increased from $13 billion to $32 billion between 1960 and 1975 (DISCUS *Facts Book*, 1977: 26), but this represents an increase in real terms (controlling for inflation) of only 36 percent. The percentage of total consumer expenditures accounted for by alcoholic beverages declined from 3.7 percent to 3.0 percent during this period. Thus as the real cost of alcoholic beverages has fallen, consumption has increased; at the same time, alcohol's share of the typical consumer's budget has shrunk.

Table 13.1. Average prices per pint of ethanol, 1960–1980

Year	Current prices[a] Beer and ale	Wine	Distilled spirits	Adjusted prices (1980 dollars)[b] Beer and ale	Wine	Distilled spirits
1960	$6.48	—	$7.79	$17.05	—	$20.50
61	6.50	—	7.84	16.89	—	20.39
62	6.53	—	7.87	16.78	—	20.22
63	6.59	$4.02	7.96	16.73	$10.21	20.21
64	6.64	4.01	7.99	16.67	10.07	20.05
65	6.70	4.03	8.01	16.56	9.96	19.80
66	6.81	4.05	8.06	16.34	9.73	19.35
67	6.93	4.10	8.16	16.14	9.56	19.01
68	7.12	4.26	8.27	15.95	9.54	18.54
69	7.30	4.44	8.36	15.47	9.41	17.73
70	7.54	4.79	8.57	15.16	9.63	17.22
71	7.82	5.02	8.68	15.01	9.64	16.67
72	7.89	5.21	8.86	14.67	9.69	16.48
73	8.01	5.55	8.91	14.01	9.71	15.60
74	8.78	6.04	9.05	13.87	9.55	14.30
75	9.72	6.32	9.31	14.09	9.16	13.50
76	9.95	6.46	9.46	13.63	8.85	12.97
77	10.10	6.64	9.59	12.93	8.51	12.27
78	10.66	7.29	9.98	12.69	8.67	11.88
79	11.77	7.95	10.39	12.60	8.50	11.12
(Jan) 80	12.40	8.27	10.74	12.40	8.27	10.74

a. Current prices were calculated as follows. *The Liquor Handbook* (1978:24) gives data on consumer expenditures and volume purchased for beer, wine, and spirits in 1976. These data yield estimates of the average price per pint of each type of beverage ($.45, .94, and 4.06 respectively). In 1976, beer averaged 4.49% alcohol, while wine was 14.6% and spirits 42.9% (calculated from data in Table 3 of Room (1977:6). Therefore, one pint of alcohol was contained in 22.3 pints of beer, or 6.85 pints of wine, or 2.33 pints of spirits. These figures for the number of pints of alcohol per pint of beverage were multiplied by the average prices per pint of beverage to obtain the 1976 figures in the first three columns. Prices in other years were derived from these 1976 prices by use of the Bureau of Labor Statistics price indexes for beer, wine, and spirits (unpublished).

b. Current prices were converted to adjusted prices (1980 dollar equivalents) by the use of the Consumer Price Index (CPI). For example, according to the CPI, 1960 dollars had 2.63 times as much purchasing power as 1980 dollars; each 1960 price was converted to 1980 dollars by multiplying by 2.63.

What accounts for the secular decline in the relative prices of alcoholic beverages? Part of the answer, particularly in the case of distilled spirits, is that excise tax rates have not kept up with inflation. Alcoholic beverages are subject to a complex array of taxes and other controls that affect retail prices. Taxes on spirits include a federal excise tax of $10.50 per proof gallon, state and local taxes and fees that averaged $5.55 per gallon in 1975 (DISCUS, 1977b), and import duties on foreign products. Beer and wine are also taxed by all levels of government, but less heavily. As a result, various direct taxes and fees account

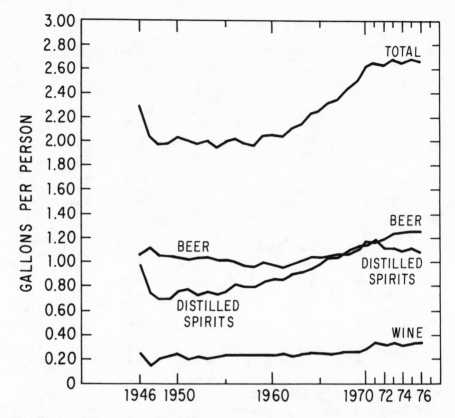

Figure 13.1. Trends in per capita ethanol consumption in U.S. gallons, based on beverage sales in each major beverage class in the United States, 1964–1976

for about one-half of retail expenditures for spirits and for about one-fifth of retail expenditures for both beer and wine (DISCUS, 1977b).

The states have legislated a considerable degree of government control on alcoholic beverage prices and sales. Nineteen states have a legal monopoly over the wholesale trade in spirits, and all but two of these also monopolize the retail trade in spirits. Most of these monopoly states also require that wine be sold only in state stores, and several have included beer as well.[2] In monopoly states, prices are set by administrative fiat. In the remaining states, retail distributors must be licensed by the state, and until recently most of these states have been subject to fair trade controls on pricing. The decline in real prices of alcoholic beverages, then, directly reflects choices made by state legislatures and regulatory agencies. More fundamentally, however, it is clear that these choices have been influenced by costs. A major component of the cost of distilled spirits is the federal excise tax; the fact that it has remained constant at $10.50 per proof gallon for the last 30 years has greatly contributed to the decline in real cost of this type of beverage. If this excise tax had been indexed to keep up with inflation since 1960, it would now stand at about $28 per proof gallon; assuming this tax increase had been passed along to the consumer with a 20 percent markup, the real price of spirits would have declined by only about 22 percent since 1960, in contrast with the actual decline of 48 percent. Hence prices of alcoholic beverages are controlled by legislation and government agencies to a considerable extent.

The Demand for Alcoholic Beverages

To what extent was the decline in real price of alcoholic beverages responsible for the increase in drinking during the 1960s? More generally, to what extent do economic variables influence drinking habits? This question has motivated a number of econometric studies in North America and Europe.[3] The principal problems in developing reliable estimates from available data are reviewed briefly below.

Problems in Estimating Demand

Price elasticities of U.S. liquor consumption estimated from state-level data have been questioned because of problems with official data on liquor sales (Waler, 1968; Smith, 1976; Hause, 1976). These data are based on reports by wholesalers to tax authorities and differ from actual liquor consumption by state residents in three potentially important respects: moonshine liquor is of course not included; wholesalers may underreport their sales in order to evade state taxes; and some consumers may import their liquor from an adjacent state if price differences between the two states make this activity worthwhile. If a state raises its tax on liquor, the resulting reduction in reported sales may overstate the reduction in consumption by state residents if moonshining increases, if wholesalers become more likely to conceal sales from tax authorities, or if consumers make more purchases in adjacent states (the "border effect"). (These problems may also affect beer and wine sales, of course.)

Next, alcohol consumption is influenced by a number of factors besides relative prices, including socioeconomic, demographic, and cultural variables and nonprice regulations on sales. Isolating the effect of price on quantity demanded requires an effort to control for these other factors. While it is possible in principle to control for other factors in the context of a multivariate regression analysis, there is considerable uncertainty about the proper specification for a regression analysis of liquor demand.

In addition, any observed relationship between prices and (apparent) quantities consumed is likely to reflect supply as well as demand conditions. In my judgment, none of the published regression analyses has succeeded in identifying the price coefficient in the demand equation. Indeed, most demand studies have simply assumed that prices are exogenous.

The econometric approach to estimating the price elasticity of demand for alcoholic beverages has dominated this empirical literature, but it is not the only available estimation technique. Simon (1966) introduced a quasi-experimental approach and argued persuasively that it offers a basis for more reliable estimates than those offered by regression analysis of cross-section or time series data.[4] Simon analyzed 23 cases in which the price of liquor in a state increased by more than 2 percent from one year to the next as a result of legislated increases in state liquor taxes. Each such price change can be viewed as an experiment, in the sense that it is induced by an external intervention in the normal market process. This intervention is exogenous unless state legislatures take market conditions into account when setting the tax rate. For each of these 23 cases, Simon calculated the proportional change in (apparent) consumption, after subtracting out (i.e. net of) the corresponding change for a group of "control" states. Simon's use of control states in this fashion is justified by the presumption that nonprice factors that influence consumption in one state in any one given year will also be influential in other states in that year. As long as the sample of 23 trial states is representative of the United States as a whole, Simon's approach yields an unbiased estimate of the apparent price effect. The median of the 23 estimates of price elasticity thus derived was Simon's choice for a point estimate of price elasticity. His median was −0.79.

Simon's method shares some of the problems discussed above in reference to the econometric studies. In particular, he makes no attempt to control for the border effect or for possible changes in the accuracy of sales reporting by wholesalers. (He does take the moonshining problem into account by excluding from his analysis states with a high incidence of moonshining.) It is possible, then, that his elasticity estimates are biased.

New Quasi-Experimental Estimates

I have replicated Simon's study using state tax changes occurring between 1960 and 1975. This study was limited to license states and excluded states in which the tax change was less than $0.25 per gallon. Alaska, Hawaii, and the District of Columbia were also excluded.[5] The resulting sample contains 39 observations.

The formula used to calculate the proportional change in liquor consumption induced by these tax changes can be written as follows:

$$D_t^s = \frac{C_{t+1}^a - C_{t-1}^a}{C_t^a} - \underset{s}{\text{Median}} \left\{ \frac{C_{t+1}^s - C_{t-1}^s}{C_t^s} \right\}, \qquad (13.1)$$

where

C_t^a = total liquor consumption divided by the population aged 21 and over in year t and state a (the state incurring the tax change).[6]

The "before" and "after" comparison is based on the calendar years preceding and following the year of the tax change, without regard to the month in which the change occurred. In all cases the median proportional change in consumption for the year in question is used as a basis of comparison. The median is calculated from the 30 license states (of the 48 contiguous states) in each year. Experiments with other approaches (e.g., using the median of the entire list of 48 states in each year, or the proportional change in total U.S. consumption) demonstrated that the choice of a basis of comparison makes little difference to the results.

The results of this analysis are reported in table 13.2. Of the 39 observations, 30 of the net consumption changes, D_i^a, calculated from this formula were negative. This is very strong evidence that other things being equal, an increase in tax reduces reported liquor sales in a state. If there were no relation between price and consumption, the probability of obtaining 30 or more negative changes out of 39 random trials would be less than one-tenth of a percent. This nonparametric sign test is a strong indication that the null hypothesis (that consumption is independent of price) should be rejected.

An estimate of the apparent price elasticity of demand can be developed by converting the statistics in table 13.2 for net change in liquor consumption by the proportionate change in price caused by the tax change for each observation. To calculate the proportionate change in price, the tax increase was multiplied by 1.2 (assuming a 20 percent markup on tax) and divided by the average retail price of liquor for the appropriate state and year.[7] The median of the resulting price elasticity estimates for the 39 observations was −1.6. This result implies that a 10 percent increase in the price of spirits results in a 16 percent reduction in quantity purchased. This is of course a point estimate and is subject to statistical error. Given the distribution of the 39 elasticity estimates, it can be shown that there is a 95 percent chance that the true elasticity is less than −1.0 (i.e., that the demand is elastic with respect to price).[8] My point estimate of −1.6 is considerably larger than Simon's estimate of −0.8, perhaps in part because he assumed a larger markup. Simon does not specify the exact rate of markup he used, but merely notes that it was the "customary retail" rate (which is surely higher than 20 percent for most commodities). If I had assumed an 80 percent markup, for example, my elasticity estimate would have been reduced to −1.07. My calculations indicate, however, that a 20 percent markup is a more realistic assumption for the retail liquor industry.

Interpretation of this elasticity estimate is complicated by the fact that in 16 of the 39 instances in which states increased the liquor tax, there was a contemporaneous increase in the state tax on beer. If beer is a substitute for liquor, then the effect of these contemporaneous changes will be to bias the liquor price elasticity upward. For this reason, the estimated price elasticity of demand for liquor may understate the true price elasticity.

For the procedure outlined above to give a valid, unbiased measure of the effect of tax changes on liquor sales, it is necessary that states' tax changes not be systematically related to historical trends in consumption in the state. It is

Table 13.2. Effects of changes in state liquor tax rates

Year	State	Tax change[a]	Net change in liquor consumption[b]	Rank[c]	Net change in auto fatality rate[b]	Rank[c]	Net change in cirrhosis death rate[b]	Rank[c]
1961	Conn.*	$1.00	-8.7%	2	13.2%	28	-9.0%	6
	Mo.*	.40	-2.5	10	-7.2	5	-5.7	10
	Nev.*	.60	-6.0	5	-39.2	1	-16.3	3
1963	Fla.*	.33	-0.1	14	-2.7	12	9.7	28
	Neb.	.40	-7.8	1	2.8	21	-7.1	7
	N.J.	.30	-1.9	7	4.7	23	-3.3	12
	N.Y.*	.75	-7.4	2	-0.0	15	2.3	21
	S.D.*	.50	-6.8	3	-17.2	4	-15.1	1
	Tenn.	.50	0.3	17	2.0	19	8.7	26
	Wisc.	.25	1.6	22	-4.3	8	-12.6	3
1964	Ga.	.50	9.8	29	-2.0	12	2.2	22
	Kans.	.30	-7.0	3	-6.1	7	-7.7	8
1966	Mass.*	.70	-6.9	3	-4.2	10	-3.0	9
1967	Calif.	.50	-4.6	6	-6.4	4	-14.7	2
	Tenn.	1.50	-11.3	2	-3.0	11	8.9	25
1968	Ariz.	.56	0.8	19	10.3	26	5.7	22
	Fla.*	1.23	-9.9	1	8.0	24	4.9	20
1969	Conn.*	.50	-9.2	1	-6.3	6	-0.9	12
	Del.	.50	0.3	16	4.5	25	-6.2	7
	Ill.*	.48	-4.8	6	-5.7	7	-3.2	9
	Mass.*	.41	14.8	30	5.3	27	-2.2	10
	Minn.	.755	-4.4	8	-9.0	4	-0.2	14
	Nev.	.50	-2.6	11	-1.7	12	11.4	23
	N.J.	.50	-8.8	2	-3.2	10	0.8	17
	R.I.*	.50	-4.3	9	-26.1	1	-17.9	2
1970	Kent.	.64	-0.5	13	0.3	16	6.7	22
	La.	.82	-0.6	12	-1.5	14	-1.0	13

Table 13.2. (Continued)

Year	State	Tax change[a]	Net change in liquor consumption[b]	Rank[c]	Net change in auto fatality rate[b]	Rank[c]	Net change in cirrhosis death rate[b]	Rank[c]
1971	Del.	$.60	−10.7%	3	−26.8%	1	3.2%	21
	Okla.	1.60	−7.3	4	−2.1	11	−11.2	3
	Minn.*	.90	−3.2	10	1.1	21	7.1	25
	Mo.*	.80	−7.1	5	0.3	17	−9.2	4
	S.D.	1.75	1.6	21	19.6	30	3.3	22
	Tex.*	.32	−3.2	11	−0.5	14	−3.4	11
	Wisc.	.35	2.9	23	0.3	18	−1.3	14
1972	Neb.	.40	−2.3	11	−20.2	1	1.5	17
	N.J.	.50	−7.2	6	−1.7	11	−8.8	5
	N.Y.	1.00	−10.0	3	−3.3	7	−9.9	2
1974	Ariz.	.50	−4.3	3	−2.2	9	−3.9	9
1975	Mass.*	.69	0.2	16	—	—	—	—

* An increase in the tax on beer was enacted in the same year.

a. A legislated change in the state tax on distilled liquor, expressed in dollars per gallon.

b. The changes in consumption, auto fatality rate, and cirrhosis death rate are proportional changes net of the corresponding change for the median state in that year.

c. Based on a ranking of the 30 license states (excluding Alaska and Hawaii), on the basis of the proportional change in the given rate.

possible that state legislatures' decisions to change liquor taxes are systematically related to trends in state sales (or tax revenue collections). Suppose that legislatures tend to raise taxes in response to an unsatisfactorily slow growth in liquor tax revenues. Then states that raise their taxes will be those with relatively slow growth in consumption. They would represent a biased sample of all states, and the statistical procedure reported above would yield misleading results; the bias in the measure of price elasticity would be negative, yielding an exaggerated notion of the degree to which reported consumption was responsive to price.

To test for this and related possibilities and, more generally, to test whether the states with tax changes can reasonably be viewed as a representative sample of all states, I calculated the net proportional growth rate in liquor consumption (the same measure as reported in table 13.2) for all states that had tax changes during the sample period, but for a period that preceded the year of the tax change by two years. Consistent with the notation defined in the formula above this statistic is denoted D_{t-2}^a. If tax changes occur at random among states and are not influenced by recent history in liquor consumption, then we would expect that it would be equally likely for any one of these values to be positive or negative. In fact, 21 of the 36 states (58 percent) for which it was possible to do this calculation[9] had negative values, while 15 (42 percent) had positive values. This result is not incompatible with the assumption that the true probability of a negative value is 0.50; the p-value from a classical hypothesis test (two-tailed) is 40 percent. In other words, this result does not provide evidence that tax changes are determined by consumption trends. In the absence of further evidence on this issue, it is reasonable to view tax changes as exogenous events.

The Effect of Tax Increases on Auto and Cirrhosis Fatalities

Introduction

The association between drinking and excess mortality from a variety of causes has been thoroughly documented. In particular, heavy drinking has been shown to be a major cause of auto accidents and cirrhosis of the liver. If an increase in the price of liquor reduces average consumption, an increase in the liquor tax rate may reduce the mortality rate due to these causes. Nevertheless, this conjecture is subject to a number of reasonable doubts, which are summarized here in three questions.

Is average liquor consumption responsive to changes in the price of liquor? While the evidence presented in the previous section demonstrates that an increase in the liquor tax rate reduces reported liquor sales, the effect on actual consumption of liquor may be smaller or nonexistent; the differences between reported sales and actual consumption, as discussed above, may be the result of moonshining, underreporting by wholesalers, and the border effect.

Is average alcohol consumption responsive to changes in the price of liquor? Even if actual consumption of liquor is reduced as a result of tax (price) increases, consumers may maintain their average level of alcohol consumption by substituting beer or wine for liquor. (Liquor accounts for only about 40 percent of beverage alcohol consumed in the United States.)

Is average alcohol consumption of heavy drinkers responsive to changes in the price of liquor? If the impact of price increases on alcohol consumption is limited to moderate drinkers, the reduction in consumption will have no effect on cirrhosis and auto fatalities. Studies of price effects on average alcohol consumption give no indication of the distribution of these effects among different types of drinkers.

There is no need to respond to these questions directly. The quasi-experimental method of measuring the price elasticity of liquor consumption, developed in the previous section, can also be used to measure the effect of tax increases on cirrhosis and auto accident fatality rates. The resulting estimates can virtually speak for themselves. If changes in liquor prices have the expected effect, it will be revealed by this method, and we can then draw the appropriate conclusions about the three questions.

Before reporting the results of this exercise, it will be helpful to review the literature on cirrhosis. For a discussion of the relationship between drinking and auto fatalities, the reader is referred to Reed (1981).

Cirrhosis and Drinking

Cirrhosis is a disease that reduces the liver's capacity to cleanse the blood and perform its other functions because of scarring of the liver tissue. Most people who die of cirrhosis have a long history of heavy drinking.[10] The liver is capable of processing a moderate level of alcohol intake without sustaining any damage. The cirrhosis disease process reflects a repeated overload of alcohol in the system.[11] If the cirrhosis victim reduces his consumption, the scarring process will be slowed or stopped and his life will ordinarily be prolonged.

A number of alcohol researchers have suggested that the cirrhosis mortality rate for a population is a good indicator of the fraction of the population that is drinking heavily (Skog, forthcoming). Thus the cirrhosis mortality rate can be used to compare relative incidence of heavy drinking in different populations or to measure trends in the incidence of heavy drinking for a single population. The main difficulty with using cirrhosis mortality in this way is that the current cirrhosis mortality rate reflects not only the current incidence of heavy drinking, but also the trend in heavy drinking during the preceding 15–20 years (Jellinek, 1947); a change in drinking habits in a population will not be fully reflected in cirrhosis mortality for this period of time. The short-run response of cirrhosis to heavy drinking, however, is not necessarily negligible. We can imagine a population to have a reservoir of cirrhosis victims whose disease has progressed to a greater or lesser extent (Schmidt & Popham, forthcoming); if this group changes its drinking patterns, there will be some effect on the cirrhosis mortality rate within a short time.

To the extent that cirrhosis mortality rates reflect the incidence of heavy drinking, they are of considerable value in alcohol research. A number of social and medical problems besides cirrhosis are related to heavy drinking.[12] If a particular alcohol-related policy is effective in reducing cirrhosis, it probably also reduces other problems associated with heavy drinking.

Seeley (1960) calculated intertemporal correlations between an alcohol price variable and the cirrhosis death rate for Ontario and for Canada, using annual data for 1935–1956. His price variable was an index representing the price of a gallon of beverage alcohol, divided by average disposable income. His work was extended to other countries and time periods by Popham, Schmidt, and deLint (1976). The reported correlations are typically close to 1.0. The authors' interpretation of these findings is that the consumption levels of cirrhosis-prone heavy drinkers are responsive to price. But these studies have two significant problems. First, the price variable confounds the price of alcohol with income level. Econometric studies of liquor demand have consistently found that the average consumption rate responds differently to changes in income and to changes in price. Johnson and Oksanen (1977), in particular, found that drinking in Canada was highly responsive to price but unresponsive to income. The second problem is that these correlation results may well be the result of "third cause" variables, not included in the analysis, that are responsible for trends both in price and in the incidence of heavy drinking.

Historical experiments with large changes in price and conditions of availability provide another source of evidence on the degree to which heavy drinkers are responsive to such environmental factors. Prohibition is an obvious case in point. Warburton (1932:240) found that alcoholic beverage prices during Prohibition were three to four times as high as before World War I. Cirrhosis death rates reached their lowest level of the 20th century shortly after World War I and remained constant at this low level (7–8 per 100,000) throughout the 1920s. Furthermore, the drop in cirrhosis death rates was apparently greater for the relatively poor than for others, suggesting that high prices were at least partly responsible for the reduction in heavy drinking during this era;[13] Warburton (1932:239) reports that the cirrhosis death rate for industrial wage-earners fell further than for city residents as a whole. Terris (1967:2007) reports that the age-adjusted cirrhosis death rates dropped further for blacks than for whites between 1915 and 1920, and that these rates preserved their new relative position through the 1920s.[14]

Results of a Quasi-experimental Study

The nature of and justification for the quasi-experimental approach to studying the price elasticity of demand for liquor have been explained above. The same approach is used here to measure the short-term effect of changes in the

Table 13.3. Analysis of tax-related changes

Rank	Net change in liquor consumption	Net change in auto fatality rate	Net change in cirrhosis death rate
1-5	16	8	9
6-10	8	8	9
11-15	6	9	6
16-20	4	4	3
21-25	3	5	9
26-30	2	4	2
Percent below median	76.9%	65.8%	63.2%
Sign test: prob-value[a]	0.001	0.037	0.072

a. Suppose that a price change had no effect on liquor consumption. Then each observation on the net change in consumption associated with a tax change would have a probability of 0.5 of being negative. This is the null hypothesis. The "prob-value" reported in the first column is the probability that 30 or more observations out of the 39 trials would be negative if the null hypothesis were true. The prob-values in the second and third columns are defined analogously. These probabilities were calculated using the normal approximation to the binomial distribution, applying the continuity correction. These procedures are discussed in T. H. Wonnacott and R. J. Wonnacott (1977).

liquor tax on the death rate due to cirrhosis and auto accidents.[15] This study uses the same 39 observations as the consumption study with one exception: data did not permit inclusion of the 1975 tax change in Massachusetts.

The results are reported in tables 13.2 and 13.3. The formula used to calculate the net change in auto fatalities is strictly analogous to the formula used in the consumption study, with the auto fatality rate replacing liquor consumption per capita. The formula used to calculate the net change in the cirrhosis death rate is a bit more complicated. It can be written as follows:

$$\frac{\sum_{i=1}^{3} D_{t+i}^{a} - \sum_{i=1}^{3} D_{t-i}^{a}}{D_{t-1}^{a} + D_{t}^{a} + D_{t+1}^{a}} - \underset{s}{\text{Median}} \left\{ \frac{\sum_{i=1}^{3} D_{t+i}^{s} - \sum_{i=1}^{3} D_{t-i}^{s}}{D_{t+1}^{s} + D_{t}^{s} + D_{t-1}^{s}} \right\}, \quad (13.2)$$

where

D_{t+i}^{a} = the cirrhosis death rate in the trial state i years after the tax change, and so forth. This formula permits delayed effects of the tax change on cirrhosis to be taken into account.

The results of this analysis are summarized in table 13.3. In the case of auto fatalities, about 66 percent of the net change observations were negative. If tax changes had no effect on auto fatalities, we would expect that only about 50 percent of these observations would be negative. The probability that 66 percent or more would be negative, given the null hypothesis of no effect, is less than 4 percent. Therefore, we can conclude with considerable confidence that a liquor tax increase tends to reduce the auto fatality rate. Additionally, about 63 percent of the net change observations for cirrhosis deaths were negative. The probability that chance alone would produce this high a proportion of negative values is about 7 percent. It appears likely, then, that increases in liquor tax also reduce the cirrhosis death rate.

Statistical findings cannot offer definitive proof of anything. The preponderance of the evidence, however, certainly supports the conjecture that the price of liquor is one determinant of the auto accident and cirrhosis death rates. The quasi-experimental technique employed here minimizes problems of interpretation and in particular minimizes doubts coucerning the causal process that underlies the results.

Despite the questions posed at the beginning of this section, there is good reason to believe that the incidence of heavy drinking responds to liquor price changes of relatively small magnitude. The magnitudes of these responses are highly uncertain but can be estimated using the same techniques employed in estimating the price elasticity of demand in the previous section. When the net change statistics of table 13.2 are converted into price elasticities, the median is −0.7 for auto fatalities and −0.9 for cirrhosis deaths. These elasticity estimates are lower than the price elasticity of demand for distilled spirits—an intuitively plausible result, given the possibility of substituting other forms of alcohol for liquor, the border effect, and so forth.

Evaluating Alcoholic Beverage Taxation

Alcoholic beverage prices have a direct effect on a chronic excess consumption and various associated problems. Three principal sources of evidence support this conclusion. First, numerous studies, including this one, have found that per capita consumption of alcoholic beverages is responsive to price changes. It is possible but unlikely that this observed responsiveness of aggregate drinking to price is due entirely to decreased consumption by light and moderate drinkers.[16] Second, large changes in price associated with Prohibition and other natural experiments have been correlated wth large reductions in the cirrhosis mortality rate and in other indicators of the prevalence of excess consumption. Third, small increases in the tax rate for spirits appear to reduce cirrhosis and auto fatality rates.

Each of these pieces of evidence is subject to legitimate scientific doubt. Taken together, however, they make a strong case for the proposition that an increase in the price of alcoholic beverages will reduce the prevalence of heavy drinking and the incidence of various problems caused by chronic excess consumption. How large an effect could be generated by, say, a 20 percent increase in the alcoholic beverage price level is highly uncertain, although it appears likely that each year thousands of lives could be saved and billions of dollars in medical and related expenses could be saved. Since they have traditionally been controlled to a considerable extent by government policy, alcoholic beverage prices can be considered public health policy instruments. This is an empirical rather than a normative conclusion; it does not imply that it would be a good thing to raise the federal excise tax on alcohol, or that higher prices are better than lower prices. A complete evaluation of a change in alcohol price policy requires consideration of other effects in addition to those related to public health. In particular, the distributive effects of a tax-induced increase in price should be considered, as should the loss in consumer benefits associated with low alcoholic beverage prices.

Incidence of Taxation

The distribution of alcohol consumption levels among individuals is very diffuse and skewed toward heavy drinkers. This characterization is valid for every population group that has been studied (Brunn et al., 1975). Roughly speaking, one-third of adults in the United States abstain, one-third drink very lightly (up to three drinks per week), and the remaining one-third account for most of the total consumption (Moore & Gerstein, 1981). Survey-based estimates indicate that for the population of the United States as a whole, 5 percent of the adults drink about half of the total alcohol (Moore & Gerstein, 1981).

Because a high percentage of consumption is concentrated in relatively few people, the incidence of alcohol taxation is necessarily very unequal. Whether this degree of inequality is good or bad depends on one's perspective. Three questions, reflecting three rather different normative perspectives on the incidence issue, are posed and discussed below.

First, how is the incidence of alcohol taxation related to consumers' ability to pay? Almost $10 billion in direct taxes and fees on alcoholic beverages was collected by all levels of government in 1976 (DISCUS, 1977b). In most jurisdictions this revenue is not earmarked for specific programs but, rather, is used to help finance a wide range of governmental activities. One traditional standard in the public finance literature is that such general public revenues should be collected on the basis of ability to pay; households with equal incomes should make equal contributions, and tax contribution should increase with income. On this principle, taxes on alcoholic beverages clearly receive low marks; households with equal incomes pay vastly different alcohol taxes, depending on their alcohol consumption levels.

Second, how much of a burden does alcohol taxation impose on members of poor households? The answer to this question is not known, but it is useful to outline the relevant issues. Individual adults and heads of households who drink clearly would not voluntarily choose to pay higher prices.[17] Their dependents may benefit, however, depending on the response of the household's drinking members to the price change. An increase in the taxes on alcoholic beverages can either increase or reduce the total expenditures of poor households on alcohol, thereby leaving less or more money for food, clothing, and shelter. For households whose demand for alcoholic beverages is elastic (price elasticity less than -1.0), an increase in price will reduce total expenditure on drinking, while expenditures will increase for other households. Surely poor households differ considerably among themselves with respect to price elasticity of demand. The evidence presented above, however, suggests that the average household's demand for spirits is quite elastic; furthermore, the demand of poor households would tend to be more elastic than that of higher income households. Therefore, for a high but unknown percentage of poor households, an increase in alcohol taxation should reduce expenditures for alcoholic beverages. Furthermore, it is quite possible that a tax-induced reduction in drinking in households at the high end of the drinking distribution may lead to reduced medical expenditures and increased earnings from employment.

Third, is the incidence of alcoholic beverage taxation related to the benefits received from government? An alternative to the ability to pay standard is the benefits standard, which links the distribution of tax liability to the distribution of benefits received from government programs. To a large extent, medical care, alcoholism treatment, minimum income maintenance, and other social services are provided and financed by government. The various health and social problems associated with alcohol consumption place expensive demands on these services. These problems are highly concentrated among the same group that pays the bulk of alcohol taxes—the chronic excess consumers. Thus there is a fairly close positive association between an individual's alcohol tax contribution and the expected value of government services he consumes for alcohol-related problems. Alcohol taxes are analogous to insurance premiums that are calibrated to one determinant of risk—the average rate of alcohol consumption—just as health and life insurance premiums are adjusted for age.

We could label this view of the alcohol tax the "drinker should pay" standard. This standard suggests that it is appropriate to set alcohol taxes at a level that will yield tax revenues equal to the total government-financed costs of alcohol-related problems. Or, by the same justification, we could structure taxes so that drinkers collectively pay the total bill for alcohol-related externalities, including private costs now borne by other individuals. For example, we all pay higher premiums for private health and life insurance policies because some insured people drink unhealthy or unsafe amounts.

Aside from the problem of actually calculating the social costs of drinking, these quantitative standards are vulnerable to a major objection: the social harm of drinking is not proportional to the rate at which an individual consumes alcohol, so that a tax that is proportional to consumption will not be strictly proportional to alcohol-related harms. Figure 13.2 illustrates a hypothetical relationship between social cost and consumption. The relationship is not strictly proportional because it incorporates two reasonable assumptions: that average

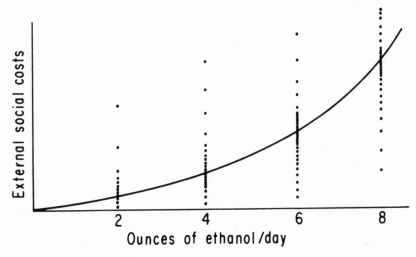

Figure 13.2. Hypothetical relationship between the individual's consumption and resulting social harm

social cost increases disproportionately with consumption and that there is a great difference in the harm caused by individuals' drinking at the same consumption level because of differences in personality, metabolism, drinking patterns, and so on. If taxes are strictly proportional to the ethanol content of alcoholic beverages, light drinkers and the safer heavy drinkers will pay more than their share of the total bill for alcoholic-related social costs. Whether this arrangement is preferable to paying these costs from general tax revenues is a matter of taste. In my judgment, the "drinker should pay" principle is not sufficiently compelling in itself to justify high taxes on alcoholic beverages. But it should be kept in mind that high taxes reduce the social costs of drinking, in addition to providing a mechanism for financing these costs.

Cost-Benefit Analysis

Besides providing a source of government revenue, alcohol taxes influence the volume of total sales and the distribution of that volume among individual drinkers. Taxation is necessary to achieve an appropriate price for alcoholic beverages (i.e., a price that reflects the negative externalities of drinking). The Pigovian principle requires that the tax on an externality-generating activity be set equal to the difference between the marginal social cost of the activity and its marginal private cost—an approach long advocated by economists for controlling environmental pollution. The objective of this type of tax is to internalize the external costs of the activity, thereby giving agents the incentive to curtail the activity to the appropriate level (i.e., the level at which every unit of the activity is valued at least as highly as its true social cost). The normative force of this principle is undermined in the case of drinking by the fact (illustrated above in figure 13.2) that the social cost of a drink depends on who consumes it and under what circumstances. Therefore, an increase in the tax on alcoholic beverages will deter some drinking that is socially worthwhile (in which the value to the consumer exceeds the social cost) as well as some that is not worthwhile. Given this situation, and ignoring the distributional issues discussed above, the appropriate tax rate should be chosen by comparing costs and benefits at each tax level.

The marginal social benefit of a tax increase is equal to the value of the reduction in negative externalities that will result from reduced consumption, plus the additional tax revenue obtained. The marginal social cost of a tax increase is equal to the value of consumer's surplus[18] lost as a result of the tax. In principle, the tax rate is too low if the additional benefit of an increase exceeds the loss in consumer's surplus. Clearly, the considerable uncertainty surrounding the actual magnitudes of these theoretical constructs would make it very difficult to implement this principle. This discussion should serve as a useful framework for further empirical research in this area.

Conclusion

Public enthusiasm for government restrictions on drinking peaked in the early years of this century, when many states and eventually the nation banned the sale of alcoholic beverages. Since the repeal of Prohibition in 1933 there has been a more or less steady decline in government restrictions on availability. Perhaps the most important aspect of this trend in recent years has been the rather sharp decline in prices of alcoholic beverages (relative to average prices of other commodities), caused in large part by the failure to increase alcohol taxes to keep pace with inflation.

While the public remains concerned about the alcohol problem, there is a widespread belief that restricting availability is not the answer. For example, a recent study by Medicine in the Public Interest (1979:31) concluded that state legislators are "generally skeptical about the effect of regulations, including taxation, on the incidence, patterns, or circumstances of use." The evidence reported above, however, suggests that the legislators' view is incorrect—that taxes do reduce total consumption, and in particular that they reduce the total consumption associated with auto fatalities and liver cirrhosis. Thus, alcohol taxation can legitimately be viewed as a policy instrument for combating alcohol-related problems, and not just as a source of revenue.

This study has not proved that taxes should be raised. A complete cost-benefit analysis would be needed to determine whether the net effect of higher taxes would be positive or negative. But the evidence presented here indicates that benefits do exist and argues for a fresh look at alcohol taxation as a policy tool.

14. Estimating Distribution Functions for Small Groups: Postoperative Hospital Stay

Michael A. Stoto

Abstract

Many policy problems involve the distribution of length of hospital stay. In particular, when studying spells of unemployment, duration of time on welfare, length of life, intervals between a mother's children, or postoperative hospital stays, we might expect substantially different distributions for different individuals. We often face the problem of having to estimate distribution functions for many small groups, when we would prefer to rely on information about the shape of the distribution gained from larger but substantially similar groups. This study develops a model that allows us to transfer information about the shape of the distribution from large groups to small groups, by using data for small groups to tailor the general shape to a specific group. Data on postoperative length of hospital stay provide an illustration of the method. We find that (a) a simple two-parameter model is effective, (b) the parameters coincide with medical logic, and (c) one common standard distribution, estimated from the data, is sufficient for estimating extreme percentiles of the distribution. These findings mean that the model is helpful for planning and evaluating changes in hospital policies, and for detecting cases whose hospital stay has been longer than expected.

With today's soaring hospital costs, the amount of time a patient spends in the hospital after an operation is an important factor in the overall cost of surgery. This chapter proposes an empirical model for studying the distribution of length of postoperative hospital stay. The model itself is quite general and is appropriate for estimating and comparing groups of probability distribution functions in a wide range of policy areas.

Hospital planners will find several uses for a good description of the distribution of length of stay. Many surgical procedures performed today are elective and can be planned in advance. To schedule patients efficiently so as not to waste hospital resources, planners must project bed usage as a function of the patient mix at a particular time. A good description of the distribution of length of stay would enable the planner to simulate the impact on length of stay of potential changes in patient mix or in policy.

Length of hospital stay is also useful as an outcome variable in studying the effects of surgery. Excessive hospital stays may indicate the occurrence of unforeseen complications. The federal government has established Peer Standard Review Organizations (PSRO) to monitor patients who have stayed in the hospital longer than expected and to check for complications. In evaluating a surgical innovation, we usually regard a shorter recuperation time as a desirable outcome.

For both planning and evaluation purposes, we recognize that different groups of patients have different distributions of length of hospital stay. For instance, we expect longer stays for older or sicker patients, or for those undergoing more serious operations. Even after stratification by such medical variables, a considerable amount of variation in the length of stay remains. In addition to purely medical standards, physicians consider, for instance, whether patients have a suitable place to go when they have been released from the hospital. Authorities also tend to release marginal patients before weekends or holidays. Because of these additional factors, which frequently are not recorded for study, it is difficult to estimate the exact length of hospital stays of individual patients. But we can get useful estimates of the distribution of length of stay for different groups of patients.

Example: Hernia Operation

Figure 14.1 shows the length of stay (LOS) curves for four groups of patients at Massachusetts General Hospital (we describe the source of the data and the calculations of the LOS curves in section II). Anesthesiologists have developed a standard score to assess the physical status of surgical patients (PSTAT), and we use this score to assign the patients to one of four groups. The healthiest patients have a PSTAT of 1 and the sickest patients have a PSTAT of 4 or 5.

Clearly, LOS increases as PSTAT increases. For instance, the proportion of patients remaining 10 days is 1.4 percent for PSTAT 1 and 50 percent for PSTAT 4 and 5. The median stay goes from about 2 days for PSTAT 1 to 10 days for PSTAT 4 and 5. The 90 percent point of the distribution is about 11 days for PSTAT 1 and 20 days for PSTAT 4 and 5. Even though the distributions of the four groups differ, there is still much variation within each group. The interquartile range is about 4 days for PSTAT 1 and about 9 days for PSTAT 4 and 5.

Stratification

For planning purposes we want estimates of the proportion of patients remaining at least t days. For evaluation of the quality of care, we want to estimate certain quantiles of the LOS distribution, the number of days until, say, only 25 percent of the patients remain in the hospital. But we must answer these questions for specific groups of patients. The stratification in the hernia example indicates how different the answers can be for patients undergoing the same operation.

With stratification, the number of individuals in some cells can be very small, even with large data sets. We used the experience of 2,331 patients to calculate

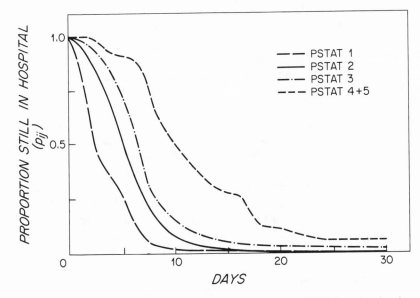

Figure 14.1. Observed length of stay (*LOS*) curves for 3800, herniorrhaphy

the curves in figure 14.1, but the number in each group ranges from 1,226 patients with PSTAT 1 to only 21 with PSTAT 4 and 5. We can confidently make statements about proportions and percentage points for patients with PSTAT 1, but cannot be so confident about those with PSTAT 4 and 5, since our data are based on only 21 operations.

Plan of the Study

Our basic goal is to estimate distribution of LOS for groups for which there are few direct observations. To do so we have developed a model that allows us to transfer information about the *shape* of the distribution from large groups of patients to small groups. We have employed four methods to check the adequacy of the model.

Examination of residuals. Systematic errors across groups may reveal inadequacies of the model, even though there are not enough data in individual cases to discover an inadequate fit.

Goodness of fit for large groups. The general applicability of the model for large groups increases our confidence that the model also applies to small groups.

Consistency across operation. Finding similar results for a wide range of operations increases our confidence in the generalizability of the model.

Medical logic. Parameter estimates that accord with a priori medical logic increase the likelihood that the proposed model is appropriate.

The second part of this chapter describes the data for the analysis. They consist of LOS distribution for nine common operations, each stratified by PSTAT. The third section presents the mathematical model for LOS. It is a flexible mathematical relationship that provides for a standard distribution for each operation and for two parameters to relate each PSTAT group to the standard. Only minimal assumptions about the mathematical form are employed. The fourth section applies the model and examines the fit in detail. We also examine two aspects of the model's general ability to fit the data. Part five looks at the interpretation and the relationship of the estimated parameters for each PSTAT group and finds that the results accord with medical logic. Finally, I compare the estimated standard distribution across operations; the results indicate that for some purposes the model can be simplified by using the same standard for each operation.

Other Policy Applications

Many policy problems have features similar to the problems involved in policy for postoperative hospital stays. Spells of unemployment; duration of time on welfare; prison stays; response times of police, ambulances, or fire trucks; time to remission or cure of a disease; and length of life itself, to name a few, are all LOS variables—they measure a length of time until something happens. Often the distributions of these variables are different for subgroups of the population. For instance, the time unemployed or on welfare is partially determined by various socioeconomic factors, including education and previous employment. The length of prison stays depends obviously on the sentence but also on previous criminal record, parole policies, and so on. Response times of police, ambulances, and fire trucks vary from one part of the city to another and depend on traffic patterns that vary over the day, week, and year.

Knowledge of the distributions of LOS variables helps policy makers in planning and evaluation. For short-term planning, LOS distributions of, say, prisoners or hospital patients help determine the future service needs of those already in the system and predict when and how many openings will arise. In the long run, LOS distributions can serve as inputs for simulation studies to determine the effect of proposed policies—for instance, the relocation of a police or fire station. For evaluation purposes, knowledge of LOS distributions can help to identify unusual cases or outliers (for instance, someone unemployed longer than usual) for further study or special attention.

All these applications rely on knowing the LOS distributions for subgroups of a population. But often data for some subgroups is very scarce while large samples are available for others. The techniques used in this chapter allow the policy analyst to estimate LOS distributions for small groups by relying on

Table 14.1. Description of dataset

S-Code	Operation	Mortality	Total N	PSTAT 1	PSTAT 2	PSTAT 3	PSTAT 4&5	Risk
406	Coronary artery bypass	7.60%	1314	4	111	827	372	High
410	Abdominal aortic aneurysm	15.91	375	11	139	185	40	High
1402	Craniotomy	11.47	784	158	349	212	65	High
208	Femoral fracture	2.29	558	122	211	197	28	Moderate
413	Extremity bypass graft	4.63	368	22	134	184	28	Moderate
731	Cholecystectomy	2.24	1321	448	609	236	28	Moderate
206	Total hip replacement	0.31	704	215	364	120	5	Low
800	Herniorrhaphy	0.33	2331	1226	783	301	21	Low
911	TUR prostate	0.58	958	111	508	316	23	Low

Note: Only live discharges with one operation are included.

information about the shape of the distribution from larger groups. Length of hospital stay is used as an example, but the statistical techniques may apply to many other problems.

Source and Calculation of LOS Curves

For our study we chose nine operations commonly performed at Massachusetts General Hospital. As part of an ongoing study of outcome from anesthesia and surgery at that hospital, anesthesiologists have collected information on every patient undergoing an operation requiring anesthesia from 1973 through 1976. In this period, about 65,000 surgical admissions led to about 75,000 surgical procedures. For a general description of the data available and the methods of collection, see Strenio et al. (1979).

The nine surgical procedures to be studied are listed in table 14.1. They are classified by "S-Code," a scheme devised by Dr. Benjamin Barnes (see Strenio et al., 1979) to group the 1,700 types of operations into a more manageable 170. Some of the categories, such as S406, coronary artery bypass graft, and S206, total hip replacement, are relatively homogeneous because they include one very specific operation, performed for a particular set of indications. Other S-Codes, such as S1402 (craniotomy), group together a more heterogeneous set of operations and patients.

We chose nine S-Codes to reflect the variety of operations performed at the hospital. The first three operations have a high overall risk of mortality. As table 14.1 shows, the overall in-hospital mortality rate for patients having one of these operations alone, or as the principal of a series of operations, ranges from 7 percent to 16 percent. The mortality of the second group of operations is lower, ranging from 2 to 5 percent, and the operations in the third group are low-risk procedures with an overall mortality rate less than .5 percent.

During the four-year study period, surgeons performed 11,064 operations of the types listed in table 14.1. Of these, 8,976, or 81 percent, were the only operations performed in that hospitalization. Because of the complicating effects that multiple operations have on postoperative length of stay, we begin our study with the 8,976 single operations. Table 14.1 gives the breakdown by type of operation.

At the time of the operation, the anesthesiologist rates the patient's general health, including the disease requiring surgical treatment, on a standard PSTAT scale of 1 to 5. We use this variable to assign the patients to one of four groups, combining PSTATs 4 and 5 because of the small number of PSTAT 5 patients. A handful of patients who had no PSTAT score recorded were excluded from the analysis. We could have used other variables to stratify patients, but since PSTAT is a good predictor of surgical outcome as measured by hospital morbidity index, we use it here to predict length of stay (Gentleman et al., 1969). The distribution of patients by PSTAT for each operation also appears in table 14.1.

We assume that shorter hospital stays are better than longer stays—a reasonable assumption for a patient who eventually recovers. But for a patient who does not recover, a shorter hospital stay may indicate more serious complications than a longer stay. Since we expect quite different behavior for the LOS distribution of patients who do not survive, we exclude these individuals from the present analysis. We study the LOS distribution for live discharges only, a more limited population, but one for which we can make more sensible conclusions. For prediction purposes, the model could just as well be applied to LOS curves for all discharges.

Table 14.1 sums up the composition of the dataset. We list nine operations, along with the number of patients experiencing each procedure, and include only patients with single operations and known PSTAT, who are live discharges. The total sample size is 8,713.

The Mathematical Model

The model we propose is based on demographic work on model life tables. In demographic analysis, a "life table" gives the proportion of individuals who survive to each age. For our analysis, we replace this concept with a "survival curve," p_{ij}, representing the proportion of patients in group i still in the hospital on day j.

Brass (1975) has developed a flexible and convenient family of life tables known as a "relational system." Simply put, he first assumes the existence of a common standard life table, p_{sj}. All other life tables, p_{ij}, are related to this standard by a simple function. Specifically, let

$$\text{logit}(p) = \frac{1}{2}\log\left(\frac{p}{1-p}\right). \tag{14.1}$$

With the factor of $1/2$, this function is similar to probit (p), the inverse of the normal cumulative distribution function. The relationship of a given life table, p_{ij}, to the standard, p_{sj}, is

$$\text{logit}(p_{ij}) = \alpha_i + \beta_i \text{logit}(p_{sj}). \tag{14.2}$$

Thus a two-parameter family of life tables is generated by a given standard. But Brass's standard for human mortality will not be a good description of hospital LOS. Instead, we have developed a model to estimate the standard appropriate to a given set of data.

Mathematical Background

We first consider under what conditions a group of similar life tables can be described by a relational system. For instance, we ask whether there is a standard life table p_{sj} and a set of α_i and β_i values which together adequately represent the four LOS curves in figure 14.1.

We begin with an unrealistic assumption, which we will soon drop. Let T be a random variable, the length of hospital stay. The life table values, p_{ij}, are

$$p_{ij} = \text{Prob}(T \geq t_j), \tag{14.3}$$

the probability that a life exeeds t_j years. The unrealistic assumption is that T has a logistic distribution, with parameters α_i and β_i, that is, that p_{ij} has the form:

$$p_{ij} = \frac{e^{2(\alpha_i + \beta_i t_{ij})}}{1 + e^{2(\alpha_i + \beta_i t_j)}}. \tag{14.4}$$

The expected value of T is $-\alpha_i/\beta_i$ and the variance is $\pi^2/(12\beta_i^2)$.

The logit function is the inverse of the logistic life table function;

$$\text{logit}(p_{ij}) = \frac{1}{2}\log e^{2(\alpha_i + \beta_i t_j)} \tag{14.5}$$

$$= \alpha_i + \beta_i t_j. \tag{14.6}$$

If all life tables represented logistic distributions, logits of all life tables would be linear functions of t_j. Thus, if we define

$$p_{sj} = \frac{e^{2t_j}}{1 + e^{2t_j}},$$ (14.7)

then

$$\text{logit}(p_{sj}) = t_j .$$ (14.8)

Hence, for all p_{ij},

$$\text{logit}(p_{ij}) = \alpha_i + \beta_i \text{logit}(p_{sj})$$ (14.9)

by our definition of terms. Under the restrictive assumptions, a relational system represents all life tables.

But we can relax the assumptions and still maintain the linear relationship. For any specific p_{ij} we can find a transformation of the time axis, $g(t)$, such that

$$p_{ij} = \frac{e^{2(\alpha_i + \beta_i g(t_j))}}{1 + e^{2(\alpha_i + \beta_i g(t_j))}} .$$ (14.10)

The transformation $g(t)$ may be simple—for instance, taking logarithms of the time scale. In general, we define $g(t)$ as

$$g(t_j) = \frac{\text{logit}(p_{ij}) - \alpha_i}{\beta_i} .$$ (14.11)

If the same $g(t)$ transforms each of a set of distributions to a logistic shape, we can represent each life table as

$$\text{logit}(p_{ij}) = \alpha_i + \beta_i g(t_j) .$$ (14.12)

If we set $g(t_j) = \text{logit}(p_{ij})$, equation (14.9) still holds.

The logit function, of course, is only one of many inverse distribution functions. The probit is an obvious alternative but is harder to calculate and gives no evidence of generally better fits. McNeil and Tukey (1975) study a family of related functions of the form $p^\lambda - (1 - p)^\lambda$ that includes $\text{logit}(p)$ in the limit as λ goes to zero, and probit (p) as an approximation.

Note that $g(t_j)$ in equation (14.12) plays the role of $\text{logit}(p_{ij})$ in equation (14.9). The search for a transformation of the time axis to make each of the observed life tables logistic is equivalent to the search for a standard life table for equation (14.9). If a set of empirical data exactly meets the above conditions, any one table of the set may serve as a standard distribution.

Our empirical life tables, p_{ij}, are observed with random variation or error. Furthermore, they do not exactly correspond to the simple model. Some summary of the observed tables should be a better standard than any individual table. The following section gives a method of specifying a standard to fit a set of empirical life tables.

Estimating a Standard Life Table

Our data consist of a rectangular array of values p_{ij}, the ith life table evaluated at the jth time period. The observation points, t_j, are the same for each table. Let us define

$$y_{ij} = \text{logit}\,(p_{ij}) \tag{14.13}$$

and

$$x_j = \text{logit}\,(p_{sj}) \ . \tag{14.14}$$

We calculate y_{ij} from the data but at the start do not know either p_{sj} or x_j. The implication of equation (14.9) is the linear model

$$y_{ij} = \alpha_i + \beta_i x_j \ . \tag{14.15}$$

The x_j as well as the α_i and β_i are unknown and to be estimated. The model is actually a simple case of factor analysis.

If the x_j were known, we would regress the values in the first column of y_{ij} on the x_j values to estimate α_1 and β_1. We would then repeat this with the other columns to estimate α_i and β_i. Similarly, if α_i and β_i were known, we could construct $y_{i1} - \alpha_i$ for the first row of y_{ij}, and regress (through the origin) these values of β_i for an estimate of x_1, and so on. Heuristically, the estimating algorithm is an iterative method based on an alternation of these two steps. Stoto (1979) provides the details of this algorithm and a computer program to carry out the estimation.

We have used weighted least squares for each regression step. The weights reflect two aspects of the data. First, there are occasional large discrepancies from the model of equation (14.15). These arise when there are errors in the original data, or when a segment of one of the observed life tables does not correspond to the linear model. To deal with these we use the bisquare weighting function (Mosteller & Tukey, 1977), which downweights very large outliers. Second, the y_{ij} do not necessarily have equal variance. Each value of p_{ij} is the proportion of the n_i patients in group i with hospital stays greater than t_j days. This has an approximately binomial distribution with expected value $E(p_{ij}) = p$ and variance $p(1 - p)/n$. Since $y_{ij} = \text{logit}(p_{ij})$, the variance of y_{ij} is approximately

$$\text{var}\,(y_{ij}) = [p(1-p)n]^{-1} \ . \tag{14.16}$$

Efficiency considerations lead to weights on y_{ij} inversely proportional to the variance of y_{ij}. We do not know $E(p_{ij})$ and hence cannot calculate the optimal

Table 14.2. Summary of fit, standard estimated

S-Code	PSTAT	n_i	α_i	β_i	$(1-R^2)_i$ in %	MAD_i in %	MAD
406	1	4	0.178	1.483	16.83	4.53	
	2	111	0.225	2.105	2.39	1.13	
	3	827	0.426	2.290	0.08	0.14	
	4&5	372	0.793	2.127	1.12	0.18	0.66
410	1	11	−0.055	1.018	7.75	2.27	
	2	139	0.271	1.740	0.68	0.21	
	3	185	0.501	1.844	1.51	0.27	
	4&5	40	0.432	1.266	11.86	2.03	1.15
1402	.	158	0.212	1.131	0.79	1.49	
	.	349	0.666	1.530	0.28	0.67	
	.	212	1.014	1.599	0.55	0.89	
	.	65	1.287	1.309	0.31	0.81	0.85
208	.	122	0.022	1.064	0.12	0.57	
	.	211	0.792	1.608	0.13	0.30	
	.	197	0.848	1.659	4.71	0.48	
	.	28	0.817	1.675	4.32	0.70	0.53
413	.	22	−0.066	1.324	2.81	2.61	
	.	134	0.408	1.954	1.07	0.28	
	.	184	0.572	1.726	0.11	0.22	
	.	28	0.785	1.683	1.39	0.94	0.61
731	.	448	0.004	2.381	0.91	0.53	
	.	609	0.437	2.100	1.42	0.23	
	.	236	1.185	1.729	8.49	2.82	0.54
206	.	215	0.605	1.890	0.93	0.37	
	.	364	0.841	1.834	0.10	0.27	
	.	120	1.003	1.620	2.66	0.72	
	.	5	1.121	1.609	15.54	3.44	0.55
800	.	1226	−1.312	1.664	0.59	0.24	
	.	783	−0.669	1.869	0.58	0.24	
	.	301	−0.237	1.709	0.23	0.35	
	.	21	0.672	1.868	2.17	2.51	0.29
911	.	111	−0.743	1.856	3.50	1.21	
	.	508	−0.480	1.751	1.34	0.81	
	.	316	−0.290	1.547	0.56	0.47	
	.	23	0.096	1.786	2.12	1.25	1.01

weights, but we lose little efficiency by using the p corresponding to the latest fitted value of $y_{ij} = \hat{\alpha}_i + \hat{\beta}_i \hat{x}_j$.

Fitting the Model

Table 14.2 summarizes the fit of the model to each operation. The columns for n_i, α_i, and β_i relate the number of patients in each PSTAT group, and the estimated α_i and β_i. In general, α_i increases with PSTAT, since sicker patients tend to have longer hospital stays.

The sample squared correlation, R^2, is a convenient statistic for assessing the closeness of a set of points to a line. Since the values of R^2 tend to be much closer to one than to zero, we calculate for group i

$$(1-R^2)_i = \frac{\sum_j (y_{ij} - \hat{\alpha}_i - \hat{\beta}_i \hat{x}_j)^2}{\sum_j (y_{ij} - \bar{y}_{i\cdot})^2}. \tag{14.17}$$

Table 2 includes another statistic that relates to the p_{ij} rather than the y_{ij}. We define the median absolute deviation as

$$MAD_i = \text{median} \{|p_{ij} - \hat{p}_{ij}|\}, \tag{14.18}$$

where $\text{logit}(\hat{p}_{ij}) = \hat{\alpha}_i + \hat{\beta}_i \hat{x}_j$.

The overall MAD is the median of the four MAD_i. We see that, in terms of MAD, operation S410 had the worst fit, S800 the best, and S208 was about average.

The MAD values range from 0.29 percent to 1.15 percent and the median value is 0.61 percent. These errors are small compared to the differences in p_{ij} from group to group. Furthermore, MAD_i is strongly related to n_i, the number of patients in group i. In other words, the larger the sample size, the better the fit.

The basic premise of this analysis is that, for certain groups with few patients, we can learn more about the LOS distribution by borrowing information about the shape of the distribution from other groups with more experience than we could by considering the original group in isolation. As a result, our estimates of the distribution for small groups may not totally agree with the directly relevant data but rely partially on observations from other groups. We cannot verify this principle by using the information in the smaller groups, since the mathematical model provides better estimates for the small groups than the data themselves could. But a justification comes from the results for the larger groups, where the model fits very well. We hope that, if the model fits well in situations with a substantial amount of data, then it will also provide a reasonable approximation where there is little data.

If the model is appropriate, variability in the calculated p_{ij} is the main source of errors in the estimated $\hat{p}_{ij}$. Since the standard deviation of the p_{ij} is proportional to $1/\sqrt{n_i}$, MAD_i will be roughly proportional to $1/\sqrt{n_i}$. If the model is not appropriate, errors in the model as well as random variation cause errors in the $\hat{p}_{ij}$, and the dependence of MAD_i on n_i will not be as strong.

Figure 14.2 shows a plot of MAD_i versus n_i for the fits based on the common standard distribution. The horizontal axis is in the reciprocal square root scale, and it appears that MAD_i is roughly proportional to $1/\sqrt{n_i}$. The linearity indicates that a large component of the residual variance comes from random error rather than from lack of fit.

In the following section, we further examine the estimated α_i and β_i for each operation and see that there is a good deal of regularity to them. We conclude the analysis of the two parameter fits with a study of the estimated standard curves, x_j. The analysis suggests a major simplification of the model, using only one standard curve for all nine S-Codes.

Analysis of Estimated Alpha and Beta Values

Standardization for Comparison

The fitting procedure employed earlier does not totally determine α_i, β_i, and x_j. for instance, α_i, $2\beta_i$, and $\frac{1}{2} x_i$ give identical predicted values for y_{ij} as α_i, β_i, and x_j. This indeterminacy is not a problem when one compares the α_i and β_i for a single operation or looks at predicted values and residuals, but we must resolve it before comparing the α_i and β_i across operations.

To explain the procedure of standardization, we must first introduce some new notation. Let k index the operation or S-code, so that p_{kij} stands for the proportion of S-Code k, PSTAT group i, remaining in the hospital on day j. Define α_{ki} and β_{ki} as the estimated α_i and β_i from operation k, and x_{kj} as the estimated standard for operation k. The model we fit is then

$$y_{kij} = \alpha_{ki} + \beta_{ki}x_{kj} , \qquad (14.19)$$

although we treat it as a separate problem for each k. We cannot compare the α_{ki}, for instance, to the $\alpha_{k+1,i}$ since they refer to different x_{kj} and $x_{k+1,j}$.

Regarding the estimated standards x_{kj} as data, we fit the model,

$$x_{kj} = a_k + b_k z_j , \qquad (14.20)$$

and thus develop a common standard z_j. To the degree that the x_{ij} are linear functions of each other—a question we explore in section VI—we rewrite equation (19) as

$$y_{kij} = \alpha_{ki} + \beta_{ki}(a_k+b_k z_j) \qquad (14.21)$$

or

$$y_{kij} = (\alpha_{ki}+\beta_{ki}a_k) + (\beta_{ki}\cdot b_k)z_j . \qquad (14.22)$$

Defining α_{ki}^* as $\alpha_{ki}+\beta_{ki}a_k$ and β_{ki}^* as $\beta_{ki}\cdot b_k$, we write

$$y_{kij} = \alpha_{ki}^* + \beta_{ki}^* z_j , \qquad (14.23)$$

and the α^* and β^* parameters are comparable across operations as well as

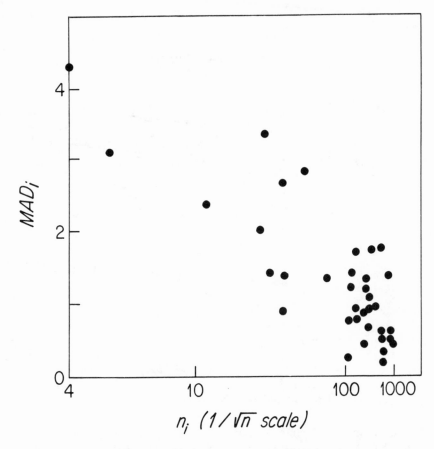

Figure 14.2. Median absolute duration of P_{ij} estimates (MAD_i) for each group versus sample size (n_i)

across PSTATs. Thus, if the operation-specific x_{kj} are linearly related, a single common standard, z_j, allows comparison of PSTAT groups across operations.

Let us examine the patterns of the α and the β individually.

Analysis of Standardized Alpha Values

Figure 14.3 plots the values of α_{ki}^* versus PSTAT. We connect the points with the same S-Code by lines. With a few exceptions, the lines are straight and increase with more or less the same slope across PSTAT. The parameter α_{ki}^* relates the location of the distribution for S-Code k, PSTAT group i, to the location of the standard distribution. Since larger values of α_{ki}^* imply a longer median LOS, medically we expect α_{ki}^* to increase with PSTAT and it does.

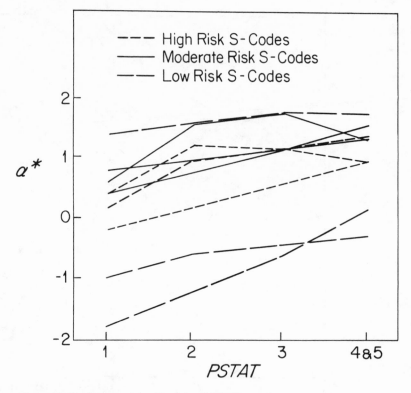

Figure 14.3. Comparison of α_{ki}^{*} by PSTAT and S-code

Furthermore, α_{ki}^{*} changes more from operation to operation than it does from PSTAT group to PSTAT group. A two-way analysis of variance of the α_{ki}^{*} indicates that while S-Code and PSTAT effects are significant ($p \ll .001$ for the null hypothesis that the effects are all zero), the operation effects explain 79 percent of the variance, and the PSTAT effects 17 percent. The PSTAT effects are: for PSTAT 1, -0.569; for PSTAT 2, -0.044; for PSTAT 3, 0.195; and for PSTAT 4 and 5, 0.418. As we would expect, S-Code plays a more important role in determining the median LOS. PSTAT, though, has a significant effect on the median or location of the LOS distribution and is a worthwhile addition to a prediction model.

We originally distinguished the nine S-Codes as high-, moderate-, and low-risk operations, and to a large extent, the α_{ki}^{*} reflect this distinction. The high-risk operations tend to have longer LOS than the low risk. Total hip replacement, S206, is an exception. Although its overall mortality is the lowest of the nine operations, S206 has the highest α_{ki}^{*} values, meaning the longest LOS. Orthopedic operations have long hospitalizations because of the special need for physiotherapy to restore joint motion as soon as possible. But in general, riskier operations involve longer hospitalizations.

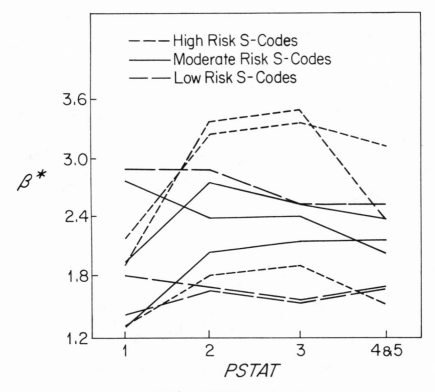

Figure 14.4. Comparison of β_{ki}^* by PSTAT and S-code

Analysis of Standardized Beta Values

We plot the β_{ki}^* values in figure 14.4. As with the α_{ki}^* values, the operation effect is strong, but the β_{ki}^* for a given operation do not vary systematically. The F test for the operation effect in a two-way analysis of variance of the β_{ki}^* shows a strong operation effect ($F = 9.45$ with 8, 24 degrees of freedom, $P \ll .001$) and a much weaker PSTAT effect ($F = 3.23$ with 3, 24 degrees of freedom, $P \approx .046$). The operation effects explain 69.2 percent of the variance, and PSTAT effects only 8.9 percent. The PSTAT effects are: for PSTAT 1, -0.267; for PSTAT 2, 0.195; for PSTAT 3, 0.135; and for PSTAT 4 and 5, -0.062.

The value of β_{ki}^* is inversely proportional to the standard deviation of PSTAT group i, operation k, in the transformed time scale. We mentioned earlier that most of the nine S-Codes consist of basically one operation and a homogeneous mix of patients. But two S-Codes, S208 (femoral fracture) and S1402 (craniotomy), are more heterogeneous. We expect the LOS distributions for these two S-Codes to be more spread out; therefore, we expect smaller than average values of β_{ki}^*. Averaging β_{ki}^* over PSTAT, S208 and S1402 have the second and fourth smallest average β_{ki}^*.

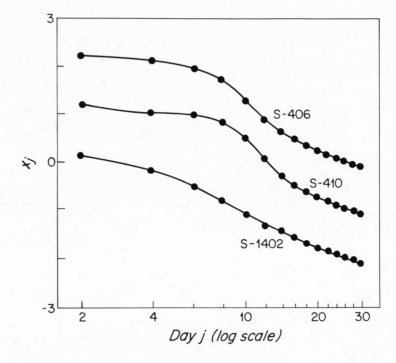

Figure 14.5. Estimated x_j for high-risk operations

Analysis of Estimated Standard Distributions

Figures 14.5, 14.6, and 14.7 plot the estimated x_j versus day j for each of the nine operations under study. We use a log scale for the time axis. The plots range from a straight line, as for S208, to a pattern with a bulge around day 8, as in S406, S410, and S413.

The straight line for S208, plotting the time axis on a log scale, has a special interpretation. We discussed the interpretation of $g(t)$, a transformation of the time variable, T, so that $g(T)$ has a logistic distribution. The estimated values x_j equal the logit of the standard distribution,

$$x_j = \text{logit}(p_{sj}) = \text{logit}(\text{Prob}(T < t_j)) \qquad (14.24)$$

$$= \text{logit}(\text{Prob}(g(T) < g(t_i))) . \qquad (14.25)$$

If $g(T)$ has a logistic distribution,

$$\text{logit}(\text{Prob}(g(T) < g(t_i))) = \alpha + \beta g(t_i) \qquad (14.26)$$

by the definition of logit(p). Since according to the plot

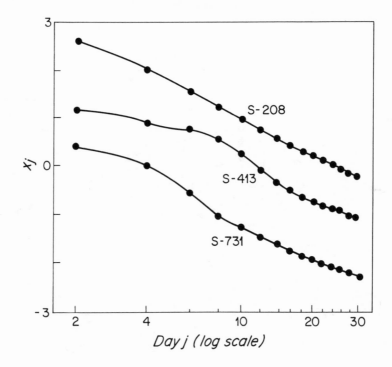

Figure 14.6. Estimated x_j for moderate-risk operations

$$x_j = \text{logit}\,(p_{sj}) \approx \alpha + \beta g(t_i)\,, \qquad (14.27)$$

we can say that in the log scale, the LOS distributions for S208 have approximately a logistic shape.

The plots of x_j versus day j for the other S-Codes cannot be as simply interpreted, but we can say that they do not have a logistic shape. The distributions are much closer to logistic in the log scale than in the untransformed time scale, however, and taking logs provides a good basis for comparison. The three cardiovascular operations (S406, S410, and S413) have a similar shape. The bulge around day 8 may reflect some belief about one-week hospital stays. The high, moderate, or low risk groups do not seem to have common patterns.

The rough similarity of the plots beyond day 10 suggests that perhaps a common standard may suffice for some purposes. Let us test whether one standard distribution, namely, the z_j estimated from the x_{kj}, sufficiently describes the distribution of LOS from different S-Codes. The fitting is simpler than the original problem of estimating α, β_i, and x_j for each S-Code. We supply the computer with z_j and it estimates α_{ki} and β_{ki} for each S-Code and PSTAT group by weighted least-squares regression, using the method of section III.

Table 14.3 presents the fitted values and goodness of fit statistics for each

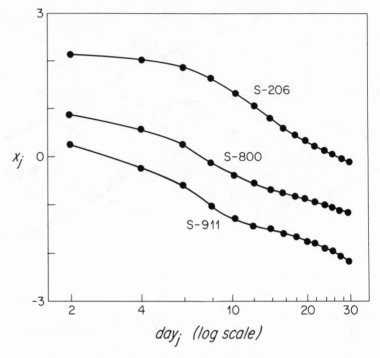

Figure 14.7. Estimated x_j for low-risk operations

PSTAT and S-Code. The MAD increases for eight out of nine S-Codes, compared to the fits with a separate x_j for each S-Code, but the median of the nine new MAD values is still only 1.11 percent, indicating a very good overall fit.

Conclusion

This chapter illustrates the application of a simple model for describing parallel distribution functions to data on length of hospital stay. The key assumption is that some transformation of the time scale exists that gives all groups a logistic distribution. If so, even if the transformation is not known, logit transformations of the survival curves are linear functions of each other and of a common standard distribution.

In summary, we have three main results. First, the simple two-parameter model adequately represents the differences in the distribution of length of stay (LOS) from one physical status group to another, even for small groups. For some operations, and to a rough approximation for others, it seems that the logarithm of LOS has an almost logistic distribution. Second, for the purpose of estimating the extreme percentiles of the LOS distribution, one standard

Table 14.3. Summary of fit, common standard supplied

S-Code	n_i	α_i	β_i	$(1-R^2)_i$ in %	MAD_i in %	MAD
406	4	0.701	2.166	14.60	4.29	
	111	1.101	3.310	5.64	0.76	
	827	1.318	3.502	1.86	0.61	
	372	1.497	3.048	1.54	0.51	0.68
410	11	0.846	2.251	20.81	2.37	
	139	1.610	3.524	4.35	0.90	
	185	1.851	3.622	2.64	0.43	
	40	1.382	2.502	40.92	2.80	1.64
1402	158	0.290	1.313	1.22	1.71	
	349	0.712	1.676	3.06	0.95	
	212	1.118	1.830	1.38	1.30	
	65	1.448	1.598	0.75	1.38	1.34
208	122	0.168	1.303	4.52	1.42	
	211	1.119	2.133	2.79	0.88	
	197	1.162	2.165	0.52	1.19	
	28	1.307	2.410	2.33	1.38	1.29
413	22	0.438	1.947	5.07	3.34	
	134	1.164	2.882	0.64	0.77	
	184	1.243	2.539	2.88	0.86	
	28	1.414	2.435	2.23	0.89	0.88
731	448	−0.222	2.851	1.89	0.19	
	609	0.157	2.224	15.86	1.34	
	236	0.433	2.205	14.60	1.07	
	28	1.178	2.172	3.19	2.66	1.21
206	215	1.553	3.058	11.07	0.63	
	364	1.766	2.984	4.91	0.59	
	120	1.834	2.660	1.25	1.21	
	5	2.000	2.712	42.84	3.09	0.92
800	1226	−1.749	2.518	7.42	0.43	
	783	−1.055	2.566	1.23	0.48	
	301	−0.539	2.184	4.08	1.74	
	21	0.245	1.801	3.98	2.04	1.1
911	111	−0.855	2.437	0.71	0.26	
	508	−0.851	1.201	8.73	0.31	
	316	−0.338	1.736	3.06	1.74	
	23	−0.131	1.691	8.17	1.41	0.86

distribution, rather than one for each operation, is sufficient. Third, the interpretations of the estimated α and β coincide with medical logic. Sicker patients have higher α's, indicating longer hospital stays. The LOS distribution has lower β's and thus is more diffuse for heterogeneous operations. Finally, the kind of operation performed has a stronger effect on length of stay than a patient's physical status does.

All three results have applications to actual hospital problems. The first result, that a two-parameter model adequately describes the LOS distribution, encourages us to believe that we can accurately predict the proportion of patients of each S-Code and PSTAT group who will still be in the hospital, say, 10 days from today, even if we have had little previous experience with some types of patients. Although we estimate proportions of patients remaining at any one time, there are usually only one or two (or zero) patients of each type in the hospital. In this situation, we interpret the estimated proportion as a probability, and calculate, for the set of patients and procedures performed today, the expected number remaining in the hospital 10 days from today.

The second result, that one standard distribution is sufficient for the long tail of the LOS distribution, means that only two parameters, α and β, are necessary to check if a patient has stayed in the hospital "too long," that is, longer than a certain percentile of the LOS distribution for similar patients. This result is relevant both for PSRO board members and for researchers using LOS as a surgical outcome variable.

The final result, about the interpretation of α and β, means that hospital planners can use the model to simulate the effects of hospital policy changes. They can alter the α and β to reflect changes in the patient mix or in policies about releasing patients and see what the effect is for the distribution of LOS.

In conclusion, a simple mathematical model well describes the length of postoperative hospital stay for many groups of patients; this model can provide reliable estimates of the LOS distribution where little direct evidence exists.

Part IV. Regulation

15. The Economic Basis for OSHA's and EPA's Generic Carcinogen Regulations

Ivy E. Broder and John F. Morrall III

Abstract

Our study explores the problem of regulating carcinogens by examining the generic policies and specific regulatory actions of two agencies: the Environmental Protection Ageny (EPA) and the Occupational Safety and Health Administration (OSHA). After briefly describing the two sets of policies, we recommend the economist's approach to regulating carcinogens and defend it against its critics. We then compare the different types of market failures that might motivate occupational and environmental regulation. We find that the case is strongest for environmental regulation, which implies that different willingness-to-pay estimates should be used for the two agencies. We calculate cost-per-death-avoided estimates for five OSHA regulations (asbestos, coke ovens, benzene, arsenic, and acrylonitrile) and for one EPA regulation (benzene). The results indicate that the agencies gave little consideration to cost-effectiveness principles in setting their standards; the estimates range from $200,000 to $20 million per death avoided for OSHA and up to $100 million for EPA's proposed benzene regulation. Cost-effectiveness calculations for given substances also show wide variation. Finally, when willingness-to-pay estimates for direct beneficiaries (adjusted for the latency periods of cancer) are compared with the cost estimates, all regulations except asbestos appear to be questionable. We conclude that decisionmakers need to advocate the desirability of additional social benefits (such as altruism or pecuniary externalities) in order to bridge the gap between private costs and public benefits, and thus to justify the cost of these regulations.

The regulation of carcinogens is one of many policy issues that have become polarized recently in the United States: Are carcinogens a major public policy problem? And if they are, what do we do about them? The answers are not obvious. Some scientists believe that cancer phobia may be a greater public policy problem than the disease itself.[1] On the other hand, some government policymakers apparently believe that a large percentage, perhaps 90 percent, of the 400,000 cancer deaths per year are caused by environmental factors broadly defined, with 40 percent or more due to occupational exposures.[2] The truth probably lies somewhere in between; however, it would not be fruitful to continue the debate about the aggregate benefits and costs expected from a government regulator policy to reduce the cancer problem. We do not need to know the total potential benefits or the total potential costs of achieving them;[3] effective policy requires less comprehensive information. Specifically, it requires knowledge of the incremental costs and benefits of controlling individual substances.[4]

Given that there is a problem of some unknown but positive magnitude, what do we do about it? In this study, we evaluate the approaches that OSHA and EPA are taking. After a brief summary of their generic policies, we analyze specific regulatory actions that have been proposed or promulgated.

OSHA's and EPA's Generic Carcinogen Policies

On January 22, 1980, OSHA promulgated a general policy aimed at the regulation of carcinogens present in the workplace.[5] The policy, which became effective on April 21, 1980, was developed after a public record of over 250,000 pages of comments and testimony had been compiled. The generic policy was proposed as a way to speed up and render more efficient OSHA's slow and uneven rate of promulgation of health standards.[6]

EPA is supposed to list hazardous pollutants and to establish emissions standards for the sources of those pollutants under Section 112 of the Clean Air Act. Two of the four pollutants that have been listed and regulated under this section are carcinogenic. On October 10, 1979, EPA proposed a general policy for dealing with airborne substances that pose a risk of cancer,[7] although the agency has not yet promulgated a generic cancer policy.

Regulating carcinogens is clearly a complex problem. Because of differences in the laws under which the agencies operate, in the professional norms of the staffs, and in the interest groups that pressure them,[8] as well as differences in the situations being regulated (ambient air versus any type of occupational exposure), one would not expect EPA's and OSHA's regulations to be identical.[9] There are differences in the way the scientific, technological, and economic judgments are made. Although space precludes a line-by-line comparison, we offer a more general comparison of the regulatory processes. Table 15.1 summarizes the major provisions of the policies of the two agencies.

An initial categorization based on the type of evidence is common to both agencies' policies, although there is more flexibility in the EPA policy because there are more categories. In the EPA proposal, a quantitative risk assessment is explicitly made part of the process of setting priorities. OSHA mentions "the extent to which regulatory action could reduce not only risks of contracting cancer but also other occupational and environmental health hazards"[10] as a factor to be considered in setting priorities. Presumably, reduction in risks can be estimated only by a quantitative risk assessment, although in the past OSHA has been reluctant to use such a method. OSHA policy states elsewhere that "because of the uncertainties and serious consequences to workers if the esti-

Table 15.1. Summary of carcinogen policies of OSHA and EPA

	OSHA	EPA
Initial screening	1) Present in workplace —brief scientific review of available data 2) No mention of extent of exposure in regulation	1) Substance found in ambient air and source emissions and searches of scientific literature 2) Screening done to determine potential extent of exposure
Catego- rization	*Category I*—meets definition of potential carcinogens or single mammalian species with or without concordance from other evidence *Category II*—evidence is "suggestive" or meets definition for single mammalian species without concordance	*Category I—High Probability*—"best" or "substantial" evidence from epidemiological and/or at least one mammalian study *Category II—Moderate Probability*—"suggestive" evidence from epidemiological, animal, or short-term studies *Category III—Low Probability*—"ancillary" evidence such as structural correlations or low probability from human or animal evidence
Prioritiza- tion of regulation	Factors include 1) number and levels of exposure 2) extent to which regulatory action could reduce risk 3) molecular structure 4) costs of substitute and other health effects	(Based on quantitative risk assessment) Factors include 1) level of emissions and exposures to population and most exposed population 2) potency and expected cancer incidence 3) other health effects
Regulation	*Category I—* 1) permissible exposure limit (PEL) set as low as feasible 2) PEL to be achieved primarily through engineering and work practice controls 3) if a substitute is available, no exposure is permitted 4) model standards, which include keeping medical surveillance, hygiene standards, etc. to be used as guideline *Category II—* 1) PEL set on case-by-case basis consistent with statutory requirement 2) - 4) same as above *Emergency temporary standards* may be set for Category I substances	*High probability substances* that impose significant risk will be listed under Section 112 as 1) General standards applied (general housekeeping) 2) Risk assessment performed to evaluate residual risks 3) Regulatory options analysis to identify alternative levels of control and their impacts 4) Existing source to be regulated at Best Available Technology levels or beyond if unreasonable residual risk remains 5) New sources will be required to meet a standard that will preclude significant risks under worst-case assumptions 6) New sources meeting specific Risk Avoidance Criteria will be permitted to meet BAT *Moderate and low probability carcinogens* 1) recommendation or requirement for further testing 2) evaluation of public exposure 3) moderate Prob/High exposure will be considered for Section III Regulation

mated risk is understated, cautious and prudent assumptions will be utilized to perform risk assessments."[11] The EPA proposal suggests using the "weight of evidence" approach, which is certainly less conservative than OSHA's policy.

Different types of regulations are required for the different categories of carcinogens. If a substance is in the highest risk category for either agency, the regulations require technology-based standards. EPA uses the concept "Best Available Technology" (BAT). OSHA's permissible exposure level (PEL) is to be set "as low as feasible." Although "feasibility" is not defined explicitly, it has been interpreted by OSHA first to mean technological feasibility and second to mean the financial capability of the industry to pay for the regulations without forcing a majority of firms into bankruptcy. This definition was affirmed by the Supreme Court on June 17, 1981 in the cotton dust case (*American Textile Manufacturers' Institute vs. Donovan*).

There is no provision for analyzing the impact of a zero PEL if substitutes are available, although presumably OSHA would determine that the substitute is less hazardous. EPA will explicitly analyze alternative levels of control if unreasonable residual risks remain after the generic standards are applied. Economic and health effects are to be considered. Standards are stricter for new sources but allow a new plant to obtain offsets or to show that exposure is not high and can thereby be regulated at BAT levels.

OSHA requires that the exposure limitation be met primarily through engineering and work practice controls. The EPA proposal requires existing sources to limit emissions to the levels corresponding to BAT levels and thus permits some flexibility in how a source meets the standard.

Finally, a major difference bearing on the question of cost effectiveness is that EPA regulates by source categories, while OSHA establishes across-the-board permissible exposure levels. Thus EPA can potentially vary its standards across industries according to cost-effectiveness criteria more readily than can OSHA.[12] EPA's potential for greater cost effectiveness is illustrated later in a discussion of EPA and OSHA benzene regulations: the proposed EPA benzene rule would apply on a plant-by-plant basis,[13] while the proposed OSHA benzene rule would apply on an industry-by-industry basis.[14]

The Economic Approach to Regulating Carcinogens

The economist's approach to regulating carcinogens is the same as for any form of regulation: the market failure is first identified and its magnitude (i.e., the expected benefit of eliminating the market failure) is estimated. The most cost effective method of obtaining those benefits is then identified among feasible alternatives. All this information is then presented to policymakers, who may use it in conjunction with information on distributional effects to maximize social welfare.

Of course, political and institutional constraints impede to various degrees the implementation of this ideal system in nearly all circumstances, and particularly in the regulation of carcinogens. The immense technical difficulties and scientific uncertainties do not invalidate the approach—which indeed is most useful when uncertainty is greatest—but do contribute to the political constraints. For example, OSHA's response to the uncertainty surrounding benefit estimates has been to eschew calculations altogether, to assume that benefits are "appreciable," and to develop technologically and financially based standards.[15]

The political or institutional constraint most often cited is the OSHA statute. For example, in defending its failure to estimate incremental benefits for the benzene standard, OSHA argued that its statute did not require it to quantify benefits. In this case, the Supreme Court ruled the benzene standard invalid because OSHA had not shown that the regulation would eliminate "significant risks of harm."[16] In the cotton dust decision of June 17, 1981, however, the Supreme Court ruled that OSHA could not balance significant risks against the costs to industry of compliance.[17] If industry is "capable" of complying, the Court decided, it must.

On a more practical level, the question of whether the carcinogen statutes allow such balancing is academic. When resources are limited and compliance costs are large, policymakers do in fact implicitly balance costs and benefits. OSHA could, of course, have issued a more protective cotton dust standard that would have further reduced risk. The question is whether the balancing should be done explicitly and systematically, or implicitly and unsystematically. Although economists and policy analysts may wonder why we bother to raise such a trivial question, experience in Washington regulatory proceedings suggests that only economists would find the answer obvious.

The democratic system functions best when the public dissemination of information is greatest and when all information is used. Cost-benefit analysis affords a systematic method of presenting information vitally necessary for regulatory decisions; moreover, it can be easily replicated, and its assumptions can be questioned by other participants in the regulatory process in ways that expose the critical elements of the analysis.

Furthermore, the alternative to this approach is greater reliance on a less democratic process (Hapgood, 1979), with policymakers claiming that statutes allow them no discretion, providing less information to the public, and tending to balance their own personal costs and benefits rather than society's. For example, Crandall and Lave (1980) noted that all regulators present at a recent Brookings Institution conference[18] on the scientific basis for safety and health regulation explicitly rejected the use of cost-benefit analysis and presumably relied on "intuitive balancing" in making their final decisions on the five regulations examined.[19] Given the politics of regulation, it is likely (especially for OSHA) that this intuitive approach will yield more regulation than society as a whole demands. For example, Kelman (1980:250) states, "The evidence suggests that the most important factor explaining OSHA decisions on the content of regulations has been the pro-protection values of agency officials, derived from the ideology of the safety and health professional and the organizational mission of OSHA."

Valid criticism of cost-benefit analysis is possible, but much of the current criticism is misguided. It has been charged, for example, that cost-benefit analysis is inherently biased against regulation because "costs are easier to express than benefits" (Ashford, 1980); because economists who do the analysis are motivated by a professional ideology that "predisposes its members to be relatively sanguine about market outcomes, wary about government intervention, and quick to note that 'there is no such thing as a free lunch' (whether the good being purchased is oranges or health)" (Kelman, 1980); and because of the "limitations of the market in allocating health, safety and environmental protection" (Green & Waitzman, 1979).

Even if one assumes that the costs of regulation are easier to estimate than the benefits, it is not clear that this difference would work against regulation. For example, reducing an unknown risk of death by cancer for an industry's 191,000 workers at an annual cost of $100 million may seem like good public policy to many citizens. They might feel quite differently, however, if they knew that the possible benefit of the policy would consist at most in the prolongation of a few lives. A threat of unknown magnitude often raises the most concern.

More specific criticisms include Ashford's (1980:71) assertion that compliance costs are overstated because they depend upon biased industry data and fail to account for economies of scale and the learning curve, while benefits are understated because they are more uncertain and include unrecognized side effects, such as the "pressure of regulation to induce industry to innovate." While it is certainly true that industry has an incentive to overstate the costs of compliance, the regulatory ageny that produces the cost estimates, as pointed out by Stokey and Zeckhauser (1978), also has an incentive to understate compliance costs. Moreover, the expressed policy of OSHA and EPA is to be conservative in estimating risks and thus in overstating benefits.[20] Morrall (1981) documents OSHA's tendency to overstate benefits and understate costs by examining an OSHA study of the cotton dust standard.

As for the relationship between regulation and innovation, it is not at all clear how this affects the cost-benefit ratio. One of industry's major complaints about health regulation is the uncertainty created by the regulatory process and its enforcement. Increased risk is thought to slow down investment and productivity. Moreover, benefit estimates never reflect the possibility that progress in medical science might reduce the incidence of cancer and increase the cure rate. And finally, to the extent that regulation reduces risk, it also reduces the rewards for research on cancer. These and other linkages between regulation and innovation may or may not have a significant bearing on cost-benefit calculations; our present point is simply that it is not obvious which way the bias runs.

Kelman's charge (1980) that economists as a profession are biased against regulation is also off the mark. Economists have spent much more time identifying market failures than identifying government failures, and they tend to propose policies that maximize social welfare rather than those that promote specific entitlements or values (e.g., occupational health, environmental quality, safe and sanitary housing, equal educational opportunity, or national defense). We believe policymakers should share the predisposition to be objective and balanced.

Finally, the criticism by Green and Waitzman (1979)—that cost-benefit analysis is inappropriate because of the limitations of the market in allocating health, safety, and environmental protection—is also incorrect. The need for cost-benefit analysis arises because of market limitations on failures: cost-benefit analysis is not needed unless the market fails.

Legitimate objections can be raised to the use of cost-benefit analysis. If process is important, cost-benefit analysis of health and safety issues may produce disutility (presumably for the noneconomists in society) while the present system is generally fair and just, producing positive utility.[21] If process produces utility just like any other good or service, however, one can have too much of it relative to other goods and services. Kelman (1980:266) expresses the dilemma well: "Still there is a point at which even the advocates of such a view would have to say 'stop'—that we cannot guarantee a right to a healthy workplace if it would cost half the GNP to save one life. Rights are not absolute. Thus the difficult decisions remain." And when markets fail, as they obviously do in providing the optimal extent of process or rights, cost-benefit analysis is useful in organizing information for these difficult decisions. Furthermore, if cost-benefit analysis of health, safety, and environmental issues does produce negative externalities, it may be because economists have not done a good job in informing the public of costs and benefits.[22]

An Economic Analysis of OSHA and EPA's Regulation of Carcinogens

For both OSHA and EPA, regulation of carcinogens is motivated by market failure, as noted elsewhere (Morrall, 1977; Zeckhauser & Nichols, 1979; Portney, 1978). There are some important differences, however, between the risks addressed by the two agencies. Those at risk from environmental carcinogens are the victims of a pure technological externality, where high transactions costs make enforcement of property rights difficult, while those at risk from occupational carcinogens are one of the two parties in the production process who are constantly negotiating with each other. In theory, to the extent that labor markets are competitive and workers know the existing information about risks,[23] compensating wage differentials equal to the worker's willingness to bear risk should prevail (see Smith, 1979; Viscusi, 1979 and forthcoming). But since not all labor markets are competitive, and since workers clearly do not have all the existing information on risks and may have difficulty processing what information they do have, risk differentials in wage rates are not likely to be fully compensating—especially for occupational hazards such as cancer.

Nevertheless, according to Viscusi (1981), the empirical evidence indicates that workers appear to be well informed and that risk premiums are significant; his latest studies show risk premiums that imply that an individual values his or her life at about $3 to $8 million.[24]

By indicating the private demand for risk reduction, compensating wage differentials can serve as guides to policymakers in evaluating lifesaving regulations. An important further implication for OSHA is that workers who now receive risk premiums may eventually pay for part of any new regulation when their compensating wage differentials are reduced. The worker's net benefits may be overstated if the effect of the differential is not taken into account.[25] If a new cancer risk is discovered, regulation and capital generally substitute for wage differentials that would otherwise have developed. If market imbalance is the cause of the market failure, then imposing additional safety by regulation will probably result in a lowering of pay (or of job quality in some other dimension) unless the underlying market power imbalance is corrected. Thus, to the extent that the market works, workers will benefit less than willingness-to-pay estimates indicate.

Two types of externalities can be used to support OSHA's cancer regulations on efficiency grounds. Both types are common to environmental regulation as well. Most individuals would be willing to sacrifice some amount of their income to reduce the risk of cancer to the rest of society, both because their taxes and insurance premiums would thereby be reduced and because of altruism.

The direct benefits of EPA regulation of carcinogens can be more accurately estimated by willingness-to-pay studies since those who benefit, unlike workers, will not have to pay part of the compliance costs.[26] Since market failures are likely to be greater for environmental than for occupational cancer risk, the benefits of environmental regulation are likely to be greater, and EPA appears to be economically justified in enforcing stricter environmental regulation than OSHA does.

Viscusi (1981) has found that jobs with higher risks tend to attract, as economic theory predicts, individuals less averse to risk than average. In fact, he finds that the value of life estimated by workers in the top quartile of risky jobs is about half the value estimated by those in the lower three quartiles. Little self-selection is involved in exposure to environmental carcinogens; thus average risk level estimates should be used in valuing the benefits of environmental regulation. In estimating the benefits of occupational regulation, on the other hand, one should use a lower risk level estimate, both because the risk-taking is partly voluntary and because the risks in occupations to be regulated are apt to be higher than average.[27]

Cost Effectiveness Comparisons

With these concepts in mind, we present some actual risk and cost effectiveness estimates implied by OSHA's and EPA's carcinogen regulations.[28] For

Table 15.2. Cost-effectiveness estimates of OSHA and EPA cancer regulations

Regulation	Date promulgated	Annualized costs (millions of dollars)	Annual cancer deaths avoided	Cost per death avoided (millions of dollars)
OSHA				
Asbestos[a]	1-12-72	75	396	.189
Coke ovens	10-22-76	160	35.4	4.5
Benzene	2-10-78	108	5.7	18.9
Arsenic	5-5-78	109	5.4	20.2
Acrylonitrile				
2.0 ppm	10-3-78	24.3	6.9	3.5
1.0 ppm[b]	not promulgated	17.3	0.6	28.8
EPA				
Benzene				
97%	proposed	1.48–1.78	.022	66.8–80.2
99%	proposed	.70–1.99	.021	33.4–96.1

a. This figure is the only one estimated computed from a secondary source and is probably an underestimate of deaths prevented and an overestimate of costs per life saved. OSHA is considering tightening the 1972 standard.

b. These are incremental cost and benefit estimates relative to the looser standard.

Source: Authors' calculations.

OSHA, we have calculated implicit costs per death avoided for five carcinogens for which standards have been promulgated: asbestos,[29] coke oven emissions, benzene, arsenic, and acrylonitrile. For EPA, we have calculated implicit values for benzene emissions for maleic anhydride plants. This regulation has been proposed but not promulgated. The results appear in table 15.2.

Except for the 1972 asbestos standard, which has an implicit cost per death avoided of less than $200,000, the OSHA standards range between $3.5 million and about $20 million per death avoided.[30] Interestingly, the arsenic and benzene standards, which have much higher costs than the others, have not gone into effect because of judicial challenge.

OSHA did not promulgate the tighter acrylonitrile standard of 1.0 ppm but instead stopped at 2.0 ppm. The reason for this is not clear. OSHA maintains that the standard of 1.0 ppm was not "feasible," but Mendeloff (1980) argues that the Regulatory Analysis Review Group (RARG) and the Council on Wage and Price Stability (COWPS) may have played a role in the decision.[31] By implication, a further reduction in risk at a cost of $28.8 million per death avoided was judged not to be worthwhile.

The table also illustrates that OSHA could have done a better job on cost effectiveness, since the implicit cost-per-death-avoided estimates differ by two orders of magnitude. The uncertainties in the cost estimates are equally great, however, and OSHA has apparently pursued a strategy of tackling the worst problem first.[32] OSHA is also presently considering tightening the asbestos standards.

Table 15.3. Incremental cost per cancer death avoided for acrylonitrile regulations by industry segment by increasingly tighter PELs (millions of dollars)

Industry segment	2.0 ppm	1.0 ppm	0.2 ppm
AN production	3.66	23.92	a
Acrylic fiber manufacturing	2.43	11.54	4.64
Nitrile elastomer latex manufacturing	8.12	98.46	860.23
ABS/SAN manufacturing	1.51	11.69	94.41
Polyols	b	91.74	232.72

a. Not technically feasible.
b. Already attained.
Source: Authors' calculations.

It is difficult to compare the OSHA results with the EPA estimates, since EPA has not yet promulgated a final standard. Moreover, the social benefits from reducing occupational risks are likely to be lower than those in the environmental case.[33] However, recent decisions by Monsanto and Tenneco to reduce emissions in their plants by 97 percent, regardless of the EPA standard, show that either the 97 percent or the 99 percent reduction standard would be extremely cost ineffective. In fact, the incremental cost per death avoided for the EPA standard is far higher than that for any OSHA standard.[34]

We can be much more confident about the cost effectiveness between different industries for the same carcinogens. Tables 15.3, 15.4, and 15.5 show cost effectiveness calculations by industry for the OSHA acrylonitrile and benzene regulations and by plant for the EPA benzene regulation. Table 15.3 also shows cost effectiveness ratios for two tighter standards than the one chosen. A comparison of tables 15.3 and 15.4 shows that the variation between industries in cost effectiveness ratios is much greater for OSHA's benzene standard than for its promulgated acrylonitrile standard; clearly, there were many opportunities to improve the cost effectiveness of the OSHA benzene standard.

Since EPA has not promulgated its benzene standard for maleic anhydride plants, the opportunities to achieve the cost effectiveness improvements shown in table 15.5 still remain.[35] In absence of any regulation, the two plants recently controlled to 97 percent (Monsanto and Tenneco) provided 95.6 percent of the potential benefits at less than 38 percent of the cost of regulating all plants to 97 percent (implying a cost-per-death-avoided estimate of only $1.9 to $2.3 million). Among the remaining uncontrolled plants, it would clearly be cost ineffective to control Reichhold-Illinois; however, the political difficulties of controlling just one plant in a competitive industry are formidable.

Table 15.4. Cost per cancer death avoided for OSHA's benzene regulations

Industry segment	Annualized costs (millions of dollars)	Workers exposed to over 1 ppm	Deaths avoided	Cost per death avoided (millions of dollars)
Benzene refiners	4.98	300	0.048	103.8
Other refiners	23.23	5,000	0.800	35.3
Coke oven light oil facilities	5.34	4,000	0.640	8.3
Petrochemical industry	4.50	552	0.088	51.1
Transportation	1.48	156	0.024	61.7
Laboratories	3.0–3.5	1,250	0.200	15–17.5
Tire manufacturing	1.99	11,400	1.82	1.1
Other rubber manufacturing	2.29	13,050	2.09	1.1

Source: Authors' calculations.

Table 15.5. Incremental cost per cancer death avoided for EPA's proposed benzene regulations for maleic anhydride plants (millions of dollars)

Plant	Current—97%	97%–99%
Monsanto	a	1.5–23.4
Reichold—III	1,777–2,233	94–1,036
U.S. Steel	73.9–91.5	3.4–52.4
Reichold—NJ	d	453.7–737.0[d]
Tenneco	a	6.3–49.1
Denka	a	485.5–789.5[d]
Ashland	38.1–46.3	44.8–600
Koppers	a	b
Pfizer	52.37	c

a. Operating at 97% in absence of EPA regulation.
b. Operating at 99% in absence of EPA regulation.
c. Calculation could not be made because of missing data.
d. Plant closed as of 1981.
Source: Author's calculations and data provided by Nichols (forthcoming).

Cost-Benefit Considerations

We have not yet determined whether the OSHA and EPA standards are cost beneficial. We believe that policymakers should make that decision. Economists have more to contribute, however, than calculations of implicit "values of life" estimates. Specifically, they should continue refining and presenting willingness-to-pay estimates for comparable risk reductions from market data (usually from labor markets, but also from seat belt usage and other markets

Table 15.6. Factors for deflating willingness-to-pay estimates

Latency period (years)	Discount rate	Divisor
10	4%	1.5
20	4	2.2
10	10	2.6
20	10	6.7

for safety). As we reported above, these estimates show a wide range, from Bailey's low estimate of $170,000 per death avoided to Viscusi's high estimate of $8 million, with best guesses of about $1.5 to $4 million for Smith and Viscusi and $400,000 for Bailey.

These estimates are based on the risk of immediate accidents; if they are to be used to determine willingness to pay for reductions of cancer risks, an adjustment should be made for the long latency period characteristic of carcinogens. Although latency periods appear to vary with the potency of the carcinogen and the dosage, the period between the onset of exposure and the clinical appearance of tumors generally ranges between 10 and 50 years (Bridbord et al., 1980). For mesotheliomas caused by asbestos, the pattern appears to be one of greater incidence appearing 15 years after exposure and thereafter at an increasing rate for 20 years (Bridbord et al., 1980). Thus the average latency period is at least 25 years.

We have calculated discount factors under the assumptions of 10- and 20-year latency periods, using real discount rates of 10 and 4 percent. Ten percent is the same discount rate used in the compliance cost calculations, while 4 percent is used to reflect the possibility that the demand for risk reduction is highly income-elastic.[36] The factors by which the willingness-to-pay estimates should be deflated under each set of assumptions are shown in table 15.6. These adjustments reduce all but the highest willingness-to-pay estimates to the $1 million range—below the costs per death avoided calculated above for EPA and OSHA standards.

Since the beneficiaries of all the regulations except asbestos apparently would not be willing to pay for the regulations, the question remains: Are there indirect beneficiaries who would be willing to pay enough to justify these costs on economic efficiency grounds? Since these benefits are not easily quantified, this question should be answered by policymakers.

Conclusion

Our review has supported the need for regulating toxic substances and for using economic analysis to do so. While OSHA's promulgated policy would permit at best some application of cost-benefit analysis, we found little positive expression of intentions to use it. Risk assessments are to be used only for determining priorities and for more positively identifying chemicals as carcinogens, rather than as useful measures of the potential benefits of regulation. Costs are estimated to determine feasibility (the financial capability of an industry to cope with the regulation) and perhaps to gauge scarce political capital, not to measure society's opportunity costs of reducing occupational risks.

EPA's proposed policy, on the other hand, seems much more receptive to economic concepts, even though it specifies that technology-based standards must be mandated. It discusses risk assessment positively and states that all sorts of factors, including risks and costs, will be considered where possible in setting the standard. But perhaps the key difference affecting the potential cost-effectiveness of the two policies is that EPA approaches the regulation of source categories one by one, while OSHA lumps all sources together. EPA's approach may allow it to regulate in a much more cost-effective way, by varying timing and enforcement as well as exposure levels.

Our review of the two agencies' regulations found room for improvements in cost effectiveness. OSHA's regulations were more cost effective than many critics might expect, however, except for the benzene and arsenic standards. For EPA, the most important recommendation is the need for an innovative approach to controlling benzene emissions for maleic anhydride plants—if there is to be any regulation of these at all.

Finally, we found that the implied costs per death avoided through EPA and OSHA regulation exceed the direct beneficiaries' estimated willingness to pay, when figures are discounted to reflect cancer's long latency period. Thus additional benefits would have to be added to justify the social cost of these regulations; such benefits might include those associated with altruism, distributional considerations, and reductions in tax and insurance bills.

16. When to Pay for Sunk Benefits

Michael O'Hare and David S. Mundel

Abstract

Incentive programs under which governments pay part of the cost of individual, institutional, or lower level government activities almost never include retroactive provisions. That is, there is no reward to the "sunk benefits" represented by past actions of the same kind that the program is designed to encourage in the future. Legislators have occasionally authorized some form of retroactivity (e.g., in the Superfund for hazardous waste clean-up). But since most programs contain no such provisions, a general expectation has been created that subsidies will not be awarded for activities already undertaken. Perversely, this assumption may work against the kinds of action that government would wish to encourage. If it seems possible that an activity will be covered by a subsidy program currently under consideration, it is likely to be delayed until subsidies are either enacted or rejected. One way around this disincentive might be to reimburse operating costs rather than capital investments of programs; this would make it possible for an established activity to benefit from a newly enacted subsidy. Limited subsidy funds will have to be stretched further if they are to cover ongoing as well as new programs. But even when retroactivity appears to dilute the impact of a specific subsidy program today, it will increase the efficiency of future programs in general.

A good way to make people do what you want them to do is to help them pay for it. Since the power of incentive is well known, a host of government programs at all levels employ it. To choose a few examples from an enormous variety: the federal government induces homeowners to repair houses in depressed areas by subsidizing the cost of loans; state governments induce local school boards to offer certain programs, or more of them, by paying some of the cost; and the federal government has paid about 90 percent of the cost of interstate highway system construction. Such a system of inducements can even operate at three levels: the federal government gives state governments money to pay some of the cost of local government acquisition of park and recreation space.

A recent incentive program, through which the federal government pays 90 percent of the cost that states incur in cleaning up abandoned hazardous waste dumps, includes an unusual and desirable provision: states can credit expenses incurred during the two years before the law's passage toward their 10 percent share of future cleanups.[1] "Sunk" benefits, like sunk costs, should not affect a rational decisionmaker's behavior, so it is not widely believed that paying someone for what he has already done affects his behavior in a useful way. The desirability of retroactivity may therefore seem paradoxical. Nevertheless, we think this provision well conceived, even though its benefits may not be obvious in the context of hazardous waste cleanup, and worthy of imitation, though its specific form in the Superfund law is imperfect.[2]

To see why we advocate retroactivity, consider the case of a state official who has just discovered an illegal hazardous waste dump under the following conditions: the private party responsible for the dumping either cannot be found or is judgment-proof, so responsibility for cleanup falls inevitably on government. No federal assistance has been suggested. The dump may or may not be leaching dangerous chemicals into the water supply, imposing an expected cost of delay (D), but the local benefits of cleaning up the dump (E) are believed in any case to exceed the substantial costs of cleanup (C) by more than D. The rational thing for the official to do, obviously, is to clean up the dump at once; if he waits, he suffers the cost of delay D with no corresponding gains. (We are collapsing, without loss of generality, the legislature that appropriates money for cleanup and the bureaucrat authorized to spend it on particular accidents.)

Consider now a change in the official's decisionmaking environment: legislation is proposed at the federal level that provides for sharing the cost of past and future hazardous waste cleanup. All is as before, except that if the bill passes, the cleanup will cost only rC ($r < 1.0$). The official's best strategy is still to clean up at once. The benefits of this action are the same as before, and the costs are the same or (if the bill passes) less. Since the costs might be less, he is to some extent more likely to clean up—perhaps the cleanup would rise on a priority ordering of projects that, in total, exceed his budget.

Finally, consider a third situation: the proposal of federal legislation to share costs of cleanups undertaken only after the bill passes. The official in this situation must consider carefully how he will feel if he spends his state's money now and the bill then becomes law; he will have avoided delay costs D, but at a price of $(1-r)C$, since he will not be allowed to share the cost of previous clean-up once the bill passes.

The more likely the enactment of such legislation seems, or the more likely it is that a second-guessing opponent will run against him in the next election and accuse him of wasting state funds, or the smaller D is—or can be made to appear—the less likely he will be to clean up quickly. Note that D is a real economic loss, while benefit rC is merely a transfer, having an exactly corresponding cost to national taxpayers; delay is undesirable in our model in aggregate terms.

The most general case is that of an official facing such a cleanup opportunity for which federal cost-sharing legislation has been proposed but has not taken final form. (For example, Senate and House versions might differ in whether

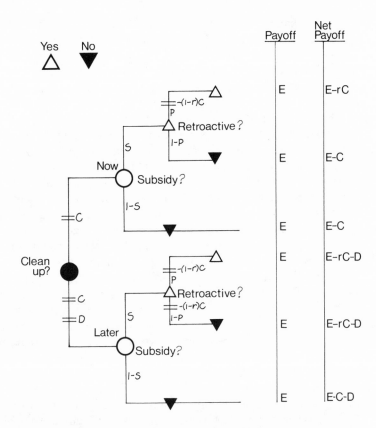

Figure 16.1. Decision tree for state official considering cleanup of a hazardous waste dump

The dump will be cleaned up eventually, at the cost of C. Delay will cost D (continued leaching, risk, etc.), and benefits from cleanup are E. The federal government may enact a subsidy program (with probability s) that bears a fraction r ($0 < r < 1$) of the cleanup costs. If it does, the program will (with probability p) or will not be retroactive, applying to cleanups undertaken before enactment.

retroactive compensation is provided.) This situation is summarized in figure 16.1, a decision tree in which s is the probability of a subsidy program being enacted, and p is the conditional probability that it will be retroactive.

The decisionmaker compares the expected values of the two major branches of this tree in order to decide what to do. The comparison reduces algebraically to the condition that the upper branch will be more attractive (have a higher expected value) if

$$s(1-p)(1-r)C < D , \qquad (16.1)$$

which means that the cost of foregone cost sharing due to quick action $((1-r)C)$ times the probability that it will occur ($s(1-p)$) is less than the cost of the delay.

The left-hand side of equation (16.1) is larger if subsidy is more likely and smaller if retroactivity is more likely. If p is very small, our third case applies and cleanups will be delayed as the subsidy program becomes more likely to pass. If p is nearly 1.0, the threat of subsidy will not delay cleanups and may encourage them (as is conventionally assumed) by reducing their expected local price.

We have assumed for this simple example that the dump will be cleaned up no matter what. But delay sometimes makes this impossible, especially if the federal program is not enacted. Sometimes costs of a particular program increase so much faster than inflation that funds that were adequate in year i will not suffice in year $i + j$. Sometimes a local administration willing to expend funds is replaced by one with a narrower view of the benefits of the investment. And sometimes the costs of delay turn out to be much greater than was predicted when the decision to delay was made. In such cases, the possibility of a cost-sharing program will have prevented the very benefits that the program was designed to promote, even if the program does pass.

What would make p (the probability of retroactivity) in figure 16.1 seem small to such a decisionmaker? Several factors are probably relevant. If the draft versions of federal legislation are moving through committees in Congress, they will or will not have retroactive provisions. Such provisions might be added or removed by amendment, of course, but if they are already in the bill and local decisionmakers are acting on that basis, it would presumably be much more difficult for Congress to remove them at the last minute.[3]

Another factor bearing on the value of p is the pattern or tradition established by previous federal legislation of similar type, if a pattern can be perceived. Before a bill is drafted, history is the only available guide. To date, a tradition of nonretroactive compensation has been nearly universal. The Interstate Highway Program is typical of traditional cost-sharing programs: some states built turnpikes before the program was conceived or funded, paying for them with tolls collected from users and local tax money. Connecticut, for example, foresaw the need for a superhighway exactly where I-95 was eventually to be. Its reward for this foresight was to receive federal funding only for the additional cost of signing (and occasional entrance and exit modifications) to meet interstate standards.

Many similar examples can be adduced, involving, for example, funding for higher education facilities and sewage treatment plant construction. The state or local decisionmaker who thinks the past behavior of Congress is any guide to its future policy will think p to be very small and will tend to delay investment in cleanup unless the expected cost of delay is proportionately large. Overall, then, this pattern of federal funding induces decisions on the part of local decisionmakers that run counter both to specific federal policy goals and to local objectives. (This may in itself be the rationale for future federal actions.)

Why then is federal cost sharing handled in this way? There are several reasons why retroactive funding of a particular project will not seem attractive to the coalition that supports it. With a fixed budget, a program that funds retroactively can obviously generate fewer new projects of the type the government is trying to encourage, since some of the funds will be soaked up in investments already made. (All too often, "new" is taken to mean "additional." If a project occurs after a program is enacted, it is clearly new but may not be additional, and it might have occurred even without the program's assistance.) Alternatively, if the program is intended to support a given amount of new investment, retroactive funding seems to increase program costs with no apparent benefits. Giving states money for investments already made obviously uses federal funds in a way that causes no new investment. In addition, the advocates of any new program have good reason to fear the "dilution expansion" effect; when limited funds are spread over many eligible targets, as in the Model Cities program, the program may be diluted to the point of ineffectuality. Congress may insist on slicing your pork into fifty very thin slices, but at least you can deny the past a share.

When we consider any single federal cost-sharing program in isolation, then, a policy of nonretroactivity may be efficient both from the narrow point of view of minimizing the budget impact for a given level of program effectiveness, and from the more general perspective of economic efficiency.[4] If the cost-sharing program moved instantaneously from concept to implementation, and the game between the federal government and the local decisionmaker were played only once, it would be advisable to design any new program without retroactivity provisions.

The inefficiency that results when local decisionmakers delay useful investments until a decision on a federal program has been reached is not simply due to the time it takes to design the new program, but also due to all those programs that have gone before. The Interstate Highway Program funding mechanism, and other programs like it, are the real source of the anxiety confronting the state decisionmakers who were considering hazardous waste cleanup in the summer of 1980. More specifically, in addition to its own direct efficiency consequences—which will encourage or discourage investments of a particular kind—every program also has a kind of temporal externality whereby the funding mechanism chosen for program A has incremental consequences for future local decisionmakers considering investment in area B (in particular, operating on their value for p in figure 16.1, above). The costs of the nonretroactivity in a subsidy program are visited upon different programs with different purposes, considered later in time, in different subcommittees, and supported by different coalitions and client groups.

Trading benefits between the present and the future in policy design is not unusual, of course; Leman has reviewed some good and bad ways this is done.[5] Unfortunately, it is most often the future that inherits such current costs as can be passed on to it, as when public employees are granted unfunded pension rights. Similarly, the people of the future pay for the nonretroactivity of today's programs.

The externality is probably more important than the delay caused by the nonretroactivity of a new program in the process of passage. Incentive programs exist as reasonable expectations or serious possibilities for much longer than they exist in the form of drafted bills. As long as a subsidy program is merely an idea in good currency, it can have the same power to stall local investments as when it is in a congressional committee, and p during the former period is estimated exclusively by reference to the convention established by previous programs.

If p were thought very small by decisionmakers at the local level—if retroactivity were the norm—an interesting second-order effect might be observed at large enough levels of s. Discussion of a retroactive program might well encourage timely local investments: some local decisionmakers who would not clean up waste dumps in the certain absence of federal aid might be motivated to proceed by the increase in expected net value of cleaning added by the possibility of subsidy. Moreover, it would be better to be early than late; the program might not be large enough to fund all claimants but would be more likely to fund (retroactively) those who had acted before its passage. But this kind of externality, with its intrinsic and universal asymmetry, is difficult to deal with; witness the "posterity ain't never done nothin' for me" response to schemes that conserve natural resources. Can anything be done about it?

One mechanism of federal support that could avoid the problem we describe is cost sharing for program operation, without maintenance-of-local-budget-effort provisions, i.e., without a requirement that the absolute local contribution to a program's cost not decrease when subsidy is provided. (If maintenance-of-effort provisions were included, localities might be inhibited from initiating efforts.) If the federal government paid a share of the cost of snowplowing, maintaining, linepainting, and patrolling highways, it would be treating the pre-existing Connecticut Turnpike in the same manner as a new road. A state considering investment in a facility whose operating costs might or might not be covered by federal funds at some future time would make the investment immediately (assuming the project to be attractive on an annual basis without the subsidy), since there would be no financial advantage to delay.

Unfortunately, operating fund subsidies are of little use in programs whose costs are intrinsically and entirely, rather than partially, capital-intensive. The federal government might subsidize hazardous waste regulation and enforcement on an ongoing basis, encourage states to set up such enforcement and regulatory programs, or even encourage state-run facilities to process waste, but there is no practical way to subsidize the cleanup of an existing hazardous waste dump by means of an operating subsidy. For programs like this, the nearest analogy to operating cost sharing would be a subsidy (additional to existing tax-exempt status) for sinking bonds or other debt floated to pay for the capital investment.

Another alternative is suggested by the temporal externality model of the problem: just as conventional externalities can be transferred back to those who impose them only by a government with power over both parties, the externality of nonretroactive programs can be corrected only by a power superior to the decisionmaker creating the program that imposes it. If the decisionmaker is the legislature, the only superior powers are a constitution and legislative tradition. The constitution is too unwieldy an instrument for this purpose, though an amendment requiring retroactivity in any cost-sharing legislation is certainly appropriate theoretically. But the deliberate shaping of legislative tradition probably deserves serious consideration; both houses of Congress and state legislatures observe many rules by longstanding convention, and do so even when they discomfit the bodies in particular cases. If it is possible to create a conventional standard of behavior through purposeful intervention, an expectation of retroactive funding would be a useful addition to these informal rules.

17. What is Regulation?

Christopher C. DeMuth

Abstract

The study of government regulation has emerged as a distinct field of policy analysis in recent years, yet it remains an open question whether "regulation" describes a distinct set of government policies—policies with features that distinguish them clearly from other policies. This chapter considers several different conceptions of regulation that have appeared in recent debate and scholarship and advances the view that regulation should be taken as the prescription by government of terms of private transactions. The arguments for this view are that it is more comprehensive and exclusive than alternative views; that it describes regulation in a neutral, functional way, free of insinuations about the purposes or consequences of regulation; and that it defines the limit of the ability of regulation either to redistribute income or to improve the efficiency of markets.

The study of government regulation has emerged as a distinct field of policy analysis. Beginning in the mid-1970s, leading universities established programs of regulatory studies, new professional journals devoted to regulation appeared, and several books on the politics and economics of regulation were published (Stigler, 1975; Owen & Braeutigam, 1978; MacAvoy, 1979; Weidenbaum, 1979; Mitnick, 1980; Wilson, 1980; Breyer, 1981). Presidents Ford, Carter, and Reagan began a tradition of appointing experts on regulation to the Council of Economic Advisors and established several new agencies to evaluate federal regulatory policies.[1]

Can the subject of all this study and debate be distinguished clearly from other endeavors of government? The word "regulation" brings to mind the various federal "alphabet agencies" and independent commissions, such as the ICC, FTC, SEC, EPA, OSHA, and so on, and the similar state agencies, such as insurance and public utility commissions. What these agencies primarily do is set prices, terms of service, and quality standards for particular firms and products. But if these activities are regulation, then we cannot stop with the alphabet agencies and commissions. We should also include the government's sporadic efforts to establish economy-wide wage and price controls and its continuing efforts to establish wages and prices by statute rather than through administrative agencies, as in the federal minimum wage requirement and municipal rent controls.

There are many other things we sometimes mean by "regulation." All organizations, including government agencies, have "rules and regulations" regarding their own operations. The agencies administering the government's expenditure programs such as Medicare, Social Security, and housing and educational subsidies have thousands of regulations concerning eligibility, reimbursement, accounting procedures, and much else, which are published in the *Federal Register* alongside the regulations of the Environmental Protection Agency (EPA) and the Occupational Safety and Health Administration (OSHA). The Internal Revenue Service (IRS) is also a prodigious author of regulations. Taxing and spending programs themselves are often described as regulatory, meaning that they alter the allocation of resources in the economy from what it would be otherwise, and legal scholars increasingly characterize common law rules as regulatory with the same thought in mind. If we add up all these usages, "regulation" means all of law viewed instrumentally.

While the meaning of the word is often clear enough in context, it is nevertheless a matter of practical interest to set more precise bounds on the idea of regulation. The automobile executive who complains that his industry is a victim of "overregulation" and goes on to demand import quotas in the next breath confuses only the economists among his listeners. But President Reagan could not be so casual once he had been elected. The "regulatory freeze" he ordered early in his administration raised a host of questions concerning scope and application and required decisions whether to exempt such regulations as IRS Revenue Rulings, Security and Exchange Commission (SEC) enforcement actions, antitrust guidelines, notices of Federal Reserve Board actions, Department of the Interior rules for leasing federal lands, and amendments to guidelines for various grant-in-aid programs. On what logical grounds could these rules be exempted from the freeze (as they were) while those of EPA were not? That the exemptions were reportedly decided with little controversy or formality is evidence that there is a particular set of government activities sharing important features that distinguish them from the rest.

This chapter advances the idea that government regulation should be taken as the prescription by government of the terms of private transactions. I attempt to distill this view from the most interesting conceptions of regulation explicit or implicit in recent scholarship. In sections II and III, I discuss two narrower views of regulation—the "public utility" approach and the "regulatory reform" approach—and argue that they are both too narrow and, in certain respects, too vague to serve as durable definitions of the subject. In section IV, I take up the question whether regulation can usefully be confined to something less than all of government action, and I draw on distinctions among types of government action suggested by several students of politics and economics. In section V, I conclude with a number of affirmative arguments for the view I suggest.

The Public Utility Approach

The traditional "public utility" approach to regulation is well exemplified by Alfred E. Kahn's *The Economics of Regulation* (1970), which is still widely used in colleges and graduate schools. Kahn treats regulation as meaning government control of public utilities and common carriers—control of entry, prices, and exit in the major infrastructure industries of power, communications, and transportation. He ignores the areas of health, safety, consumer protection, and environmental regulation, although regulation for such areas was conspicuous even in 1970.[2]

Kahn acknowledges at the outset that government influences the operation of private markets in many ways other than utility regulation, e.g., by regulating the money supply, enforcing contracts and property rights, providing subsidies and tariffs, and imposing product and packaging standards. He argues, however, that in these cases government is simply "maintaining the institutions *within* whose framework the free market can continue to function" (Kahn's emphasis). By contrast, in the "regulated sector" (i.e., the utility and common carrier sectors), government is supplanting the market itself by directing what should be produced, by whom, and at what price (Kahn 1970:I, 2).

Kahn seems to have been clearing the deck in these passages, describing the scope of his book rather than propounding a rigorous distinction. His distinction between "influencing" and "supplanting" markets is, in any event, untenable. Public utility programs certainly do not supplant markets entirely. Even the ideal utility or common carrier commission described in textbooks merely limits the total revenues (or rates of return) regulated firms may earn and resolves controversies over particular rates, services, and investments. Innumerable other decisions remain market decisions, left to the discretion of the firms' managers, investors, suppliers, customers, and competitors. Many such decisions are beyond the legal authority of even the most comprehensively endowed commission. For example, except in the case of automobile liability insurance, consumers cannot be forced to purchase any particular goods or services under any regulatory regime in the United States. And with or without legal authority, many important matters will always be arranged privately in a manner satisfactory to all concerned (or at least in a manner not unsatisfactory enough to inspire a complaint to a commission), and many will simply be immune to effective administrative control. In practice, moreover, utility and common carrier commissions exercise only haphazard control even over total revenues (Joskow, 1974).

At the same time, many non-utility policies mentioned by Kahn, such as product quality standards and monetary controls, do supplant markets to some extent—they dictate certain aspects of market transactions or forbid certain kinds of transactions. In many cases—drug regulation, for instance—they manifestly amount to deciding what should be produced and by whom. While utility controls have in common the setting of prices, non-utility controls frequently set prices too, as in SEC regulation of brokerage commissions, the minimum wage requirement, and state regulation of agricultural goods and professional services. Only some of the government policies mentioned by Kahn, such as taxes and subsidies and common law doctrines, can properly be characterized as merely influencing private markets, insofar as they stop short of prescribing the terms of private transactions; and these are precisely the kinds of policies least likely to be described as "regulation."

Kahn's is the best of the traditional regulatory economics textbooks, and probably the last. Just as it was being published, many of the framework regulatory programs began to grow rapidly in mission and political importance and soon were housed in several new federal agencies of their own, such as OSHA (1970), EPA (1971), and the Consumer Product Safety Commission (CPSC) (1972).

These programs were at first considered a distinct variety of policy—"social regulation" rather than "economic regulation." The distinction seemed rhetorically useful at first. It was said that business favored economic regulation but despised social regulation, because the former restricted competition whereas the latter imposed costly social obligations, while, for the same reasons, consumer and "public interest" groups favored social regulation but despised economic regulation. But no sooner was the distinction made in these terms than it began to melt away, for it became evident that consumer groups sometimes profited from economic regulation, as in the case of natural gas (Breyer and MacAvoy, 1973), and that producer groups sometimes profited from social regulation, as in the case of product standardization (Cornell, Noll & Weingast, 1976; Leland, 1979; Thomas, 1979). In the mid-1970s, as price controls were extended to all levels of the petroleum industry—apparently at the expense of most sectors of the industry—and then became increasingly tangled in the administration of pollution and automobile safety controls, it was difficult even to remember what the differences between economic and social regulation had been. Today it seems obvious that the distinction was a confusion from the start: railroad rates were as much a social issue as was meat quality a century ago, and the newest regulatory policies governing medical care, such as requirements for "certificate of need" and price regulations, are reinventions of public utility controls.

The Regulatory Reform Approach

The regulatory reformers have a very different conception of regulation, one which treats regulation as a method of government administration rather than as a cluster of programs applied in certain markets or in response to certain problems. By "regulatory reformers" I mean those scholars and government officials, mainly economists, who argue that public objectives should usually be pursued through economic incentives rather than through government command and control. In the usage of most regulatory reformers, command-and-control policies *are* regulation, and reform consists of replacing them with other policies that alter the economic incentives facing organizations and individuals in private markets. Other reformers speak of economic-incentive policies as "regulatory alternatives," but their meaning is identical: that command and control typifies current regulatory practice and ought to be minimized in favor of economic alternatives (United States Regulatory Council, 1980a, 1980c).

The policy recommendations of the regulatory reformers follow a rough division between economic regulation and social regulation; they usually recommend deregulation (abolition of regulatory programs) for utilities and common carriers, but only reform (the infusion of economic-incentive techniques) for programs of health, safety, and environmental regulation (Schultze, 1977; Joskow and Noll, 1978; Breyer, 1981). The difference arises, however, not because they see any fundamental difference between social and economic regulation, but rather because their approach is to identify market failures justifying government intervention and then to recommend the most economically efficient corrective intervention. Most programs of utility and common carrier regulation have been applied in cases where the market-failure argument —that monopoly is natural—is spurious (e.g., in the case of truck transportation), and where the appropriate reform is therefore to eliminate the government intervention itself. On the other hand, in cases where a market failure appears real and serious—e.g., in plausible natural monopolies (electricity distribution) as well as in other sorts of failures—intervention is appropriate but should correct the failure as efficiently as possible. In both cases the regulatory reformer prescribes maximum reliance on economic incentives and market forces. But this reliance actually involves no intervention at all in the case of spurious natural monopolies, and only some intervention, of a less "regulatory" sort, in the case of true natural monopolies and other market failures.

A prominent example of the regulatory reform approach is Charles L. Schultze's *The Public Use of Private Interest* (1977), which has become well known for its advocacy of greater reliance on private incentives and of the price system in federal policymaking. Schultze's advocacy is encased in a larger and more descriptive argument, which is briefly this: (*a*) Our libertarian political tradition in the United States has created a "rebuttable presumption" against government intervention in private markets, and as a result we usually intervene only when there is wide agreement that shortcomings in certain markets need correction. (*b*) Paradoxically, our libertarian tradition has also created the rule that government, when it does intervene, may "do no direct harm" to any identifiable individual or group, and as a result our government policies are less automatic and private-market oriented than they could and should be, since they rely too heavily on case-by-case decisionmaking.

The nature of the distinction between actual and desirable policies is suggested in the book's opening passages (1977:5–6,13):

> there is a growing need for collective influence over individual and business behavior that once was the domain of purely private decisions. But as a society we are going about the job in a systematically bad way. . . . We usually tend to see only one way of intervening—namely, removing a set of decisions from the decentralized and incentive-oriented private market and

transferring them to the command-and-control techniques of government bureaucracy. . . .

. . . Once the decision to intervene has been taken, there remains a critical choice to be made: should intervention be carried out by grafting a specific command-and-control module—a regulatory apparatus—onto the system of incentive oriented private enterprise, or by modifying the informational flow, institutional structure, or incentive pattern of that private system. Neither approach is appropriate to every situation. But our political system almost always chooses the command-and-control response.

Here and throughout the book Schultze neglects to say just what command-and-control techniques are. Perhaps he thought a definition would seem pedantic; the book abounds with examples, and the term "command and control," borrowed from military parlance, is highly suggestive. In particular it suggests centralized regimentation, the attempt to move society in a particular direction simply by ordering people to march that way—policy that is all stick and no carrot. The difficulty with this imagery is that, where government is concerned, there is no difference between sticks and carrots. The essence of government is command, the use of coercion to change behavior. Virtually any act of state can be characterized in this way, and all such acts alter the incentive pattern of private markets—inevitably, and often deliberately.

Consider Schultze's (and other regulatory reformers') favorite example of the superiority of economic-incentive techniques over regulatory command and control: the emission fee. His argument, now widely familiar, is that charging a fee based on the level of pollutant emissions would permit firms to respond differentially according to their differing marginal costs of abatement. By contrast, the uniform emission standard (the predominant approach in practice) requires all firms to abate in the same degree regardless of their abatement costs—some too much and some too little to minimize the total costs of a given amount of abatement. Variable emission standards might set abatement requirements according to costs but would place enormous information-gathering burdens on regulatory agencies, burdens that can be avoided, or at least delegated to the market, with an emission fee.

The argument is persuasive as far as it goes, but why wouldn't a program of emission fees actually be a "regulatory apparatus" grafted onto incentive-oriented private enterprise? There is certainly no inherent logic in calling an emission fee an economic-incentive policy and an emission standard a command-and-control policy. A standard affects incentives and a fee is a command made in order to control, and both require administration and enforcement at some level of government. Indeed, an emission standard, enforced by a civil fine that varies with the degree of violation and not with the abatement costs of individual firms, is economically equivalent to an emission fee with a "deductible" in the amount of the standard. A revealing irony is that one of the most touted achievements of regulatory reformers has been the calibration of pollution-control enforcement fines according to the abatement costs of individual firms—that is, according to firms' differential savings from noncompliance with emission standards.[3] While this policy has been described as the substitution of economic incentives for command and control, it is rather conspicuously a move in the opposite direction: its purpose is to achieve uniform compliance with administratively determined abatement standards regardless of differential abatement costs.

Schultze elaborates his distinction with the argument that economic-incentive policies are "process-oriented, seeking to correct the faulty process," while command-and-control policies are "output-oriented, seeking to bypass the process and determine outputs directly" (1977:29, 65–66, 74). At times, the difference appears to be that "process-oriented" policies like taxes on cigarettes and gambling aim only to moderate the general tendency or degree of disapproved private behavior rather than to achieve the precise result or "output" of a perfect market. Schultze says, for example, that the appropriate level of emission fees is "stiff" and that fees could be adjusted to achieve "any desired set of water-quality standards" (1977:35, 53–54). At other times, however, he undermines the distinction by suggesting that economic-incentive policies actually "correct" market failures by incorporating social considerations into the price system, and that "one of the major efficiency gains from use of a price system is precisely its ability to induce individuals and firms to balance costs against gains. . . . The trick is to make sure that the costs and gains they confront also reflect, as far as possible, *true* social costs and gains" (Schultze's emphasis; 1977:81).

An emission fee calibrated according to the marginal social benefit of pollution abatement might or might not be "stiff." It certainly would not be merely stiff, nor would it be adjustable to obtain "any desired" level of air or water quality. A fee calculated in this manner most emphatically would be "output-oriented," since its whole purpose would be to maximize total economic output, not simply to minimize the total costs of achieving some degree of abatement that might or might not be optimal. It would also supersede the market with an administrative order: the fee would necessarily be set by administrative procedures rather than by the price system, since the absence of a market generating true supply-and-demand-based prices would be the very problem being addressed.

A more complete example of the use of the price system to avoid administrative command and control is the institution of private, marketable property rights to some naturally occurring resource. This would have happened in the 1920s if the government had established a system of property rights in the electromagnetic spectrum rather than an administrative allocation of broadcast frequencies (Coase, 1959). Such a system might have developed spontaneously, as in the case of land, without any government action other than provision for a public filing system and for judicial resolution of conflicting claims. Or the government might have coaxed things along by designing and running an initial auction. But even this is a false example of an economic-incentive alternative to regulation, since the solution (an effective market) is simply the absence of the problem (a failing or nonexistent market). Schultze recognizes this in noting that the economic case for government intervention, and the dilemma of choosing between command-and-control and economic-incentive intervention, arises only when the institution or improvement of property rights to resolve a market failure is for some reason infeasible (1977:29–32).[5]

It seems impossible to erect any unique conception of regulation upon generalizations about command and control or output orientation or the efficiency of emission fees. Indeed, in the context of Schultze's larger argument about the policy consequences of the American political tradition—that our distrust of government has led us to hobble public policies with excessive legal protections of individual interests—the contrast between regulation and economic incentives pales to a contrast between the actual and the (economic) ideal. At the end of his book, he concludes that what we need is not economic-incentive techniques themselves, but rather the political maturity and economic sophistication to let them work their magic (1977:76–90). In the meantime, presumably, even the most elegantly conceived programs for harnessing private incentives to public purposes will be disfigured by judicial doctrines and political pressures until they become mere regulatory programs, marred by absolute-sounding standards, detailed exemptions, special conditions, deadlines, precedent, and waste. Notably, when Schultze himself was chairman of the Council of Economic Advisors and architect of President Carter's regulatory reform program, he devoted himself to applying economic analysis within the existing structure of regulatory policy—attempting to conform regulatory decisionmaking to cost-benefit analysis—rather than to replacing existing policies with economic incentives (DeMuth, 1980).

Schultze is no doubt correct that a policy proposal aimed at adjusting marginal economic incentives so that "costs and gains reflect *true* social costs and gains" would be molded by the political process until it departed substantially from its original conception. The interesting question is whether the results would significantly differ from existing regulatory policies. Policies in the form of taxes and expenditures involve different political institutions than policies in the form of standards. An emission fee in the form of a flat national tax would have to be initiated by the House of Representatives and would have no success without the support of the Treasury Department. Such a tax would fall under the jurisdiction of several congressional committees, composed of representatives with interests and constituencies different from those which influenced the writing and administration of the present environmental laws. Because the tax would be a statute rather than an administrative order, it could not be thrown out by a court for lack of evidence or an incomplete hearing record. On the other hand, an emission fee scheme that required greater administrative supervision and held little potential as a revenue raiser, such as one whose fee schedules varied according to different marginal damages in different locales, might evolve out of the current EPA program of administrative fines and might require only minor tempering to gain the approval of congressional finance committees and the courts. Political contingencies are surely different in different cases, and if they are systematically different, approaching problems in certain ways may produce certain distinctive results.

Roger G. Noll, in a recent paper whose title I have borrowed (1980), argues explicitly that institutional forms make a difference. He begins where Schultze leaves off, by noting that the need to define regulation as a distinct form of policy arose when reform-minded economists began to analyze the effects of "different institutional approaches to the same policy objective" in order to recommend the most economic approach. In an earlier paper he wrote with Alain Enthoven on the problem of rising medical care expenditures, Noll argued that altering "the basic financial incentives facing [medical care] providers" was preferable to "imposing economic and technical regulation on providers" in an attempt to defeat their (perverse) financial incentives. To make his case Noll had to explain how "economic and technical regulation" differed from what he was proposing (Enthoven & Noll, 1979:215):

> regulation refers to a type of social control of transactions that is characterized by its procedures as well as by the substantive purpose of the regulation. The two key characteristics of regulation are as follows. First, the regulatory authority is not a party to the transactions it regulates. Instead, it acts as the referee of transactions between other parties. By contrast, eligibility requirements and cost reimbursement formulas for Medicare and Medicaid recipients are not, in this sense, regulations because they are written by the purchaser of the service. These controls are more properly regarded as terms of a contract between a purchaser and a vendor. . . . Second, regulation is operated according to procedural rules that were developed from case law and formalized after the fact in the Administrative Procedure Act of 1946. The most important features of these rules are that decisions must be based on evidence that is presented in formal proceedings, that substantial evidence must be submitted in support of each decision, and that the courts may review a decision if it is appealed by a participant in the regulatory proceeding.

The first prong of this definition may seem a little odd at first, until one realizes that many of the things we customarily call regulations are really only terms of voluntary transactions. Regulations concerning military dress, teaching loads in universities, and vacations and promotions in private firms and government agencies are all terms of contracts between organizations and employees, just as Medicare reimbursement regulations are terms of contracts between government and medical providers, and just as procurement regulations are terms of contracts between government and suppliers. Regulations such as these pertain sometimes to an organization's internal management and sometimes to its dealings with the outside world, but as a class their function is to define an organization's own purposes and manner of operation. They might, therefore, be called "organizational regulations." Distinguishing them from "government regulation" was important in the Enthoven-Noll paper because their alternative to "regulating" medical care costs was to revise the terms of government payments under Medicare, Medicaid, and other programs so as to strengthen the incentives of doctors and hospital administrators to minimize their costs (1979:221–223). The concept of "command and control" would not have helped to distinguish regulation from what they were proposing, but the distinction between a referee and a contracting party did.

A more direct approach would be to say that the medical care reimbursement provisions are aspects of public finance, which taxes some activities and subsidizes others. Public finance also covers the other nonregulatory proposal in the Enthoven-Noll paper—to revise the tax deductions for medical care and medical insurance expenditures to give consumers greater incentives to minimize medical costs—and it puts both in the same category as other economic-incentive proposals such as emission fees. Of course, all tax and subsidy programs necessarily involve terms and conditions; even farm subsidies are not just showered over the fields of Kansas. But farm subsidies are surely different in kind from the terms of the government's "organizational regulations"—from the terms of a contract between the government and its clients when the government is purchasing or selling goods and services to operate weather stations, naval bases, or medical insurance programs.

Most people would consider it euphemistic to call the government a "contractor" when it is taxing and subsidizing, or to call those who are taxed and subsidized "clients." Even those who assume that all government activities are determined by the pressures of private economic interests would almost always distinguish activities in political markets from those in conventional economic markets; the provision of additional government jobs, for example, has probably been an insignificant motivating factor in the growth of Medicare and Medicaid. Moreover, if we wish (with Enthoven and Noll) to distinguish public policies according to institutions and procedures, then it is surely important to recognize that taxing and spending programs are largely the product of legislative action, while the government's organizational regulations, such as civil service rules, are largely the product of administrative action.

If we put organizational regulations aside and distinguish other government actions as either "regulation" or "taxing and spending" (public finance), we can then dispense with the second prong of the Enthoven-Noll definition, the application of procedures of administrative law. While there are exceptions, the Administrative Procedure Act (APA) generally does not apply to taxing and spending programs. Indeed, administrative law may be described as a set of restraints that has grown up because government sometimes acts outside the restraints of public finance and yet acts purposively—not as a referee in the manner of a court. Moreover, administrative law does not apply at all to policies involving neither taxing and spending nor administrative action other than prosecutorial discretion. Especially at the state and local level, statutes themselves often prescribe the terms of specified private transactions; examples are building codes, rent control, drug substitution laws, and California's law entitling artists to a 5 percent commission on resales of their works. Even federal statutes, such as the Fair Labor Standards Act and the Clean Air Act, may stipulate ultimate regulatory standards, leaving little to the discretion of administrative agencies (Ackerman & Hassler, 1981). To say that regulation is policy developed according to the APA is incomplete and obscures the interesting question why legislatures sometimes dictate regulatory standards and sometimes delegate the task to administrative agencies.

Noll's paper (1980) suggests that administrative procedures may determine the content of policy in a predictable fashion; his examples, however, are very brief and tentative. He notes that the regulations of the Consumer Product Safety Commission have occasionally been baldly anticompetitive, presumably because of the influence of trade organizations in the administrative process, and that this is also a well-known effect of the work of traditional "producer protection" regulatory commissions such as the Interstate Commerce Commission (ICC). Yet nonadministrative safety regulation, such as building codes, is often anticompetitive too. Noll also suggests that administrative procedure, with its eternal delays and preoccupation with "equity" to protect interests in the status quo, strengthens the hypothesis that the dominant purpose of regulation is to reduce economic risk by dampening the rate of economic and technological change (Owen & Braeutigam, 1978:1–42). But counter-examples abound here in both directions. Building codes and rent controls (nonadministrative) retard economic adjustments and preserve the status quo, while environmental and automobile safety regulations (administrative) are often explicitly "technology forcing." The very flexibility, and hence the uncertainty of administrative policymaking appears recently to have increased economic risk in several sectors of the economy, such as electrical power generation.

Is Regulation All of Law?

The most expansive conception of regulation is that of the theorists of the Chicago School, who in their efforts to understand regulation as an arm of the government's redistributive apparatus have tended increasingly to treat "regulation" and "redistribution" interchangeably. Their work recognizes no distinction between economic and social regulation, nor between policies that do and do not apply to business or even to explicit markets, nor between policies that operate through rules and those that operate through taxing and spending. Thus, in three influential articles during the 1970s, Richard Posner (1971) argued that regulation could be considered a branch of public finance, George Stigler (1971) incorporated tariffs and other differential taxes into the regulatory fold, and Sam Peltzman (1976) built a formal model of redistribution-by-regulation whose most obvious application was to direct fiscal redistribution.

The Chicagoans' usage departs boldly from the conventional understanding of regulation, for they have lost interest in regulation as it is conventionally understood. They propose to explain the pattern of government policies in strict economic terms, specifically in terms of the costs and gains of political action by differently situated groups. Their interest is thus in the economics of politics, and it may be no more than happenstance, or a vestige of earlier interests, that they have called the supply side of the political market "regulation" rather than "legislation" or "state action." Eventually it may turn out that "regulation" in some narrower sense is systematically more or less costly in supplying the state's favors than other kinds of policies, but only then will a redefinition of terms be necessary.

The idea of regulation has tended to expand in the hands of political scientists as well as economists. James Q. Wilson's *The Politics of Regulation* (1980), a collection of case studies by political scientists and an explicit challenge to the Chicago economists, exhibits a similarly broad conception of what regulation is. His book contains, for example, a chapter on the Antitrust Division, which enforces laws that have conventionally been considered as alternatives to regulation, and a chapter on the Office of Civil Rights, which polices racial and other discrimination in organizations receiving federal grants (schools and other institutions of local government). Noll would have omitted both chapters, since the first does not involve the APA and the second involves terms of government contracts. Wilson differs from the members of the Chicago School in thinking that political and institutional detail is more important than "cosmic generalization" for understanding regulation, but nowhere does he suggest that the details are fundamentally different between regulation and other sorts of policies. He concludes his book with an essay setting forth a typology of "regulatory politics" based upon distributions of costs and benefis (e.g., "entrepreneurial politics" when regulatory benefits are dispersed and costs are concentrated, "client politics" when benefits are concentrated and costs are dispersed—a typology that might also be applied to "tax politics" or "welfare politics." It is noteworthy that Stigler, in a scathing review of *The Politics of Regulation*, described this typology as "simply a primitive version of the economic theory of regulation" (1980:12).

That scholars as diverse as Wilson and Stigler have found it unnecessary to distinguish sharply between regulatory politics and other kinds of politics obviously bodes ill for the hopes of regulatory reformers (such as Noll) that political institutions may have a determining effect upon policy. There are, however, two glimmers of hope in the recent work of Richard Posner (1981) and Friedrich Hayek (1973, 1976, 1979). Posner argues that while legislative law may typically promote redistribution of wealth and income, judge-made common law typically promotes allocative efficiency in the sense of maximizing economic product or wealth (1981:88−115). He argues that legislative policies can have distributive effects that are "substantial and nonrandom" with respect to identifiable groups, so that individuals with similar interests have incentives to organize and exert political pressure to obtain economic benefits through legislation. Their success typically brings them benefits smaller than the consequent losses to those outside the successful coalitions, and thus diminishes the wealth of the whole society. In contrast, common law adjudication of discrete, individually small disputes cannot confer substantial and nonrandom benefits on identifiable groups, so individuals have little incentive to organize and exert pressure on the process. The best anyone can do is to favor the efficient (wealth-maximizing) resolution of all common law disputes, since this confers the greatest benefits on each individual group.

Posner's argument leaves room (implicitly) for treating regulation as an intermediate case. Consider his example of the redistributive potential of legislation, progressive versus proportionate taxation (1981:101–102). If tax revenues were held constant, lower income taxpayers could realize higher after-tax incomes under progressive taxation than under proportionate taxation, even though higher income taxpayers would do better—and aggregate income would be higher—under proportionate taxation. This could happen even if, as today's "supply side" tax-reduction advocates maintain, higher income taxpayers earn less taxable income under progressive taxation. For they still might earn enough to generate greater tax revenues under higher progressive tax rates, thus permitting lower income taxpayers to enjoy lower tax rates and higher after-tax incomes. Posner's contrasting example of the redistributive deficiency of common law adjudication is landlord-tenant law. Deciding all landlord-tenant disputes in favor of tenants would be an ineffective means of redistributing wealth from landlords to tenants, since landlords would simply react to the increased risk (and other costs) of doing business by raising their prices, or if this were ineffective or legally prohibited, by withdrawing their investments.

The crucial difference in these examples lies in the elasticity of response to the two policies. Faced with the respective common law and legislative policies, landlords have greater alternative opportunities than higher income taxpayers. But high response elasticity is also a characteristic of regulatory policies. Indeed, rent control is said to be an ineffective means of aiding low-income apartment dwellers for precisely the reason given by Posner in his example of landlord-tenant law. The principal normative argument against using regulation as a device for redistribution is that it is bound to produce greater allocative inefficiency than broad taxes on earnings or consumption; there is less elasticity of response to raising the price of all earnings, or the price of all or most of the things earnings can buy, than to raising the price of just one or a few of the things earnings can buy. But this argument, like Posner's, is at the same time a positive argument. Redistribution by regulation is ineffective—and hence an unpromising source of governmental benefits around which to organize—to the degree it is inefficient.

Of course, taxes may be narrowly targeted and regulatory programs may be more comprehensive than the setting of apartment rents. But the most pervasive regulatory programs, such as the public-utility programs, which cover not only price but quality of service and service initiation and discontinuance, apply at most to one or a few markets. And the regulatory programs applying to many markets, such as the safety and environmental programs, cover at most one or a few terms of transactions in any one market. While there is a powerful tendency for regulatory controls to expand in an attempt to defeat compensating reactions to earlier policies (McKie, 1970), the consistently negative conclusions of studies of regulation in many different fields suggest that the regulative effort is usually futile—that human behavior has many more, and more subtle and tenacious, facets than can be controlled, monitored, or even imagined by the regulator.

Friedrich Hayek's *Law, Legislation and Liberty* (1976, 1976, 1979) introduces a different pair of categories. Hayek divides all social rules (not just those established by governments) into two types: (*a*) general rules, such as customs, manners, and commercial and social standards of all sorts, which emerge spontaneously through social evolution and may or may not be adopted in legislative or common law, but "have no purpose" conceived or desired by any particular individual or group; and (*b*) purposive rules, which are adopted by private or public organizations in an effort to achieve some purpose. His argument, very briefly, is that the only proper function of purposive rules is to direct the activities of individuals within organizations—within the context, that is, of voluntary relations. When enacted by governments in pursuit of social goals, in an attempt to move society as a whole in a particular direction, purposive rules are based on the dangerous illusion that society can be managed as if it were a single organization, or that it can have any singular or consistent purpose at all.

Hayek's formulation encounters serious difficulties when one gets down to identifying social rules that evolved purely through chance and competition and hence "have no purpose." Individuals formulate their interests consciously, use persuasion as well as outright coercion to engage others in cooperative ventures, and observe and form opinions about their fellows. As a result, we can speak of any of our social rules as "having a purpose" without being teleological, whether we are speaking of rules that emerged out of the mists of the past or rules enacted by identifiable legislative coalitions. (That we may disagree endlessly over the "true" purposes of laws and other rules is a separate matter.)

For example, Posner's essay discussed above is an explanation of the content of common law rules in terms of purposive individual action, and it evidently grew from his and others' dissatisfaction with attempts to explain common law rules in strictly evolutionary terms (Landes & Posner, 1979; Rubin, 1977; Priest, 1977). Even seemingly neutral rules of social coordination, such as those of measurement and timekeeping, invariably involve divergent interests. There is a distinct politics of daylight-saving time: people in different geographic and occupational situations wish to have it observed for longer or shorter periods, beginning earlier or later in the year, or not at all (Bartky & Harrison, 1970).[6] And every machinist or manufacturer knows the large economic stakes involved in the choice between metric and American-British measurement. Presumably, so long as England and the United States remain major industrial powers, the American-British system will persist, however superior the metric system may be in the abstract.

The question of purposiveness can be avoided by the similar but less problematic distinction between general and specific rules, which often seems to be what Hayek has in mind. Common law, and informal social rules such as customs and moral conventions, consist almost entirely of general rules. They are standards rather than stipulations of conduct. They do not prescribe the exact terms of either deliberate or circumstantial relations among individuals, but rather establish boundaries for acceptable conduct within which individuals are free to gauge their actions or negotiate joint actions with others. Whether the boundaries should be declared violated is left for *ex post* determination in the event of a dispute. This conception is a departure from Posner's argument that common law is typified by its very specificity. A court decision in a landlord-tenant case, he suggests, alters only one term of a contract, leaving contracting parties to alter all of the other terms in the future. While common law can do no more than this, it often does less. A single court decision is both highly specific *and* limited to the case at hand; the decision rests upon an interpretation of the behavior of the disputants under particular circumstances and is important for the future primarily as a guide to behavior under arguably analogous rather than identical circumstances. In other words, common law consists not so much of specific rules as of general guidelines implied by a stream of specific decisions. There are arguable exceptions. The common law of contract occasionally adds fairly specific terms, such as implied warranties, to certain kinds of contracts. But even the "implied warranty of habitability" in landlord-tenant law is much more general, and more open to interpretation in a particular case, than the terms of a rent-control ordinance. Of course, this way of looking at the matter only strengthens Posner's argument about the difficulty of effecting redistribution through common law.

The legislative and administrative agencies of the modern state are more versatile than the courts, and their actions tend to be more specific. Certainly they are highly specific in defining the terms of rights and obligations between the government itself and others, whether the others are citizens, in the case of programs of taxation and expenditure, or employees and other contractors, in the case of the government's organizational regulations. When, on the other hand, legislatures adopt rules for behavior *among* citizens, they often do so in fairly general terms, as in most traditional criminal law, which incorporates standards of conduct from the common law. But the legislative and administrative branches also, and apparently increasingly, spell out rules for behavior among citizens that are highly specific, to the point of prescribing the exact terms of private transactions. This seems to come closest to what we mean by regulation, and to set regulation apart in an unambiguous and useful way from other government actions.

Conclusion

The view of regulation suggested here defines a clear subset of government actions—those that prescribe the terms of specified private transactions. Only some statutes and agencies do this, and those that do usually do little else. The terms, of course, may be price terms, quantity terms, or quality terms. Minimum-wage laws and direct wage controls prescribe price terms in labor markets; maximum-hour laws prescribe quantity terms in labor markets; and OSHA, pension fund, and equal employment regulations prescribe quality terms in labor markets. Even "full disclosure" and "truth in advertising" requirements are no more than the prescription of quality terms in certain information markets. Economic regulation and social regulation are thus appropriately consolidated.

The suggested view is not entirely comprehensive. Regulatory agencies may do less, as in denying a proposed price reduction without specifying what price is "just." And the prescription may be implicit, as when an agency awards compensation based on an existing term (a price or business practice) it finds to be discriminatory. But prescribing certain terms of certain transactions is the most any regulatory authority can do. Even prohibitions, as of child labor, the manufacture of certain chemicals and other products, or the making of certain advertising claims, are simply the limiting case of banning certain transactions altogether. Thus, this approach captures the essence of regulation more completely than general references to "a type of social control of transactions" (Enthoven-Noll), because it specifies the extent of any regulator's powers of social control.

The suggested view is exclusive, distinguishing regulation from other forms of government action discussed in this chapter: taxation and expenditure, the government's own organizational regulations, general rules of common law, and specific rules of coordination such as those of measurement and timekeeping. All these actions influence private transactions—sometimes massively, sometimes trivially—but none stipulates their terms. If regulation is indeed a distinctive form of policy for any of the reasons mentioned by the leading authors in the field, the distinction is likely to rest upon the circumstance of setting one or a few terms of a transaction to which one is not a party, leaving a multitude of other terms to readjust according to the interests of those who *are* parties. As an approximation, regulation is less effective than taxing and spending but more effective than common law in redistributing income. The normative side of the same proposition, and the essential argument of the regulatory reformers, is that regulation is also less effective than taxing and spending in correcting market failure.

Another virtue of the approach suggested here is that it reduces the idea of regulation to pure function, stripping away accretions that are not descriptions at all but rather arguments over purposes and consequences. We may debate whether the ICC or the EPA is correcting market failures, balancing the interests of producer and consumer groups, promoting safety or national integration or regional development, providing political vent to the power of certain factions, redistributing income in a worthy or unworthy manner, or reducing market uncertainty and the rate of economic change. But surely it is best not to identify regulation itself with the pursuit of any of these goals. The purposes of regulatory policies are deeply ambiguous. For example, competing firms that agree to standardize their products in some respect (through regulation or otherwise) may know it is in their interest to do so, but neither know nor care whether this is because standardization will "widen the market or narrow the competition" (in Adam Smith's phrase). Moreover, even if their intention is exclusively to narrow the competition, they may very well end up promoting a wider interest that is no part of their intention (as Smith again puts it). Even the original Act to Regulate Commerce of 1887, long regarded as an imperfect effort to shore up a disintegrating cartel, is now regarded by at least one careful scholar (a Chicagoan) as having been plausibly related to the promotion of general economic welfare (Kitch, 1979).

A degree of reductionism would be a healthy thing for political debate as well. Consider, as a small example, the perennial debates over the inclusion of certain expenses in the rate bases of utilities, such as expenses for political advertising, charitable contributions, and construction work in progress on generating plants not yet producing power. These debates are almost always cast in terms of whether consumers or owners should pay for the activity in question, or whether it is fair to charge today's customers for tomorrow's power. Yet the utility commissions cannot decide these questions; all they can decide is what rates the utilities may charge. Depending on how financial and consumer markets react, the ultimate results may be just the opposite of those envisioned in the debates, and recent research suggests that they often are just the opposite (Lehn, Benham, & Benham, 1980; Navarro, 1980; Comptroller General of the United States, 1980).

Finally, the suggested formulation is compatible with current economic thinking about market failure, which consolidates all of the various "failures" into the same underlying phenomenon—the costs of market transactions. Emphasizing that regulation is in fact no more than the prescription of terms of transactions brings out the important point that, in any regulatory controversy, the issue is not whether a failure should be corrected, but whether a government agency can formulate appropriate terms of transactions at lower cost than the market can. Monopoly, externality, and poor information are not problems unique to markets or amenable to technical administrative solutions, even by thoroughly disinterested government agencies. Rather, they are problems that may be transferred from market settings to administrative settings, with attendant advantages and disadvantages. Every contention for government regulation based upon market failure is more precisely a contention that economies of larger scale decisionmaking remain somehow to be exploited.

Part V. Management

18. The Search for Implementation Theory

Erwin C. Hargrove

Abstract

This study presents a set of testable propositions about the implementation of federal programs. "Implementation" is defined as having two main components: (a) that the actions required by law are carried out, and (b) that those actions encompass both formal compliance with the law and organizational routines consistent with compliance. It is assumed that the process of implementation will vary according to the character (or class) of policy being implemented. Employing Lowi's classification of policies as either distributive, regulatory, or redistributive, the study discusses propositions regarding the implementation of these classes of policies.

Policy analysis that lacks theoretical underpinning is incomplete. Theory that is not tested through applications remains academic. The premise of this chapter is that assessments of how proposed programs might work would be enhanced by empirically grounded theories of policy implementation. And the very effort to apply theoretical insights to analysis will infuse vitality into the search for theoretical understanding.

The purpose of this study is to present a set of testable propositions about the implementation of federal programs. Policy analysts who must make implementation estimates would find propositions of this kind useful in predicting how implementation would proceed under varying conditions. The propositions presented here do not form a comprehensive, logically tight theory, nor do they encompass all aspects of implementation. Rather, statements about how American ideology and politics shape implementation processes are presented in a loosely joined framework.

A full theory of implementation may not be possible, but the following components would be needed to anticipate most implementation situations: (*a*) propositions about how the efforts of contending parties to shape and control programs affect their initial design and implementation; (*b*) propositions about how the organizational incentives of implementing administrators affect implementation; and (*c*) propositions about the effect of politics and bureaucracy upon the implementation of programs.

Politics shape the institutional characteristics of programs. For example, categorical and block grant programs reflect different national political patterns, but bureaucratic institutions have independent power of their own to shape programs and even to create new patterns of politics. So politics and organization would be both independent and dependent variables in a complete theory of implementation.

Any assessment of the degree of implementation requires criteria by which to judge the extent to which implementation has occurred. The ultimate impact of the policy itself must be excluded. One would like to know, for example, whether the air is cleaner as a result of the Clean Air Act, but that is a question for evaluation research. Those concerned with implementation must ask whether the implementing actions required by law were in fact carried out. But verifying the simple facts of compliance or noncompliance is not enough. If the law is vague or contradictory, it may be difficult to know what should be implemented. Moreover, full implementation goes beyond compliance to incorporate the required actions into the organizational routines of the implementing agencies (Berman & McLaughlin, 1975).

These uncertainties make it very difficult to use a clear criterion of implementation as a normative standard by which to judge results. The best solution is to treat the question empirically. If a statute states clearly what is to be done, then one asks whether it has been done, remembering that both compliance and incorporation may be important. If the statute is unclear or calls for incompatible actions, then one documents the consequences for implementation and draws the appropriate conclusions.

It is thus possible to compare the implementation of a program with the actions required by law. A remaining difficulty is that programs change over time. Within what boundaries should we assess the degree of implementation? This is a particular problem when comparing programs. Does one compare only "mature" programs, and what are the criteria for maturity? My answer is practical rather than theoretical. It makes sense to compare programs that were enacted at roughly the same time, e.g., the social programs of the Great Society. The underlying politics may be similar and the programs may exhibit common developmental dynamics. But, for one or several programs, the observer must finally make a judgment about whether the program has fulfilled the normative goals it was designed to meet. Beyond this evaluation point, the program may be restructured and then transformed, but it then becomes a new program.

The working definition of implementation employed in this chapter therefore includes two components: (a) the actions required by law are carried out; and (b) those actions encompass both formal compliance with the law and organizational routines consistent with compliance.

Policy Analysis and Political Theory

In graduate schools of public policy, instruction in implementation estimates has normally been based on prudential rather than on theoretical knowledge. The two best examples of intelligent prudential analysis are the classic Massachusetts Medical School case assessed by Graham Allison (1974: chap. 19) and

Gordon Chase's (1979) comprehensive framework of implementation problems that should be flagged in advance.

The Massachusetts medical case is a critique of economic cost-benefit analysis that fails to consider the institutional and political feasibility of carrying out policy options. The policy analyst is asked to complement economic analysis by making an implementation estimate of feasibility. For example, if Massachusetts were to decentralize the two required clinical years of medical education to four regional medical school teaching hospitals, what problems of uniformity and control of curriculum would result? One might conclude either that decentralization was feasible or that difficulties would overwhelm the attempt. Considerable factual knowledge about doctors, hospitals, and medical education is required for such analysis, and it would also be helpful to have a theory of bureaucratic coordination. In the absence of such a theory (and I know of none), the analyst must live by his wits and his concrete knowledge. Much writing about implementation, and perhaps much actual analysis, is guided by the social scientist's implicit general theories about institutions. We know it is difficult for coequal organizations to coordinate mutual business. But few of us can summon up propositions about the conditions under which such coordination works or fails and then apply the propositions to cases.

Chase's article (1979) identifies a number of obstacles to implementation and ways around them; his speculations cry out for theoretical elaboration through research. For example, writing about the New York City methadone program, he concludes that one way to minimize the number of veto points in a program is for government to contract out to a private organization. He cites both advantages and disadvantages of such a strategy, presumably based upon his experience, but such a balance sheet is not quite the same as a theory.

A few political scientists have attempted to develop theoretical propositions about implementation that could enrich prudential policy analysis and strengthen implementation efforts. Some of these efforts have been very broad, others quite focused and specific. Sabatier and Mazmanian (forthcoming), for example, sum up the conditions under which federal programs are successfully implemented with such broad propositions as the following:

1. The enabling legislation mandates clear and consistent policy objectives.
2. The enabling legislation incorporates a sound causal theory giving implementing officials sufficient jurisdiction to attain, at least potentially, the desired goals. . . .
3. The leaders of the implementing agency possess substantial managerial and political skill and are committed to statutory goals.

These are the best propositions we have, but they are not rooted in a historical context and give us no sense of the historical possibilities. Propositions of this kind are often adduced from the study of implementation failure rather than of its success: one discovers flaws and then imputes their opposites as a basis for success. Such ideal conditions, however, are seldom fully present in concrete historical situations. If they are not present, what is the analyst to do?

It might be argued that I misstate the problem—that in fact there is sufficient theory around to be applied to cases. One could cite organization theory in general or, more specifically, the rich literature of public administration. Very little of this work, however, deals with the contemporary problems of policy implementation that preoccupy political scientists and analysts. (This is what Pressman and Wildavsky meant when they wrote in 1973 that they could find no literature on policy implementation.) The more focused kind of theory has been developed from the analysis of classes of contemporary implementation problems. It addresses problems often not addressed in the older public administration literature. For example, Paul Hill has developed the idea that the successful implementation of Title I of the Elementary and Secondary Education Act has depended upon the development of informal regulatory strategies to supplement the formal federal role. He cites as an example the creation of networks of state and local officials, whose careers depend upon Title I. Hill links his list of informal strategies to other literature on regulation in an insightful way (1979: v–ix).

Still, the critical question remains: What is the relationship between compliance by school systems with Title I requirements and effective teaching of disadvantaged students in schools? There is a literature on compliance and a literature on delivery of services within bureaucracies, including schools, but the two fields have not been joined in research. These are the kinds of gaps in implementation theory that focused research can fill.

A Middle Range Theory

This chapter develops a third approach to theory which stands between the very general and the very specific. Its unit of analysis is classes of programs. Its intention is to set contexts and conditions with greater specificity than is possible for generalizations that embrace all policy, and also to build the kinds of insights developed by Hill into an understanding of classes of problems. Such an approach to theory requires a typology.

First, different kinds of policy issues will involve different sets of participants and levels of intensity according to the stakes presented by the issue. Pork barrel legislation that appears to benefit all congressional districts and to harm none will stir much less interest than a measure that benefits one region or social group.

A second fundamental assumption is that processes of implementation will vary according to the character of the policy being implemented, and that policies can be classified so that the categories can be used as a basis for predicting the implementation processes. (Obviously, to avoid circularity, implementation processes themselves cannot be part of the category definition.)

Third, the language of the statute itself is the basis for the classification of a program. Even if it is ambiguous or internally contradictory, statutory language is the most reliable guide to the intent of a program and thus the best benchmark for assessment of the actual degree of implementation. The behavior associated with programs within the typology is not part of the definition of types. Of course, the typology itself is a result of insights about implementation that preceded and shaped its creation.

The value of any such typology lies in its capacity to capture the reality of American government and to enhance prediction. A good typology makes it possible to group discrete policy areas, such as agriculture and environmental issues, according to crosscutting categories, and thus permits generalizations about processes common to more than one issue. The typology must also capture the fact that policy is a seamless web in which policy formation influences implementation and the administration of policies and also affects new policy. Although policy formation and administration are not the same thing, they cannot be divorced.

The classification scheme used here is that developed by Theodore Lowi, who characterizes policies as either distributive, regulatory, or redistributive (1964, 1970, 1972, 1978). The distinctions lie in the degrees and types of coercion by government, and the basis for classification is found in the language of the statutes by which the policy is formulated.

Distributive policies express the purpose of creating public goods for the general welfare. Great discretion in the distribution of resources is given to government authorities because the population of recipients is diffuse. Public works programs and government-supported research activities fall in this category; the National Defense Education Act of 1958, for example, made funds available to schools and universities for the furtherance of general objectives at the discretion of government administrators. Distributive policies are characterized in the literature as non-zero-sum, since they appear to create only winners and no losers—everybody who counts gets something (Ripley & Franklin, 1980: chap. 4). Such a situation requires many tacit understandings and few rules.

Regulatory policies are those in which the statute specifies rules of conduct, with sanctions for failure to comply. We distinguish two kinds of regulatory policies: those that seek "public goods," such as the Clean Air Act, and those that protect specific populations, such as the 1964 Civil Rights Act. In both cases, central government is ordering citizens, producers, and other governments to respond positively to specific rules, although latitude in modes of compliance and enforcement may be granted.

Redistributive laws specify categories of citizens who are to receive benefits or services according to specific rules of accountability. Redistributive policies are generally understood as attempts to change allocations of wealth or power in favor of some social groups at the expense of others, with clear implications about the winners and losers. Such measures can benefit the wealthy, as do many subsidies to corporations, or try to redress injustices to the poor or minorities. They may also create broad entitlements, such as old-age pensions.

Redistributive programs may have a greater or lesser distributive component.

Table 18.1. Distributive program types

Program	Distributive component	Goal
Medicare	High	Welfare
Medicaid	Low	Welfare
Title I Elementary and Secondary Education Act	High	Human development
Head Start	Low	Human development

The distributive principle tends to broaden both the group of beneficiaries and the stringency of the rules governing the policy, so that policy purposes become both more general and more vague. In contrast, pure redistributive policies are governed by specificity and stringent rules. Also significant is the distinction between redistributive programs that serve goals of human development (such as education programs) and those that seek goals of material welfare (such as health and income security policies). Table 18.1 illustrates these distinctions. Finally, redistributive policies often include regulatory components as a means to insure compliance; the strength of regulatory provisions may vary inversely with the importance of the distributive element.

The hypotheses proposed below are limited in at least two ways. First, they are derived primarily from comparisons of programs that were enacted in the 1960s and 1970s and reflect certain characteristics of American politics during this period that are ignored in the propositions. The character of that historical context will be considered below in the conclusion. Second, the hypotheses emphasize politics as the prime factor influencing implementation and understate the importance of organization; when organization is considered, it is as a dependent variable reflecting political factors. This is admittedly an incomplete formulation for a full theory of implementation, but one must begin somewhere.

Distributive Policy

(*a*) Distributive policies are characterized by fragmented demand and decision patterns (Salisbury, 1968). Further, the fragmentation reflects an "invisible hand" that allocates resources without overt political conflict; and this lack of conflict, which characterizes the policy formation process, carries over into the administration of programs. (The political bargains that were necessary to achieve policy agreement among many parties are adhered to throughout implementation.)

(*b*) Distributive programs are characterized by a congruence of bureaucratic incentives throughout the intergovernmental system. Each level of the implementing bureaucracy shares the goals of the level above it, and the tacit agreements that guided legislative passage operate within bureaucratic spheres in the guise of administrative discretion.

(*c*) Distributive policies are characterized by agreement on the appropriateness and efficacy of the technology required to implement programs. This certainty gives distributive programs an air of predictability so as to reinforce the tacit bargains that permeate them.

(*d*) When there is political and bureaucratic agreement on goals and appropriate technology, distributive programs are very likely to be implemented in accordance with statutory language.

(*e*) Distributive programs do not typically include a systematic search for evidence about outcomes or impact. The organized constituencies that seek and support distributive policies focus on immediate outputs rather than long-run objectives.

(*f*) The chief cause of implementation failure in distributive programs is corruption. The implementation problem can take two forms: either funds are so directed to private purposes that public goals are disregarded, or controversy over corruption kills the program. But corruption is usually localized; national policies are brought into question only if corruption appears to be endemic in the program.

The Interstate Highway Act created a classic distributive program. Its benefits were guaranteed to all states. Each level of the implementing bureaucracy knew what was expected of it, and all shared common administrative and engineering technologies. Almost no emphasis was given to the long-run impact of the program upon society, but the immediate benefits were clear and widely accepted.

The National Defense Education Act (NDEA) of 1958 was much the same in the area of social policy. The federal government developed efficient mechanisms to pass funds to states and local school districts with maximum discretion and minimal requirements. The funds were used to support new curricular programs with obvious financial and educational benefits to school systems. Whether the NDEA has had a salutory effect on American education and society in the long run is a moot question.

Regulatory Policy

(*a*) Regulatory programs are characterized by active support from organized groups, tacit support from diffuse publics, and opposition by those regulated. Most legislators tend to support the initial enactment of such measures more vigorously than their subsequent implementation, since their political incentives are served by actions in the short term. If diffuse public support continues to be strong, regulatory policy will possess the legitimacy necessary for the imposition of rules upon those regulated. If diffuse public support weakens, however, the political difficulties of implementing policy increase, and regulators find that they must compromise with those regulated; as a result, policy is often diluted, without any change in law (Sabatier, 1977).

(*b*) Unresolved disputes about the strength and scope of regulation are passed by legislatures to bureaucracies.

(c) Bureaucracies develop two alternative strategies in coping with unresolved disputes about the strength and scope of regulation. They may seek to mobilize support for regulation by stimulating organized groups to demand regulation; they may bargain with the regulated and dilute the law. Finally, the strategy chosen depends as much on the character and composition of regulatory agencies as on the balance of external political forces.

(d) The successful implementation of regulatory programs requires agreement upon an implementable technology. Without such agreement, regulatory rules, and the statutes from which they are derived, are subject to legal challenge. A legal counterforce to such challenges is provided by policy supporters who couch their arguments in the rhetorical objectives of the law, quite aside from questions of the feasibility of implementation. Bureaucracies tacitly pass conflicts between technological uncertainties and rhetorical objectives on to the courts, which thereby become agencies of implementation.

(e) Compliance with regulatory rules is a function of a clear statute and regulations, a political environment supportive of regulation, agreement on technology, and the organizational capacity of the regulated to act.

(f) Regulation that requires extraordinary organizational change in those regulated will fail if formal rules are not sufficient to induce such change. The implementation of regulatory rules requires the search for informal strategies that will induce change in the regulated organizations.

A comparison of different kinds of regulatory policies will show that the degree to which they are successfully implemented depends on a combination of political and organizational factors. The examples given below begin with a case in which the degree of implementation was high and work toward the other end of the continuum:

The 1965 Voting Rights Law. This law illustrates the capacity of the federal government to enforce basic constitutional provisions. President Johnson had used public rhetorical persuasion, coupled with dramatic events in Selma, Alabama, to persuade Congress and the public that the right of black southerners to vote should not be impeded. The technology was very simple. If the voting registrars in seven southern states did not register black citizens to vote, they were replaced by federal registrars. Complex organizational change was not required.

The 1964 Civil Rights Act. This act denied federal funds to segregated school districts, but there was little federal aid to education in 1964. The law, therefore, lacked teeth until the Elementary and Secondary Education Act of 1965 provided funds badly needed by southern school districts, funds which would then be withheld for noncompliance. The subsequent history of how these two statutes worked together on behalf of desegregation is complex and unfinished, and it illustrates the kinds of partial victories that characterize federal regulation in a volatile political setting (Orfield, 1969).

Amendments to the Clean Air Act. Environmental policy is a search for public goods which initially met the political needs of Congress and the president for popular symbolic action, and which had the support of diffuse publics influenced by the intense activity of policy advocates. The amendments to the Clean Air Act placed the burden of proof on the automobile industry to reduce auto exhaust emissions despite the absence of an effective technology. As a result, the Environmental Protection Agency faced an administrative dilemma: it could moderate enforcement in accordance with technological uncertainties, or, to protect its credibility with environmental groups (Marcus, 1980: chap. 8), it could demand stringent compliance from the industry. The decision to deny requests for delay in compliance achieved the latter objective but also brought the courts into the situation and, moreover, was ineffective in resolving the technological difficulties. This is a familiar story in the implementation of environmental laws. An atmosphere of favorable political support is necessary but not sufficient in the face of other obstacles to implementation.

"Client politics." Certain regulatory social programs are characterized by what James Q. Wilson calls "client politics" (1980: 369). These are programs in which the benefits are concentrated and the costs are widely distributed. A well-organized group prevails in securing government protection and others have little incentive to organize in opposition, if they even know of the policy. Wilson uses this concept to characterize a "producer dominance" model through which industries and occupations enjoy subsidies and protective regulations, but the concept can easily be applied to social policy—particularly if one adds a dash of another Wilson concept, "entrepreneurial politics" (1980: 370–371). In this case, action is initiated by political entrepreneurs who tap latent public sentiments for actions supported by widely shared values. The passage of one law prepares the way for subsequent extensions of the principle. Client politics on behalf of social regulation result in specific legislation passed in the wake of more general measures which established the general principle. The overwhelming legitimacy of the general principle is one reason that opposition groups do not form. Thus the Civil Rights Act prepared the way for subsequent statutes on behalf of women, the handicapped, and the aged.

Peter Schuck describes the factors that made possible the passage of the Age Discrimination Act (ADA) of 1975: "It promised benefits to a visible, politically influential group that all Americans hoped someday to join; its sponsors argued that it could confer these benefits at no additional cost; its redistributional implications were not clear, or at least not noticed; and it was a small and inconspicuous part of a large omnibus bill that both Congress and the Administration supported. Perhaps most important, it drew strength from the moral legitimacy and rhetorical force of the 1960s and early 1970s. . . ." (1980:75)

The legislative rhetoric, however, obscured some important ambiguities and contradictions in the ADA. For example, the definition of age discrimination which was to be outlawed, was so broad as to be useless ("any act or failure to act, or any law or policy that adversely affects an individual on the basis of age") (Schuck, 1980:79). There were no boundaries to the definition, and its goal was not reconciled with other social goals in which values other than age might take priority. Possible conflicts between different age groups were not considered. For example, if a community Mental Health Center devotes more resources to young than to old people because money is limited and therapeutic prospects are better with the young, is this age discrimination?

Such hard questions cannot be avoided. Consequently, although they do not change their rhetoric, agencies make selective compromises in enforcement. One reason is limited resources for inspection and litigation. But an even more compelling reason is the inability of government to force private institutions to accept policies that are very expensive or require great organizational change, even if the regulated subscribe to the principles underlying regulation (Rabkin, 1980: 351–352). The result is often that many regulations are never fully enforced. But this is never admitted, lest it appear that government is willing to tolerate a compromise in civil rights.

Redistributive Policy

This section will deal only with the redistribution of resources and power in the class structure through social policies. Economic subsidies to industries are excluded.

(*a*) Redistributive programs with a high distributive component have greater political legitimacy during implementation than those with a low distributive component. The presence of a distributive element appeals to a wide population and saves these programs from the taint of purely redistributive welfare programs.

(*b*) The implementation of redistributive programs with a high distributive component reveals an ambiguity about program goals: is their purpose primarily distributive or redistributive? School administrators, for example, sought to distribute funds authorized under Title I of the Elementary and Secondary Education Act to as many school districts as possible; more recently, however, redistributive values have been affirmed in federal implementation of the law (Goettel, 1978: chap. 6). The enforcement of redistributive values in such mixed programs entails a strong regulatory component, which presents implementation problems of its own. Administrative methods to insure compliance with redistributive goals must be contrived, and the success of such strategies will depend upon the general degree of political support for them. One thus finds the politics of regulative protection encapsulated within some redistributive programs.

(*c*) Redistributive programs with a low distributive component have more severe implementation problems than those with a high distributive component, since their recipient population is more suspect. Government imposes rules to restrict benefits to the eligible. Such programs frequently suffer from insufficient funding, because of low political legitimacy, and from cumbersome bureaucracy, which alienates recipients and stifles the discretion of those who deliver services. Here the contrast between Medicare and Medicaid is instructive. The former serves all social classes and therefore, while redistributive to the elderly, is distributive to all in that category. The resulting legitimacy of the program simplifies its implementation. The existing Social Security old-age pension, which possesses legitimacy and administrative simplicity, is an appropriate administrative vehicle for Medicare. Medicaid, in contrast, serves the poor—a more suspect group—and not even all of them. Program beneficiaries must undergo an income test with all its attendant administrative problems. The regulatory apparatus required by Medicaid is therefore far more complex than that for Medicare (Feder, 1977; Stevens & Stevens, 1974).

(*d*) Redistributive programs directed solely to lower class recipients have greater legitimacy and are easier to implement if they pursue a human development goal rather than a welfare goal. "Human development" matches the American ethic of equality of opportunity better than the idea of welfare does. The Head Start program, for example, aims to enhance educational opportunity for the children of disadvantaged families; it has provoked less political conflict than has Medicaid, and its administration has been easier.

(*e*) Redistributive programs are constantly moving toward either distributive or regulatory goals. There is continuous pressure to increase the distributive character of programs with a balanced distributive-redistributive character. An increased distributive emphasis gives greater political legitimacy and better reflects the politics of American pluralism and federalism. The politics of implementing such mixed programs are fought out in policy and administrative decisions about who will and will not be served. Should the redistributive forces prevail, the regulatory battle begins. The implementation problems that attend such regulation have already been described.

The Comprehensive Employment and Training Act (CETA) and Title XX of the Social Security Act are two programs that currently serve distributive and redistributive goals in a roughly even balance, with predictable results for implementation (Hargrove & Dean, 1980). Their social purposes and implementation strategies and problems are intertwined. These two programs grew out of earlier programs for the poor but serve a wider range of the population. The decentralized structures of the programs have served the political incentives of local elected officials to provide services for more voters than just the poor; whether this is considered an implementation problem depends upon whether the goal of the programs is thought to be primarily distributive or redistributive. The programs succeed very well in the former case and less well in the latter.

Moving these programs in redistributive directions would require a stronger, more authoritative federal regulatory role. (We have already discussed the implementation problems that follow from this course.) CETA might be expected to encounter less severe problems that Title XX, however, since employment training, as a human development goal, has greater political legitimacy than social services tied to welfare principles. Both CETA and Title XX have been administered so as to gain broad legitimacy as distributive programs without abandoning redistributive goals. This appears to have been the intent of the legislation. As a result, the implementation process has been loose, relaxed, and decentralized, with a minimum of regulation. (Hargrove & Dean, 1980).

Title I of the Elementary and Secondary Education Act (ESEA) could have gone in the same direction. Certainly many of its adherents, in Congress and the school systems, attempted to write the allocation formulae so that as many children in as many schools as possible would be covered. (Murphy, 1971). But the momentum of the civil rights movement and corresponding legal and political pressures appear to have strengthened both the regulatory and the redistributive character of the implementation of Title I, so that federal funds have been primarily directed to schools with large concentrations of disadvantaged students (Goettel, 1978). Furthermore, there is a tradeoff in implementation between distributive smoothness and the attainment of redistributive goals. The former may sacrifice evaluation of outcomes for distributive principles; the latter requires a stronger regulatory component with corresponding political support in order to achieve implementation.

(*f*) Regulatory redistributive programs that combine goals of equity and service delivery are the most difficult to implement. Formal regulatory strategies designed to secure compliance by local providers with policy goals are insufficient. They must be supplemented by the development of informal strategies that can activate formal approaches. Hill (1979), for example, has developed a theory of the relation between formal and informal strategies of regulation in regard to the implementation of Title I, ESEA: informal strategies consist of the development of networks of state and local education officials whose careers depend upon the continuance of Title I, the federal use of nonfiscal sanctions such as public audits, and national program evaluations which may stimulate parents and advocates to mount local watchdog efforts. According to Hill, formal regulations will not suffice because Congress will not permit federal agencies to withhold funds for noncompliance. In addition, Title I's specification of objectives is only an invocation of principles; nothing is added about how to achieve them. And finally, because federal knowledge of local school systems is inherently limited, the state of compliance in general cannot be known. Formal regulations, then, are levers to be invoked by informal strategies. The key to success is to strengthen local incentives to comply.

The experience of redistributive programs that require a strong, authoritative federal enforcement role reveals that efforts to insure compliance are a necessary but not sufficient condition for the actual implementation of programs. Federal regulations that require services or benefits to be delivered to disadvantaged groups are not implemented and incorporated by the organization that is to deliver the services without mutual adaptation between federal directives and local organizational goals and routines (Berman & McLaughlin, 1975). Moreover, federal regulations that are imposed from the top down in a uniform fashion across many jurisdictions will be blunted by the variety of requirements for mutual adaptation in local settings. Hence federal implementation strategies directed toward influencing the local practices necessary for mutual adaptation, implementation, and incorporation are more likely than top-down strategies to be effective in achieving implementation (Elmore, 1979–80). The power to implement or erode lies at the grassroots level among those who deliver services: federal and state officials can support or inhibit positive initiatives at the grassroots level, but they can do little directly to enforce implementation.

The foregoing propositions attempt to bring together two bodies of literature that have seldom been joined in actual research. Research on compliance with court or bureaucratic directives typically determines whether the regulated institution is in formal compliance and does not ask whether compliance is incorporated into routines for the delivery of services. (Wasby, 1970; Handler, 1978). On the other hand, research on effective modes of service delivery with organizations generally focuses upon internally generated sources of innovation and does not examine the possible links of such change to external stimuli or mandates (Berman & McLaughlin, 1977).

We need theory that can join the two. The author's recent study of the implementation of the Education for All Handicapped Children Act of 1975 illustrates some fruitful ways to join regulation and service delivery in a more detailed and specific manner (Hargrove et al., 1981; Hargrove et al., forthcoming).

(g) A strong emphasis in a regulatory redistributive program upon compliance may work against effective delivery of services. An insistence on uniform compliance with federal rules makes it impossible to differentiate among organizations in terms of their varying capacities to deliver services, so that complying organizations tend to move toward a mean of pro forma compliance. The deficient improve and the effective may regress, but in neither case is the question of quality of services faced.

The Education for All Handicapped Children Act (P.L. 94-142) was inspired by the belief among special educators that the labeling of mentally handicapped children was harmful to their development. Labeling by category, such as learning disability (LD) or educable mentally retarded (EMR), was said to have been substituted for diagnosis and treatment according to individual needs. Critics charged that such categories served political and bureaucratic purposes. Advocates were organized to press for funds and services for particular categories—categories which also governed the training and placement of special education teachers. Under the act, an individualized education plan (IEP) superseding the old categories was to be designed for each child. It was assumed that schools and teachers would and could make the necessary adaptations by debureaucratizing, that individual needs would take precedence over labels. Yet the actual effect in many places may have been to increase bureaucracy and reduce individuation: the IEP is not necessarily used as a device for improved educational treatment (Weatherly, 1979), but is often used simply as part of the bureaucratic requirement to process all children.

If these have been the unintended effects of the law, they have been caused by naiveté about bureaucracy. Reformers assumed that school systems and schools could debureaucratize for greater attention to individual needs. In fact, in the response to bureaucratically administered regulations, concern with compliance may have crowded out concern for developing individual programs.

In a recent paper, Mark Yudoff (1980:7–8) develops these ideas more fully with respect to the strategies of the courts in ordering and fostering racial desegregation of schools. The big steps in bringing school systems into compliance with federal law came after passage of the Civil Rights Act of 1964, when the courts were aided by the Office of Civil Rights and the Department of Justice in bringing potential sanctions to bear on recalcitrant systems. Such firm and direct approaches to compliance, however, have been of limited value to courts and federal agencies in the second generation of problems (such as tracking, discipline, and policies about teacher location and tenure). The courts have therefore resorted to strategies of organizational development, in which direct coercion has been replaced by efforts to obtain the cooperation of local judges and attorneys, advocate groups, and school administrators.

In sum, any theory of implementation for such different cases, and any strategies that follow from it, must embrace the perspectives both of compliance and of implementation.

Assumptions about American Politics

The observations of this study reflect a certain understanding of American politics of the 1960s and 1970s. All middle-range propositions, which are necessarily bounded by time and culture, rest on such invisible foundations. Such propositions are inevitably manifestations of unstated regularities of culture, politics, and government in a given society during a certain historical period. Specifically, the following assumptions have guided the propositions set forth here:

(a) The United States has a "liberal" political culture, as described by Louis Hartz (1955). Neither classical European conservatism nor socialism has taken root; there is, rather, a tension between acquisitive and egalitarian values, with a consensus on equality of opportunity rather than of condition (Lipset, 1963: chaps. 6, 7). This fact helps explains the weak legitimacy accorded welfare policy and the greater support for Great Society policies of human development.

(b) The political incentives of American congressional politicians strengthen distributive policies at the expense of redistributive policies, with a consequent lessening of concern for effectiveness. This proposition helps explain why so many of the seemingly redistributive social programs of recent years were, in fact, distributive both in latent intent and in actual effect.

(c) The political incentives of congressional politicians cause an emphasis on symbolic expression of principles of equity in regulatory policy, with little thought given to implementation. This hypothesis helps explain why so much regulatory legislation in recent years appears to have been designed to win immediate support from mobilized constituencies. Members of Congress seek political credit for highly visible acts in the short term; by the time long-term problems of implementation emerge, they have moved on to new issues (Hargrove, 1975).

(*d*) The difficulty of implementing social programs in a geographically large federal system causes government administrators to present the form and symbolic appeal of policy as its reality. We are left with the irony that public bureaucracy, which is supposed to join means to ends in rational action, shows very little interest in ends at all (Meyer & Rowan, 1978: 363–364).

Conclusion

The opportunities for analysis to influence policy are bounded by the prevailing structure of politics. Implementation analysis becomes sterile and technocratic when practiced apart from the political context. A new majoritarian politics of redistributive cast, whether of the ideological right or left, would change all of the foregoing propositions and present analysis with unforeseen possibilities. But assuming there are no such fundamental changes in the structure of politics, how can implementation analysis build on the propositions presented here? Let me suggest a few possibilities.

Analysts can predict the consequences of proposed program characteristics and structures and ask policymakers if that is what they really intend. Would congressional entrepreneurs reconsider the regulatory legislation they write if they could foresee the actual consequences? Second, analysts can suggest strategies that might enhance policy effectiveness, e.g., explicit boundaries and specifications of priorities and goals in regulatory legislation. (Of course, such ideas must match the grain of politics.) Third, analysts can suggest methods of program management that might enhance implementation. Finally, analysts can point out the tradeoffs in efforts to make redistributive programs more palatable politically by adding a distributive dimension. For example, CETA and other block grant programs achieve certain broad political objectives, but at what price of help for the most disadvantaged?

The framework and propositions presented here may be helpful to policy analysts and program managers by showing how specific decisions fit into a larger context. But the chapter is perhaps more suggestive as an illustration of how the search for theory properly unites research and policy analysis.

19. Compensating When the Government Harms

Joseph J. Cordes, Robert S. Goldfarb,
and James R. Barth

Abstract

An increasing number of federal programs compensate individuals harmed by government policy changes; the list has grown to include trade adjustment assistance, federal relocation assistance to households displaced by public works projects, transitional aid features of environmental regulations, compensation provisions in the Airline Deregulation Act, and compensation to displaced redwood loggers. To determine whether government compensation schemes are appropriate, one must resolve two important issues. First, under what conditions can compensation ever be conceptually justified? Second, if a conceptual justification exists, can a practical scheme be developed that achieves the conceptual objective of compensation to an acceptable degree? This study examines some conceptual rationales for compensating those harmed by public actions. One issue is whether public policy changes per se impose compensable economic losses. We show that the likelihood that public policy shifts will generate potentially compensable losses depends on how accurately such shifts are anticipated by those affected. Determining that a given policy change is appropriately unexpected does not, however, guarantee that compensation is ethically justified. Specific equity rationales must be considered. Applying these rationales to such actual situations suggests three broad conclusions. First, although the rationales need not conflict, they are sufficiently different that in some instances they may yield different evaluations of whether compensation is required. Second, the various rationales provide a clear basis for rejecting payment of compensation under some plausible circumstances. Third, if those affected by public policy changes are capable of forming correct anticipations, the equity rational for compensation is weakened considerably—regardless of how equity is defined.

To determine whether government compensation schemes are appropriate, one must resolve two important issues. First, under what conditions can compensation ever be conceptually justified? This issue has been addressed by Harold Hochman (1974), Cordes and Weisbrod (1979), Goldfarb and Cordes (1979), and Tullock (1978), among others. Second, if a conceptual justification exists, can a practical scheme be developed that achieves the conceptual objective of compensation to an acceptable degree? Goldfarb (1980) argues that practical considerations may dissuade even those who strongly favor compensation in principle from adopting a particular compensation scheme. Others (e.g., Bale & Mutti, 1978; Cordes, 1979) have considered particular compensation schemes, such as Trade Adjustment Assistance and Relocation Assistance, to determine the extent to which these programs have achieved their objectives. Although these more narrowly focused studies typically do not evaluate compensation schemes in general, they do provide important evidence on the feasibility of designing such schemes.

While some conceptual justifications have been offered for compensation, the earlier study by Goldfarb and Cordes (1979) warrants further elaboration, which we offer here. Goldfarb and Cordes (GC) identify several alternative rationales for severance pay compensation and then examine which of these rationales are consistent with the actual compensation provisions in the Airline Deregulation Act of 1978. Two distinct types of rationales are discussed: (*a*) those based on practical considerations of efficiency, and (*b*) those based on ethical judgments of equity. The two practical rationales referred to by GC as "political buyout" and "better calculations" are fairly straightforward conceptually and are therefore not discussed here.[1] Instead, we address two additional and important issues.

The first is whether government policy changes per se impose identifiable, systematic economic losses that require compensation. Since the behavior of economic agents operating in a world of uncertainty is based upon expectations, the economic impacts of government policy shifts should depend on the expectations formed by those affected. If agents can perfectly anticipate government policy changes and their consequences (in the sense to be explained below), the ethical basis for compensation is diminished. If, on the other hand, policy changes are completely unanticipated, a strong case can be made for full compensation. A more realistic and interesting case arises when expectations about government policy are such that a policy change comprises both anticipated and unanticipated components.

The second issue is whether there are ethical as opposed to purely pragmatic justifications for compensation. Recent experience suggests that compensation is often provided to mute the opposition of politically powerful groups to policy changes. Is this desirable policy, or should compensation also be provided to potentially weak yet deserving groups?

Compensation and Expectations

In a recent paper, Harold Hochman (1974) argues that procedures be seriously considered for offsetting the "windfall declines in the absolute wealth of some individuals that occur when the community-at-large . . . alters its *rules and institutions* [emphasis added]." In Hochman's view, such procedures—which include paying compensation—are required to preserve the individual's belief in the fairness of a system of laws and rules: "Most often, individual behavior presumes the permanence of preexisting rules. Indeed, if law and the concept of rules are to be credible, individuals must hold this presumption with a high degree of confidence. Not just existing rules, but change in these rules, must be justifiable, and the process through which change is effected must itself be fair. . . . Rules changes that disappoint such expectations may themselves be unjust. . . . The process of change, if considered arbitrary, can itself make individuals feel it is irrational to accept the limits that rules imply" (pp. 323–24).

Hochman's view is readily interpreted as favoring compensation of those harmed by public actions or by adverse changes in private markets. This follows from the important, albeit implicit, role of anticipations in Hochman's framework. From Hochman's perspective, for example, there would be no reason to compensate someone losing a job in an industry where jobs are known to be short-lived. Presumably, a rational worker choosing between a "short-lived" and "long-lived" job would accept the short-lived job only at a wage appropriately higher than that offered by the long-lived job. Those employed in short-lived jobs would, therefore, already receive compensation through higher wages. An unanticipated switch to compensation for loss of such jobs would double payment and would violate the spirit of Hochman's argument.[2]

Hochman's defense of compensation for government rules changes underscores the importance of expectations. However, the relevance of expectations in the design and evaluation of compensation schemes has been largely unexplored.[3] We shall therefore examine the way assumptions about expectations can alter compensation schemes.[4]

Consider an economic agent who maximizes profit (Π). For simplicity, assume that profits depend upon the government policy (R) and other economic variables (V). That is,

$$\Pi = \Pi(V, R) . \tag{19.1}$$

Assume further that the economic agent must formulate his behavior today on the basis of the government policy he expects to be in effect in the future, so that his behavior is based upon some anticipated government policy (R^e). The maximization of profit based upon this anticipated policy will yield an optimal profit (Π^e) defined as follows:

$$\Pi^e = \Pi^e(V, R^e) . \tag{19.2}$$

In many cases, the actual government policy will turn out to be different, so that an economic agent's expectations will in general not be fully realized. The difference between the actual government policy (R^r) and the anticipated policy (R^e) represents the anticipation error. Had the actual government policy been known when an agent committed himself to particular actions, maximizing behavior would instead have produced an optimal profit:

$$\Pi' = \Pi'(V, R') .\tag{19.3}$$

The loss resulting from anticipation error would therefore be formulated as

$$\Pi' - \Pi^e = f(R' - R^e) .\tag{19.4}$$

In other words, the loss in profits resulting from government policy changes depends upon the extent to which such changes are anticipated. When anticipations are perfect, so that R' equals R^e, Π^e equals Π' and there are no losses. When anticipation are less than perfect, however, R' will not equal R^e and Π' will not equal Π^e. Hence, only unanticipated government policy changes generate losses, and the accuracy of an economic agent's expectations affects the magnitude of losses generated by changes in public policies. Since individuals and firms are likely to base their behavior on expected government policies, it seems appropriate to provide compensation only for those losses resulting from anticipation errors.

Since economic agents will use all available information in forming expectations about R, the case for compensation is weak when the government provides accurate information in advance about a policy change, or if the policy shift is of a sort that can be easily anticipated. If, however, little information is provided about future policy changes, or if policy shifts are of a type difficult to anticipate, economic agents are likely to make relatively large and systematic anticipation errors. This implies that compensation is less warranted when a policy change is preceded by a period of discussion and debate, giving those affected the opportunity to acquire and process information about the policy change.

The case for compensation is thus most compelling when government policies are changed in such a way as to generate large and systematic anticipation errors. Even if such anticipation errors were small and random, however, compensation might still be justified in specific circumstances. In particular, if economic agents must incur real costs in adjusting their behavior, some losses will be suffered even if anticipations are correct. In such cases, however, compensation should only be based on specific adjustment costs rather than on any observed changes in profits or incomes of those affected by the policy change.

Equity Rationales for Compensation

Even if a policy change is unexpected by some or all of those adversely affected and therefore imposes real economic losses, it does not necessarily follow that there is an ethical obligation to compensate losers. This raises the issue of whether there are ethical as well as pragmatic rationales for compensation.

The fact that compensation is often extended to politically powerful groups is one reason why ethical factors should be considered. Without an ethical rationale, appropriate social policy would adopt the compensation scheme that purchased political acquiescence at the lowest possible cost. But the recognition of ethical rationales would imply that society should also compensate deserving though politically weak groups.

A second reason for examining ethical rationales is the long-standing controversy about whether income distributional factors should be included in benefit-cost analyses. Some argue that maximization of social welfare requires that income distributional considerations be explicitly included in the form of distributional weights assigned to benefits and costs.[5] Others reject this view, maintaining that social welfare is best advanced by choosing projects that maximize the difference between unweighted benefits and costs and then relying on government tax and transfer programs to achieve the desired final distribution of benefits and costs.[6]

Establishing explicit equity criteria for compensation requires a compromise between these two positions. Rather than assigning distributional weights in benefit-cost calculations or relying on periodic income redistribution through taxes and transfers, one may use compensation to redress, at least partially, any harmful distributional effects of government actions. This particular approach has recently been suggested by Alan Williams (1979:71):

> I have come round to the view that we shall have made a small but important immediate gain if we can merely ensure that the major unintended distributional effects of public projects are neutralized, by putting renewed emphasis on devising and implementing better compensation arrangements. After all, our initial difficulties over distributional matters stemmed partly from the fact that the efficiency calculus works on hypothetical compensation tests, while the distributional calculus works on actual compensation arrangements, and there is often considerable divergence between the two. So we should, perhaps, re-examine the scope for improving compensation arrangements so as to narrow this gap, since even small improvements on this front may lead to disproportionately large reductions in people's sense of injustice.

Rawls-Michaelman Fairness View

One way of identifying equity criteria for payment of compensation has been proposed by Frank Michaelman (1967), who applies John Rawls's concept of justice. According to Rawls, the most reasonable principles of justice for structuring society are those that would be accepted by free, rational, self-interested persons in a hypothetical original position where no one knows what his or her particular place and needs in the society will be. Rawls argues that rational individuals, if placed in the original position, would choose social practices that conformed to two principles. The first would require equality in the assignment of rights and duties. The second would allow inequalities only to the extent that they resulted in compensating benefits for all, especially for the least advantaged members of society.

These concepts are the foundation of Michaelman's principles for evaluating compensation schemes. Michaelman's first criterion, based on the Rawls equality principle, would require full compensation whenever public programs impose concentrated welfare losses. But Michaelman's second criterion, based on Rawls's second principle, would permit departures from strict compensation under certain circumstances. In general, departures would be permitted if a less rigorous rule were chosen.

More specifically, Michaelman performs the following "thought experiment." The decisionmaker in an original position must choose a compensation rule. If compensation is not paid to losers, the decisionmaker risks suffering losses he or she could avoid if compensation were paid. Conversely, if compensation is required, the real costs of paying compensation—the transactions or settlement costs—may be so high that otherwise economically efficient projects are abandoned. By choosing stringent compensation rules, then the decisionmaker may forego future opportunities for real gains in national income in which he or she would share. The problem in choosing between a more stringent and a less stringent compensation rule is therefore to determine which alternative is potentially least costly to the decisionmaker.

A requirement to compensate losers fully would be adopted whenever the expected costs of full compensation were less than those of a less strict compensation rule. Presumably, the costs associated with stringent compensation would be lower whenever the costs of identifying the losers, estimating the losses, and delivering the compensation—i.e., the transactions or settlement costs—were low. Conversely, the expected costs of not paying compensation would be high whenever the losses resulting from public programs were large and/or when the individuals sustaining such losses were not likely to receive significant offsetting benefits from the program responsible for generating such losses.[7]

The distinctive feature of Michaelman's adaptation of Rawls is that it provides an ethical argument for a rather pragmatic, efficiency-oriented approach to determining whether compensation should be paid. Consider, for example, the proposition that paying full compensation is fair if the costs of doing so are low, while the costs of failing to do so are high. In principle, such a tradeoff calculation could provide an ethical rationale for compensating groups simply because their political power enables them to block socially desirable policy changes. This line of reasoning could also, however, justify denying compensation because of administrative difficulties encountered in identifying losers, measuring losses, and delivering compensation—particularly if the group to be compensated lacks political power.

Moreover, compensation criteria based on the Rawls-Michaelman principles are not simply poverty criteria. To be sure, Rawls-Michaelman criteria would, other things being equal, favor compensating low-income as opposed to high-income losers, although they would not preclude compensation of high-income losers. Furthermore, low-income status would not guarantee compensation since other factors, such as transaction costs, would also have to be taken into account. This follows from a fundamental difference between Rawls's philosophical orientation and more traditional distributional equity arguments. Whereas the latter arguments are often based on a moral obligation to help the poor, Rawls's conception of fairness rests on the assumption that individuals would pursue their own best interests in a pre-social-contract state of the world.

Dynamics of Status Change

Those who criticize compensation arrangements often object that such programs are a piecemeal, haphazard means of remedying more general income distribution problems. As evidence, these skeptics point to compensation programs that fail to benefit many who are poor but provide benefits to others who are not poor. An important rebuttal is that equity can pertain to changes in status as well as to the static income distribution.

Suppose two societies have identical income distributions, that each has the same percentage of individuals (or of families) at every income level. In the first society, individuals' positions within the income distribution are not affected by government rules changes, while in the second society the government changes rules every year so that the positions of 20 percent of the population are altered. Specifically, assume that some high-income people become low-income people, and vice versa. By construction, the static income distribution in each society is identical. An equity view stressing only income distribution would view these societies as equally fair. Unlike the first society, however, the second experiences substantial government-caused change in relative positions. If this difference is perceived as a difference in equity, then equity can be defined as a function not only of income distribution but also of the fairness of changes in status. If significant changes of relative position caused by government actions are considered unfair, compensation to maintain relative positions would have considerable ethical appeal.

Compensation and Tax Equity

Losses imposed by government policy changes can also be viewed as prices that must be paid if such activities are to be undertaken. Such losses would be equivalent to implicit taxes which certain individuals might have to bear in addition to explicit taxes. From this perspective, the problem of determining how much compensation to pay, and to whom, is formally equivalent to that of determining the desired incidence of a tax.

If uncompensated losses are treated as taxes, actual compensation criteria can be evaluated according to standard tax equity criteria. One such criterion is the ability-to-pay principle of taxation. Under this rule, a tax is equitable if and only if (a) burdens are distributed in a horizontally equitable manner, with equally situated persons paying equal amounts of tax, and (b) burdens are distributed in a vertically equitable manner, with persons in unequal positions paying appropriately unequal amounts of tax.

Horizontal equity. If equality of situation is defined in terms of income, failure to compensate those harmed by policy change would violate horizontal equity if such harms were unevenly distributed among individuals in any given income class. If horizontal equity were regarded as an important tax-sharing norm, compensation might then be justified on equity grounds. In this case, the actual amount of compensation paid would depend upon the variance in the distribution of individual losses. If strict horizontal equity were desired, for instance, equalization of implicit tax rates within income classes would require that the amount of compensation, C_{ij}, received by the ith member of income group j be specified as

$$C_{ij} = (L_{ij} - L_j^*) , \qquad (19.5)$$

where L_{ij} is the loss sustained by the ith individual in the jth income group, and L_j^* is the minimum loss sustained in income group j. If the government program imposed losses that fell on *some* but *not all* members of income class j, L_j^* would equal zero, and horizontal equity would require that each person receive full compensation equal to L_{ij}. However, if everyone in income class j suffered equal losses, so that $L_{ij} = L_j^*$ for all i, horizontal equity could be achieved without payment of any compensation. These comments suggest that notions of horizontal equity based on income are both too restrictive and too broad to guide decisionmakers in determining whether conpensation should be paid. For example, horizontal equity would not require that any compensation be paid so long as all members of income class j suffered equal losses, $L_{ij} = L_j^*$, even though those losses might be large.

The recent optimal taxation literature includes some reformulations of the horizontal equity concept which suggest that the fairness of status changes should be considered an important feature of equity. Several tax scholars have argued that large changes in relative tax liability because of arbitrary rules changes are fundamentally inequitable. For example, Harvey Rosen (1978) adopts as an equity criterion Feldstein's conception of horizontal equity in utility terms, which requires that two conditons be fulfilled.[8] First, if two persons would be equally well off (that is, achieve equal levels of utility) in the absence of taxation, they should also be equally well off with taxation. Second, for taxpayers who would not be equally well off in the absence of taxation, taxation should not alter their ordering of well-being. This notion, that changes in tax policy are equitable if they do not disturb existing orderings of well-being, is consistent with the view presented above, that relative change in status creates issues of equity.

Vertical equity. In the design of compensation rules, attention should also be given to the distribution of losses and of compensation payments among individuals in unequal positions. Vertically equitable compensation criteria might be based on an explicit social welfare function (SWF). This SWF would translate changes in income or utility of individuals into social welfare changes. In practice, however, such a SWF cannot be observed directly. Instead, institutional arrangements, such as tax codes, are observed. If one assumes that such arrangements reflect value judgments embodied in some (unobservable) SWF, the existing tax structure can identify compensation criteria judged by the political structure to be vertically equitable.

Equation (19.6) shows how tax structure information might be used to form value judgements concerning compensation. The amount of compensation, C_k, paid to any household k, would equal

$$C_k = L_k - gT_k , \tag{19.6}$$

where L_k is the gross loss imposed by some public policy change on household k and T_k is the total tax liability of household k. The parameter g would be determined by the decisionmaker. For example, setting $g = 1$ ($g = \frac{1}{2}$) would represent an explicit judgment that households should bear uncompensated losses equal to no more than the amount (half the amount) normally paid in taxes, and so forth.

This approach implies that, regardless of the value of g, whenever T_k equals zero, C_k will equal L_k, and full compensation will be paid. Taxes are often structured so that households at or below a specified income level pay no tax at all. Presumably, this reflects an implicit judgment that the ability of such households to pay is minimal. If some limitations are placed on the burdens imposed by explicitly mandated taxes, these limitations should also apply to implicit taxes imposed by unexpected policy changes.[9]

If g is held constant across income classes, equation (19.6) further reveals that compensation payments will decrease as the tax liability, T, increases.[10] Moreover, holding tax liabilities constant, more adequate compensation—measured in terms of the ratio of compensation to losses suffered—would be provided under equation (19.6) for large losses than for small losses. To see this, divide equation (19.6) through by L_k:

$$\frac{C_k}{L_k} = 1 - g\frac{T_k}{L_k} . \tag{19.7}$$

For constant gT_k, the percentage compensated, C_k/L_k, rises as L_k (the absolute loss) rises.

Equation (19.6) is but one possible example of how tax structure information can be used to determine desired levels of compensation. While many such potential relationships exist, reference to the tax structure does limit the universe of acceptable compensation equations.

The benefit principle.   The benefit principle is a second broad criterion of tax equity. Under this criterion, an equitable tax is one that distributes the burdens of financing public programs according to the benefits received from public programs. If this standard were applied to compensation schemes, the appropriate procedure would be to compare the losses imposed by public programs or public policy shifts with the benefits received. Failure to provide some compensation to those who bear cost-benefit ratios exceeding the politywide average ratios of probram costs to benefits would violate the benefit principle.

A significant practical implication of the benefit principle is that the amount of compensation paid should depend on whether a given public project or policy shift is structured to provide offsetting gains to losers. Thus government rules changes that restrict certain economic activities may be viewed as fair if they are accompanied by grandfather clauses or by other property rights that benefit those whose behavior has been restricted.[11] (An explicit example of this principle is discussed below.) The benefit principle also explains the strong ethical appeal of compensating those harmed by public actions which both impose concentrated losses and provide widely diffused benefits.

Evaluating Ad Hoc Compensation Arguments

Thus far, several distinct criteria for evaluating the desirability of compensation have been identified. In this section our framework is used to evaluate two popular ad hoc arguments, one in favor of compensation, and one skeptical of it.

Transitional Aid Rationale

The existence of such programs as unemployment compensation indicates that there is considerable social support in some cases for provision of "no-fault transitional aid." Specifically, the transitional aid rationale eschews making moral distinctions among potential recipients, holding instead that it is ethically desirable to cushion individual transitions over painful adjustment periods, but that compensation should be extended only if costs are not excessive and if perverse incentive effects can be avoided. These conditions are more likely to be met if payments are explicitly transitional and of short duration.

Our analysis above suggests that both the level and the incidence of transitional adjustment costs depend on the accuracy of expectations concerning the timing and the impact of policy shifts. On the one hand, transitional adjustment costs are more likely to be painful and systematically imposed when the timing and impact of governmental policy changes are difficult to anticipate accurately. It may further be argued that it is more difficult to anticipate changes in the rules of the game (i.e. laws, regulations and procedures) than to anticipate other types of public policy shifts, such as changes in government spending levels. These arguments suggest that the transitional aid rationale will be more compelling if expectations are inaccurate and/or the policy shift involves a change in the rules of the game.

On the other hand, many industries have predictable patterns of seasonal or cyclical unemployment. Individuals enter these industries with expectations of regular periods of unemployment. In these cases, the existence of unemployment insurance enables the industry to attract individuals at lower wages. That is, because unemployment is expected, unemployment insurance reduces the labor costs faced by seasonal and cyclical industries. Unemployment insurance may appear to be a compensation for adjustment, but it is actually a shifting of the source and pattern of wage payment. This is an apt illustration of how expectations can invalidate an apparently plausible compensation policy.

Monopoly Gains Limitation

One argument for explicitly limiting compensation maintains that payment should not be made when government policy changes destroy monopoly positions previously created by government regulation: since the government created the monopoly position, and artificially created monopoly returns are unfair, the government should not pay compensation for the removal of an economic rent.

One may view monopoly gains quite plausibly as having provided offsetting benefits to those who are adversely affected when a policy change destroys government-supported monopolies; if so, the monopoly-gains limitation on compensation would thus appear consistent with the benefit principle. Two crucial issues, however, must be resolved. The first is whether the individuals affected by the rules change are in fact those who reaped the monopoly gains. If they are, the second question is whether the policy change simply returns these individuals to the same economic position they occupied before the creation of monopoly gains.

Resolving the first issue may be quite difficult. A relevant case is the recent deregulation of the trucking industry. Before deregulation, entry into certain markets was legally permitted only if new entrants purchased operating licenses from existing firms. Deregulation will eventually permit entry into new markets without the purchase of such licenses. Several observers have noted that any "monopoly returns" flowing from restricted entry into particular markets should have been reflected in higher selling prices for entry licenses. Thus, the firms reaping monopoly gains would be those initially given the legal right to serve particular markets, not firms who subsequently had to purchase the right to do so. It is largely this latter group of firms, however, that would be affected by deregulation. Since deregulation would render any entry permits virtually worthless, such firms could well suffer losses without the offsetting benefit of past monopoly gains.

Even if one assumes that those affected by the rules changes have also reaped monopoly gains, the benefit principle requires that one distinguish between two different consequences of eliminating government-created monopoly positions. One possible outcome would be a reduction in losers' income to the level they would have attained in the absence of monopoly. The implication of the benefit principle is fairly clear in this case. Those affected would be no worse off in the future than they would have been if the monopoly position had not been created. They would, however, have enjoyed the benefits conferred by the monopoly position during its existence. Compensation would therefore not be warranted.

An alternative outcome would be a reduction in losers' income below the level they would have attained in the absence of monopoly. Determining whether compensation is justified in this case is more complex. Those affected would be worse off in the future than they would be in the absence of the publicly created monopoly, but such losses would be offset by excess earnings received while the monopoly position was in effect.

The Fairness of an Actual Compensation Scheme

To illustrate the application of the criteria described above, we shall consider the case of compensation for limiting fishing rights. Legislation enacted in 1976 extends U.S. coastal jurisdiction to 200 miles and establishes eight regional fishery management councils to develop fishery management plans. The intent of this legislation was to regulate fishing activity in order to promote conservation and to prevent over-exploitation of particular species. The economic argument for such legislation is that particular fishery resources are subject to economic overfishing because of a common property problem.[12] But it has been argued that some of the existing councils have failed to regulate fishing activity effectively, resulting in a serious danger of over-exploitation.[13]

Suppose a fishery is to be regulated so as to limit the existing fishing rights and practices of individuals. The issue then arises whether compensation is warranted and, if so, what this implies for different regulatory schemes. If the aim of regulation were to reduce the volume of fishing from its unregulated level, at least three alternative schemes to achieve this objective might be adopted. One would be to levy appropriate taxes per unit of catch. Another would be to limit the catch directly through fishing quotas. A third alternative would be to simultaneously impose quotas and issue licenses transferable in perpetuity.[14] Further, if each alternative were implemented so as to impose the same limitation on the amount of fishing,[15] the issue then is whether any scheme would be preferable to the others on compensation equity grounds.

Imposing a tax per unit catch would restrict fishing by raising the marginal cost of catching fish. The economic theory of the firm implies that this would force some marginal producers to leave the industry. At the same time, the government would collect revenue from the catch tax. A quota, allocated to fisherman or vessels on the basis of prior catch, would give any rents generated by limiting free entry to those fortunate enough to receive quotas. Auctioning off the quotas, on the other hand, transfers the rents to the government in the form of proceeds from the sale.[16] Licenses in perpetuity are similar to quotas, with the exception that they assign permanent ownership rights to license holders, however selected. Whether rents are received by the government or by license holders depends on whether the licenses are auctioned. Note that the various alternatives differ as to whether the rents go directly to favored producers or instead go initially to the government. If the government initially receives the rents, one must consider how this new source of public renvenue is to be spent.

The major distributional difference among these alternative forms of regulation may be illustrated by comparing the catch tax with one of the licensing schemes. In the comparison, we assume that licenses are distributed freely rather than auctioned off, and that the amount of fishing permitted for each licensee is based on that licensee's prior fishing activity.

The catch tax forces out some marginal producers without simultaneously compensating them for the loss in fishing rights. The government could use the tax proceeds to finance compensation, but compensation would require additional legislative action and is not an automatic feature of the tax. The licensing scheme, on the other hand, automatically compensates those marginal fishermen who would no longer find it worthwhile to fish. Each former producer receives a license allowing him to catch in perpetuity a certain percentage (based upon his own past catch) of each year's quota. Since licenses are marketable, marginal producers who choose to leave the industry could sell their licenses to others who wish to obtain a quota large enough to make fishing profitable. Hence the proceeds from selling licenses would, at least partially, compensate marginal fishermen forced out by the limitation on fishing.

The distributional effects of a nonauctioned quota, issued each year and based on the individual's past year's fishing activity, are similar to those of the nonauctioned license. Conversely, the distributional effects of quotas and licenses auctioned by the government are similar to the catch tax. From the perspective of compensation equity there are, therefore, three competing regulatory alternatives: (a) regulation through nonauctioned quotas or licenses which provide automatic compensation, (b) regulation through a catch tax or auctioned quotas and licenses, with compensation financed by government revenues resulting from the tax or sale of quotas and licenses; and (c) regulation through a catch tax or auctioned quotas and licenses without compensation.

If the expectations of fishermen concerning impending regulation are imperfect, the equity rationales identified above provide some basis for choosing either of the first two alternatives over the third. For example, most of the equity criteria support—or at least do not oppose—provision of compensation when a nonmonopoly property right is removed. In addition, the type of automatic compensation provided by the first two alternatives would limit sudden status changes, would help relatively disadvantaged fishermen, would provide transitional aid, and so forth.

In terms of the equity criteria, a major difference between the first and the second "regulation with compensation" alternatives is that the first provides compensation automatically—no explicit government action is required, and the amount of compensation is determined by the market—to anyone leaving the industry, while the second alternative does not. Hence the first alternative, while it has the advantage of providing automatic compensation, has the associated disadvantage of inflexibility in the way in which compensation is distributed. Conversely, the second alternative does not automatically compensate but allows the government to design an explicit compensation scheme with any desired income distribution characteristics.[17]

Given these differences, different equity criteria may favor one alternative or the other. For example, both the Rawls-Michaelman criteria and the vertical tax equity variant place considerable emphasis on the income distributional features of compensation schemes. These criteria will therefore tend to favor a well-administered tax or auction scheme, since this alternative allows the government the greatest flexibility in varying the amounts of compensation received. On the other hand, the "dynamics of status change" criterion and the benefit principle would favor the nonauctioning schemes, since granting nonauctioned quotas or marketable licenses automatically preserves the economic status of firms in the regulated industry. Similarly, such quotas and licenses automatically provide offsetting benefits to those likely to bear concentrated losses.

It must, of course, be recognized that this discussion has ignored numerous practical difficulties with each scheme. For example, can nonauctioned quotas or licenses in fact be accurately distributed on the basis of past fishing activity? If compensation is financed out of, say, tax revenues, will such compensation be distributed according to accepted equity criteria or according to practical political considerations? Detailed discussion is beyond the scope of this paper, but careful consideration of these practical difficulties might well alter the ranking of the regulatory alternatives. We have also assumed that firms in the industry would form only imperfect expectations concerning the imposition and form of regulation. If, however, fishermen were able to anticipate such regulation correctly and to change their behavior accordingly, the nonauctioning schemes would create a behavioral incentive that would be absent in the case of the catch tax or auctioning schemes. Specifically, if fishermen expected regulation to be accompanied by nonauctioned quotas or licenses, each firm would have an incentive to increase its fishing activity above normal levels in order to receive the largest possible quota or license.

It seems quite plausible that the firms most likely to succeed in inflating their catches would be the relatively more efficient firms in the industry. In addition, some firms would be encouraged to enter the industry simply to obtain an entitlement to a quota or license. If so, granting nonauctioned quotas or licenses would provide automatic compensation to precisely those firms least worthy of compensation according to the equity criteria presented above.

Thus, if firms were able to form correct anticipations, the case for automatic compensation would be substantially weakened. Regulatory schemes that allowed the government more discretion in determining eligibility for compensation, as well as the amount of it, would be more defensible. It is conceivable, however, that no compensation arrangement would be equitable, so that the ethical imperative to compensate may depend quite directly on the assumed abilities of affected groups to anticipate government policy and/or rules changes.

Summary

This study has discussed several rationales for compensating those harmed by public actions. One issue is whether public policy changes per se impose compensable economic losses. We have shown that whether policy shifts generate potentially compensable losses depends greatly on the extent to which such shifts can be accurately anticipated by those to be affected by them.

Determination that a given policy change is appropriately unexpected does not, however, guarantee that compensation is ethically justified. Specific equity rationales must be considered, and several have been identified and discussed. Applying these rationales to actual situations has suggested three broad conclusions. First, although the rationales need not conflict, they are sufficiently different that in some instances they may yield different evaluations of whether compensation is required. Second, the various rationales provide a clear basis for rejecting payment of compensation under some plausible circumstances. Third, if those to be affected by public policy changes are capable of forming correct anticipations about them, the equity rationale for compensation is weakened considerably—regardless of how "equity" is defined.

20. The Fundamentals of Cutback Management

Robert D. Behn

Abstract

During periods of retrenchment, public managers are responsible for making their organizations smaller and also for maintaining efficiency and effectiveness. The task is difficult but not impossible. Managers must understand how their basic responsibilities are complicated by a shift from growth to contraction. Then, they must apply some fundamental principles of leadership for cutback management to the particular problems facing their own agencies.

In the history of human organizations, retrenchment is a modern problem. Many organizations have contracted and disappeared over the centuries, but the idea of managing an organization so as to make it smaller but still effective is quite contemporary. In the past, the inevitability of growth—economic, population, and technological growth—made the task of cutback management unimportant. If an organization lost its market or its clientele, it simply shrank or disappeared while other, expanding organizations absorbed those functions for which some private or public demand still existed. Moreover, for most organizations, growth itself was a primary goal. In business, the imperative of market share motivated this quest. To obtain economies of scale and to move further along the learning curve, firms sought greater market share. Their reward for this growth was increased profit.

Governments have different motivations and rewards, yet they also pursue growth. Organizations whose funds come from budgets rather than markets have no criterion like profit—a simple ratio that specifies how effectively the organization is using its resources to achieve its objectives—to measure success. For several reasons, governments have a difficult time measuring the impact of their actions and thus cannot easily compare resources used with results produced. Consequently, size itself becomes a surrogate measure of success and a key to power. The bigger an agency and its budget, and the more rapid its growth, the more successful it is considered to be.

But growth, in government or business, is no longer inevitable. Business is learning to cope with stable or declining markets. And government can no longer assume that it will be permitted to allocate an increasing (or even a constant) share of the nation's resources. That does not mean that all organizational growth will cease. It does mean, however, that some organizations will have to stop growing and that others will have to contract. And the more successfully public and private managers handle the process of retrenchment, the more resources they will free up for growth—both by other organizations and by their own—to meet new demands, new opportunities, and new needs.

In government, the contraction of resources is forcing retrenchment at all levels. President Reagan's budget, public referenda, and continued inflation without economic growth are creating new fiscal realities for NASA and the Department of Agriculture, for New York City and Cleveland, for state highway departments and local school systems (which also face a drop in demand due to declining enrollments). In such an environment, public managers can create opportunities for growth, for expanding existing activities and starting new ones, only if they can cut back on some of their existing programs.

Thus, public managers may have several reasons to learn about cutback management: the current clamor for smaller government, the competing demands for limited resources in a barely expanding economy, a drop in the demand for particular public services, or simply the desire to expand some other components of the organization. Being able to take an agency and make it smaller, while still maintaining morale and productivity and fulfilling the agency's most basic purposes, will be an important, and perhaps essential, responsibility of public managers during the coming decade.

The Fact of Retrenchment

The Assumption of Real Retrenchment

The analysis of any managerial problem depends upon assumptions about its severity. Indeed, worrying about cutback management is worthwhile only if the required retrenchment is major. If the following three conditions are met, it is safe to assume that the problem is real and significant—that it cannot be solved with some simple economies or by a technological fix.

Retrenchment is necessary. Real resources are declining, for whatever reason (tax cuts, shifting priorities, a steady budget combined with inflation). Moreover, the agency cannot easily expand by creating new programs with new clients who will supply new resources. The agency will simply have to get along with less.

The problem is serious. It cannot be solved simply by cutting out the fat. The required retrenchment is greater than whatever organizational slack the manager has been able to accumulate. Representative Delbert L. Latta (R-OH) observed, "If I were President, I'd say cut back spending without cutting back services" (Leman, 1980). This second assumption precludes such a miracle, since the retrenchment necessitates some real cuts in services.

The manager's responsibility is to make the retrenchment work. Naturally, the temptation is to resist—to make cuts in such a way that the natural forces of politics will restore them. (This has been called "the Washington Monument strategy" after a success by the National Park Service: Forced to make budget cuts, NPS eliminated elevator service at the Washington Monument and suggested to out-of-town tourists that their representatives just down the Mall were responsible for this unfortunate cutback in service. Soon the funds and the elevator service were restored.) But the other two assumptions preclude this possibility; there will be fewer resources and the manager will simply have to make the agency function as well as possible under this constraint.

Still, the public manager does not have to manage. Confronted by contradictory demands—for contractions and cuts, but also for services and performance—he or she can simply resign. Or, without officially resigning, the manager can abdicate responsibility, surrendering control to superiors, to the legislature, to the public employee unions, to the banks, or to the most powerful interest groups. Some managers, however, will accept the challenge. Recognizing the reality of retrenchment, they will seek to lead their organizations through the process and to create a smaller, more efficient (and perhaps more effective) organization. To such managers—Andrew Glassberg (1978:328) calls them "revitalizing entrepreneurs"—this chapter is addressed.

The Basic Responsibilities of Cutback Management

The necessity of retrenchment presents the leaders of an organization with a number of tasks. Their ability to handle these basic responsibilities of cutback management will determine how productive the organization is when it emerges from the retrenchment process.

Decide what to cut. This is, of course, the fundamental dilemma of retrenchment: Which functions should be abandoned and which continued? Which organizational subunits should be eliminated and which maintained? Which employees should be laid off and which retained? How intelligent the manager is in choosing—and how effective he or she is in obtaining the necessary support for the decisions—will determine how well the organization copes with retrenchment.

In choosing what to cut, the basic issue—for it applies to all organizations—is whether to favor equity or efficiency. Equity considerations suggest a share-the-burden strategy. Across-the-board cuts are attractive, for not only can they be defended as equitable but they also avoid the necessity of making real choices about priorities. If the required cuts are large, however, across-the-board retrenchment does not make sense. It is silly to require every unit, regardless of the importance of its mission or the effectiveness of its work, to absorb, for example, a 30 percent cut. Such a decision could well destroy the effectiveness of all the subunits. Since some units may require a critical mass of personnel and equipment to function effectively, a 30 percent cut may result in more than a 30 percent loss of effectiveness. Moreover, across-the-board cuts punish the most efficient units, for they have little of the fat that the sloppily managed units can use to absorb the cuts.

Further, what principle of ethics states that organizational subunits deserve equal protection? Ethical considerations should concern people, not organizations; and in human terms, retrenchment is inherently unfair. Some people will lose their jobs; others will not. To the people who are laid off, it hardly matters whether the layoffs come proportionately from every subunit of the organization or from just a few. True equity would require that everyone make an equal sacrifice: instead of a 30 percent cut in the workforce, everyone would take a 30 percent cut in pay. (This approach has been employed in some industries, with union acceptance and support.)

An effective manager of an organization undergoing retrenchment must consciously decide whether to target the cuts. Yet this decision will not be easy. The targets will naturally complain, and with all the political force they can mobilize. Further, a variety of legal constraints—seniority, veteran's preferences, bumping rights, entitlements, mandated programs—will limit a manager's ability to focus the cuts. But if the organization must undergo a 30 percent cut in resources, the manager will have to decide what 70 percent is the most essential and the most productive, and concentrate the cuts so as to maximize the organization's post-retrenchment effectiveness.

Maintain morale. Since growth has been the traditional measure of performance, retrenchment can have a devastating impact upon morale. Employees, constituents, legislators, and journalists see the organization becoming smaller and conclude that it is becoming less important and less successful as well. Such an inference can easily destroy morale and affect the motivation of employees to work, of legislators to appropriate funds, of constituents to provide support, and of journalists to provide attention. The result can be what Richard Cyret (1978:345) calls the "vicious circle of disintegration": a first set of cutbacks leads to declining morale, which leads to poorer performance, which leads to a second round of cutbacks, which leads to a further decline in morale, and so on. To keep the agency productive, the manager will have to find some way to turn retrenchment into a positive force that actually boosts morale.

Attract and keep quality people. As morale begins to decline, the best people, who are by definition the most mobile, will begin to leave. This trend can be further aggravated by across-the-board cuts, which fail to distinguish between productive and unproductive people and subunits. Indeed, the consequence (if not the intent) of across-the-board cuts may well be to lay off the organization's best workers. Cutback management requires the ability to recognize good performance and reward it. Otherwise, the most productive workers will simply leave—Charles Levine (1979:180) calls this the "Free Exiter" problem—contributing still more torque to Cyret's vicious circle of disintegration.

Develop the support of key constituencies (and legislators). Any agency needs outside support. Yet how can it continue to attract such support when it has less to offer? Which constituencies should the agency's managers continue to court? Which should it risk alienating, perhaps turning into enemies? These decisions are obviously related to the choices about where to make the required cuts. The functions and units that the managers wish to retain, emphasize, and strengthen will need constituent and legislative support. Managers must concentrate remaining resources so that these target constituencies will have something worth supporting.

Create opportunities for innovation. Even in retrenchment, an organization can improve if it increases productivity. This requires flexibility, the ability to experiment with innovations. When cutbacks are required, however, such experiments seem like a luxury; how can we think of funding new activities which will (implicitly) necessitate cutting back further on existing units and laying off even more personnel? Still, the organization faced with retrenchment cannot survive unless it learns to do new things, or to do old things better. For a growing organization, innovation is desirable and occurs automatically as the agency experiments to find the best use of each increment of resources. For a contracting organization, innovation is essential; yet it will not occur unless the manager makes a conscious effort to create the opportunities (and find the resources) for it.

Avoid mistakes. While stimulating innovation, however, the manager must be careful to avoid any disastrous mistakes. In the middle of retrenchment, the organization is vulnerable enough. One serious error can twist the circle of disintegration into a cyclone of destruction.

The desire to avoid mistakes will come naturally—too naturally, perhaps. Even managers of stable or growing agencies are conservative in their style, seeking (at all costs, it often appears) to avoid mistakes that could create reasons for budget cuts. When cuts are already occurring, the natural tendency is to be even more conservative. Thus, public managers faced with retrenchment must find a balance between encouraging innovation and avoiding mistakes. They must not make the one error that can end the organization's chances for recovery and success. At the same time, however, they need to experiment with innovations that might increase productivity, improve morale, and recapture stability.

The (Marginal) Economies of Retrenchment

These six responsibilities are not unique to cutback management. Deciding what to cut is really just the traditional chore of allocating resources; in retrenchment, however, this means deciding who must absorb the decrements rather than who will be awarded the increases. And all managers must maintain morale, attract and keep quality people, develop the support of key constituencies (and legislators), create opportunities for innovation, and avoid mistakes. Whether resources are growing or shrinking, the challenge of management is to organize the productive activities of individuals into a coherent enterprise so that they can accomplish more working together than they could separately. Consequently, whether the organization is growing or contracting, the basic responsibilities of the manager remain the same.

In retrenchment, however, these responsibilities are much more difficult to carry out. For example, the task of allocating growing resources is relatively simple. The manager need only decide who will get how much of this year's increase. He or she will, of course, make some mistakes in allocating resources, but these can be easily rectified. For example, the manager may have overestimated the ability of subunit A to make productive use of additional resources and underestimated the ability of subunit B to do so. As a result, the manager allocates to A some resources that would have better been given to B, and the entire organization is less productive than it could be. Still, both B and A are alive and functioning, and the mistake can easily be corrected with the next round of increases by allocating more of the increase to B and less to A. Thus, the manager's mistake is not disastrous in the short run (both A and B continue to function quite well) and can be corrected in the long run (by allocating the next round of increases differently).

In retrenchment, however, the managerial responsibility of allocating resources is qualitatively different. Now the manager must decide which units will absorb the greatest portion of the losses, and the consequences of any error can be significant, indeed disastrous. For example, suppose that more cuts should be made in A than in B, but the manager decides wrong and cuts more from B than from A. In the short run, A will continue to function more or less as it has, but B may be significantly wounded. Moreover, the manager may not be able to correct the problem in the next round of cuts. Subunit B may already have been permanently damaged; even if extra cuts are made in other subunits to give B a real increase, the loss of key personnel may make recovery an extremely expensive process. In retrenchment, a mistake in allocating resources can be much more disastrous than in growth.

Indeed, growing resources facilitate all of the basic managerial chores. More money can help resolve the inevitable conflicts between subunits over resources or policy. Morale is much easier to maintain when funds exist to reward productive subunits and individuals; even if there are limitations on salary increases, quality personnel can be recruited and retained by using the growing resources to provide perquisites, staff, equipment, and promotions. And just as such resources can win support inside the organization, they can also be used to develop support from key constituencies, for there will be programs and benefits to offer them.

Moreover, managers blessed with growing resources will find it easier to avoid mistakes. Not only will their mistakes be less serious and more easily corrected, managers of growing organizations can afford the analytical capability to make better decisions. In retrenchment, however, the analytical staffs are often the first to be cut. In an effort to maintain the line units—the productive components of the organization—as close to full strength as possible, the organization sacrifices some of its ability to avoid mistakes. The decrease in resources makes all of the tasks of management more difficult.

The Two Stages of Retrenchment

Who has the motivation to declare that the reality of retrenchment has arrived and to initiate the cutbacks? Unfortunately, very few public officials do. Indeed, they have a strong incentive to avoid the immediate abuse they will receive for even suggesting that retrenchment is coming. Who will cheer the announcement of impending cutbacks? Very few. Who will boo? All of us. Most public managers have very short time horizons (compared, at least, with managers in the private sector) and will see little benefit in making unnecessary enemies. After all, the discrepancy between revenues and expenditures can always be disguised for a little longer with "creative financing" or deferred maintenance.

The process of retrenchment can be divided into two stages: before and after the organization's leaders publicly recognize that cutbacks are necessary. Both before and after this milestone, the organization is coping with the mismatch between revenues and expenditures. In the first stage, however, the tactic is to borrow against the future, to make the future pay for the deficits of the present. Yet unless some future miracle increases revenues significantly, this approach only exacerbates the problem. The longer the organization's managers delay making cutbacks, the worse the problem becomes—the greater the operating debt that is accumulated (no matter how "creative" the financing) and the longer the maintenance will be deferred. The sooner the reality of retrenchment is recognized, the sooner the organization moves to the second stage of retrenchment and the easier it will be to solve the problem.

The rub is that other people—employees, constituents, legislators, even journalists—often will not believe the reality. They, too, have little incentive to believe it or to do anything about it. They have experienced the growth of the past and want it to continue. Any momentary imbalance between revenues and expenditures, they hope, will surely correct itself; some miracle will happen to make everything better again. Levine (1979:181) calls this the "Tooth Fairy Syndrome." Eventually, however, reality will arrive, either because the bridges fall down or because the banks refuse to lend any more money. If retrenchment is required, it will come. The only question is who will announce its approach: the organization's leaders, who recognize the reality and are willing to take the risk of doing something about it, or some outsiders, who—in return for their continued, essential cooperation—insist that something be done. For example, in the cases of Cleveland, New York City, and Antioch College these outsiders were the banks, who as a condition for their continued support demanded that revenues and expenditures be brought into balance.

It is, unfortunately, in most people's collective interest but in few people's individual interest that the second stage come quickly. The debilitating impact of remaining in the first retrenchment stage for too long is dramatically illustrated by the plight of Cleveland. During the eight years under mayors Ralph Perk and Dennis Kucinich (November 1971 to November 1979), the city's budget was never in balance. In Ohio, no city can increase taxes without a voter referendum, and in 1970 and 1971 Cleveland Mayor Carl Stokes failed in three attempts to increase the city's income tax. Both Perk and Kucinich campaigned on promises not to increase taxes. Both followed the example of New York City and used debt to cover operating expenses. Only in December 1978, after the city defaulted on $15 million in short-term notes, did Mayor Kucinich agree that more taxes were needed; the city's citizens then voted to increase the income tax (Humphrey, Peterson, and Wilson, 1979).

The failure to advance quickly from the first to the second stage of retrenchment has been particularly destructive to Cleveland's fiscal and physical condition. A study by the Urban Institute examined the city's capital plant (its street, sewer, bridge, water and transit systems) and found that "Cleveland now faces a backlog of some $700 million in basic improvements to its infrastructure systems. . . . Many facilities have outlived their expected service lives or have become functionally obsolete" (Humphrey, Peterson, and Wilson, 1979:75). Specifically, the report concluded:

> The city-owned water system, which serves most of the metropolitan area, needs $250 to $500 million in replacements and renovation. One treatment plant is in hazardous condition, and clogged and corroded pipes have reduced the system's capacity to deliver water at acceptable pressures. The condition of 30 percent of the city-owned bridges has been rated as unsatisfactory or intolerable, and in need of more than $150 million in major repairs. The city's sewer collection system is plagued with frequent overflows and basement floodings; an estimated $340 million would be needed to alleviate floodings alone. (Humphrey, Peterson, and Wilson 1979:xv)

Cleveland's capital plant has clearly been a primary victim of its financial plight; deferred maintenance and the use of debt for operating expenses were the chief means of handling declining resources during the 1970s. The Urban Institute team found that "maintenance spending has borne more than a proportionate share of Cleveland's budget retrenchment, primarily because of its lesser urgency or less visibility" (Humphrey, Peterson, and Wilson, 1979:42–43). Cleveland delayed, for nearly a decade, moving from the first stage of retrenchment to the second, and that delay has proved extremely costly to the city and its residents.

The Role of Leadership

Leadership Fundamentals

In this type of environment, how can public managers carry out their basic responsibilities? How can they lead their organizations into the second stage of retrenchment and take them through the necessary cutbacks so as to rejuvenate and not demolish them? Five fundamentals of retrenchment leadership are important.

Explain the reality. Unless the manager is willing to let the banks (or whoever is covering the deficit) decide when the organization should enter the second stage of retrenchment, he or she must educate the organization to this reality. This educational process takes time and ideally should be initiated long before the first cuts are even suggested. Before people can begin the painful process of actually making cuts, they need time to adjust their thinking from growth to contraction. In retrenchment the chief difficulty, both emotional and intellectual, lies not in deciding what must be done to close the gap, but in accepting the fact that a problem exists—that there exists a gap that must be closed.

In addition to recognizing the imbalance between resources and expenditures, people must also realize that there are significant costs to not cutting back. The costs of cutting back will be very clear; they are direct, out-of-pocket costs imposed on particular individuals and groups. In contrast, the costs of not cutting back will be much more obscure; they are indirect, opportunity costs imposed on larger, less well-identified, and less well-organized groups. As leader and thus as educator, the manager needs to explain who will bear what costs if the organization does not cut back.

Take a long-term view. Retrenchment cannot be managed on an ad hoc basis. The leaders of an organization must have a long-term perspective on the problem. They must understand where they are going and how they can get there. And they must recognize the subtle steps that need to be taken today to ease the more difficult cutback decisions that must be made tomorrow. For example, the Department of Defense has had for nearly 20 years an ongoing and very successful program of closing military bases across the country. And when the Pentagon announces that it is closing a base, the base is usually closed. Part of the reason for such success lies in the characteristics of the department—its budgeting process and the nature of its military mission—and part in the inability or unwillingness of Congress to overturn its decisions. But part of the secret also lies in the department's long-term approach to its program of cutback management. The Department of Defense is consciously shrinking its base structure. Consequently, it can plan ahead. If it believes that it may want to phase out a base in five years, it begins now by not putting any new facilities on the base, by not modernizing existing equipment, by letting the base become slightly obsolete. Then, when the time comes for some base to be closed, any unbiased individual can see that this base is the best choice for closing, and that the other alternatives are simply in much better shape. The department's willingness to take a long-term approach in this program—to act ahead as well as think ahead—is one of the keys to its success (Behn and Lambert, 1979).

For two important reasons, cutback management requires a long-term view. First, retrenchment can produce few short-term gains. Unless layoffs are massive, the costs of any cutbacks may well exceed the gains during the first year. Closed facilities must be put in mothballs. Individuals who are fired or "retired" must be given severance payments. Consolidating units involves transitional costs. Most of the sensible tactics for reducing the scale of an organization produce benefits only in the long run. One observer of cutback management in school systems reported, "The gurus of decline say it takes about 10 years for a district to realize any substantial saving from retirement after enrollment decline" (Divoky, 1979:87).

The second reason for taking a long-term perspective is that decisions based on short-term considerations may only exacerbate the problem. Ad hoc decisionmaking does little to fulfill any of the six basic responsibilities of cutback management. Indeed, the primary impact may be to worsen morale. Hostility and suspicion will be particularly high in an organization undergoing retrenchment. A promise that "this is the last set of layoffs" will be viewed skeptically. A second such promise (after a first round of layoffs) will be taken as a deliberate lie. Yet if managers do not know where their organizations are going, they will be sorely tempted to make such promises in an attempt to mitigate the consequences of any cutback.

Ad hoc decisionmaking, which is responsive to the crises and pressures of the moment rather than to an overall plan, is the easiest way to enter Cyert's vicious circle and to make it spin faster. The organization's leaders need to know where the cutbacks can stop, where the retrenchment can level off, and how they can get the organization to stop there. Only then can they take actions and make commitments that will be realistic, not just expedient. Everyone in the organization will be suspicious of deals that involve present sacrifices for future benefits; everyone will believe that the deal will be forgotten. The managers need to convince employees, clients, supporters, and observers that they know where they are going and that they can and will honor their commitments to get there.

Develop a new "corporate strategy." To provide the basis for such long-term thinking, the organization needs a new plan of its basic purposes, programs, and resources. Such a comprehensive plan makes clear what the new equilibrium of the organization will be (i.e., at what point the organization will be able to establish a new balance between resources and programs) and how it will get there. Such a plan provides a basis for sustaining employee morale by empha-sizing the positive aspects of the organization's future—the things it *will* be doing. It clarifies the types of innovations the organization should most enthu-siastically promote, and the types of people it needs to retain and recruit. Finally, it provides the criteria for deciding what should be cut and what should not.

In the business world, such a comprehensive plan is called a "corporate strategy" (Andrews, 1971). Unfortunately, governments rarely develop explicitly corporate, organizational, or agency strategies. As a result, government agencies tend to expand in a disorganized, incoherent manner, responding to the pres-sures of the moment. Without an explicit overall statement of purposes, pro-grams, and resources, agencies become a menagerie of programs which have little in common other than the fact that they are funded with taxpayer dollars.

In a period of growth, the lack of an organizational strategy is merely costly. Without a clear statement of purpose, there can exist no criteria for allocating resources between competing interests. Resources cannot be concentrated on the agency's most fundamental purposes, for these have not been defined. As long as the agency is expanding, however, each year's growth in resources can be allocated so as to minimize conflicts between competing interests. Everyone can have a little more, and so no one feels neglected.

In retrenchment, however, the absence of an explicit corporate strategy upon which to base key decisions is disastrous. For without a clear purpose, the debate over where to make cuts quickly deteriorates into a childish squabble with everyone making demands on the basis of personal selfishness. (Little wonder that across-the-board cuts are so attractive; without any clear purpose, there is no justification for any other mode of decision, and the equity argument can dampen the whines.) A healthy, productive organization must have a purpose; otherwise, how can it be said to be productive? Further, to lead an organization through a retrenchment process and have it emerge healthy and productive, a manager must be able to articulate a clear, specific mission for the organization. The manager who tries to muddle through without such an ex-plicit corporate strategy cannot lead but can only react (Behn, 1980).

Develop measures of performance. In deciding which functions to empha-size in the corporate plan and which to cut during retrenchment, the perfor-mance of different subunits is important. Yet how does the manager know which units are performing well? How can he or she know which units are sustaining productivity while cutting back and which units are deteriorating rapidly? How can the manager recognize and reward those who are performing well? To carry out all these basic functions, the manager needs to be able to measure performance.

During retrenchment, people and subunits will have obvious and credible explanations for why performance is deteriorating. The manager needs to know what is really happening and where the major weaknesses lie, and to be able to compare various subunits to each other and to reasonable standards. More-over, he or she needs to determine who is performing well despite the cutbacks; morale will be bad enough anyway during retrenchment, and the manager needs to be able to recognize and reward those who are still performing well.

Create incentives for cooperation.   Few people believe that retrenchment is in their self-interest. Indeed, many members of the organization will have both the incentive and the ability to resist the cutbacks, if not to sabotage the process and the manager too. People can hide resources, complain to higher authorities about cutback priorities, create rumors, and purposefully underperform to prove the evils of the cutback process. In retrenchment, the members of the organization see only the prospect for punishment; they perceive no chance for reward and thus have little reason to cooperate. Yet without cooperation the manager cannot manage.

As Robert P. Biller (1980) has emphasized, managers need to create incentives for cooperation and participation in the retrenchment process. This will not, of course, be easy. People see clearly why they should cooperate in increasing their budget; it is not at all obvious, however, what they have to gain by decreasing it. A clear corporate strategy can provide one reason, for this plan will state which units will remain stable (and perhaps even expand) as well as which units will be cut or disappear. Those whose relative or absolute impor-tance will be enhanced by the retrenchment will have a reason to cooperate.

Moreover, the budget process can be redesigned to create incentives for managers of subunits to make their own cuts. Permitting managers to carry forward some fixed fraction of unused funds from one fiscal year to the next would encourage savings. Under present rules, all unspent funds revert to the treasury at the end of the fiscal year. Official commandments not to spend unused funds at the end of the fiscal year have little impact when compared with the incentives which the rules create for managers: not to spend the money is to lose it. Yet if managers were rewarded rather than punished for not spending money, they might not engage in traditional end-of-the-year spending sprees. If they could keep some unspent money to be used as they saw fit during the coming year, the incentive to spend could be turned into an incentive to save.

Governments have traditionally relied upon commands rather than incentives to achieve their purposes. The results are often unsatisfactory and sometimes counter-productive. When the natural incentives are clear and work against cooperation, as is the case in retrenchment, managers need to think carefully and creatively about how they can establish positive incentives for cooperation. For example, Irene Rubin (1980) has discussed how the budgetary process in cities could be redesigned to curtail the ability of the city council and others to hide operating deficits. Hidden deficits prevent the city from moving into the second stage of retrenchment; consequently, creating incentives to expose defi-cits can help the city cope with its unfortunate fiscal realities in a realistic manner.

At the University of Southern California, reports Biller (1980:607), a system of across-the-board cuts has been used to create extra funds for which departments can compete. Every department might be required to take, for example, a 5 percent cut, with some of these funds put into a special pool. Departments submit proposals for new undertakings to a committee that then awards funds from the pool. The outcome is a system of targeted, not across-the-board, cuts, but the process itself creates the incentive for departments to cooperate, since they all have a chance to win some of the awards from the special pool.

Be compassionate. Retrenchment is not a happy time. People are losing their jobs, their benefits, their expectations. Their world is changing suddenly and drastically, and they have trouble coping with the uncertainty. Managers who want to sustain the morale of staff, to recruit and keep talented people, and to maintain the support of key constituencies will have to demonstrate that they understand the hardships retrenchment imposes on people. As one observer of cutback management in school systems has concluded, "A cold-blooded approach won't work. The [school] board and administration must make it clear that this is an extremely unpleasant decision. The number one concern must be people" (Mazzarella & Barber, 1978:32). Managers who seek the cooperation of individuals, although they have been deprived of the resources usually available to promote such cooperation, must demonstrate that they recognize the human problems caused by retrenchment and that they truly sympathize with the plight of the members of their organizations.

The Necessity of Leadership

Public agencies with declining resources require conscious and effective management. An organization cannot simply drift through retrenchment. Centralized decisionmaking and centralized leaderhip are essential. A public manager who is responsible for an organization when it is forced to cut back faces a particularly demanding assignment. Nevertheless, such a task is not impossible. But unless a manager is able to think ahead and to learn from similar managerial endeavors (and records now exist of a variety of such experiences), he or she may overlook some of the fundamentals of cutback management and thus lose the opportunity to convert a declining organization into a smaller but more stable and effective one.

Postscript

21. The Creation of a Profession

Joel L. Fleishman

Abstract

The former president of the Association for Public Policy and Management (APPAM), reviews the origins of the discipline, of the profession, and of the research behind the current volume.

There is insufficient space to give credit to the intellectual progenitors of policy analysis from Aristotle to Jeremy Bentham, to Harold Lasswell, to Herbert Simon, and to Robert McNamara. For an organization launched by the institutional teachers and practitioners of policy analysis and management, however, it would be an inexcusable omission to fail to acknowledge our debt, if not our very being, to those boldly imaginative scholar-teachers at Harvard, Michigan, and Berkeley who created the new professional academic field. Without the intellectual power, vision, and boldness of Frederick Mosteller, Richard Neustadt, Don Price, Howard Raiffa, and Tom Schelling, as well as their junior colleagues Graham Allison and Richard Zeckhauser at Harvard, Pat Crecine at Michigan, and Aaron Wildavsky at Berkeley, it is extremely unlikely that APPAM would be doing what it is doing today, or that we would be meeting as a group anywhere. We are all, therefore, personally in their debt; without those great and imaginative architects, the public policy analysis and management programs probably would never have been born.

This bold new conception of education for public policy and decisionmaking survived and flourished because of the good judgment and generosity of foundation officials who nurtured it and facilitated its spread throughout the country. Even compelling ideas will languish and die without sufficient nourishment. To McGeorge Bundy, Harold Howe, Frederick Bohen, Peter de Janosi, Arthur Cyr, Peter Bell, and later Richard Sharpe at the Ford Foundation, the new curriculum became a personal commitment. They saw immediately that it would yield better trained officials for the public sector than any other form of education then available, and they provided the necessary funds to most of the universities with public policy analysis or management programs.

Simultaneously, the Alfred P. Sloan Foundation, under the leadership of Arthur Singer and Steven White, with support from Nils Wessel, Robert Kreidler, and James Koerner, took a very special interest not only in strengthening the existing graduate programs and in creating bridges between public policy and engineering through technology and public policy programs, but also in establishing undergraduate public policy programs. While I cannot speak for other universities, I know that Duke's undergraduate public policy studies major could never have been created without the initial and continuing support of the Alfred P. Sloan Foundation. Nor could our graduate program have been launched without the support of the Ford Foundation. Today, both programs are supported by Duke University funds. But neither the Sloan nor the Ford Foundation limited its support to the academic programs. Both knew well that a new field of learning needs infrastructure as well as educational institutions. Accordingly, during the past decade, both foundations have generously supported the institution-building activities in which we have engaged.

Furthermore, the Ford Foundation and the Sloan Foundation provided support for the Duke/Rand Public Policy Curricular Materials Development Program (PPCMDP), which was created to generate teaching cases and other curricular materials for the new public policy analysis and management program. The PPCMDP Advisory Committee, convened at the insistence of the Ford Foundation, represented the first continuously meeting group of public policy teacher-administrators and practitioners. Without the insight and wisdom of Graham Allison, Charles Christenson, Pat Crecine, Peter Goldmark, Frederick Hayes, Andrew Marshall, William Morrill, Alice Rivlin, and John Steinbruner, PPCMDP could never have thrived.

Moreover, the Ford and Sloan program officers were not content to let us stop with the production of curricular materials. They insisted that we take the initiative in training public policy faculty members to use them and to develop their own new materials. Accordingly, with support principally from the Sloan Foundation, the Hilton Head summer workshop of 1978 brought together for the first time about 40 members of the teaching faculty of public policy analysis and management programs.

There, Arnold Meltsner argued that a new organization was indeed needed, and Richard Zeckhauser persuaded us that its central focus should be the exchange of ideas and findings about research. Hence both APPAM and the annual Research Conference can be credited in part to the Alfred P. Sloan Foundation.

In 1977, the strong wish of Peter Bell and Richard Sharpe at Ford and of Arthur Singer at Sloan that we actively disseminate teaching materials led to the creation of the Clearing House for Public Policy Education, under Robert Weinberg's leadership and with Steven Hitchner's enthusiastic cooperation. Both foundations supported the Clearing House, and the Sloan Foundation financed its transformation into the Council on Public Policy and Management, cosponsored jointly by the Intercollegiate Case Clearing House. Under James McKenney's leadership, again with support from the Sloan Foundation, the council has worked to legitimate the production of the teaching materials as a creditable activity of faculty members. To this end, and to create a substantial peer review mechanism to increase the quality of teaching materials, the council has appointed an editorial board, along with panels for each curricular area of public policy and management programs.

The first foundation grant to APPAM came from the Sloan Foundation, for the vital purpose of helping public policy and management programs identify and provide summer enrichment and fellowships to prospective minority graduate students in our programs. Both the Ford and Sloan foundations facilitated our development in countless other ways, too—Ford by bringing the directors and deans together informally at various times over the decade, Sloan by sponsoring the Amelia Island Conference in 1977.

As a sometime student of philanthropic behavior, I cannot imagine a more convincing example of the effectiveness of foundation seed money in creating a new field, new educational programs, and new life in the older social sciences. Whether the generosity of these foundations ultimately works to the benefit of society is up to us and our colleagues. The progenitors have done their part, and the foundations have done theirs. It is now our turn, and I am confident we shall live up to the challenge to our profession.

Notes and References

1. The Role of Television in American Politics

1. An American University survey of media coverage in the 1980 primaries concluded, "Too often, they cover the story as if it were a fire, a ball game, or just another speech at the National Press Club. With few exceptions, seldom is more than a silhouette of a candidate's philosophy provided" (Groff et al., 1980:2). A study of CBS Evening News coverage of the 1980 campaigns from January 1 through June 4 concluded, "CBS coverage has been *extensive, nonpartisan, objective,* and . . . *superficial. . . .* above all, the Evening News has shown an overriding interest in who's winning" (Robinson, Conover, & Sheehan, 1980:41, 45).

2. The networks' 1980 election-night coverage—particularly the projection of Ronald Reagan as the victor well before the polls had closed in the West—raises new questions about the capacity of television to distort the political system. For a general discussion of this issue, see, for example, Skelton (1980) and Wolfinger (1980).

References

Alexander, Herbert. 1976. *Financing Politics: Money, Elections, and Political Reform.* Washington, D.C.: Congressional Quarterly Press.

Atkins, Charles, and Gary Heald. 1976. "Effect of Political Advertising." *Public Opinion Quarterly* 40 (Summer): 216–228.

Bonafede, Dom. 1980a. "The Press Makes News in Covering the 1980 Primary Election Campaigns." *National Journal* 12 (July 12): 1132–1135.

———. 1980b. "The New Political Power of the Press." *Washington Monthly* 2 (September): 24–27.

———. 1980c. "Campaigning by TV—It's Expensive, But Does It Make Any Difference?" *National Journal* 12 (October 11): 1702–1706.

———. 1981. "A $130 Million Spending Tab Is Proof—Presidential Politics is Big Business." *National Journal* 13 (January 10): 50–52.

Brandon, Henry. 1980. "The Role of Television and Political Realities." *Washington Star* (September 25): A15.

Common Cause. 1979. *How Money Talks in Congress: A Common Cause Study of the Impact of Money on Congressional Decision-Making.*

Gans, Curtis B. 1979. "How to Take the Big Money Out of Politics." *Washington Monthly* 11 (April): 40–42.

Graber, Doris A. 1980. *Mass Media and American Politics.* Washington, D.C.: Congressional Quarterly Press.

Groff, Donald; Francine R. Schwadel; Lynda DeWitt; William B. Fulton; Harriet C. Johnson; Linda McCormick; Chad Randolph; and Cynthia L. Skrzycki. 1980. *The Press and the 1980 Presidential Campaign: In the Shadows of an Economic Crisis.* Washington, D.C.: The National Center for Business and Economic Communication, The American University.

Halberstam, David. 1981. "How Television Failed the American Voter." *Parade Magazine* (January 11): 4, 7–8.

Institute of Politics. 1978. *Increasing Access to Television for Political Candidates: A Report with Recommendations Released by the Campaign Study Group, Institute of Politics.* Cambridge, Mass.: Institute of Politics, Harvard University.

Kaiser, Robert G. 1980. "TV on the Trail: A Three-Course Menu for Fluff." *Washington Post* (October 10): A1, A3.

Leff, Laurel. 1980. "Candidates' Campaign Budgets are Squeezed By Inflation and '74 Law's Limits on Donations." *Wall Street Journal* (September 30): 56.

MacNeil, Robert. 1980. "The Edge of Apathy." *The Dial* 1 (September): 33, 36–37.

Patterson, Thomas E. 1980a. *The Mass Media Election: How Americans Choose Their President.* New York: Praeger.

———. 1980b. "The Mass Media Election: Findings from a Panel Survey and Election News Analysis of the 1976 Campaign." Paper presented at 1980 American Political Science Association Annual Meeting, Washington, D.C. (August).

Phillips, Kevin. 1975. *Mediacracy: American Parties and Politics in the Communications Age.* Garden City, N.Y.: Doubleday.

Reeves, Richard. 1980. "Reason to Cry Over This Year's Political Carnival." *Washington Star* (August 18): A9.

Robinson, Michael J. 1978. "TV's Newest Program: The 'Presidential Nominations Game.'" *Public Opinion* 1 (May/June): 41–46.

————, Nancy Conover, and Margaret Sheehan. 1980. "The Media at Mid-Year: A Bad Year for McLuhanites?" *Public Opinion* 3 (June/July): 41–45.

———— & Margaret Sheehan. 1980. "How the Networks Learned to Love the Issues: The Eleventh Hour Conversion of CBS." *Washington Journalism Review* 2 no. 9 (December): 15–17.

Roper, Burns W. 1979. *Public Perception of Television and Other Mass Media: A Twenty Year Review 1959–1978.* Report by the Roper Organization (April).

Skelton, George. 1980. "Carter's Early Concession Had Little Effect on Results." *Los Angeles Times* (November 23): 1, 8–9.

Swerdlow, Joel. 1981. "A Question of Impact." *Wilson Quarterly* 5 (Winter): 86–98.

Thayer, George. 1973. *Who Shakes the Money Tree?* New York: Touchstone Books.

U.S., Congress, House, Committee on Interstate and Foreign Commerce. 1971. *Political Broadcasting 1971.* 92nd Cong., 1st sess., 8, 10, 11, 15, and 16 June.

————. 1980. *Repeal of "Equal Time" Requirements.* 96th Cong., 2nd sess., 7 February.

U.S., Congress, Senate, Committee on Commerce. 1971. *Federal Election Campaign Act of 1971.* 92nd Cong., 1st sess., 2, 3, 4, 5, 31 March and 1 April.

U.S., Federal Communications Commission. 1980. *The Law of Political Broadcasting and Cablecasting: A Political Primer.*

U.S., General Accounting Office. 1979. *Selected FCC Regulation Policies: Their Purpose and Consequences for Commercial Radio and TV.*

Washington Journalism Review 2. 1980. "Candidates and Their Gurus Criticize Coverage." (September): 28–31.

The Washington Post. 1980. "Raising The Limits." (April 1): A16.

Wertheimer, Fred. 1980. "The PAC Phenomenon In American Politics." *Arizona Law Review* 22:603–626.

White, George H. 1978. *A Study of Access to Television for Political Candidates.* Cambridge, Mass.: Institute of Politics, Harvard University.

Wolfinger, Raymond E. 1980. "Network Election Day Predictions and Western Voters." Unpublished paper, University of California, Berkeley (December).

2. The Presidential Nominating System: Problems and Prescriptions

1. The morning-after banner headline in the *Baltimore Sun*, for example, was "Anderson runs strong in two states." Evidently, Sen. Edward Kennedy's spokesmen were a bit too bold in claiming that apparent defeats really were victories. "If you should *lose* an election, how would we know?" one exasperated reporter finally asked Kennedy.

2. For more detail, see Lanouette (1979).

3. The summary history that follows is drawn primarily from Ranney (1974a), Crotty (1977), Young (1966), Davis (1967), and Schlesinger (1972).

4. Interview with the author, March 7, 1980.

5. Interview with the author, March 6, 1980.

6. Interview with the author, March 5, 1980.

7. If this turns out to be so, it reverses a recent trend toward drawing presidential nominees from the Senate. Being in Washington—an advantage under the prereform rules—means being tied to Washington, a disadvantage nowadays, according to Senator Howard Baker: "Those of us who are already in government and public life [don't] have the time and the resources to run soon enough and early enough to succeed."

8. Among the definitional characteristics of "polyarchal democracy," as Robert Dahl (1956:67) defines it, are these: (*a*) "In tabulating . . . votes, the weight assigned to the choice of each individual is identical." (*b*) "The alternative with the greatest number of votes is declared the winner." As is argued

above, the present nominating system fails to meet the first standard and, on occasion, could fail to meet the second as well.

9. In this case the policy is that some public officials be chosen democratically; the selection system is the method of implementation.

10. Barber's typology is flawed but still useful; see Nelson (1980). For a not dissimilar psychological assessment of recent presidents, see Hargrove (1974:chap. 2).

11. Strangely, in defending the superior judgement of party leaders, "pro-pros" commentators most often put forward the example of fondly remembered losers. Terry Sanford (1980:31) writes: "Adlai Stevenson and Charles Evans Hughes would never have been candidates had they been required to gear up for a present-day campaign survival exercise"; Ranney (1978b:246) notes that "where the prereform Democratic party was able to turn back a Kefauver for a Stevenson and a McCarthy for a Humphrey, the postreform party was easily captured by outsiders."

12. Ranney (1978b:220-221). The percentage of Democratic senators, representatives, and governors present at the national conventions also was declining before 1969 (*ibid.*: 237).

13. This study considers only those proposals for change that have been introduced in Congress, in part in the interest of brevity, and in part because only they have reached a stage in the agenda-setting process at which there is any reasonable possibility that they will be acted upon. It is worth noting, however, that among those proposals consequently not considered here are several that would mandate a turning away from primaries. Former Gov. Terry Sanford (1980), for example, has urged that the national conventions become the locus of decision-making in presidential nominating politics. He urges the election of "thinking delegates . . . who are uninstructed" and thus could constitute a "contemplative convention." Sen. Gary Hart, a Democrat from Colorado, has urged that national convention delegates be selected at local and state party caucuses, and that a national primary be held among those candidates who received 20 percent or more of the convention vote. This plan has the advantage—and disadvantage—of offering something for everyone. Among the drawbacks born of its complexity is that it would require electors in the nominating process to participate two times in two different ways in two kinds of forums.

14. Other recent versions of the national primary proposal, such as those offered by Sen. Mike Mansfield (D-MT) and Sen. George Aiken (R-VT) in 1972, and by Rep. Albert Quie (R-MN) in 1977 differed from Weicker's in that they would not have allowed independent voters to participate. The Mansfield-Aiken bill also would have defined 40 percent as sufficient for victory in the first primary.

15. Interview with the author, March 7, 1980.

16. Drawing from an ABC News poll of New Hampshire primary voters that asked them which candidates were acceptable to them, Brams (1980) deduced that under an approval voting system, Reagan would have risen 8 percentage points, from 50 percent to 58 percent; Bush 16 points, from 23 to 39; and Baker 28 points, from 13 to 41—and into second place. For an even more speculative treatment of the 1976 contest, see Kellett and Mott (1977).

17. Distressingly, a major short-run obstacle seems to be the lack of seriousness of the proposal's present sponsor in Congress. To wit: When I called Sen. Weicker's office in March 1980 to ask for an interview with the senator about his national primary bill, his press secretary's honest response was, "Do we have a national primary bill?" And when I sat down with Weicker in his office the following week, he told me that he did not know if his bill had attracted any cosponsors, did not know if there were comparable bills being looked at in the House of Representatives, and was not sure whether hearings had been scheduled on it in the Senate or not. He thought there might be hearings in 1981. (Hearings were to be held by the Senate Committee on Rules and Administration on Sept. 10, 1980.)

References

Arterton, F. Christopher. 1977. "Strategies and Tactics of Candidate Organizations." *Political Science Quarterly* 93 (Winter).

———. 1978. "Campaign Organizations Confront the Media-Political Environment" and "The Media Politics of Political Campaigns." In *Race for the Presidency,* ed. James David Barber, pp. 3-25, 26-54. Englewood Cliffs, N.J.: Prentice-Hall.

Barber, James David. 1977. *The Presidential Character.* Englewood Cliffs, N.J.: Prentice-Hall.

———. 1980. *The Pulse of Politics.* New York: W. W. Norton.

Brams, Steven. 1978. *The Presidential Election Game.* New Haven, Conn.: Yale University Press.

———. 1979. "Approval Voting: A Practical Reform for Multi-candidate Elections." *National Civic Review* 68 (November 1979).

_____. 1980. "Baker Could Have Survived N.H." *Concord Monitor* (March 9).

Bryce, James. 1959. *The American Commonwealth*. New York: G. P. Putnam's Sons.

Cronin, Thomas, 1980. *The State of the Presidency*, 2nd ed. Boston: Little, Brown.

Crotty, William J. 1977. *Political Reform and the American Experiment*. New York: Thomas Y. Crowell.

Dahl, Robert. 1956. *A Preface to Democratic Theory*. Chicago: University of Chicago Press.

Davis, James W. 1967. *Presidential Primaries*. New York: Thomas Y. Crowell.

Gallup, George. 1978. "Six Political Reforms Americans Want Most." *Reader's Digest* 113 (August): 59-62.

Gallup Opinion Index. 1980. "Two in Three Back Nationwide Primary Plan." (January): 19-20.

Hargrove, Erwin. 1974. *The Power of the Modern Presidency*. New York: A. A. Knopf.

Hargrove, Erwin, and Michael Nelson. 1981. "Presidents, Ideas, and the Search for a Stable Majority." In *A Tide of Discontent: The 1980 Elections and Their Meaning*, ed. Ellis Sandoz and Cecil Crabb. Washington, D.C.: Congressional Quarterly Press.

Kellett, John, and Kenneth Mott. 1977. "Presidential Primaries: Measuring Popular Choice." *Polity* 9 (Summer).

Lanouette, William J. 1979. "As Many Candidates as Strategies for the 1980 Presidential Primaries." *National Journal* 11 (October 20): 1737-1741.

Matthews, Donald. 1978. '"Winnowing': The News Media and the 1976 Presidential Nominations." In *Race for the Presidency*, ed. James David Barber, pp. 55-78. Englewood Cliffs, N.J.: Prentice-Hall.

Mayo, Henry. 1960. *Introduction to Democratic Theory*. New York: Oxford University Press.

McCarthy, Eugene. 1980. "After New Hampshire." *New York Times* (February 28).

Nelson, Michael. 1979. "Power to the People: The Crusade for Direct Democracy." *Saturday Review* 6 (November 24).

_____. 1980. "James David Barber and the Psychological Presidency." *Virginia Quarterly Review* 56 (Fall).

Pressman, Jeffrey, and Aaron Wildavsky. 1973. *Implementation*. Berkeley: University of California Press.

Ranney, Austin. 1974a. "Changing the Rules of the Nominating Game." In *Choosing the President*, ed. James David Barber. Englewood Cliffs, N.J.: Prentice-Hall.

_____. 1974b. *Curing the Mischiefs of Faction*. Berkeley: University of California Press.

_____. 1977. *Participation in American Presidential Nominations, 1976*. Washington, D.C.: American Enterprise Institute.

_____. 1978a. *The Federalization of Presidential Primaries*. Washington, D.C.: American Enterprise Institute.

_____. 1978b. "The Political Parties." In *The New American Political System*, ed. Anthony King. Washington, D.C.: American Enterprise Institute.

Robinson, Michael. 1975. "The Presidential Nominating Caucus." *Congressional Record* (June 19).

Rossiter, Clinton. 1968. *1787: The Grand Convention*. London: MacGibbon and Kee.

Sabato, Larry. 1980. "Caucus Finds New Favor." *Baltimore Sun* (March 2).

Sanford, Terry. 1980. "Picking the President." *Atlantic Monthly* 246 (August).

Schattschneider, E. E. 1966. *The Semi-Sovereign People*. New York: Holt, Rinehart, and Winston.

Schlesinger, Arthur M., ed. 1972. *The Coming to Power*. New York: Chelsea House.

_____. 1979. "Crisis of the Party System." *Wall Street Journal* (May 10).

Stearns, Richard. 1979. "Is There a Better Method of Picking Presidential Nominees." *New York Times* (December 2).

White, Theodore H. 1980. "The Making of a President Ain't What It Used to Be." *Life* (February 3).

Young, James Sterling. 1966. *The Washington Community, 1800-1828*. New York: Harcourt, Brace and World.

3. Morality, Democracy, and the Intimate Contest

1. See his article by that title in *The Public Interest*. It goes without saying that he should not be held liable for the use to which I put his brilliant, elegant piece, a use quite different from his.

4. Transfer Recipients and the Poor during the 1970s

1. The federal share of a state's AFDC expenditures is between 50 and 83 percent. The exact percentage varies inversely with the ratio of state-to-national per capita income.

2. Throughout this paper, the term "AFDC benefit" refers to the national or regional average, weighted by 1979 state AFDC caseloads, of the maximum AFDC benefit paid by the various states to a family of four with no other income. This measure is preferable to the average of actual payments because it controls for the substantial shifts in the incomes of recipients and the sizes of their families that occurred during the 1970s.

3. Options G and H were adapted from a study, *AFDC Standards of Need: An Evaluation of Current Practices, Alternative Approaches, and Policy Options*, conducted by Urban Systems for the Social Security Administration in 1980.

5. Labor Supply Response to a Negative Income Tax

1. For a discussion of these labor supply studies as well as descriptions of the various experiments, see Keeley (1981) and Moffitt and Kehrer (forthcoming) and the references cited therein.

2. See Keeley et al. (1978a, 1978b), Robins and West (1980a), Cogan (1978), Robins (1978), Burtless and Greenberg (1979), and Ashenfelter (1980). Throughout this paper, the terms "participating" and "not participating" are used interchangeably with the terms "below the breakeven level" and "above the breakeven level," respectively.

3. The average labor supply response in the experimental sample is equal to the response of participants times the proportion of the sample that participates, assuming nonparticipants do not respond. This implies that the response of participants can be derived from the response of eligibles and knowledge of the proportion of the eligible population that participates. If the response of participants in the experimental sample is similar to the response of participants in the U.S. population, the experimental results can be generalized by applying the participant response to the portion of the U.S. population that is predicted to participate.

4. See Keeley et al. (1978b) for an illustration of the way this distinction facilitates interpretation of aggregate responses.

5. In the New Jersey and Seattle-Denver experiments, eligibility is randomly assigned within several strata, the most important of which is normal income. When we present the eligibility model in this paper, we discuss the implications of the assignment model for estimating treatment effects. Also see Robins and West (1980d) and Keeley and Robins (1980).

6. When participation is defined for the period at enrollment, we refer to it as initial participation. When participation is defined for the same period in which labor supply is being measured (in this paper, the second year of the experiment), we refer to it as current participation. Robins and West (1980a) and Cogan (1978) focus their analyses on current participation. Keeley et al. (1978a, 1978b) focus on initial participation. Robins (1978) and Burtless and Greenberg (1979) consider both definitions of participation. Clearly, other definitions are also possible.

· 7. In principle, this need not be the case for several reasons. First, one of the major determinants of participation (other than labor supply) is nonwage income. Certain types of nonwage income, such as AFDC benefits, can cause persons with low labor supplies to be above the breakeven level. Second, the experiments tested several programs and these were not randomly assigned within the experimental population. In particular, persons with higher initial labor supplies were more likely to be assigned to the more generous programs. If generosity of the treatment (as measured by the breakeven level) rises faster than average labor supply in the sample, it is possible that participants have higher average labor supply than nonparticipants. Third, persons with initially low labor supplies (participants) are more likely to have transitorily low incomes and may experience greater increases in income over time than persons with initially high labor supplies (nonparticipants).

8. For a description of SIME/DIME, see Spiegelman and Yaeger (1980) and Keeley, Spiegelman, and West (1980).

9. The second year is chosen for analysis because it is a period in which SIME/DIME families are assumed to be unaffected by adjustment to either the beginning or the end of the experiment.

10. The regression equations estimated in this paper also include several additional variables, which are described in our section describing models.

11. A more elaborate (structural) version of this model, which is extrapolated to the national population, is presented in Keeley et al. (1978a), where two variables are specified for initial participation and three variables are specified for initial nonparticipation.

12. Initial breakeven status also depends on several other variables (such as nonwage income other than the NIT payment), but these do not affect the formal argument.

13. In the case where a_0 is not assumed to be zero and $A_0 F$ is included in the equation, it can be shown that the bias in b_0 is equal to the difference between the mean of μ for experimentals below the breakeven and the mean of μ for controls.

14. As we shall see in the next section, a substantial number of initial participants are not affected by the program (i.e., they are above the breakeven level) in the second year. Hence, the initial status model will combine the response of such persons with the response of persons who are actually below the breakeven level in the second year.

15. This does not imply the absence of a labor supply response to the experiment; it just means that breakeven status is unaffected by the experiment.

16. A discussion of the predicted probabilities is given in an appendix available from the authors upon request. The use of instrumental variables greatly reduces the precision with which we can estimate experimental effects in the current status model.

17. Jonathan Dickinson has pointed out to us that this procedure is subject to a small-sample bias because the participation probability equation is estimated on a sample of experimentals only. Consequently, the predicted participation probabilities fit actual participation more closely for experimentals than for controls. This leads to a bias in the estimate of the experimental effects. Although the bias approaches zero as the sample size increases, in some cases the bias can be shown to be sizable even in samples as large as those used here. However, the bias is small if the nonexperimental effect of the participation probability (b_2') is small or if the fit of the estimated probability equation is reasonably good. For a detailed discussion of this bias and some suggested estimation procedures see Dickinson (1980).

18. The husband and wife sample sizes are not the same because of differential attrition after marital separations.

19. It is not possible to generate for controls a simulated breakeven status variable comparable to the reported breakeven status variable of experimentals. The simulated breakeven status variable calculated from interview-reported income is used as a proxy in models using reported breakeven status.

20. Cogan (1978), in his study of the New Jersey Experiment, uses official payments records. Official payments records are probably the best source for construction of measures of participation, but the records were not available when this study was undertaken. In earlier SIME/DIME studies, Robins and West (1980a) and Robins (1978) use interview reported payments while Keeley et al. (1978a, 1978b), and Burtless and Greenberg (1979) construct a definition of participation on the basis of interview-reported income.

21. About one-half of the control families filed income report forms (equivalent to those filed by experimental families) to test whether this administrative feature of the experiment leads to differential reporting behavior. The variable is included in the equation to control for such an effect.

22. See Spiegelman and Yaeger (1980) for a description of the manpower treatments in SIME/DIME.

23. The test for differences between the initial and current status models (models 2 and 3 in the tables) cannot be performed because the null hypotheses are not tested.

24. This finding is consistent with the means reported in table 5.2 and the coefficients of the simulated breakeven status variables.

25. The percentage effects are calculated from the results that include the simulated breakeven status variables and are based on the means in table 5.2.

26. It is interesting that for husbands and single female heads, the responses estimated using the IV technique and including the simulated treatment variables are larger (in absolute value) than the responses estimated using OLS and excluding the simulated treatment variables. Apparently, the bias caused by endogeneity of participation more than offsets the bias caused by sample selection. A significant positive response for nonparticipating single female heads in estimates using the IV technique is perplexing, however. It is also interesting that the direction of the selectivity bias reverses for husbands and single female heads when the IV technique is used.

References

Ashenfelter, Orley. 1980. "Discrete Choice in Labor Supply: The Determinants of Participation in the Seattle and Denver Income Maintenance Experiments." Research Report, Socioeconomic Research Center, SRI International. March.

Burtless, G. 1979. "Family Decisions To Receive Experimental Transfers in the Seattle and Denver Income Maintenance Experiments." Unpublished paper, Office of Income Security Policy, U.S. Department of Health, Education, and Welfare. March.

Burtless, G., and D. Greenberg. 1979. "Measuring Treatment Effects in Social Experimentation: Estimates of the Work Response to Income Maintenance." Unpublished paper, Office of Income Security Policy, U.S. Department of Health, Education, and Welfare. November.

Cain, Glen G., and Harold W. Watts, eds. 1973. *Income Maintenance and Labor Supply*. Chicago: Markham.

Cogan, J. 1978. "Negative Income Taxation and Labor Supply: New Evidence from the New Jersey-Pennsylvania Experiment." R-2155. Santa Monica, Cal.: Rand Corporation. February.

Danzinger, Sheldon, and Robert Haveman, "The Reagan Budget: A Sharp Break with the Past," *Challenge* 24 (May/June 1981): 5-13.

Dickinson, J. 1980. "Differential Imputation Bias in Analysis of Experimental Response." Unpublished paper, SRI International. May.

Garfinkel, Irwin. 1976. "Review of the Seattle-Denver Labor Supply Paper." Memorandum to Stanley Masters, Glen Cain, and Robert Lerman, Institute for Research on Poverty, University of Wisconsin, Madison. October 18.

———. 1979. "Sample Selection Bias as a Specification Error." *Econometrica* 47 (January): 153-162.

———. 1978. "Dummy Endogenous Variables in a Simultaneous Equation System." *Econometrica* 46 (July): 931-959.

Heckman, J. J. 1976. "Simultaneous Equation Models with Continuous and Discrete Endogenous Variables and Structural Shifts." *Studies in Nonlinear Estimations*, S. Goldfeld and R. E. Quandt, eds. Cambridge, Mass.: Ballinger.

Keeley, Michael C. 1981. *Labor Supply and Public Policy: A Critical Review*. New York: Academic Press.

Keeley, M. C., and P. K. Robins. "The Design of Social Experiments: A Critique of the Conlisk-Watts Assignment Model." *Research in Labor Economics*, Vol. 3, R. Ehrenberg, ed. Greenwich, Conn.: JAI Press. Pp. 293-333.

Keeley, M. C., P. K. Robins, R. G. Spiegelman, and R. W. West. 1978a. "The Labor Supply Effects and Costs of Alternative Negative Income Tax Programs." *Journal of Human Resources* 13, (Winter).

———. 1978b. "The Estimation of Labor-Supply Models Using Experimental Data." *American Economic Review*, December, 873-887.

Keeley, Michael C., Robert G. Spiegelman, and Richard W. West. 1980. "Design of the Seattle/Denver Income Maintenance Experiments and an Overview of the Results." *A Guaranteed Annual Income: Evidence from a Social Experiment*, P.K. Robins, R.G. Spiegelman, S. Weiner, and J. Bell, eds. New York: Academic Press.

Keeley, Michael C. and Hoi S. Wai. 1981. "Earnings Mobility, Program Participation, and the Labor Supply Response to a Negative Income Tax Program." Research Report, Socioeconomic Research Center, SRI International. March.

Maddala, G. S., and L.-F. Lee. 1976. "Recursive Models With Qualitative Endogenous Variables." *Annals of Economic and Social Measurement* 5 (Fall): 525-545.

Moffitt, Robert A. "The Labor Supply Response in the Gary Experiment." *Journal of Human Resources* 14 (Fall 1979): 477-487.

———, and Kenneth C. Kehrer. (forthcoming.) "The Effect of Tax and Transfer Programs on Labor Supply: The Evidence from the Income Maintenance Experiments." *Research in Labor Economics* 4, R. Ehrenberg, ed. Greenwich, Conn.: JAI Press.

Palmer, John, and Joseph A. Pechman, eds. 1978. *Welfare in Rural Areas: The North Carolina-Iowa Income Maintenance Experiment*. Washington, D.C.: The Brookings Institution.

Pechman, Joseph A., and P. Michael Timpane, eds. 1975. *Work Incentives and Income Guarantees: The New Jersey Income Maintenance Experiment*. Washington, D.C.: The Brookings Institution.

Robins, P. K. 1978. "Breakeven Status and the Labor Supply Response to a Negative Income Tax Program." Mimeographed, Center for the Study of Welfare Policy, SRI International. July.

Robins, P. K., and R. W. West. 1980a. "Program Participation and Labor Supply Response." *Journal of Human Resources* 15 (Fall): 499-523.

———. 1980c. "Labor Supply Response to SIME/DIME: Alternative Estimates of a Structural Model." Research Report, Socioeconomic Research Center, SRI International. January.

———. 1980d. "Labor Supply Response to SIME/DIME: Analysis of Six Years of Data." Research Socioeconomic Research Center, SRI International. May.

Spiegelman, Robert G. and K.E. Yaeger. 1980. "Overview." *Journal of Human Resources*, 15 4 (Fall): 463-79.

Watts, Harold W., and Albert Rees, eds. 1977. *The New Jersey Income-Maintenance Experiment: Volume II, Labor Supply Responses.* New York: Academic Press.

West, R. W., and G. Stieger. 1980. "The Effects of the Seattle and Denver Income Maintenance Experiments on Alternative Measures of Labor Supply." Research Memorandum No. 72, Socioeconomic Research Center, SRI International. May.

6. Measuring the Distribution of Personal Taxes

The authors benefited from the comments of Carl Simon, Kerry Smith, and Kenneth Wertz and those on an earlier version of Bruce Davie, Emil Sunley, and Randy Weiss. However, responsibility for errors remains with the authors. Financial support from the Office of Tax Analysis, U.S. Department of the Treasury, is gratefully acknowledged.

1. A "winner-loser" count contains little information about the horizontal equity implications of the proposal, and implicitly assumes that current law is a proper benchmark, even though current law contains distortions. Thus, a wide dispersion in the winner-loser count for a given income bracket may actually accompany an increase in horizontal equality. Similar arguments exist for looking at winner-loser counts as a vertical measure, and for using the two dollar measures of tax changes.

2. See, for example, Theil (1972) for an application of inequality analysis to housing data by race.

3. It should be observed that a SWF is usually thought to be open-ended in value, so that higher levels of the SWF denote more well-offness to society. Index numbers, to be useful, may be bounded, as the Gini is between zero and one. On the other hand, there are index numbers, widely used, which are not normalized or bounded, and may then be thought to be structured in form identical with an SWF. In the index numbers developed in this paper, care is taken to distinguish between normalized and unnormalized versions both for numerical and evaluation purposes.

4. In particular, the axioms are: separability in the sense of Gorman (1968), continuity, essentiality, and consistency as well as several minor technical assumptions such as a range condition.

5. It should be noted that the rate difference approach, although intuitively less plausible, is the weighting scheme used by Suits (1977) and Wertz (1978).

6. Feldstein (1976) and Atkinson (1979) discuss in some detail the conceptual problems of horizontal equity. Our approach here is simply to examine disparities in tax treatment of tax units with the same economic income, and abstract from the complex issues of differential behavioral response to preferential tax treatment of certain sources of income. We differ in our analysis of horizontal equity from Atkinson (1979) in that we view horizontal equity as a two-variable measurement problem, pretax economic income and tax rate, rather than a univariate measurement problem involving income.

Our approach to measuring horizontal equity differs also from Brennan (1971), in that the number of unequal comparisons, weighted by the extent of the relative tax rate disparity, is analyzed, rather than the money value of the disparities. Brennan's approach would appear to be undesirably unit-dependent.

7. Because data collection necessarily entails the passage of considerable periods of time, inferences about the effects of policy proposals on the current income distribution must be made with historical data projected or extrapolated to current presumed levels. The extrapolation process used is due to Wyscarver (1978).

8. Economic income is defined in this data base as the sum of wages and salaries, dividends, interest, nonfarm business income, total capital gains before carryover, income from estates and trusts, and pensions and annuities. Items which are in personal income but which are not included in this income measure are certain tax-exempt incomes such as the interest on state and local bonds and transfer payments as well as accrued (but not realized) capital gains. The income and taxes due are

static representations of the population, except that it is assumed that taxpayers in the sample will choose to itemize their deductions when doing so minimizes their tax liability.

9. As noted, the empirical analysis was performed with 112 tax-rate intervals and 25 income intervals. Such bracketing of the data was performed to keep the computations tractable, for performing $(n - 1)$ n comparisons for 50,000 taxpayers would lead to 2.5 billion comparisons which would be unduly expensive in terms of computer time. The choice of income intervals was made with the aim of having roughly 4% of the taxpayers represented in each bracket, while the choice of 112 tax rate brackets was made to permit 1%-wide brackets.

The question naturally arises as to how sensitive our results are to changes in the size of the income and tax brackets. While a complete answer would entail computations well beyond the original scope of the project, we did examine the impact of widening brackets by a factor of 4. That is, we widened the tax-rate intervals to 4% widths and computed the vertical and horizontal measures at 1978 tax law and at 1978 income levels. The results indicate that the vertical scores are relatively unaffected by changes in tax brackets. On the other hand, the equity results do display some major changes. This is, of course, expected since with wider tax brackets we are counting such tax-rate differences of 2 and 3% as being the same, whereas with the 112 brackets these would be counted as disparities. With 112 brackets, we observe 1978 law to contain only 17.5% equitable comparisons, while with 30 tax rate brackets, 35.0% of the comparisons display horizontal equity. Thus, a quadrupling of the bracket width is accompanied by roughly a doubling in observed horizontal equity.

References

Arrow, K. J. 1965. "Aspects of the Theory of Risk Bearing." Helsinki.

Atkinson, A. B. 1970. "On the Measurement of Inequality." *Journal of Economic Theory*, No. 2. pp. 244–63.

Atkinson, A. B. 1980. "Horizontal Equity and the Distribution of the Tax Burden." in H. Aaron and M. J. Boskin, eds., *The Economics of Taxation*. Washington, D.C.: The Brookings Institution, pp. 3–18.

Berliant, M., and R. P. Strauss. 1980. "An Axiomatic Theory of Index Numbers," Carnegie-Mellon University.

Blackorby, C., and D. Donaldson. 1976. "Measures of Equality and Their Meanings in Terms of Social Welfare," University of British Columbia Discussion Paper, No. 76–20.

Bourguignon, F. 1979. "Decomposable Income Inequality Measures." *Econometrica* 47, No. 4 (July): 901–20.

Brennan, G. 1971. "Horizontal Equity: An Extension of an Extension." *Public Finance/Finance Publiques* 26, 3:(437–56).

Bridges, B., Jr. 1978. *Intertemporal Changes in Tax Rates*. Studies in Income Distribution, No. 11. Washington, D.C.: Social Security Administration, Office of Research and Statistics, SSA 79–11776.

Dalton, H. 1920. "The Measurement of the Inequality of Incomes." *Economic Journal* no. 30:348–61.

Feldstein, M. S. 1976. "On the Theory of Tax Reform." *Journal of Public Economics* 6, no. 1-2:77–104.

Fields, G. S., and J. C. H. Fei. 1978. "On Inequality Comparisons," *Econometrica* 46:303–16.

Gorman, W. T. 1968. "The Structure of Utility Functions." (in Symposium on Aggregation) *Review of Economic Studies* 35:367–90.

Kendall, M. 1947. *The Advanced Theory of Statistics*. London: Griffin & Co.

Kolm, S. C. 1976. "Unequal Inequalities." *Journal of Economic Theory*, no. 12 and 13:82–112.

Kondor, Y. 1975. "Value Judgments Implied by the Use of Various Measures of Income Inequality." *Review of Income and Wealth* 21:309–21.

Okner, B. A. 1979. "Distributional Aspects of Tax Reform During the Past Fifteen Years." *National Tax Journal* 32, no. 1 (March): 11–28.

Pechman, J. A., and B. Okner. 1974. *Who Bears the Tax Burden?* Washington, D.C.: The Brookings Institution.

Pratt, J. W. 1964. "Risk Aversion in the Small and Large." *Econometrica*, no. 32 (January-April): 122–36.

Sen, A. 1973. *On Economic Inequality*. Oxford: Clarendon Press.

Shorrocks, A. F. 1980. "The Class of Additively Decomposable Inequality Measures." *Econometrica* 48, no. 3:613–25.

Suits, D. B. 1975. "Measurement of Tax Progressivity." *American Economic Review* 67, no. 4:747–52.

Theil, H. 1967. *Economics and Information Theory.* Amsterdam.

Theil, H. 1972. *Statistical Decomposition Analysis.* Amsterdam.

Wertz, K. L. 1975. "Empirical Studies of Tax Burdens: Design and Interpretation." *Proceedings.* Houston: National Tax Association, pp. 115–22.

Wertz, K. L. 1978. "A Method for Measuring the Relative Taxation of Families." *Review of Economics and Statistics* 60:145–50.

Wyscarver, R. A. 1978. "The Treasury Personal Individual Income Tax Simulation Model." *OTA Paper 32.* Washington, D.C.: U.S. Treasury Department, Assistant Secretary for Tax Policy, Office of Tax Analysis.

7. Private Sector Unions in the Political Arena: Public Policy vs. Employee Preference

1. A much more exhaustive and rigorous treatment is given in Freeman and Medoff (1976).
2. For a more detailed discussion of the pension fund issue, see Bennett and Johnson (1981).

References

Bennett, James T., and Manuel H. Johnson. 1980. *Pushbutton Unionism.* Fairfax, Va: Contemporary Economics and Business Association.

———. 1981. "Union Use of Employee Pension Funds." *Journal of Labor Research* 2 (Fall): 181-190.

Freeman, R. B., and J. L. Medoff. 1976. "Where Have All The Members Gone? The Dwindling of Private Sector Unionism in the U.S." Unpublished paper, Harvard University.

Heldman, Dan C. 1979. "Making Policy in a Vacuum: The Case of Labor Relations." *Policy Review* 10 (Fall): 75-88.

Kochan, Thomas A. 1980. *Collective Bargaining and Industrial Relations.* Homewood, Ill.: Irwin.

Marshall, F. Ray, Allan G. King, and Vernon M. Briggs, Jr., *Labor Economics: Wages, Employment, and Trade Unionism,* 4th ed. (Homewood, Ill.: Richard D. Irwin, Inc., 1980).

Mitchell, Daniel J. B. 1980. "Some Empirical Observations of Relevance to the Analysis of Union Wage Determination." *Journal of Labor Research* 1 (Fall): 193-215.

Rifkin, Jeremy, and Randy Barber, *The North Will Rise Again* (Boston: Beacon Press, 1978).

Thieblot, A. J. 1978. *An Analysis of Data on Union Membership.* St. Louis: Center for the Study of American Business.

8. The Davis-Bacon Act

1. I am indebted to Professor David T. Ellwood of the Kennedy School of Government, Harvard University, for this point and for a number of incisive comments. Professor Richard E. Bernstein of Temple University and Dr. Jerome Staller of the Center for Forensic Economic Studies have also provided many helpful suggestions.

2. If there is excess capacity (unemployment) in construction, downward pressure on wage rates would be expected. During contract periods, union wages are expected to be inflexible, while the nonunion average may be more flexible. Over sufficient time to renegotiate, at a time when prices and wages are generally rising, it is not clear that there would be a great difference between nonunion and union wage pressures, or a significant change in the differential.

3. This was viewed as a problem because it limited the contractor in assigning the same workers to different jobs at different times; a worker going from a federal to a private sector contract job would be assigned a lower pay rate, and one assigned to a federal project would be paid higher wages than colleagues on other jobs.

4. This analogy is not wholly applicable, since all millers pay the same support price for wheat for all uses. All contractors pay the same (prevailing) wage rate under government contracts, but wage rates for private sector construction may differ substantially.

References

Bourdon, Clinton C., and Raymond E. Levitt. 1978. *A Comparison of Wages and Labor Management Practices in Union and Nonunion Construction.* Cambridge, Mass.: Department of Civil Engineering, Massachusetts Institute of Technology, Research Report R78-3, Publication no. 593.

Building Construction and Trades Department, AFL-CIO. 1977. *In Defense of Davis-Bacon.* Washington, D.C.

Ehrenberg, R.G., M. Kosters, and M. Maskow. 1971. "The Economic Impact of Davis-Bacon Type Legislation: An Econometric Study." Unpublished paper, U.S. Department of Labor.

Employment Standards Administration. 1978. *Guide to the Service Contract Act.* Washington, D.C.: Department of Labor.

Federal Personnel Manual System. 1978. *Federal Wage System.* Washington, D.C.: Civil Service Commission. FPM Supplement 523-1.

Fulton, Joseph F. 1978. *The Davis-Bacon Act: History, Administration, Pro and Con Arguments, and Congressional Proposals.* Washington, D.C.: Library of Congress. Report 78-161E.

Goldfarb, Robert S., and John F. Morrall, III. 1976. "An Analysis of Certain Aspects of the Davis-Bacon Act." U.S. Council on Wage and Price Stability. Mimeograph.

Gould, John P. 1971. *Davis-Bacon Act: The Economics of Prevailing Wage Laws.* Washington, D.C.: American Enterprise Institute.

Gujarathi, D.N. 1967. "The Economics of the Davis-Bacon Act." *Journal of Business* 40 (July): 303–316.

King, Alan G. 1979. "A Brief in Support of the Davis-Bacon Act." Unpublished paper, University of Texas, Austin.

Lehner, Urban C. 1979. "Labor Letter." *Wall Street Journal,* December 4, p. 1.

Mills, David Quinn. 1972. *Industrial Relations and Manpower in Construction.* Cambridge, Mass.: M.I.T. Press.

Northrup, Herbert R., and Howard J. Foster. 1975. *Open Shop Construction.* Philadelphia: University of Pennsylvania.

Solomon, Arthur P., and Clinton C. Bourdon. 1979. *The Inflationary Effects of the Davis-Bacon Act: A Summary and Analysis of the Research Literature.* Washington, D.C.: Department of Housing and Urban Development.

Thieblot, Armand J., Jr. 1975. *The Davis-Bacon Act.* Philadelphia: University of Pennsylvania.

U.S. Comptroller General. 1979. *The Davis-Bacon Act Should be Repealed.* Washington, D.C.: General Accounting Office.

9. OPEC II and the Wage-Price Spiral

1. The nature of the appropriate policy response to an oil-price shock depends not only on the nature of wage- and price-setting institutions, but also on the relative welfare costs of inflation and unemployment. See Gordon (1979) for a brief summary of these issues, and Gramlich (1979) for a more detailed analysis. Gramlich demonstrates (132–133) that under a set of fairly restrictive conditions, the optimal policy response to an oil-price shock is to accommodate—even if the shock is incorporated into the trend rate of increase in industrial costs and prices. Under a more realistic set of assumptions, however, the case for accommodation is not so clear-cut and will in general be influenced by the degree of real wage and non-oil price flexibility in the economy. Horwich (1980) highlights the importance of determining the impact of an oil-price shock on potential output in assessing the optimal policy rule.

2. A more complete description of the accelerationist model may be found in any recent macroeconomics textbook. See, for example, Dornbusch and Fischer (1981) or Turnovsky (1977).

3. See Blinder and Newton (1978) for a more sophisticated approach to the analysis of the Nixon program.

4. Some recent proposed modifications and alternatives to this traditional approach have not been pursued here. Sachs (1979) offers a modified specification—designed to include the effects of long-term contracts in a more explicit fashion than in the traditional approach—which includes the lagged rate of change of wages as an additional explanatory variable. Taylor (1980) derives an alternative wage equation employing staggered, long-term contracts and a relative wage hypothesis.

5. We also examined the impact of the effective personal income tax rate on hourly compensation. It was statistically insignificant.

6. See Blinder (1980) for a more complete discussion of these issues. Of course, any index that measures period-to-period changes in averages of prices is a less-than-ideal counterpart to theoretical constructs which postulate behavioral responses to changes in prices at the margin; the PCE index, which measures average oil prices instead of marginal oil prices, is no exception. However, for a part of the sample period, governmental regulation of the domestic oil market forced equality of these two

measures; for most of the rest of the period, the difference between average and marginal prices was small.

7. Both lag structures were third degree, with the coefficient on the last quarter constrained to zero.

8. The parameters and their standard errors for the equation estimated from quarterly data for 1964:1 to 1978:2 are

$$\text{3-year T-note rate} = .39 + .89 \times \text{real 3-month T-bill rate}$$
$$(.29)\,(.06)$$
$$+ .11 \times \text{sum of lags on real bill rate}$$
$$(.08)$$
$$+ .89 \times \text{percent change in } PCE \text{ deflator}$$
$$(.06)$$
$$+ .23 \times \text{sum of lags of percent change in } PCE \text{ deflator}$$
$$(.06)\,,$$

where the real 3-month T-bill rate is the nominal rate minus the percent change in the PCE deflator. R-bar squared $= .95$; $D.W. = 1.08$.

9. An alternative approach to the construction of an inflation expectations variable, suggested by Sargent (1973), would employ directly the one-period-ahead inflation estimate generated by the linearized reduced form of a complete macro model. Such an estimate would include not only past rates of change of prices but, *inter alia*, past rates of change of the money stock. The extent to which changes in the money stock are important direct and independent determinants of inflation expectations remains an unresolved issue. The existence of strong direct effects of monetary growth on inflation expectations would alter the properties of the simulations reported later in this study.

10. Other measures similar to this concept, such as the "core" inflation rate or the "underlying" inflation rate, could also be used.

11. The negative coefficient on the farm deflator is a consequence of the fact that the dependent variable is a measure of value-added in the private nonfarm (excluding housing) sector. It may also reflect the particular procedures used in the construction of that deflator.

12. It is interesting to note the role that the inclusion of a constant term plays in obtaining the result that the sum of the coefficients on factor costs is less than one. As Gordon found (1975:634), the inclusion of a constant term can lead to a reduction in the sum of the coefficients on factor prices. Estimation of our equation for the nonfarm (excluding housing) deflator without a constant term yielded coefficients on current and lagged standard unit labor costs that summed to 0.85; on the farm deflator, $-.03$; and on the current and lagged value of the import deflator that summed to 0.10. The motivation for estimating an equation with a constant term is the familiar one of allowing the average value of the disturbances in the equation to differ from zero. In our particular specification, the constant term represents the possibility of a non-zero trend in, for example, the shift parameter representing tastes in the demand function used to derive our specification, or alternatively, in the institutional environment in which wages and prices are set.

13. As noted in n. 1, the optimal policy response to a supply shock is conditioned by the effect of that shock on potential output. Further, as noted in n. 9, were our model to include direct effects of monetary growth on inflation expectations, we would have to specify precisely the path that such a monetary accommodation implied. This path, in turn, would alter the simulation properties of our model, in that the path of wage and price inflation induced by the oil-price shock would be higher, and it would take the inflation "bubble" caused by the oil-price shock longer to dissipate. As Taylor (1980) notes, a high degree of monetary accommodation may initially minimize output loss, but at the cost of a high degree of inflation persistence.

14. See Fellner (1976), Lucas (1972), Sargent (1973), and Sargent and Wallace (1975).

15. This is the result due to Fischer (1977).

16. For a description, see the recent annual reports of the Council of Economic Advisers (CEA, 1979, 1980).

17. If one assumes that low-wage groups had wage increases at least as large as the high-wage groups, then this estimate of one-third is an upper bound. Given the large increase in the minimum wage over that period, the assumption may not be so bad. On the other hand, the influx of lower-wage workers might have been expected to slow wage growth for such workers.

References

Blinder, A. 1980. "The Consumer Price Index and the Measurement of Recent Inflation." *Brookings Paper on Economic Activity* 2:539–565.

———, and W. Newton. 1978. "The 1971-1974 Controls Program and the Price Level: An Econometric Post-Mortem." National Bureau of Economic Research Working Paper 279. Cambridge, Mass. September.

Council of Economic Advisers. 1979. *Annual Report*. Washington, D.C.: Government Printing Office.

———. 1980. *Annual Report*. Washington, D.C.: Government Printing Office.

———. 1981. *Annual Report*. Washington, D.C.: Government Printing Office.

Dornbusch, R., and S. Fischer. 1981. *Macroeconomics*. New York: McGraw-Hill.

Fellner, W. 1976. *Toward a Reconstruction of Macroeconomics: Problems in Theory and Policy*. Washington, D.C.: American Enterprise Institute.

Fischer, S. 1977. "Long-Term Contracts, Rational Expectations, and the Optimal Money Supply Rule." *Journal of Political Economy* 85 (February): 191-205.

Gordon, R.J. 1971. "Inflation in Recession and Recovery." *Brookings Papers on Economic Activity* 1:104-158.

———. 1975. "The Impact of Aggregate Demand on Prices." *Brookings Papers on Economic Activity* 3:613-662.

———. 1979. "Monetary Policy and the 1979 Supply Shock." *National Bureau of Economic Research Working Paper* 418. Cambridge, Mass. December.

Gramlich, E.M. 1979. "Macro Policy Responses to Price Shocks." *Brookings Papers on Economic Activity* 1:125-166.

Horwich, G. 1980. "Government Contingency Planning for Petroleum Supply Interruptions: A Macro Perspective." Paper presented at the Conference on Policies for Coping with Oil Supply Disruptions, American Enterprise Institute, Washington, D.C. September 8-9.

Lucas, R.E. 1972. "Expectations and the Neutrality of Money." *Journal of Economic Theory* 4 (April): 103-124.

Modigliani, F., and R. Sutch. 1966. "Innovations in Interest Rate Policy." *American Economic Review* 56 (May): 178-197.

———. 1967. "Debt Management and the Term Structure of Interest Rates: An Empirical Analysis of Recent Experience." *Journal of Political Economy* 75 (August): 569-595.

Nordhaus, W. 1972. "Recent Developments in Price Dynamics." In *The Econometrics of Price Determination*, ed. O. Eckstein. Washington, D.C.: Board of Governors, Federal Reserve System. Pp. 16-49.

Perry, G. 1980. "Inflation in Theory and Practice." *Brookings Papers on Economic Activity* 1:207-242.

Sachs, J. 1979. "Wages, Profits, and Macroeconomic Adjustment: A Comparative Study." *Brookings Papers on Economic Activity* 2:269-320.

Sargent, T.J. 1973. "Rational Expectations, the Real Rate of Interest, and the Natural Rate of Unemployment." *Brookings Papers on Economic Activity* 2:429-472.

———, and N. Wallace 1975. "'Rational' Expectations, the Optimal Monetary Instrument, and the Optimal Money Supply Rule." *Journal of Political Economy* 83 (April): 241-254.

Taylor, J.B. 1980. "Aggregate Dynamics and Staggered Contracts." *Journal of Political Economy* 88 (February): 1-23.

Tobin, J. 1972. "The Wage-Price Mechanism: Overview of the Conference." In *The Econometrics of Price Determination*, ed. O. Eckstein. Washington, D.C.: Board of Governors, Federal Reserve System. Pp. 5-15.

Turnovsky, S. 1977. *Macroeconomic Analysis and Stabilization Policy*. Cambridge: Cambridge University Press.

10. The Political Economy of Wage and Price Regulation: The Case of the Carter Pay-Price Standards

1. See the "Recommendations of the Pay Advisory Committee with Respect to the Wage Guidelines Program and Regulations," Washington, D.C., November 17, 1980.

2. See Kosters (1975) and Dunlop (1975) for discussion of the Nixon program.

3. Eckstein and Brinner (1972) provide a thorough empirical assessment of the guidepost program.

4. Some of these tensions were widely publicized, as in the article "Wage-Price Official Upsets White House," *New York Times*, April 17, 1980, pp. D1, D4.

5. It did, however, vary by industry. Petroleum companies were particularly vulnerable to this sanction.

6. Suppose, for example, that the enterprise's profits would be different if it faced no price constraint from what they would be if it reduced its prices to be in compliance with the standard. The firm will choose to comply only if profits during compliance exceed profits with no price constraint. Adverse publicity for noncompliers imposes a cost that reduces profits. Clearly, for companies with large violations and consequently large costs for compliance, the potential reductions in profit must be very large to induce compliance. As a result, when wielding a small sanction, the greatest gains can be reaped by focusing on small violations. See Viscusi and Zeckhauser (1979) for further analysis of these issues.

7. See Galbraith (1981) for a lucid discussion of the World War II controls program.

8. This tally of noncompliers omits the flurry of noncompliance decisions after Carter lost the election, since the program had by then lost all its effectiveness.

9. Exceptions for unusually great inefficiencies can be justified on equity grounds. In addition, there may be an efficiency-oriented justification for attempting to equalize the distortions across firms. The efficiency argument hinges on the degree of variability of the social loss from these distortions.

10. An independent overview of these trends is provided by Meyer (1980).

11. See pp. 27 and 37 of the Council on Wage and Price Stability, *Issue Paper*, July 8, 1980.

12. See, for example, the article by Oi (1976), which surveys work in this area.

13. This sample period was dictated by the availability of average hourly earnings index data. This series begins in 1964:1. Since the price equation includes a lagged unit labor cost variable (calculated using the average hourly earnings index), the estimation period begins in 1964:2.

14. The PAY variable represents the rate of increase in the Bureau of Labor Statistics average hourly earnings index multiplied by the ratio of total compensation to the value of wages and salaries, using these two Department of Commerce series. Thus it includes fringe benefit costs, employers' Social Security tax payments, and base rates of pay.

15. The PCE variable enters contemporaneously (unconstrained) and through a 12-quarter third-order polynominal-distributed lag.

16. The form of SSTAX used was the percentage change in the inverse of one minus the employer's tax share. This variable is identical to that used by Gordon (1971).

17. This variable assumes a value of zero when the ESP was not in effect and a value of one throughout the 1971:3 to 1974:2 period of operation, except in the instances in which the program was in operation for only a fraction of the quarter, in which case this fraction becomes the dummy variable. Thus ESP1 assumes a value of 0.5 in 1971:3 and 0.167 in 1973:1, while ESP2 assumes a value of 0.833 in 1972:4 and 0.333 in 1974:2. Each of these variables takes on a value of one in the intervening quarters and zero otherwise.

18. The trend productivity measure was obtained by regressing nonfarm output per manhour on a time variable and two dummy variables to capture shifts in productivity growth.

19. Since the PPI energy components were not as comprehensive as the CPI-based measure, a retail energy price variable was used.

20. To complete the wage-price equation system, a bridge equation relating PCE to PCE' was used in the case of the TSLS estimates.

21. Gordon (1975) argues that the sum of the unit-labor-cost coefficients should be 1.0, and his empirical results generally indicate an effect that differs from 1.0 by about 0.1. Since his analysis pertains to the case in which the input prices are not included explicitly, as in the equations here, Gordon's results are not too dissimilar from those in this paper.

22. See, for example, Blinder and Newton (1979).

23. The PAY simulation results in table 10.5 and the PCE' simulation results in table 10.6 use the actual value of the other endogenous variable rather than its predicted level in order to isolate the quarterly patterns of influence for each variable.

24. Period 1 is 1978:4–1979:1; period 2 is 1979:2–1980:1; and period 3 is 1980:2.

25. In this case, this variable should perhaps be a dependent variable rather than an explanatory variable. Because of the long time lag between the violation and the correction action, it is not a good measure of current program effectiveness, though it may imperfectly reflect staff activity. As the results below will indicate, corrective actions are not positively related to any restraining effect.

26. There is no theoretical basis for constraining the energy effect to have the same three-year length as the overall price terms in the wage equation. Even if energy shocks do not affect labor demand but simply alter price expectations, it is doubtful whether the standard three-year distributed lag is appropriate.

References

Blinder, Alan S., and William J. Newton. 1979. "The 1971-1974 Controls Program and the Price Level: An Econometric Post-mortem." Princeton University and NBER, Working Paper.

Dunlop, John T. 1975. "Inflation and Incomes Policies: The Political Economy of Recent U.S. Experience." *Public Policy* 23 (1975): 135-166.

Eckstein, Otto, and Roger Brinner. 1972. *The Inflation Process in the United States, A Study of the Joint Economic Committee.* Washington, D.C.: Government Printing Office.

Galbraith, John Kenneth. 1981. *A Life in Our Times.* Boston: Houghton Mifflin.

Gordon, Robert J. 1971. "Inflation in Recession and Recovery," *Brookings Papers on Economic Activity* 1 (1971): 105-158.

Gordon, Robert J. 1975. "The Impact of Aggregate Demand on Prices." *Brookings Papers on Economic Activity* 3 (1975): 613-662.

Kosters, Marvin. 1975. *Controls and Inflation: The Economic Stabilization Program in Retrospect.* Washington, D.C.: American Enterprise Institute.

Meyer, Jack E. 1980. "Wage and Benefit Trends under the Carter Administration Guidelines," in W. Fellner, ed., *Contemporary Economic Problems.* Washington, D.C.: American Enterprise Institute. Pp. 193-226.

Oi, Walter. 1976. "On Measuring the Impact of Wage-Price Controls: A Critical Appraisal," in K. Brunner and A. Meltzer, eds., *The Economics of Price and Wage Controls.* Amsterdam: North-Holland Publishing Company.

Perry, George. 1980. "Inflation in Theory and Practice." *Brookings Papers on Economic Activity* 1 (1980): 207-241.

Viscusi, W. Kip, and Richard Zeckhauser. 1979. "Optimal Standards with Incomplete Enforcement." *Public Policy* 26 (1979): 437-456.

11. The Value of a Life: What Difference Does It Make?

1. The "human capital" measure is based on estimates of the present value of earnings foregone because of premature death. The "willingness-to-pay" measure is derived from estimates of how much individuals are willing to pay to reduce their probability of death by a small amount.

2. For the lower bound, see Acton (1973); for the upper bound, see Jones-Lee (1976).

3. For a review of these studies, see Smith (1979).

4. The mean value of a life in the willingness-to-pay studies was $1,288,000; in the foregone-earnings studies it was $204,000.

5. The dust appears to have settled after the battle between foregone-earnings advocates and the proponents of the willingness-to-pay concept. Most economists and policy analysts agree that the foregone earnings method is theoretically inappropriate and that estimates of peoples's willingness to pay for safety should be used in benefit-cost studies. See, for example, Mishan (1976:298-320).

6. Let p_i be the proportion of those individuals whose lives would be saved who are age i and let e_i be the life expectancy of individuals age i. Then, average life expectancy gained is given by the sum over all ages i of the product of p_i and e_i. We used life expectancy data for the U.S. population for 1976 as given in the "Monthly Vital Statistics Report," 26, no. 11 (Feb. 1978).

7. Of course, if a study considers a continuous range of alternatives rather than a few discrete alternatives, the value of a life will influence which policy is optimal.

8. In most cases, all three kinds of statistics should be presented to provide a variety of perspectives.

9. These life-expectancy statistics are based on the assumption that victims, if saved, would face the same life chances as nonvictims. Victims, however, may be frailer or more accident-prone, on average, than non-victims. By making some estimates about this difference, Zeckhauser and Shepard (1976) estimate an average life expectancy gained of 25 years, rather than 41 years, for victims of motor vehicle accidents. Also see Vaupel, Manton, and Stallard (1979).

10. The Supreme Court's Benzene Decision, Secretary of Labor vs. API, July 2, 1980. The Court cites Richard Wilson's work suggesting that the 1 ppm benzene standard would avert only 2 cancer

deaths every six years. Ignoring capital costs and using OSHA's estimate of $34 million per year in operating costs, it appears that the 1 ppm standard would cost $102 million per life saved.

11. In a more recent paper, Graham (in press) has explored in detail some possible explanations for disparities between OSHA and NHTSA investments.

References

Acton, Jan P. 1973. *Evaluating Public Programs to Save Lives: The Cost of Heart Attacks.* Santa Monica, Cal.: Rand Corporation.

Arnould, Richard J., and Henry T. Grabowski. 1981. "Auto Safety Regulations: An Analysis of Market Failure." *Bell Journal of Economics and Management Sciences.* 12 (Spring): 27–48.

Ashford, Nicholas. 1980. *Benefits of Environmental, Health and Safety Regulation.* Prepared for the Senate Government Affairs Committee, Center for Policy Alternatives, MIT, March 26.

Bailey, Martin. 1980. *Reducing Risks to Life: Measurement of the Benefits.* Washington, D.C.: American Enterprise Institute.

Baram, Michael S. 1979. *Regulation of Health, Safety and Environmental Quality and the Use of Cost-Benefit Analysis.* Final Report to the Administrative Conference of the United States, March 1.

Castle, Gilbert. 1976. "The 55 MPH Limit: A Cost-Benefit Analysis." *Traffic Engineering* 46 (January): 11–14.

Colfelter, Charles T., and John C. Hahn. 1978. "Assessing the National 55 MPH Speed Limit." *Policy Sciences* 9:281-294.

Coleman, William T. 1976. "Benefit-Cost Analysis of Motor Vehicle Occupant Crash Protection." *Federal Register,* June 14, pp. 24078–79.

Council on Environmental Quality. 1980. *Annual Report.* Washington, D.C.: GPO.

Council on Wage and Price Stability. 1976a. "Exposure to Coke Oven Emissions: A Proposed Standard." Washington, D.C.: Executive Office of the President, May.

———. 1976b. "Council Comments on OSHA's Proposed Standards on Arsenic." Washington, D.C.: Executive Office of the President, September 14.

———. 1977a. "Council Urges More Study on Saccharin Ban." Washington, D.C.: Executive Office of the President, June 15.

———. 1977b. "Occupant Crash Protection Standard." Washington, D.C.: Executive Office of the President, May 31. CWPS–244.

———.1978a. "Comments Submitted to the EPA on the Proposed Drinking Water Regulations." Washington, D.C.: Executive Office of the President, September 5.

———. 1978b. "Council Comments on Proposed Standard for Occupational Exposure to Acrylonitrite." Washington, D.C.: Executive Office of the President, May 22.

Crocker, Thomas D., William D. Schulze, Shaul Ben-David, and Allen V. Kneese. 1979. *Methods Development for Assessing Air Pollution Control Benefits.* Experiments in the Economics of Air Pollution Epidemiology, Environmental Protection Agency, Washington, D.C. vol. 1. Prepared for the EPA. February.

Dardis, Rachel, Susan Aaronson, and Ying-Nan Lin. 1978. "Cost-Benefit Analysis of Flammability Standards." *American Journal of Agricultural Economics* 60 (November): 697-699.

Ford Motor Company. 1979. "Benefits and Costs Related to Fuel Leakage Associated with the Static Rollover Test Portion of FMVSS 208." Reprinted in *Chicago Tribune,* October 14, p. 1.

Freeman, A. Myrick, III. 1979. *The Benefits of Air and Water Pollution Control: A Review and Synthesis of Recent Estimates.* Prepared for Council on Environmental Quality. Washington, D.C., December.

Gates, Howard P., Jr. 1975. "Review and Critique of NHTSA's Revised Restraint System Cost-Benefit Analysis." *Fourth International Congress on Automotive Safety.* July. Pp. 209–233.

General Accounting Office. 1976. *Effectiveness, Benefits and Costs of Federal Safety Standards for Protection of Passenger Car Occupants.* Washington, D.C.: Government Printing Office, July.

Graham, John D. In press. 1982. "Some Explanations for Disparities in Lifesaving Investments." *Policy Studies Journal.*

Jones-Lee, M. W. 1976. *The Value of Life.* Chicago: University of Chicago Press.

Koplan, Jeffrey P., Steven C. Schoerbaum, Milton Weinstein, and David W. Fraser, 1979. "Pertussis Vaccine: An Analysis of Benefits, Risks, and Costs." *New England Journal of Medicine* 301 (October).

Koshal, Rajindar, and Manjulika Koshal. 1973. "Environmental Urban Mortality—An Econometric Approach." *Environmental Pollution* 4:247–59.

Lave, Charles A. 1979. "Energy Policy as Public Policy." In *Changing Energy Use Futures*, vol. IV, ed. Faggolare and Smith. Second International Conference on Energy Use Management, October 22–26. Pp. 2046–53.

Lave, Lester B., and Eugene Seskin. 1977. "The Benefits and Costs of Air Pollution Abatement." In *Air Pollution and Human Health. Resources for the Future.* Baltimore: The Johns Hopkins University Press. Pp. 209–34.

Mishan. E.J. 1976. *Cost-Benefit Analysis.* New York: Praeger.

Muller, Andreis. 1980. "Evaluation of the Costs and Benefits of Motorcycle Helmet Law." *American Journal of Public Health* 70 (June): 586–92.

National Academy of Sciences. 1974. *Air Quality and Automobile Emission Control.* Prepared for the U.S. Senate Committee on Public Works. The Costs and Benefits of Automobile Emission Control, vol. 4. Washington, D.C., September.

Nichols, Albert. 1980. "Alternative Regulatory Strategies for Controlling Benzene Emissions from Malcic Anhydride Plants." Mimeo, Harvard University, Cambridge, March.

Perry, Charles, and Randall Outlaw. 1978. "Safe and Healthful Working Conditions—The Vinyl Chloride Experience." Mimeo Philadelphia: University of Pennsylvania.

Potter, J. M., M. L. Smith, and S. S. Lanwalker. 1976. "Cost-effectiveness of Residential Fire Detector Systems." Mimeo Texas Technical University, November.

Raiffa, Howard, William Schwartz, and Milton Weinstein. 1978. "Evaluating Health Effects of Social Decisions and Programs." *EPA Decision Making.* Washington, D.C.: National Academy of Sciences.

Robertson, Leon S. 1977. "Car Crashes: Perceived Vulnerability and Willingness to Pay for Crash Protection." *Journal of Community Health* 3 (Winter): 136–41.

S.R.I. 1979. Decision Analysis of Strategies for Reducing Upholstered Furniture Losses. Washington, D.C.: Department of Commerce, June.

Smith, Robert S. 1979. "Compensating Wage Differentials and Public Policy: A Review." *Industrial and Labor Relations Review* 32 (April): 339–52.

Swint, J. Michael, Judith M. Shapiro, Virginia L. Corson, Linda W. Reynolds, George H. Thomas, and Haigh Kazazian Jr. 1979. "The Economic Returns to Community and Hospital Screening Programs for Genetic Disease." *Preventive Medicine* 8:463–70.

U.S. Department of Transportation. 1976. *National Highway Safety Needs Report.* Washington, D.C.: Government Printing Office, April.

Vaupel, James W., Kenneth G. Manton, and Eric Stallard. 1979. "The Impact of Heterogeneity in Individual Frailty on the Dynamics of Mortality." *Demography* 16 (August): 439–54.

Warner, Charles Y., Michael A. Wither, and Richard Peterson. 1975. "Societal Priorities in Occupant Crash Protection." *Fourth International Congress on Automotive Safety.* U.S. Dept. of Transportation, Washington, D.C. July. Pp. 907–60.

Waterman, T.E., K.R. Minszewski, and D.G. Spadoni. *Cost-Benefit Analysis of Fire Detectors.* Chicago: IIT Research Institute, September.

Wilson, Richard. 1980. Cited in Supreme Court Case, *Industrial Union Dept. (AFL-CIO) versus The American Petroleum Institute*, 448 US 607(1980).

Zeckhauser, Richard. 1975. "Procedures for Valuing Lives." *Public Policy* 23 (Fall): 419–64.

———, and Donald Shepard. 1976. "Where Now for Saving Lives." *Law and Contemporary Problems* 40 (Autumn): 5–45.

12. The Formation of Health-Related Habits

1. The health belief literature uses the term "health preventive action," but this term suggests that the action prevents health. We prefer the terms "health-related action" and "health-beneficial action."

2. We have chosen to use annual time periods, but this is arbitrary.

3. Some of these variables also affect the level of consumption of the other commodities in the utility function. This joint production phenomenon is analyzed in Grossman (1970).

4. These results are available upon request from the authors.

References

Abt, C. C. 1977. "Lifestyle and Health." In *Costs, Risks, and Benefits of Surgery,* ed. J. P. Bunker, B. A. Barnes, and F. Mosteller. New York: Oxford Publishing.

Auster, R., I. Leveson, and D. Sarachek. 1969. "The Production of Health, An Explanatory Study." *Journal of Human Resources* 4:411–36.

Belloc, N. B. 1973. "Relationship of Health Practices and Mortality." *Preventive Medicine* 2 (March): 67–81.

Becker, M. H., D. P. Haefner, S. V. Kasl, J. P. Kirscht, L. A. Maiman, and I. M. Rosenstock. 1977. "Selected Psychosocial Models and Correlates of Individual Health-Related Behaviors." *Medical Care* 15 (supplement): 27–46.

Berry, R. E. Jr., and J. P. Bowland. 1977. *The Economic Cost of Alcohol Abuse.* New York: Free Press.

Breslow, L., and B. Klein. 1971. "Health and Race in California." *American Journal of Public Health* 61 (April): 763–75.

Delbanco, T. L., and J. Noble. 1975. "The Periodic Health Examination Revisited." *Annals of Internal Medicine* 83 (August): 271–73.

Folkins, C. H., S. Lynch, and M. M. Gardner. 1972. "Psychological Fitness as a Function of Physical Fitness." *Archives of Physical Medicine and Rehabilitation* 53 (November): 503–8.

Fuchs, V. R. 1974. *Who Shall Live? Health, Economics, and Social Choice.* New York: Basic Books.

Gordon, T., and W. B. Kannel. 1973. "The Effects of Overweight on Cardiovascular Diseases." *Geriatrics* 28 (August): 80–88.

Grossman, M. 1970. "The Demand for Health: A Theoretical and Empirical Investigation." Ph.D. dissertation, Columbia University.

——— . 1972. "On the Concept of Health Capital and the Demand for Health." *Journal of Political Economy* 80 (March–April): 223–55.

Kannell, W. B., A. Kagen, T. R. Dawber, and N. Revotskie. 1962. "Epidemiology of Coronary Heart Disease: Implications for the Practicing Physician," *Geriatrics* 17 (October): 675–90.

Knox, E. G. 1974. "Screening for Disease: Multiphasic Screening." *Lancet* (December): 1434–36.

Lalonde, M. 1974. *A New Perspective on the Health of Canadians; A Working Document.* Ottawa: Ministry of National Health and Welfare, Government of Canada.

Lewin, K. 1948. *Resolving Social Conflicts: Selected Papers on Group Dynamics.* New York: Harper.

Maiman, L. A., and M. H. Becker. 1974. "The Health Belief Model: Origins and Correlates in Psychological Theory." *Health Education Monographs* 2:336.

Mann, G. V., H. L. Garrett, A. Farhi, H. Murray, and F. T. Billings, with the assistance of E. Shute and S. E. Schwarten. 1969. "Exercise to Prevent Coronary Heart Disease." *American Journal of Medicine* 46 (January–June): 12–27.

Nelson, E. C., W. B. Stason, R. R. Neutra, H. S. Soloman, and P. J. McArdle. 1978. "Impact of Patient Perceptions on Compliance with Treatment for Hypertension." *Medical Care* 16 (November): 893–906.

Rosenstock, I. M. 1966. "Why People Use Health Services." *Millbank Memorial Fund Quarterly* 44 (part II): 94–127.

——— . 1974. "Historical Origins of the Health Belief Model." *Health Education Monographs* 2: 328–35.

Silver, M. 1972. "An Economic Analysis of Spatial Variations in Mortality Rates by Race and Sex." In *Essays in the Economics of Health and Medical Care,* ed. V. Fichs. New York: National Bureau of Economic Research. Pp. 161–227.

Society of Actuaries. 1959. *Build and Blood Pressure Study.* Chicago: Society of Actuaries.

Taubman, P. 1976. "The Determinants of Earnings: Genetics, Family, and Other Environments; A Study of White Male Twins." *American Economic Review* 66 (December): 858–70.

U.S. Department of Health, Education, and Welfare, Public Health Service. 1964. *Smoking and Health: Report of the Advisory Committee to the Surgeon General of the Public Health Service.* Washington, D.C.: Government Printing Office. PHS no. 1103.

Wilhelmsen, L., G. Tibblin, M. Aurell, J. Bjure, B. Ekström-Jodal, and G. Grimby. 1976. "Physical Activity, Physical Fitness and Risk of Myocardial Infarction." *Advances in Cardiology; Physical Activity and Coronary Heart Disease* 18:217–30.

13. The Effect of Liquor Taxes on Drinking, Cirrhosis, and Auto Fatalities

1. See Bruun et al. (1975); Popham, Schmidt, and deLint (1976 and 1978); Medicine in the Public Interest (1979).

2. Details on state regulation are given in *DISCUS* (1977).

3. A review of this literature is included in an earlier version of this paper, published under the same title in Moore and Gerstein (1981). A number of other reviews of the econometric literature are available. Bruun et al. (1975:74–78) and Medicine in the Public Interest (1979:64–68) present non-technical summaries. More detailed reviews are in Lau (1975) and Ornstein and Levy (ca. 1978).

4. The seminal discussion of quasi-experimental methods is in Campbell and Stanley (1963).

5. Monopoly states were excluded since pricing and other supply-related decisions are made by public agencies in these states, rather than by the market. Very small changes in tax were ignored because I was concerned that their effects would be masked by random noise in consumption. The decision to exclude Hawaii, Alaska and Washington, D.C., was based on an initial judgment that consumption patterns in these jurisdictions may reflect some unique forces. Each of these decisions is somewhat arbitrary, and none was tested in any fashion.

6. These data were taken from various issues of *The Liquor Handbook*.

7. The prices used for this calculation were taken from data in various issues of *The Liquor Handbook* on "retail prices of leading brands." Average prices for each state and year were calculated by analysis of variance, with main effects for each state and each brand. Separate analyses of variance were run for each year. The coefficients on the state effects were used as a measure of average price. (The null category for brand was Bacardi's Rum.)

To calculate the markup on tax changes, I proceeded as follows: For each year, price changes for all 30 license states were calculated and standardized by subtracting that year's median price change. The resulting net price changes for states with tax changes in that year were divided by the tax changes. The median of the 39 ratios calculated in this fashion was 1.1875, suggesting a typical markup of 18.75 percent. This estimate was rounded to 20 percent in the elasticity calculations reported here.

8. This test is explained in Wonnacott and Wonnacott (1977:475f.).

9. Since no data were available for 1958, it was not possible to include the three states that had tax changes in 1961.

10. Not all cases of fatal cirrhosis are alcohol-related. Schmidt (1977) estimated that the death rate in Canada from causes other than excess drinking is about 4 per 100,000. If this base rate of alcohol mortality is applicable to the United States, then almost three-quarters of cirrhosis deaths are alcohol-related.

11. Schmidt (1977) reports evidence that drinkers who consume as little as three ounces of ethanol per day for long periods have a heightened risk of cirrhosis. A large percentage of those who die of alcohol-related cirrhosis have a history of drinking that is more moderate than that of a clinical alcoholic population.

12. See Polich and Orvis (1979) for an analysis of the relationship between consumption level and the incidence of a variety of alcohol-related problems in a sample of U.S. Air Force personnel.

13. Economic theory and common sense both suggest that the price elasticity of demand for a normal commodity will tend to be relatively high for households whose expenditures on the commodity constitute a relatively large fraction of their budgets.

14. A related bit of evidence is given in Terris (1967:2086). He notes that in England and Wales in 1950, the cirrhosis death rate increased strongly with socioeconomic class. (No such correlation was found in the United States.) His explanation is that "spirits have been taxed out of reach of the lower social classes in the United Kingdom, where only the well-to-do can really afford the luxury of dying of cirrhosis of the liver."

15. Mortality rates for cirrhosis and auto accidents were calculated from frequency counts published in National Center for Health Statistics, *Vital and Health Statistics of the U.S.*, in Table 1-13 ("Deaths from 69 Selected Causes: United States, Each Division and State—1975") and in related tables in previous editions. Annual state population estimates were taken from two publications of the Bureau of the Census: "Population Estimates and Projections," Series P-25 (No. 460 and No. 727).

16. There is considerable evidence that the consumption levels of the median drinker and the heavy drinker are closely related. When one compares population groups that differ widely in per capita

consumption, it appears that levels of the typical drinker and the heavy drinker are subject to the same environmental and cultural influences, and/or that drinking patterns are interdependent or "contagious."

17. That is, drinkers would prefer a lower price to a higher price for their personal consumption. But for political reasons they may also prefer a higher price (tax) in order to discourage others from drinking too much. A few may even welcome a higher tax as a device for protecting themselves against a failure in their own willpower.

18. "Consumer's surplus" is defined as the maximum amount consumers would be willing to pay for their current consumption level, minus the amount they actually are required to pay. This difference is positive because consumers value inframarginal units of the commodity at more than their price, and this is reflected in the fact that demand curves have a negative slope.

References

Bruun, K. et al. 1975. *Alcohol Control Policies in Public Health Perspective*. Forssa, Finland. The Finnish Foundation for Alcohol Studies, vol. 25.

Campbell, Donald, and Julian Stanley, 1963. *Experimental and Quasi-Experimental Designs for Research*. Chicago: Rand McNally.

Distilled Spirits Council of the United States (DISCUS), 1977a. *Summary of State Laws and Regulations Relating to Distilled Spirits*. 22nd ed., Washington, D.C.

———— 1977b. *1977 Tax Briefs*. Washington, D.C.

———— 1977c. *Facts Book 1977*. Washington, D.C.

Hause, J.C. 1976. "Comment." *Journal of Law and Economics* 19:431-435.

Hogarty, T., and K. Elzinga. 1972. "The Demand for Beer." *Review of Economics and Statistics* 54 (May): 195-198.

Houthakker, H.S., and L.D. Taylor. 1966. *Consumer Demand in the United States, 1929-1970*. Cambridge: Harvard University Press.

Jellinek, E.M. 1947. "Recent Trends in Alcoholism and in Alcohol Consumption." *Quarterly Journal of Studies in Alcohol* 8:1-42.

Johnson, J.A., and E.H. Oksanen. 1977. "Estimation of Demand for Alcoholic Beverages in Canada from Pooled Time Series and Cross Sections." *Review of Economics and Statistics* 59 February: 113-118.

Lau, Hung-Hay. 1975. "Cost of Alcoholic Beverages as a Determinant of Alcohol Consumption." In R.J. Gibbins et al., eds.; *Research Advances in Alcohol and Drug Problems*, vol. II. New York: John Wiley and Sons.

Ledermann, S. 1956. *Alcool, Alcoolism, Alcoolisation*. Vol. 1. Paris: Presses Universitaires de France.

The Liquor Handbook. 1978. New York: Gavin-Jobson Associates, Inc.

Medicine in the Public Interest. 1979. *The Effects of Alcohol-Beverage Control Laws*. Washington, D.C.

Moore, Mark H., and Dean Gerstein. 1981. *The Alcohol Problem*. Washington, D.C.: National Academy of Sciences.

Niskanan, W.A. 1962. "The Demand for Alcoholic Beverages: An Experiment in Econometric Method." Santa Monica, Cal.: Rand Corporation P-2583.

Ornstein, S.I., and D. Levy. ca. 1978. "Price and Income Elasticities of Demand for Alcoholic Beverages." Graduate School of Management, University of California at Los Angeles. Unpublished paper.

Polich, J.M., and B. Orvis. 1979. *Alcohol Problems: Patterns and Prevalence in the U.S. Air Force*. Santa Monica: The Rand Corporation.

Popham, R.E. 1970. "Indirect Methods of Alcohol Prevalence Estimation: A Critical Evaluation." In R.E. Popham, ed., *Alcohol and Alcoholism*. Toronto: University of Toronto Press.

Popham, R.E., W. Schmidt. and J. deLint. 1976. "The Effects of Legal Restraint on Drinking." In B. Kissin and H. Begleiter, eds., *Social Aspects of Alcoholism*. Vol. 4. New York: Plenum Press.

————. 1978. "Government Control Measures to Prevent Hazardous Drinking." In J.A. Ewing and B.A. Rouse, eds., *Drinking*. Chicago: Nelson-Hall.

Reed, David. 1981. "Reducing Drinking/Driving Costs." In M. Moore and D. Gerstein, eds. *The Alcohol Problem*. Washington, D.C.: National Academy of Sciences.

Room, R. 1978. "Evaluating the Effect of Drinking Laws on Drinking." In J.A. Ewing and B.A. Rouse, eds., *Drinking*. Chicago: Nelson-Hall.

_____ 1977. "The Prevention of Alcohol Problems." Draft report for *Alcohol and Health III*, National Institute of Alcohol Abuse and Alcoholism.

Schmidt, W. 1977. "The Epidemiology of Cirrhosis of the Liver: A Statistical Analysis of Mortality Data with Special Reference to Canada." In M.M. Fisher and J.G. Rankin, eds., *Alcohol and the Liver*. New York: Plenum Press.

Schmidt, W., and R.E. Popham. 1980. "Skog's 'Lagged' Consumption Variable: A Comment on Liver Cirrhosis Mortality as an Indicator of Heavy Alcohol Use." *British Journal of Addiction.* 75:363–65.

Seeley, J.R. 1960. "Death by Liver Cirrhosis and the Price of Beverage Alcohol." *Canadian Medical Association Journal* 83:1361–66.

Simon, J.L. 1966. "The Price Elasticity of Liquor in the U.S. and a Simple Method of Determination." *Econometrica* 43:193–205.

Skog, O.J. Forthcoming. "Liver Cirrhosis Mortality as an Indicator of Heavy Alcohol Use: Some Methodological Problems." *British Journal of Addiction*.

Smith, R.T. 1976. "The Legal and Illegal Markets for Taxed Goods: Pure Theory and an Application to State Government Taxation of Distilled Spirits." *Journal of Law and Economics* 19:393–429.

Terris, M. 1967, "Epidemiology of Cirrhosis of the Liver: National Mortality Data." *American Journal of Public Health* 57:2076–88.

U.S. Department of HEW, NIAAA. 1978. *Third Special Report to the U.S. Congress on Alcohol and Health*. Washington, D.C., Government Printing Office.

Waler, T. 1968. "Distilled Spirits and Interstate Consumption Effects." *American Economic Review*, 58:853–63.

Warburton, Clark. 1932. *The Economic Results of Prohibition*. New York: Columbia University Press.

Wonnacott, Thomas H. and Ronald J. Wonnacott. 1977. *Introductory Statistics for Business and Economics*. 2nd ed.; New York: Wiley/Hamilton.

14. Estimating Distribution Functions for Small Groups: Postoperative Hospital Stay

The author is grateful for discussions with and comments from Benjamin Barnes, David Ellwood, John Gilbert, Nathan Keyfitz, Nan Laird, Bucknam McPeek, Frederick Mosteller, Donald Shepard, Judith Strenio, and Richard Zeckhauser. The work was supported in part by grant GM 15904 from the National Institute of General Medical Sciences to Harvard University.

References

Anesthesiology. 1963. New Classification of Physical Status, Vol. 24, No. 111.

Brass, William. 1975. *Methods for Estimating Fertility and Mortality from Limited and Defective Data*. An Occasional Publication, International Program of Laboratories for Population Statistics. Chapel Hill: University of North Carolina.

Gentleman, Morven W., John D. Gilbert, and John W. Tukey, 1969. "The Smear-and-Sweep Analysis." In *The National Halothane Study*, ed. John P. Bunker et al., Bethesda, Md.: National Institutes of Health.

McNeil, D.R., and J.W. Tukey. 1975. "Higher-Order Diagnosis of Two-Way Tables, Illustrated on Two Sets of Demographic Empirical Distributions." *Biometrics* 31:487–510.

Mosteller, Frederick, and J.W. Tukey. 1977. *Data Analysis and Regression: A Second Course in Statistics*. Reading, Mass.: Addison Wesley.

Strenio, Judith et al. 1979. "Description of Surgical Experience at the Massachusetts General Hospital 1973–1976." Working paper of the Surgery Group of the Faculty Seminar in Health and Medicine of Harvard University.

Stoto, Michael A. 1979. *A Generalization of Brass' Relational System of Model Life Tables with Applications to Human Survival and Hospital Post-Operative Length of Stay*. Ph.D. dissertation, Harvard University.

_____. "General Applications of Brass' Relational Life Table System." Paper presented at the annual meeting of the Population Association of America, Denver, Colo.

15. The Economic Basis for OSHA's and EPA's Generic Carcinogen Regulations

We would like especially to thank Art Fraas and David Harrison for comments on an earlier draft. Jim Miller, Marvin Kosters, Kip Viscusi, and Nick Nichols also provided useful comments.

1. Whelan (1978). She states, "Indeed, there appears to be a legitimate question as to whether, after all, the expenditures and sacrifice of our government will succeed in preventing even one case of human cancer."

2. Dr. David Rall, director of the National Institute of Environmental Health Science, quoted the 90 percent estimate, while the second estimate is endorsed by OSHA in the preamble to the OSHA cancer regulations. See *Federal Register*, (hereinafter *FR*) 45:5027 and 5033 for the two estimates, respectively.

3. Upper estimates of the aggregate costs of regulating carcinogens are also high. For the OSHA cancer policy, Booz, Allen and Hamilton estimated direct compliance costs of up to $88 billion annually, while James Miller extrapolates the costs of seven promulgated OSHA cancer standards to estimate $55 billion in annual costs for the estimated remaining 571 carcinogens. See Miller (1980).

4. Of course, these aggregate estimates do serve to attract the attention of the media and the politicians. It is not clear, however, whether this kind of attention is helpful in the pursuit of reasoned regulatory policy.

5. *FR* 45:5282–5296.

6. Ten health standards had been promulgated in the ten years of OSHA's existence. The carcinogen regulations concern asbestos, "the 14 carcinogens," vinyl chloride, coke ovens, arsenic, benzene, DBCP, and acrylonitrile. Cotton dust and lead are the two noncarcinogenic agents that are the focus of health standards. OSHA does, of course, have many other health standards, but they were adopted informally as "consensus standards." For reviews of OSHA see Ashford (1976).

7. *FR* 44:58653.

8. For a discussion of these factors see Kelman (1980), on OSHA, and Marcus (1980), on EPA.

9. Both the Regulatory Council, a coordinating agency for all regulatory activities, and the Interagency Regulatory Liaison Group (IRLG), a group composed of five agencies with regulatory responsibility for carcinogens, have tried to make the two policies consistent. See *FR* 44:39858 for the IRLG recommendations and *FR* 44:60038 for the Regulatory Council's.

10. *FR* 45:5285.

11. *FR* 45:5284.

12. Only one OSHA standard (cotton dust) has established different exposure levels for different industries, and the motive there was probably to minimize the differences in risk of byssinosis by sector rather than to promote cost-effectiveness (Morrall, 1981).

13. Although the analysis presented in the next section is by plant, EPA may not necessarily regulate at such a disaggregated level.

14. For another comparison of the two policies that emphasizes the scientific aspects, see Havender (1980).

15. In the preamble to the benzene regulation in 1978 (*FR* 43:5491), OSHA stated: "Having determined that the benefits of the proposed standard are likely to be appreciable, OSHA is not obligated to carry out further exercises toward more precise calculations of benefits which would not significantly clarify the ultimate decision. Previous attempts to quantify benefits as an aid to decision-making in setting health standards have not proved fruitful: (*FR* 41:46742). The reference is to the coke oven standard.

16. See *Industrial Union Department, AFL-CIO* vs. *American Petroleum Institute*, p. 31, Supreme Court of the United States, Nos. 78–1253,–1257,–1486,–1676,–1677,–1707,–1745, July 2, 1980.

17. See *American Textile Manufactures et al.* vs. *Donovan*, p. 17, Supreme Court of the United States, Nos. 79–1583, June 17, 1981.

18. See Crandall and Lave (1980).

19. The five cases studied were: Sulphur dioxide and airborne carcinogens for EPA, cotton dust for OSHA, saccharin for the Food and Drug Administration and airbags for the National Highway and Traffic Safety Administration.

20. In addition to OSHA's expressed policy of overestimating benefits by "erring on the side of caution" (*FR* 43:5419), OSHA states that "unfortunately this tendency toward overestimation of costs

and underestimation of benefits allows decisions to be biased on the side of current economic situation at the expense of future benefits to society, and tends to preserve the status quo" (OSHA, 1975:57).

21. We include in this group Kelman (1980), Zeckhauser (1975), Mendeloff (1979), and Rhoads (1978). Kelman criticizes cost-benefit analysis because it fails to weigh basic "rights" such as justice, fairness, and the "right to a healthy workplace" (p. 266).

22. Another way out of this dilemma has been proposed by Rhoads. He argues that since cost-benefit analysis is necessary but demoralizing, it should be done but kept out of the public view. We believe this is just as undemocratic as not doing it (see Rhoads, 1978).

23. To the extent that risks are later discovered that no one initially knew existed, workers will bear the risk without compensation. The use of vinyl chloride in the 1970s and perhaps asbestos in U.S. shipyards in the 1940s are examples. This is not a market failure, but a failure of science.

24. Other estimates are somewhat lower. Smith (1979) bounds the estimate between $200,000 and $3 million while Bailey (1980), after surveying a wide variety of studies, making third-party adjustments, and inflating to 1978 dollars, estimates a plausible average of $170,000 to $715,000.

25. Much of the decline in the differential resulting from the decline in risk is a transfer to employers, but there is a net efficiency loss to workers who preferred the income to the risk reduction. The loss depends upon either the marginal rate of substitution between risk and income or the cost of finding new jobs with similar risk-pay characteristics.

26. In fact, to the extent that the pollution is localized, the nearby property owner will be the beneficiary of a windfall gain.

27. Comparing the regulation of coal mining and nuclear power, Viscusi argues that a given reduction in nuclear risk should be valued over twice as highly as the same occupational risk reduction (pp. 17-18).

28. One cannot be completely certain that the methods used to calculate expected costs and benefits were identical. Given the data provided by the agencies, however, the analysis presented here is consistent across regulations.

29. We have less confidence in this estimate than in the others, since it is the only one not calculated from primary sources.

30. Although we present point estimates, the actual numbers could be an order of magnitude off in either direction. We also believe these numbers are conservative (biased downward) because of the linear extrapolation models used, and because exposure levels were generally higher when the epidemiology data was gathered than just before the standards were proposed.

A study of vinyl chloride regulation by Perry and Outlaw (1978), reported in Smith (1979), estimates costs at $5 to $10 million per death avoided.

31. The acrylonitrile standard was the first RARG filing and our estimates are based on that filing. See Morrall (1978a).

32. The exception is acrylonitrile, but that was triggered by a 1977 epidemiologic study by DuPont.

33. It should be noted that we used EPA's risk estimate for benzene (adjusted for the lower occupational exposure) in estimating the risks for the OSHA standard. Also, since a linear extrapolation model is used, which is widely acknowledged to overestimate very low risk, the EPA upper cost estimate should probably be used. The environmental risks for benzene are over 1,000 times less than for the occupational risks.

34. When the standards were first proposed by EPA, Monsanto and Tenneco were not controlling to 97 percent. Originally, when those plants were included, the incremental cost per death avoided for the 97 percent option ranged from $4.8 to $6.0 million.

35. See also Nichols (1981). The author performed an analysis similar to, but more comprehensive than, the one presented here.

36. Zeckhauser (1975), however, argues that there is no evidence of this.

References

Ashford, N. 1976. *Crisis in the Workplace: Occupational Disease and Injury.* Cambridge, Mass.: MIT Press.

Ashford, N. 1980. "The Limits of Cost-Benefit Analysis in Regulatory Decisions," *Technology Review*, (May): 70.

Bailey, M. 1980. *Reducing Risks to Life.* Washington, D.C.: American Enterprise Institute.

Bridbord et al. 1980. "Estimates of the Fraction of Cancer in the U.S. Related to Occupational Factors." Washington, D.C.: NCI, NIEHS, and NIOSH.

Crandall, R., and L. Lave. Forthcoming. *The Scientific Basis for Health and Safety Regulations.* Washington, D.C.: Brookings Institution.

Green. M., and N. Waitzman. 1979. *"Business War on the Law: An Analysis of the Benefits of Federal Health/Safety Enforcement."* Testimony before the House Subcommittee on Oversight and Investigation. October 9, 1979.

Hapgood, F. 1979. "Risk-Benefit Analysis: Putting a Price On Life." *The Atlantic.* (January): 33–38.

Havender, W. 1980. "Regulating Cancer." *Regulation* (May).

Kelman, S. 1980. "OSHA." In *The Politics of Regulation,* ed. J. Q. Wilson, New York: Basic Books.

Marcus, A. 1980. "EPA." In *The Politics of Regulation,* ed. J.Q. Wilson. New York: Basic Books.

Mendeloff, J. 1979. *Regulating Safety.* Cambridge, Mass.: MIT Press.

———. 1980. "Reducing Occupational Health Risks." *Technology Review* (May): 66–78.

Miller, J. 1980. "Supreme Court to Issue Ruling On Economic Criteria For OSHA." *Journal of Commerce* (May 16).

Morrall, J. 1977. "OSHA and U.S. Industry." In *Economic Effects of Government-Mandated Costs* ed. R. Lanzillotti. Gainesville: University of Florida Press.

———. 1978a. "Report Submitted to RARG On Occupational Exposure to Acrylonitrile." Washington, D.C.: COWPS-272. Council on Wage and Price Stability, Report 272, Washington, D.C.

———. 1978b. "The Cost and Benefits of the Proposed Standard for the Control of Cotton Dust." *Review of Industrial Management and Textile Science* (Spring): 11–27.

———. 1979. "Exposure to Occupational Noise." In *Benefit Cost Analyses of Social Regulation,* ed. J. Miller and B. Yandle. Washington, D.C.: American Enterprise Institute.

———. 1981. "An Economic Analysis of OSHA's Cotton Dust Standard." In *The Scientific Basis for Health and Safety Regulation,* ed. R. Crandall and L. Lave. Washington, D.C.: Brookings Institution, pp. 93–108.

Nichols, A. 1981. "Choosing Regulatory Targets and Instruments, with Applications to Benzene." Ph.D. dissertation, Kennedy School of Government, Harvard University.

Northrop, H. et al. 1978. *The Impact of OSHA.* Philadelphia: University of Pennsylvania Press, Industrial Research Unit.

OSHA. 1975. *Inflation Impact Analysis of the Proposed Standard for Coke Oven Emissions.* Washington, D.C.: Government Printing Office.

Portney, P., ed. 1978. *U.S. Environmental Policy.* Baltimore: Johns Hopkins Press.

Rhoads, S. 1978. "How Much Should We Spend to Save a Life?" *The Public Interest* (Spring).

Scalia, A. 1980. "A Note on The Benzene Case." *Regulation* (July/August): 25–28.

Smith, R. 1976a. *The Occupational Safety and Health Act.* Washington, D.C.: The American Enterprise Institute.

———. 1979. "Compensating Wage Differentials and Public Policy: A Review." *Industrial and Labor Relations Review* (April): 339–52.

Stokey, E., and R. Zeckhauser. 1978. *A Primer for Policy Analyses.* New York: W. W. Norton.

Viscusi, K. 1979. *Employment Hazards.* Cambridge: Harvard University Press.

———. 1981. "Occupational Safety and Health Regulation: Its Impact and Policy Alternatives," *Research in Public Policy Analysis and Management,* Greenwich, Conn. JAI Press, Inc., *Proceedings of the 1979 Research Conference on Public Policy Analysis and Management.*

Whelan, E. 1978. "Cancerphobia: The Enemy Within." *Los Angeles Times* (August 30).

Zeckhauser, R. 1975. "Procedures for Valuing Lives." *Public Policy* (Fall): 419–64.

———., and A. Nichols. 1979. "The Occupational Safety and Health Administration: An Overview." *Study of Federal Regulation.* Washington, D.C.: U.S. Senate. 95th Congress, 1st Session, Volume 6.

16. When to Pay for Sunk Benefits

The authors appreciate the assistance of Douglas Smith and the insights of Andrew Reschovsky, Martin Levin, and several conferees on the occasion of this study's oral presentation. Shanta Deverajan clarified and generalized the analysis. This chapter does not necessarily reflect the positions of either the Commonwealth of Massachusetts or the City of Boston.

1. The Comprehensive Environmental Response, Compensation, and Liability Act of 1980, P.L. 96–510.

2. Reimbursement for pre-enactment cleanups is limited to a credit against a 10 percent share of

future cleanup. States that have spent more than 10 percent of their dump costs will thus be rewarded less than those that have cleaned less.

3. Notice that the reliance is not upon the enactment of the program per se but upon the conditional probability that, given the bill's enactment, it will be retroactive.

4. Another efficiency issue bearing on the general advisability of federal subsidies to states has been much discussed elsewhere: where the benefits received as the result of a given investment are all, or nearly all, local (within the recipient decisionmaking unit of government), it can be argued that any federal subsidy will encourage inefficient investments. We consider this question important, and we think programs would benefit from a more critical review on this basis, but in the present study we choose to focus on the second-order problem detailed in the text.

5. Leman, C., "How to Get There From Here: The Grandfather Effect and Public Policy." *Policy Analysis* 6, 1 (1980).

17. What is Regulation?

Financial support for work on this study was provided by the Harvard Faculty Project on Regulation. I received many helpful criticisms of an earlier draft from Michael Brewer, Albert Nichols, and Richard Zeckhauser.

1. The appointees were Paul W. MacAvoy (1975-1976), Charles L. Schultze and George C. Eads (1976-1980), and Murray L. Weidenbaum (1981−82). Presidents Ford and Carter established offices in the Council on Wage and Price Stability for analyzing and making recommendations on all major regulations proposed by the executive-branch regulatory agencies (DeMuth, 1980). President Carter also established the interagency Regulatory Analysis Review Group to review major regulatory proposals, and the Regulatory Council, chaired by the administrator of the EPA, to oversee many of the activities of 35 other regulatory agencies (DeMuth, 1980; United States Regulatory Council, 1980b). President Reagan has abolished the Council on Wage and Price Stability, the Regulatory Analysis Review Group, and the Regulatory Council but has established his own regulatory analysis program, administered by the Office of Management and Budget and the new cabinet-level Task Force on Regulatory Relief (Executive Office of the President, 1981; Office of the Vice President, 1981).

2. Among the non-utility regulatory agencies doing business in 1970 were the Food and Drug Administration (FDA), the Federal Aviation Administration (FAA), the Federal Trade Commission (FTC), the Securities and Exchange Commission (SEC), the National Highway Traffic Safety Administration, the Atomic Energy Commission (AEC), innumerable state licensing boards, and rudimentary pollution control agencies in the federal and state governments. Noll (1980:6) notes that "[i]n Kahn's two volumes, FDA is mentioned once in a footnote, and the AEC is not mentioned at all." Kahn does discuss SEC regulation of brokerage commissions in his chapter on "destructive competition" (1970:II, 193-209).

3. A report of EPA's regulatory reform initiatives lists as its prime example of "Alternatives to Traditional 'Command and Control' Regulatory Approaches" the assessment of noncompliance penalties equal to "the amount of money the violator has saved by not installing pollution control equipment" (U.S. Environmental Protection Agency, 1978:2). The EPA policy is listed as a "regulatory reform highlight" by the U.S. Regulatory Council (1980a:41).

4. The "purpose" of taxes on cigarettes and gambling may be either to discourage people from smoking and gambling or to raise public revenues efficiently because they will not discourage people very much (and thus will interfere little with "consumer welfare"). Either way, there is no suggestion that such taxes are calibrated so as to internalize some measure of the external costs associated with smoking and gambling.

5. The other alternative to pollution regulation suggested by economists—the sale of "marketable rights" to emit specified amounts of pollution—is also output-oriented command and control, requiring an authoritative determination of the total amount of pollution to be permitted. The quantity of resources available for trade is an artifact of government, as in the case of FCC broadcast licenses and municipal taxi medallions, rather than an apolitical, technological fact, as in the case of land. In practice, the development of marketable rights has gotten much further than emission fees in environmental policy, taking such forms as EPA's "offset" policy (under which firms violating pollution standards may purchase the right to do so from other firms that exceed the standards) and its proposal to auction off rights to manufacture and use chlorofluorocarbons (U.S. Regulatory Council, 1980a:38−39). As in the case of the long-standing private markets in taxi medallions and broadcast licenses, it

appears that once the government has created valuable rights or costly obligations by administrative action, there is little political resistance to permitting them to be traded.

6. Standard time was introduced by the railroads in the 19th century; before railroading no one much cared that the time in Washington, D.C., measured by the sun, was a few minutes earlier than the time in Baltimore (Bartky and Harrison, 1979). Standard time was conceived and implemented by the railroads to make scheduling more convenient, and it undoubtedly increased their profits. So we may say that the immediate purpose of standard time was to enrich the railroads—although it benefited many others as well.

References

Ackerman, Bruce A., and William T. Hassler. 1981. *Dirty Air/Clean Coal*. New Haven, Conn.: Yale University Press.

Bartky, Ian R., and Elizabeth Harrison. 1979. "Standard and Daylight-Saving Time." *Scientific American* 240 (May): 46–53.

Breyer, Stephen G. 1981. *Regulation and its Reform*. Cambridge: Harvard University Press.

Breyer, Stephen G., and Paul W. MacAvoy. 1973. "The Natural Gas Shortage and the Regulation of Natural Gas Producers." *Harvard Law Review* 86:941–73.

Coase, Ronald H. 1959. "The Federal Communication Commission." *Journal of Law & Economics* 2 (October): 1–40.

Comptroller General of the United States. 1980. *Construction Work in Progress Issue Needs Improved Regulatory Response for Utilities and Consumers*. Washington, D.C.: Government Printing Office.

Cornell, Nina W., Roger G. Noll, and Barry Weingast. 1977. "Safety Regulation." In *Setting National Priorities: The Next Ten Years*, ed. Charles L. Schultze, pp. 457–504. Washington, D.C.: The Brookings Institution.

DeMuth, Christopher C. 1980. "Constraining Regulatory Costs: The White House Review Programs." *Regulation* 4 (January-February): 13–26.

Enthoven, Alain, and Roger Noll. 1979. "Regulatory and Nonregulatory Strategies for Controlling Health Care Costs." In *Medical Technology: The Culprit Behind Health Care Costs?* ed. S.H. Altmann and R. Beldon, p. 216. U.S. Department of Health, Education and Welfare, PHS # 79–3216. Washington, D.C.: Government Printing Office.

Executive Office of the President. 1981. Executive Order 12291—"Federal Regulation." *Federal Register* 46 (February 19): 13193.

Hayek, Friedrich A. 1973 (vol 1), 1976 (vol 2), and 1979 (vol 3). *Law, Legislation and Liberty*. Chicago: University of Chicago Press.

Joskow, Paul L. 1974. "Inflation and Environmental Concern: Structural Change in the Process of Public Utility Price Regulation." *Journal of Law and Economics* 17 (October): 291–328.

———, and Roger G. Noll. 1978. "Regulation in Theory and Practice: An Overview." Social Science Working Paper No. 213 (May). Pasadena: California Institute of Technology.

Kahn, Alfred E. 1970. *The Economics of Regulation: Principles and Institutions*. New York: John Wiley & Sons.

Kitch, Edmund W. "Economics of the Interstate Commerce Act of 1887 and its Antecedents." Unpublished paper, University of Chicago Law School.

Landes, William M., and Richard A. Posner. 1979. "Adjudication as a Private Good." *Journal of Legal Studies* 8 (March): 235–84.

Lehn, Kenneth, Lee Benham, and Alexandra Benham. "Ideology, Investor Expectations, and Economic Efficiency." Unpublished paper, Department of Economics, Washington University, St. Louis.

Leland, Hayne E. 1979. "Quacks, Lemons, and Licensing: A Theory of Minimum Quality Standards." *Journal of Political Economy* 87:1328–46.

MacAvoy, Paul W. 1979. *The Regulated Industries and the Economy*. New York: W.W. Norton & Company.

McKie, James W. 1970. "Regulation and the Free Market: The Problem of Boundaries." *Bell Journal of Economics and Management Science* 1 (Spring): 6–26.

Mitnick, Barry M. 1980. *The Political Economy of Regulation*. New York: Columbia University Press.

Navarro, Peter. "Public Utility Regulation and National Energy Policy." Unpublished paper. Energy and Environmental Policy Center, Kennedy School of Government, Harvard University.

Noll, Roger G. 1980. "What Is Regulation?" Social Science Working Paper No. 324 (June). Pasadena: California Institute of Technology.

Office of the Vice President. 1981. *Fact Sheet—Executive Order on Regulatory Management* (February 17).

Owen, Bruce M. and Ronald Braeutigam. 1978. *The Regulation Game.* Cambridge, Mass.: Ballinger Publishing Company.

Peltzman, Sam. 1976. "Toward a More General Theory of Regulation." *Journal of Law and Economics* 19 (August): 211–40.

Posner, Richard A. 1971. "Taxation by Regulation." *Bell Journal of Economics and Management Science* 2 (Spring): 22–50.

_____. 1981. *The Economics of Justice.* Cambridge, Mass.: Harvard University Press.

Priest, George L. 1977. "The Common Law Process and the Selection of Efficient Rules." *Journal of Legal Studies* 6 (January): 65–82.

Rubin, Paul H. 1977. "Why is the Common Law Efficient?" *Journal of Legal Studies* 6 (January): 51–64.

Schultze, Charles L. 1977. *The Public Use of Private Interest.* Washington, D.C.: The Brookings Institution.

Stigler, George J. 1971. "Theory of Economic Regulation." *Bell Journal of Economics and Management Science* 2 (Spring): 1–21.

_____. 1975. *The Citizen and the State: Essays on Regulation.* Chicago: University of Chicago Press.

_____. 1980. "Trying to Understand the Regulatory Leviathan." *The Wall Street Journal* (August 1): 12.

Thomas, Lacy Glenn. "The Economics of Producer Developed Safety Standards." Department of Economics, University of Illinois. Mimeographed.

U.S. Environmental Protection Agency. 1978. *Regulatory Reform Initiatives, Quarterly Progress Report* (August). Washington, D.C.: Government Printing Office.

U.S. Regulatory Council. 1980a. *Regulatory Reform Highlights: An Inventory of Initiatives, 1978-1980* (April). Washington, D.C.: Government Printing Office.

_____. 1980b. *Calendar of Federal Regulations* (May). Washington, D.C.: Government Printing Office.

_____. 1980c. *Innovative Techniques in Theory and Practice: Proceedings of a Regulatory Council Conference* (July). Washington, D.C.: Government Printing Office.

Weidenbaum, Murray L. 1979. *The Future of Business Regulation.* New York: AMACOM.

Wilson, James Q. 1980. *The Politics of Regulation.* New York: Basic Books.

18. The Search for Implementation Theory

I wish to thank the following colleagues who were kind enough to read drafts of this paper and give me critical thoughts, not all of which have been heeded: Eugene Bardach, David Beam, Kenneth Betsalel, James Blumstein, Richard Elmore, George Graham, Robert Hauck, Willis Hawley, Paul Hill, Robert Hudson, Theodore Lowi, Duncan MacRae, Jr., Lawrence Mead, Jerome T. Murphy, Robert Nakamura, Michael Nelson, John Oneal, Randall Ripley, Byron Shafer, Evert Vedung, Benjamin Walter, Richard Weatherley, and Aaron Wildavsky.

References

Allison, Graham T. 1974. "Implementation Analysis: The Missing Chapter." In *Benefit-Cost Policy Analysis,* ed. Richard Zeckhauser et al. Chicago: Aldine.

Berman, Paul, and Milbrey Wallin McLaughlin. 1975. *Federal Programs Supporting Educational Change,* vol. IV, *The Findings in Review.* Santa Monica, Cal.: Rand Corporation.

_____. 1977. *Federal Programs Supporting Educational Change,* vol. VII, *Factors Affecting Implementation and Continuation.* Santa Monica, Cal.: Rand Corporation.

Chase, Gordon. 1979. "Implementing a Human Services Program: How Hard Will It Be?" *Public Policy* 27 (Fall): 387–435.

Elmore, Richard F. 1979-80. "Mapping Backward: Using Implementation Analysis to Structure Policy Decisions." *Political Science Quarterly* 94 (Winter): 601–16.

Feder, Judith. 1977. *Medicare: The Politics of Federal Hospital Insurance.* Lexington: D.C. Heath.

Goettel, Robert J. 1978. "Federal Assistance to National Groups: The ESEA Title I Experience." In

The Federal Interest in Financing Schooling, ed. Michael Timpane. Cambridge, Mass.: Ballinger.

Handler, Joel. 1978. *Social Movements and the Legal System*. New York: Academic Press.

Hargrove, Erwin C. 1975. *The Missing Link: The Study of the Implementation of Social Policy*. Washington, D.C.: The Urban Institute.

———, and Gillian Dean. 1980. "Federal Authority and Grass-Roots Accountability: The Case of CETA." *Policy Analysis* 6 (Spring): 127–49.

——— et al. 1981. "School Systems and Regulating Mandates: A Case Study of the Implementation of the Education for All Handicapped Children Act." In *Organizational Analysis of Schools and School Districts*, ed. Samuel Bacharach. New York: Praeger. Pp. 97–123.

———. Forthcoming. *Regulation and Schools: The Implementation of the Education for All Handicapped Children Act*.

Hartz, Louis. 1955. *The Liberal Tradition in America*. New York: Harcourt, Brace and World.

Hill, Paul. 1979. "Enforcement and Informal Pressure in the Management of Federal Categorical Programs in Education." A Rand note prepared for the U.S. Department of Health, Education and Welfare, N-1232-HEW. August.

Lipsit, Seymour Martin. 1963. *The First New Nation*. New York: Basic Books.

Lowi, Theodore. 1964. "American Business, Public Policy, Case Studies, and Political Theory." *World Politics* 16 (July): 677–715.

———. 1970. "Decision Making vs. Policy Making: Toward an Antidote for Technocracy." *Public Administration Review* 30 (May-June): 317.

———. 1972. "Four Systems of Policy, Politics and Choice." *Public Administration Review* 32 (July-August): 298–310.

———. 1978. "Public Policy and Bureaucracy in the United States and France." In *Comparing Public Policies*, ed. Douglas E. Ashford. Beverly Hills, Cal.: Sage Publications.

Marcus, Alfred. 1980. "Environmental Protection Agency." In *The Politics of Regulation*, ed. James Q. Wilson. New York: Basic Books.

Meyer, John W., and Brian Rowan. 1978. "The Structure of Education Organization." In *Environments and Organizations*, ed. Marshall W. Meyer. San Francisco: Jossey-Bass.

Murphy, Jerome T. 1971. "Title I of ESEA: The Politics of Implementing Federal Educational Reform." *Harvard Educational Review* 41 (February): 38.

Orfield, Gary. 1969. *The Reorientation of Southern Education: The Schools and the 1964 Civil Rights Act*. New York: John Wiley and Sons.

Pressman, Jeffrey, and Aaron Waldavsky. 1973. *Implementation*. Berkeley: University of California Press.

Rabkin, Jeremy. 1980. "Office for Civil Rights." In *The Politics of Regulation*, ed. James Q. Wilson. New York: Basic Books.

Ripley, Randall B., and Grace A. Franklin. 1980. *Congress, the Bureaucracy and Public Policy*. Homewood, Ill.: The Dorsey Press.

Sabatier, Paul. 1977. "Regulatory Policy-making: Toward a Framework of Analysis." *Natural Resources Journal* 17 (July): 415–60.

———, and Daniel A. Mazmanian. 1982. "Policy Implementation." *The Encyclopedia of Policy Studies*, ed. Stuart Nagel. Marcel Dekker.

Salisbury, Robert H. 1968. "The Analysis of Public Policy: A Search for Theories and Roles." In *Political Science and Public Policy*, ed. Austin Ranney. Chicago: Markham Publishing.

Schuck, Peter H. 1980. "The Graying of Civil Rights Law." *The Public Interest* 60 (Summer): 75, 79.

Stevens, Robert, and Rosemary Stevens. 1974. *Welfare Medicine in America: A Case Study of Medicare*. New York: The Free Press.

Wasby, Stephen L. 1970. *The Impact of the United States Supreme Court: Some Perspectives*. Homewood, Ill.: The Dorsey Press.

Weatherly, Richard A. 1979. *Reforming Special Education: Policy Implementation from State Level to Street Level*. Cambridge, Mass.: MIT Press.

Wilson, James Q. 1980. "The Politics of Regulation." In *The Politics of Regulation*, ed. Wilson. New York: Basic Books.

Yudof, Mark G. 1980. "Implementing Desegregation Decrees." 1981. In Willis D. Howley (ed.), *Effective School Desegregation*, Beverly Hills, CA: Sage Publications, Pp. 245–64.

19. Compensating When the Government Harms

1. Briefly, "political buyout" refers to the argument that compensation should be paid to politically powerful groups who may block otherwise desirable policy changes that would harm them. "Better calculations" refers to the argument that requiring publicly financed compensation is desirable because it will encourage government agencies to balance more carefully the costs of their actions against the benefits. O'Hare (1977) discusses political buyout, while Tullock (1978) discusses better calculations.

2. The word "unanticipated" is crucial because, if compensation were expected as a matter of course, short-lived jobs would not have to command a much higher wage. The reason is that compensation itself would be a part of the expected remuneration from the job; if compensation is expected, wages adjust. The implication is that what appears to be compensation (a net transfer to the recipient) may not actually be a net increase in the recipient's income over time. This issue is explored more completely in Section IV, where unemployment insurance is considered as an example.

3. The potentially important role of expectations is also alluded to by Michaelman (1967), though not examined in detail. See the discussion in section IIIA.

4. For a more detailed and thorough discussion of the role of expectations in economic models, see Kantor (1979), and the references cited therein. Also, see Swamy, Barth, and Tinsley (1982) for a discussion of some of the difficulties associated with modeling expectations.

5. See, for example, Weisbrod (1968).

6. See Harberger (1978) and Hylland and Zeckhauser (1979).

7. No mention has been made of the possibility of purchasing private insurance against losses due to public policy change, and this omission is intentional. A private insurer would have little incentive to provide such insurance because the possibilities for spreading risk are small, since the insurable event—e.g., airline deregulation—would simultaneously affect all those holding insurance. A "moral hazard" problem would also arise because the insured would have less incentive to oppose an unfavorable public policy shift.

8. For an extended discussion, see Feldstein (1976a). For a briefer treatment, see Feldstein (1976b).

9. Current tax provisions permit deductions for casualty losses, which presumably are unexpected.

10. Total tax payments that increase with income are a property of most regressive tax systems, as well as of proportional and progressive income tax systems.

11. We abstract here from behavioral restrictions such as alcoholic beverage and narcotics laws.

12. For an important early discussion of the common property problem, see Gordon (1954). For a more recent discussion, see Peterson and Fisher (1977).

13. To the best of our knowledge, this argument has been made most explicitly by conservationists. See, for example, "Petition of the Environmental Defense Fund for the Amendment of Guidelines for Fishery Management Plans," Oct. 10, 1979, a document submitted to the National Marine Fisheries Service of the U.S. Department of Commerce.

14. There are many other types of regulation the councils might impose, but many of these do not have as their major aim the restriction of catch per se. Thus, some regulation attempts to deal with conflicts of equipment between different types of fishermen, with limiting the catch of "too small" (too young) fish (as opposed to limiting the quantity of catch), and so forth.

15. There is, in fact, a considerable problem of uncertainty and enforcement in regulating fisheries. While our discussion does not consider these problems, an informed choice among regulatory alternatives would have to consider how each scheme will deal with them. For a discussion of the nature of these problems and how alternative schemes approach them, see Council on Wage and Price Stability, "Comments on Guidelines for Development of Fishery Management Plans," CWPS-382, July 15, 1980.

16. The term "rents" refers to above-normal returns to economic activity. Economic models of fishing activity suggest that, without entry limitation, rents are zero. Limiting entry produces above-normal returns (rents) to those allowed to fish (assuming quotas are obtained at no cost).

17. For a more detailed and general analysis see Cordes and Weisbrod (1980).

References

Bale, Malcolm, and John Mutti. 1978. "Income Losses, Compensation and International Trade." *Journal of Human Resources* 13 (Spring): 278-285.

Cordes, Joseph. 1979. "Compensation Through Relocation Assistance." *Land Economics.* 55 (November): 486–98.

Cordes, Joseph, and Burton Weisbrod. 1979. "Governmental Behavior in Response to Compensation Requirements." *Journal of Public Economics.* 11 (February): 47–58.

―――. 1980. "Compensating Losers From Economic Change When Lump-Sum Transfers Are Not Possible." *Discussion Paper* no. 608-80, Institute for Research on Poverty, University of Wisconsin-Madison, May.

Feldstein, Martin. 1976. "The Theory of Optimal Tax Reform." *Journal of Public Economics* 6 (July/August): 77–104.

―――. 1976. "Compensation in Tax Reform." *National Tax Journal* 29 (June): 123–30.

Goldfarb, Robert. 1980. "Compensating 'Victims' of Policy Change." *Regulation* 4 (Sept./Oct.): 22–30.

―――, and Joseph Cordes. 1979. "Alternate Rationales for Severance Pay Compensation (With An Application to Airline Deregulation)." Paper presented at the American Economic Association Meetings, Atlanta, December 28–30.

Gordon, H.S. 1954. "The Economic Theory of a Common Property Resource: The Fishery." *The Journal of Political Economy* 62 (April): 124–42.

Harberger, Arnold. 1978. "On the Use of Distributional Weights in Social Cost-Benefit Analysis." *The Journal of Political Economy* 86, 2 (April): S87–S121.

Hochman, Harold. 1974. "Rule Change and Transitional Equity." In *Redistribution Through Public Choice,* ed. Harold M. Hochman and George E. Peterson. New York: Columbia University Press for the Urban Institute.

Hylland, Aanund, and Richard Zeckhauser. 1979. "Distributional Objectives Should Affect Taxes But Not Program Choice or Design." *Scandinavian Journal of Economics* 81:264–84.

Kantor, Brian. 1979. "Rational Expectations and Economic Thought." *Journal of Economic Literature* 17 (December): 1422–76.

Michaelman, Frank. 1967. "Property Utility and Fairness: Comments on the Ethical Foundations of 'Just Compensation' Law." *Harvard Law Review* 80 (April): 1165–258.

O'Hare, Michael. 1977. "Not on My Block, You Don't. Facility Siting and the Strategic Importance of Compensation." *Public Policy* 25: 407–59.

Peterson, Frederick, and Anthony Fisher. 1977. "The Exploitation of Extractive Resources: A Survey." *The Economic Journal* 87 (December): 681–722.

Rawls, John. 1971. *A Theory of Justice.* Cambridge: Harvard University Press.

Rosen, Harvey. 1978. "An Approach to the Study of Income, Utility and Horizontal Equity." *Quarterly Journal of Economics* 92 (May): 307–22.

Swamy, P. A. V. B., James Barth, and Peter Tinsley. 1982. "The Rational Expectations Approach to Economic Modelling." *Journal of Economic Dynamics and Control* (May): 125–47.

Tullock, Gordon. 1978. "Achieving Deregulation—A Public Choice Perspective." *Regulation* 2 (November-December): 50–4.

Weisbrod, Burton. 1968. "Income Redistribution Effects and Benefit-cost Analysis." In *Problems in Public Expenditure Analysis,* ed. Samuel Chase. Pp. 177–209. Washington, D.C.: Brookings Institution.

Williams, Alan. 1979. "Income Distribution and Public Expenditure Decisions." in *Public Expenditures,* ed. M. V. Posner. Cambridge, England: The University Press. Pp. 65–81.

20. The Fundamentals of Cutback Management

This essay draws freely upon the ideas developed by a small community of scholars who have investigated the problems of policy termination and cutback management: Eugene Bardach, Garry D. Brewer, Robert P. Biller, Richard M. Cyret, Andrew Glassberg, Charles H. Levine, and Irene Rubin.

References

Andrews, Kenneth R. 1971. *The Concept of Corporate Strategy.* Homewood, Ill.: Dow Jones-Irwin.

Behn, Robert D. 1980. "Leadership for Cut-Back Management: The Use of Corporate Strategy." *Public Administration Review* 40 (November/December): 613–20.

―――, and David P. Lambert. 1979. "Cut-back Management at the Pentagon: The Closing of Military Bases." Paper presented at the Research Conference on Public Policy and Management, Chicago, Ill., October 19.

Biller, Robert P. 1980. "Leadership Tactics for Retrenchment." *Public Administration Review* 40 (November/December): 604–9.

Cyret, Richard M. 1978. "The Management of Universities of Constant or Decreasing Size." *Public Administration Review* 38 (July/August): 344–49.

Divoky, Diane. 1979. "Burden of the Seventies: The Management of Decline." *Phi Delta Kappan* 61 (October): 87–91.

Glassberg, Andrew. 1978. "Organizational Responses to Municipal Budget Decreases." *Public Administration Review* 38 (July/August): 325–32.

Humphrey, Nancy, George E. Peterson, and Peter Wilson. 1979. *The Future of Cleveland's Capital Plant.* Washington, D.C.: The Urban Institute.

Leman, Nicholas. 1980. "Fiscal Conservative's District: A Lot of Bucks Stop Here." *Washington Post* (January 29).

Levine, Charles, 1979. "More on Cutback Management: Hard Questions for Hard Times." *Public Administration Review* 39 (March/April): 179–83.

Mazzarella, Jo Ann, and Larry Barber. 1978. "Facing Declining Enrollment: Considerations and Procedures." School District No. 4J, Eugene Public Schools, Eugene, Ore. Mimeographed.

Rubin, Irene. 1980. "Preventing or Eliminating Planned Deficits: Restructuring Political Incentives." *Public Administration Review* 40 (November/December): 621–26.

Index

Contributors

Gerard F. Anderson, Economist, Office of the Secretary, U.S. Department of Health and Human Services; also teaches at American University

James R. Barth, Professor of Economics, George Washington University, and Visiting Scholar, Federal Reserve Bank of Atlanta

Robert D. Behn, Associate Professor, Institute of Policy Sciences and Public Affairs, Duke University

James T. Bennett, Professor of Economics, George Mason University

Marcus C. Berliant, Assistant Professor, Department of Economics, University of Rochester

Anthony E. Boardman, Professor, School of Commerce and Business Administration, University of British Columbia

Ivy E. Broder, Associate Professor of Economics, American University

Stephen G. Cecchetti, Assistant Professor of Economics, Graduate School of Business Administration, New York University

Philip J. Cook, Associate Director, Institute of Policy Sciences and Public Affairs, and Associate Professor of Public Policy Studies and Economics, Duke University

Joseph J. Cordes, Associate Professor of Economics, George Washington University

Christopher C. DeMuth, Executive Director, Presidential Task Force on Regulatory Relief, and Administrator of Information and Regulatory Affairs, Office of Management and Budget

Joel L. Fleishman, Director, Institute of Policy Sciences and Public Affairs, and Vice Chancellor, Duke University

Robert S. Goldfarb, Professor of Economics, George Washington University

John D. Graham, doctoral candidate, Carnegie Mellon School of Public Affairs

Erwin C. Hargrove, Director of Institute for Public Policy Studies and Professor of Political Science, Vanderbilt University

Randy Huwa, Lobbyist, Common Cause

Robert P. Inman, Professor of Finance and Economics, The Wharton School, University of Pennsylvania

Manuel H. Johnson, Associate Professor of Economics, George Mason University

Richard A. Kasten, Director of Income Security Policy Analysis, U.S. Department of Health and Human Services

Derek Leebaert, Associate Editor, *Journal of Policy Analysis and Management*, and visiting scholar, Harvard University

David S. McClain, Assistant Professor of Economics and Finance, School of Management, Boston University

Michael J. McKee, Senior Staff Economist, Council of Economic Advisers

John F. Morrall, Deputy Assistant Administrator for Regulatory Analysis, Office of Management and Budget

David S. Mundel, Director, Employment and Economic Policy Administration, City of Boston

Michael Nelson, Assistant Professor of Political Science, Vanderbilt University

Michael O'Hare, Lecturer in Public Policy, Kennedy School of Government, Harvard University; formerly Assistant Secretary of Environmental Affairs for Policy, The Commonwealth of Massachusetts

Arnold H. Raphaelson, Professor of Economics, Temple University

Philip K. Robins, Senior Economist, Stanford Research Institute International, and Professor of Economics, University of Miami

Daniel H. Saks, Professor of Economics and Education Policy and Guest Scholar, The Brookings Institution

Gary L. Stieger, Policy Analyst, Stanford Research Institute International

Michael A. Stoto, Assistant Professor of Public Policy, Kennedy School of Government, Harvard University

Robert P. Strauss, Professor and Associate Dean, School of Public Affairs, Carnegie-Mellon University

John E. Todd, Director, Short Term Information Division, Office of Energy Markets and End Use, Energy Information Administration, Department of Energy

James W. Vaupel, Associate Professor of Policy Sciences and Business Administration, Duke University, and Associate Editor, *JPAM*

W. Kip Viscusi, IBM Research Professor of Business and Policy Sciences, Director of the Center for Study of Business Regulation, Fuqua School of Business, Duke University; written as Deputy Director, Council on Wage and Price Stability

Fred Wertheimer, President, Common Cause

Richard W. West, Senior Economist and senior executive, Socio-Economic Research Center, Stanford Research Institute International

Richard J. Zeckhauser, Professor of Political Economy, Kennedy School of Government, Harvard University